AFTERNOON LIGHT

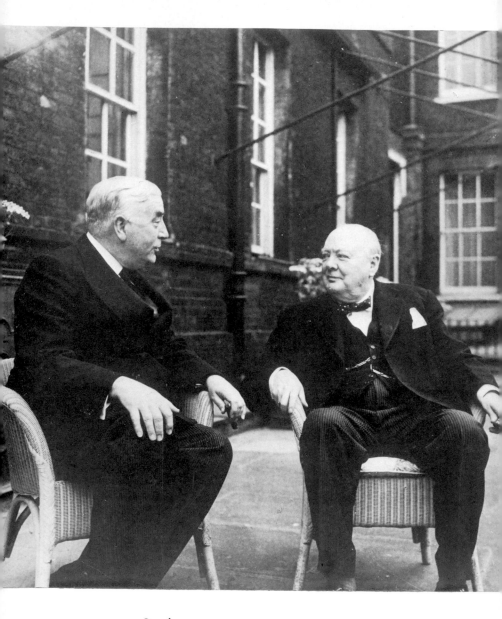

On the terrace at 10 Downing Street

The Right Honourable
SIR ROBERT GORDON MENZIES
K.T., C.H., Q.C., F.R.S.

(Prime Minister of Australia, 1939–41 and 1949–66)

Afternoon Light

SOME MEMORIES OF
MEN AND EVENTS

CASSELL · LONDON

CASSELL & COMPANY LTD
35 Red Lion Square, London WC1
Melbourne, Sydney, Toronto
Johannesburg, Auckland

© Sir Robert Menzies 1967
First printed October 1967
Second edition November 1967
Third edition December 1967

S.B.N. 304 91508 4

Printed in Great Britain
by Ebenezer Baylis and Son, Limited
The Trinity Press, Worcester, and London
1167

for
FRANK GLADSTONE MENZIES, C.B.E.
Brother, counsellor, and friend

ACKNOWLEDGEMENTS

I am indebted to Sir Arthur Goodhart for permission to quote his published opinion on the validity of President Nasser's 'nationalization' decree; to Mrs Verwoerd, of South Africa, for permission to quote from a correspondence I had with her late husband; to the Hon. Winston Field for permission to use a document he sent me, relating to Rhodesian attendance of Prime Ministers' Conferences; to the proprietors of Wisden's *Cricketers' Almanack* for permission to quote from an article I wrote for the Centenary Number; and to the *Daily Express* and Cummings for permission to use the cartoon reproduced on page 211.

I should also express my thanks to my secretary, Miss Hazel Craig, C.B.E., for her help in assembling material, and to her, Miss Gladys Munro, and Mrs Eleanor Kett of the University of Virginia, for their uncanny skill in the deciphering of my handwriting.

R.G.M.

CONTENTS

INTRODUCTORY

THIS IS NOT A HISTORY. The man who sets out to write 'history' essays a most difficult task. If he writes about the more remote past he will inevitably find himself plundering treasures gathered by others, though he may add to them by his own records and may illuminate them by his own reflections. I am not an historian; my resources are inadequate, and my inclination lacking.

As for contemporary history, I have no great faith in it. What is the source material? All too frequently, in my experience, it consists of newspaper material (almost all of which is slanted one way or another), and does not stop short of the gossip column. History, as the great French sceptic once wrote, is 'nothing but a received fable'; though at its best it can throw light on the past and therefore provide some guidance for the future. But its adequate writing requires a degree of objective scholarship to which I can lay no claim. In spite of these reservations, or perhaps because of them, I think that those of us who have known some of the actors in the world drama, or who have had even a walking-on part in some of the acts of that drama, should if possible set down our impressions, *our own first-hand impressions,* for the assistance of tomorrow's historian. Added to the observation of others, such memoirs will help that historian to see his human beings 'in the round', and to form something like a balanced judgement on great events.

In a lecture at the Smithsonian Institution at Washington on 31 March 1966, that brilliant and remarkable American, Dean Acheson made a point which we shall do well to remember. He was dealing with the cant phrase 'the verdict of history' (on which many prominent men in public life repose either their hopes or their fears). He said: 'Now a verdict is the product of a jury under the Anglo-American legal system, its unanimous opinion, and its opinion upon the facts. The law is given to the jury by the judge; but both come out in the verdict as a rather scrambled egg.' And then, some people 'regard it [the jury] as an excellent method of administering law tempered by justice. But its most ardent admirer would hardly advocate it as an adequate way of establishing truth, at least as truth is conceived by a physical scientist.'

So, he argues that when we talk of the verdict of history, we are talking of the verdict of historians.

His remarks served to remind me, at least, of this. I am a layman, interested in the reading of history. What are my 'facts' about past people and events? For the most part, the works of the historians using, to a perceptible extent, the works of earlier historians. They may, by good fortune, perpetuate truth; they may equally perpetuate error. For if we could trace it all back far enough, we would find that such contemporary records as were made and added to over the centuries were as prone to prejudice or error of observation as any twelve observers of a motor collision in our time will be prone. In my experience, at least six different versions will emerge. Which version the jury has accepted no one will ever know, perhaps not even the members of the jury which, in these days of compulsory third-party insurance, usually decides for the plaintiff anyway!

The verdicts of the future jury of historians on the events of today will, of course, not be unanimous, and will be even more susceptible to error, since these historians will not have the benefit of direct observation and will therefore be obliged either to select their witnesses at will or to make a compromise decision long after the event. And no lawyer ever believed that a compromise verdict had much relation to a precise and authoritative ascertainment of the facts.

Now you may well wonder where these observations are taking me. Are we to discard history, either now or in the future? Not at all. For myself, the great advantage of history is that its study tends to give one a sense of time and therefore of continuity. We are not bound to accept as gospel truth all of the facts recorded; we would be very naïve to do so. King Alfred and the burnt cakes; Bruce and the spider; such anecdotes remain in our memories of our young reading, but almost certainly they were quite untrue. Even King Canute, who has been reported to have sat by the sea and ordered the waves to retreat, is popularly regarded as having been an ignorant booby, whereas I have never doubted that, if the event occurred at all, he was aiming to convince his superstitious courtiers not of his own folly, but of theirs.

But the sense of historical continuity is, in any people, a powerful instrument for the production of sanity and responsibility. If, in any generation, we believe that, to adapt the words of Omar Khayyám, we came like water, and will go like the wind, then we shall have no sense of responsibility. Our instinctive motto will be: 'Eat, drink, and be merry, for tomorrow we die.' So the scramble for individual wealth and prosperity will go on, with all its accompaniments of selfishness. The short view, the demand for immediate and increasing personal benefits, will place great obstacles in the way of statesmanship and the steady march of civilization.

The archer in *Ivanhoe* may have been somewhat rhetorical when he said: 'My grandsire drew a stout bow at the battle of Hastings, and I trust not to dishonour his name,' but he expressed an unspoken attitude which I could clearly discern in the England of 1941.

Winston Churchill was himself the most eloquent embodiment of that sense of historical continuity, and I will have much to say about him in the course of this book. His great wartime speeches are in no sense derivative, but, allowing for differences in the mode of expression, are reminiscent of those of the Younger Pitt, confronting the Napoleonic threat to England.

Two years ago, I was appointed by the Queen to succeed Winston Churchill as Lord Warden of the Cinque Ports and Constable of Dover Castle, and was installed at Dover. In this ancient office, which goes back to King Harold in 1066, and which, over the last two centuries has been occupied by such historic personages as William Pitt, the Duke of Wellington, Lord Palmerston, the Marquess of Salisbury, Lord Curzon, Lord Reading, the Marquess of Willingdon, and Churchill himself, a sense of continuity is inevitable. You almost see the procession of history. You know that you are in what has been the 'invasion area' of England for centuries. Along the coast, there are physical proofs of this, from Henry VIII's castles, built as fortresses, through Pitt's Martello towers, built to repel Napoleon, to the remains of more recent gun-emplacements and searchlight posts, built under Churchill to repel Hitler. It is this sense of continuity which has helped to produce, in the British people, a confidence in survival, a quiet good humour, and a capacity for endurance which have carried them through crisis after crisis, in the course of a frequently difficult history.

I have agreed with my friend Dean Acheson about the phrase 'the verdict of history,' a reliance on which can serve only to distract the statesman's attention from the stern need for decision and action. But I attach vast importance to a 'sense of history', a phrase which I use to describe a state of mind which draws inspiration and light from the recorded past, not a state of mind which is anxious to be regarded well in the un-recorded future.

Now Churchill both made history and recorded it. What are lesser people, who have been close to some of the events of modern history, and played some small part in some of them, to do about it? The answer is to be found in what Mr Justice Frankfurter, of the United States Supreme Court, once said:

> But if history be the ultimate judgment seat, a man's contemporaries have a special claim to be heard before it. It has been wisely said that if the judgment of the time must be corrected by that of posterity, it is no less true that the judgment of posterity must be corrected by that of the time.

For myself, I have no intention to be tedious, or to attempt to be definitive. What I will set down will be a series of vignettes of people and events as I knew them; not accompanied by a mass of footnotes and documents; not necessarily in continuous chronology; but everything at first hand. Perhaps some day, an historian may find in them some assistance in his task of seeing people clearly and understanding the facts more accurately. This is a modest enough ambition. If parts of this book are somewhat autobiographical it does not mean that I am producing an autobiography. On the contrary. This is a book of personal memories. It is not an essay in self-justification; such things are wearisome, and frequently distorted by personal bias. And, in any case, 'history', or the historians, will be more interested in many of the people of whom I write than, I profoundly suspect, they will be interested in me.

Last, but not least, I want to make it clear that these are 'some memories'; by no means all. I have omitted many notable events and many people richly deserving of record. But one should not set out to be comprehensive in a hurry. At my age, I must do what I can when I can. Some critic may properly call this book a 'patch-work quilt'. And so it is; but its colours light up the past for me, and I hope for you, and its substance warms me as the afternoon draws on.

[4]

CHAPTER TWO

A PORTRAIT OF MY PARENTS

THE STREAM CAN RISE NO HIGHER than its source. It is not the fault of my parents if the stream of my life has sometimes run sluggishly, sometimes meandered, and sometimes been turbulent. For they were a remarkable pair of people, with great talents, high moral purpose, and an intense and self-sacrificing desire to see their children make some unselfish but competent contribution to life.

My father's father, Robert Menzies, came to Australia in 1855, from Dumfries in Scotland. With a partner (Joseph Pawsey, whose grandson became a celebrated scientist with world recognition) he carried on, in the mining city of Ballarat, a typically Scottish business in machinery. His wife hailed from St Andrews, and bore him ten children, seven sons and three daughters. My father, James Menzies, was the fourth son, and was born in Ballarat in 1862.

While still only forty-six, my grandfather Menzies, hearing the fire-bell on a wintry night, rushed outside to see where the fire was, caught a chill, and before long died, leaving his family indifferently provided for. This event altered the course of my father's life. He was sixteen years old. He had shown some artistic ability; the family legend is that there was a movement in Ballarat, a city in which there was already a civic sense of beauty, the products of which are still notable, to send him abroad to study. On his father's death, the *res angusta domi* drove him into a different course. He turned his talents to use by becoming a coach-painter. Those were the days when both horse-vehicles and locomotive engines were decorated by pictures of flowers and the like. So my father found himself hard at work (and he had a passion for hard work) painting for current pay. Ballarat at that time had a works called the Phoenix Foundry which built locomotives for the Victorian Railways; and I can remember, in my early youth, a few survivors, old-fashioned things, still carrying the faded remains of some of my father's work.

It was at this time that a red-headed son of a farmer, Hugh Victor McKay, invented and began to produce the first stripper-harvester, which combined the two functions of stripping the heads of the grain, and winnowing them to separate out the grain from what used to be called, delightfully, 'cocky chaff'.

And so H.V. produced the first 'Sunshine' harvester and began a progress which made him the greatest maker of farm implements in Australia; as I think, our greatest industrial pioneer.

My father painted and decorated that first harvester. Last time I visited the great establishment, in an outer suburb of Melbourne, a suburb re-named 'Sunshine', they produced as a curiosity the account rendered and the receipt of payment!

At this stage my father met and married my mother, Kate Sampson. This was an enduringly happy event in his life.

Kate Sampson was the daughter of John Sampson, a Cornishman from Penzance, born there in 1834, who had emigrated and had become a gold-miner in Creswick, a few miles out of Ballarat. One of her brothers, Sydney Sampson, was to sit in the Federal Parliament as Member for Wimmera for thirteen years. John Sampson and W. G. Spence, who became a well-known Labour Member of Parliament and Minister, were active in a dispute with the mine-owners and formed the Australian Miners' Union. My grandfather was promptly dismissed and was never employed in a mine again. This was radical action with a vengeance. Yet, in spite of speculation to the contrary, I think he would have approved of my own political activities and policies. As a schoolboy in Ballarat, living in a little cottage with my little widowed Scots grandmother, I went down into East Ballarat once a fortnight, to see my Cornish grandfather. I was young (about thirteen at the time I write about), but the old man had the divine faculty of not talking down to children. He would sit back in his chair and ask me to read aloud the leading article in that week's *Sydney Worker,* a devoutly Labour and vigorous journal. I would read it, and then be asked what I thought of it. Even then I suppose I was an instinctive Conservative, and I usually disagreed with it, I would say so politely, and give my reasons. The old man was delighted, even though I was laying rude hands on what, to him, was a sort of Ark of the Covenant.

He used to say to my mother—who was a great favourite of his— 'Kitty, I see a great deal of myself in the boy Robert!'

I remember him clearly; he was in the seventies at this time, and died a few years later; an upright man with a good forehead—marked by the usual accidents of underground mining—and a full white beard. Like so many miners of that period, he was keenly political, though not rigidly partisan (he was a great one for Alfred Deakin, Member for Ballarat, and for some years Prime Minister of Australia, though Deakin was a non-Labour leader) and, in spite of a limited formal education, he was a keen and discriminating reader. My mother inherited the essence of her own remarkable talents from him.

By the early nineties, my parents had three children, two sons and a daughter, all born in Ballarat. Father, possessed of an almost violent physical and nervous energy, was over-working at his trade and earning what we now call 'good money' at it. He was threatened with a breakdown. So my parents decided to move to the country—'fresh woods and pastures new' (though as it turned out the woods were not all that fresh, and the pastures withered easily)—and open a general store. This was a new enterprise for which they had no qualifications except courage, character, and a will to succeed. For the reasons I have recounted, my father's formal education was prematurely ended; while my mother, out in Creswick, had ended her schooling when she was about thirteen. But they both understood what many people with University degrees do not understand; that very frequently true education begins when formal studies end. For formal studies are but a means of securing a later enlargement of the mind and spirit; they are not an end in themselves.

They went to a small township with a main street and a few score houses, called by the curious name of Jeparit, in what later became accepted as part of the Wimmera District, but was then precariously perched at the far extremity of the Railway system, in an area which formed part of the Mallee. There, on 20 December 1894, I was born, my birth being ushered in by the greatest series of bank failures in the history of the State of Victoria. The question was being loudly posed—'Is the Mallee worth saving?' The land itself had been, and to a large extent still was, covered mainly by a stunted Mallee scrub, growing from a light sandy loam with the assistance of a sparse rainfall.

As clearing went on, the scrub being rolled and burned, the hot winds of summer would blow the sand into hillocks and drifts. There were tremendous dust-storms which darkened the skies. The summer

[7]

heat was intense and dry. One of my childhood memories is of one week in which the shade temperature rose by steady degrees, to 120°F. Business was inevitably poor. The neighbouring farmers had little money until after the wheat harvest came in, and therefore had to be given credit for long periods. Life for my parents was, in a financial sense, difficult and even grim.

But they never gave up. There were some physical alleviations in the facts that the Wimmera River flanked the township, and that three miles away there lay the wide but shallow expanse of a large lake, Lake Hindmarsh. So as children we had fishing, and bathing.

In 1902, there came the Great Drought. Our district had $2\frac{1}{2}$ inches of rain for the year, and all at the wrong time. What grass there was withered, and was blown away, so that the soil lay burnt, and pale brown, and vacant. The river receded into a series of unrelated and stagnant pools. The lake dried up, the sandy floor naked to the sun. All seemed lost. I was seven years old; and it remains a vivid memory. Then an astonishing thing happened. Up from the bed of the lake there came a green tuberous growth, fibrous but succulent. Cattle were brought in by the hundred. Everything was organized. A little metal disc—a sort of licence and registration—was hung about the neck of each beast. My mother took charge of the issuing of the discs, and kept the records. I can still remember the trampling sound of the cattle as they came up the road past our house, in the dead of the night, with salvation ahead.

There are two other things about that year of disaster which deserve to be told. The first is that the wheat farmers, having literally no harvest, had no seed wheat for the next sowing. So the State Government made advances totalling a few hundred thousand, for seed wheat. They were accepted. The next season, as is not uncommon after a drought, brought in a bumper harvest. Within three months of its gathering and sale, all of the advances had been repaid. These, as I need hardly add, were the years before a new political philosophy had arisen, under which, in times of trouble, we look first to that mystical giver of all good things, 'the Government', and only second to ourselves.

But I was lucky. I was the son of people of fierce independence, and learned early the importance of standing on my own feet.

My father, James Menzies, was a strongly built man of little more than medium height. His hair was prematurely grey, and became a splendid silver. He had a fairly full moustache, in which he took some pride. The nervous tension which he had tended to make him both dogmatic and intolerant; in a very modified sense, a 'Barrett of Wimpole Street'. His temper was quick. We, his sons, got to know that 'whom the Lord loveth, he chasteneth'. We were not a little frightened of him, and found our regular refuge in the embracing arms of our mother who afforded us the comfort of her own understanding, balance, and exquisite humour. As I recall W. J. Locke saying, in one of his books, 'She had the divine gift of laughter which rainbows the tears of the world'. Everybody loved her. She was a handsome and wide-eyed woman. She became a sort of mother confessor to the local women. She worked herself to the bone, and cheerfully performed tasks which we now call menial.

She had a wonderful faculty which I shall always recall with affection. She could go through an experience of the greatest difficulty, in the course of which no saint, however cheerful by nature, could have smiled. Yet, a few weeks later, she could have all of us rocking with laughter at what had happened. Like the sundial, she numbered only the sunny hours.

At the age of about four and a half, I went to school. I remember vividly the school that was built a couple of years later. It was built of wood. It stood on a little sandy rise between the township and the river. There were, in my time, about thirty pupils, with a bearded headmaster inevitably known as 'Daddy' Livingston, and one assistant, or monitor, who was one of his sons. His family are still active and prominent in Jeparit.

At that time, as I have already hinted, independence still lived, and people did not look to 'the Government' as much as they do now. At least a dozen of the pupils walked three or four miles in from their parents' farms.

I became, over a few years, a sort of infant prodigy; a purely comparative term. The reason was not far to seek. My parents were both great readers. I grew up on a fascinating *mélange* of books. Henry Drummond for evangelistic theology; Jerome K. Jerome for humour; the 'Scottish Chiefs' for historical fervour. In the winter evenings, with

[9]

the fire burning, I found myself, at the ripe age of ten or eleven, awarded the task of reading aloud to the family; a task to which I brought the faculty, rare in the family at that time, of being able to read the most excruciatingly funny passage in *Three Men in a Boat* with a dead-pan face.

My uncle Sydney, who, with my mother's other brother John, lived at Warracknabeal, about twenty-five miles away, would drive across (in horse and buggy) to see us in Jeparit. He was a wise and widely-read man. When I was no more than twelve or thirteen years old, he would talk to me, as if I were years older, about such matters as the American Constitution! Needless to say, he soon had me ransacking the meagre resources of the local 'Mechanics' Institute' Library.

Then and later, he had a great influence upon my mind.

It was, of course, inevitable that my father, in a small township of under two hundred people, surrounded by a series of wheat farms, should become a civic leader. He became a Shire Councillor, and in due course Shire President. The railway line was extended north to a small town called, somewhat lyrically, Rainbow. A great argument then arose as to the route to be followed by a proposed 'spur' line to a wheat-farming centre called Lorquon—out 'west of the Lake'. Should it go from Jeparit, or from Nhill, on the Adelaide line? The distances were not entirely dissimilar.

Father was, of course, for Jeparit. He went before the Railways Standing Committee of that time, and eventually won.

There was no Presbyterian Church, so we attended the little Methodist Church. My father, who had great but somewhat emotional talents as a speaker, soon became a local preacher (or lay reader). The pews in the church were of varnished pine, and, as money was scarce, the varnish was cheap and sticky. As a small boy, I can remember sitting forward after the sermon and disentangling my hair from the varnish with considerable difficulty!

Some years later my father went into the State Parliament as Member for Lowan. We moved soon after that to Melbourne.

My parents had a passionate faith in the procuring of an education for their children better (if that is the right word) than that which they had themselves had. So, by stages, we went off to school in Ballarat, where I won the scholarship necessary to take me to secondary school, and then to open the door to the University.

My eldest brother, James Leslie, became an Australian Trade Commissioner, and died some years ago. Frank Gladstone, the second, became the Crown Solicitor for the State of Victoria. My sister, Isabel Alice, was a great pioneering wife in the Soldier Settlement at Redcliffs, near Mildura; later, as a widow, she was Secretary to the Melbourne Exhibition Trustees, and now, in retirement, is, in spirit and gaiety, the youngest of us all. My younger brother, Sydney Keith, born at Jeparit ten years after me, is the Managing Director of a well-known manufacturing enterprise.

So it will be seen that each child achieved position and personal repute; from all of them I received great affection and encouragement. Indeed, but for Frank's unselfish attention to my private financial affairs, inevitably neglected by me while I was Prime Minister, my present state of mind, in retirement, could have been much less calm and settled.

When my father went into the State Parliament, he was a mass of nervous energy. The nerves took charge when he made his maiden speech. After a few sentences he paused, and collapsed. He made a good recovery, but it was an inauspicious beginning. He did not become a Minister, but he was listened to. Even as a youngster, I thought he had some disabilities. He was eloquent, but over-emotional. He had no originating humour, and so took everything in the House too much *au grand serieux*. The first 'disability', as I have called it, had a curiously contrary effect upon me. Temperamentally linked as I was with my mother, and although I have always had a lot of emotion in me, I learned to distrust its public expression. When my father was in full spate at some meeting, and drew the tears from his audience, I am ashamed to say that I used to shrink back in my seat and say to myself, 'I wish Father wouldn't do that!'

In effect, in my own later public and political life, I distrusted emotion, and aimed at a cold, and as I hoped, logical exposition. It was years before I ever exhibited emotion either in the House or on the platform. It was only in my later years that the feelings in me would occasionally break through. But, even then, I could never become emotional by design; such a technique, which I have occasionally heard employed, strikes me as cheap and theatrical. But every now and then, if you make speeches and do not read essays, a strong feeling will leap into your heart and mind, and then it happens.

My father's emotional character derived from a deep-seated faith and belief. He had not been through the disciplined experiences of the Law, and so, paradoxically, was nearer to the surface in the expression of things that were deepest in his heart. I wish today that there were more like him. It is one thing to be the coldly reasoning product of the schools; the objectivity thus produced is needed badly in a world in which there is so much passion and prejudice, 'malice, hatred, and all uncharitableness'. But there is a great place in life for beliefs so strongly held that they must find utterance and sway the hearts of men.

My mother was, in the most remarkable way, father's complement. They were each quite different, but together one. Where he was explosively intolerant, she was calm, human and understanding and in the end, with patience, would secure a victory for sweet reasonableness. Father was a great one for getting things done. In this he was completely unselfish, for all his greatest crusades were for others. But in the battle he could inflict wounds. My mother healed them. She had a calm and, I think, beautiful face. At no time, until her later years, was her life easy. But she harboured no bitterness. She was always the first port of call for those who needed comfort. She had what I came to recognize and admire, the judicial temperament. Somehow she found time to read widely. She spoke educated English, as did my father. Which shows, as I said before, that schooling is wonderfully advantageous, but is not all.

I owe an immense debt to both of them, and, now that they are long since dead, I send my love to them in heaven.

CHAPTER THREE

TWO CRUCIAL YEARS: 1939-41

1. Coming into office

WHEN MR LYONS DIED in February 1939 the Prime Minister-ship of Australia temporarily devolved upon the Deputy Prime Minister, Sir Earle Page, who was the Leader of the Country Party, the minority Government party. Practice dictated that the Parliamentary members of the majority Government party, the United Australia Party, should select a new leader, who would then become Prime Minister.

I had, some time earlier, resigned from the Government when it decided to abandon its recently enacted National Insurance scheme, largely under pressure from Page, and returned to practice at the Bar.

When the party met, it elected me as Leader, and therefore entitled me to ask the Governor-General for a commission as Prime Minister.

Page, who had no friendly feelings towards me, was furious. His temper, which he could seldom control, got the better of him. On the floor of the House, speaking still as Prime Minister, he made a bitter and entirely false attack upon me; in the making of which he did himself more harm than he did me. Several of his own party members sat apart thereafter, to mark their disapproval of his performance.

My wife was in the gallery when this abuse was hurled at me. And, although one who is in politics learns to take the rough with the smooth and to live with even an enemy, as I did when I made Page a Minister in a subsequent government, my wife never forgave him, and never spoke to him again. Women achieve a remarkable skill in these matters.

The Governor-General at the time of my election as Leader was Lord Gowrie, a brave soldier and a gentleman of immaculate honour. I went out to Government House and presented myself for a commission, though at that time I literally did not know whether a commission was in writing or by word of mouth. He put me at my ease at once. 'If I commission you to form a government, how long do you think you will last?' Well that was a question, for Page had withdrawn the sup-port of the bulk of the Country Party, and my government would therefore be in a minority. I therefore said, 'Six weeks, your Excellency.' He smiled and said, 'Well, that will do for a start. I commission you, and will look forward to receiving the names of your Ministers.'

And that's how in April 1939 I began my first Prime Ministership, which in fact lasted until August 1941. Conducting a minority government is a great training ground in political tactics. With two parties to watch, the Labour opposition and Page's party, a lot of 'cross-trumping' was called for. Issues must be promoted on which those two parties could not and would not agree. Hitler's added pace in Europe began to make war seem inevitable. It was a strenuous period for me. The House usually sat until Friday afternoon; and when I returned to the Lodge for dinner my usual greeting to my wife was 'Well, my dear, the House is up. Nothing but death can put me out before Tuesday.'

In spite of the precarious nature of my government's tenure, we did many essential things by way of preparing for the contingency of war. The Defence Department was reorganized, and Service Departments created. A Ministry of Supply was set up. Compulsory military training, which had been abandoned in Scullin's time, was re-established.

2. *The coming of war*

In the last week of August 1939 war seemed inevitable.

We received news early on 23 August that Germany and Soviet Russia had reached agreement on a Pact of Non-aggression. A period of acute tension began. In a press statement, I said that if Great Britain was forced into war she would not go alone. I said something which it may be interesting to recall, now that the structure and spirit of the Commonwealth have sustained such changes.

Some misapprehension appears to exist in foreign countries as to the effect of the modern constitutional development in the British Empire. It is quite true that each of the great British Dominions has had full recognition accorded to its nationhood and to its equality in all things with other members of the British Commonwealth, including Great Britain. But this independence does not indicate separatism. On the contrary, we are still members of one family, and our family feeling is reinforced rather than weakened by our adult growth. I speak unhesitatingly for Australia, and I am confident that the same could be truly said of the other Dominions, that in this time of testing and strain Great Britain has, and will continue to have, the fullest co-operation from us in her magnificent efforts to avoid the insanity and injustice of war. If her great efforts fail, we will still stand with her. It would be a cardinal error for any other country to assume that there is any disunity among the British people on these matters.

Australia stands where it stood twenty-five years ago.

By the following day I was saying that 'the state of tension is such that no preparation for war can be neglected'.

We instituted emergency measures on 25 August.

On 1 September, I drove down to Colac, in the Western District, to address a meeting. (I will make some reference to this in my chapter on President Truman.)

News reached me that the Germans had invaded Poland. I cancelled my speech, and returned to Melbourne at 11 p.m., conferring immediately with such Commonwealth Ministers as were available. At 3 a.m. on 2 September, I made a broadcast from the studios of the Australian Broadcasting Commission, uttering a grave warning about events. At 4.30 a.m., I went home for a few hours rest. All of my Ministers were assembling from various States.

We met on Sunday morning, and adjourned for further news. I went into my office and devoted some hours to writing the statement I would have to make if, as seemed certain, war was to come. Cabinet met again at 8 p.m., a wireless announcement having been made by Mr Chamberlain stating that Great Britain was at war with Germany. After a brief discussion, in which there was complete unanimity, I made, at 9.15 p.m., my statement over a network which included every national and commercial broadcasting station in Australia.

Though I stated with care the sequence of events, to show that the guilt was that of Germany alone, the essence of my announcement was in one paragraph:

It is my melancholy duty to inform you officially that in consequence of a persistence by Germany in her invasion of Poland, Great Britain has declared war upon her, and that, as a result, Australia is at war. No harder task can fall to the lot of a democratic leader than to make such an announcement.

I concluded with these words:

I know that, in spite of the emotions we are all feeling, you will show that

Australia is ready to see it through. May God in His Mercy and compassion grant that the world may soon be delivered from this agony.

Early next morning I sent a message to Mr Chamberlain:

Your broadcast message moved Australia deeply. We ourselves have proclaimed a state of war, and I have broadcast on behalf of the Commonwealth Government that we stand with Great Britain. We firmly believe we have right on our side, and in that strength victory is sure.

The Federal Parliament met on 6 September, and I made a full statement of the events, and the action we had taken. There was no audible dissent.

So far, there was unanimity. But, two years later, a criticism arose, about which I should say something. It began to be said that by saying that 'Great Britain has declared war . . . and, as a result, Australia is at war' I had abandoned Australia's independent status as a nation; that there could be no automatic involvement; that Parliament should have been convened, and a formal declaration of war submitted for its approval.

I am quite unrepentant on this matter; and for reasons which can be quite simply stated.

First, I believed, and rightly, that my announcement expressed the overwhelming sentiment of the Australian people, and that they would have been shocked to be confronted by formalities and delay.

Second, the country in the immediate firing line would be Great Britain, and what could be done to encourage her people should be done at once. It would have been an intolerable thought, for me, that for even two or three days they should wonder whether they were standing alone.

Third, those were the days when the Commonwealth was a Crown Commonwealth, its constituent nations, Great Britain, Canada, Australia, South Africa, and New Zealand, bound together by a common allegiance to a common Crown. The modern notion of neutrality or non-alignment had not then been devised. How could the King be at war and at peace at the same time, in relation to Germany? I am well aware of recent Commonwealth developments, with the admission of Republics and neutrals to membership. I have even lived long enough to see one Commonwealth country sever diplomatic relations with another! But these developments were, in 1939, beyond the scope of reasonable prophecy.

So, from my point of view in 1939, neutrality for Australia in a British war was unthinkable, unless we were prepared to add secession to neutrality. These notions may, for all I know, be out-dated today. But they were very much alive in 1939, when every British country went to war. Not one of them surrendered its independent nationhood; they all faced the inevitable facts of life, and death.

We then called for volunteers for a Second Australian Imperial Force, and got them in great numbers. We dispatched to the Middle East under General Blamey the famous 6th Division, which was to fight with great success at Bardia, Tobruk, and Benghazi. We raised and sent the 7th Division, under Laverack, which earned fame in Syria, and later the 9th Division which, under Morshead, was to play a great part in the defence of Tobruk and later in the crucial battle of El Alamein.

We dispatched the cruiser *Sydney,* under Collins, to the Mediterranean, and sent the famous 'scrap-iron flotilla' of destroyers, which had for years been laid up in Sydney harbour, first to Singapore and then to the Mediterranean.

When France fell in 1940, and Dunkirk had heavily depleted British military equipment, it became clear that Australia must become more self-supplying in munitions. Up to that time we had made our own small-arms and ammunition, but little more.

So I sent for the celebrated Essington Lewis, the executive head of the Broken Hill Proprietary, the great iron and steel company, and asked him to become the Director-General of a new Munitions Department I was about to create; with the widest possible charter to produce what the armed Services required, and with direct access to myself as Prime Minister and to the War Cabinet which had previously been set up.

His appointment was an enormous success. He gathered around him a splendid team of industrial leaders, and carried through a volume of production which was one of the outstanding features of the Australian war effort.

During this period, I led a minority government. On 13 March 1940, I was sitting in my office at Parliament House, Canberra.

Minority though we were, I had many good friends and colleagues. But I confess that I had a special feeling for three of my Ministers—Sir Henry Gullett, Geoffrey Street, and 'Jim' Fairbairn. They were all men of character, capable of being difficult, but never capable of disloyalty. It was a bright and sunny day, and I was at work.

A knock came on my door, and somebody walked in. There had been a dreadful air crash, almost within sight of my windows. Gullett was dead; Street was dead; Fairbairn was dead; the most scholarly and technically talented soldier in Australian history, Sir Brudenell White, whom I had recalled from retirement to be Chief of the General Staff, was dead. And dead with them were other younger men whom I knew, and for whom I had an affection.

This was a dreadful calamity, for my three colleagues were my close and loyal friends; each of them had a place not only in my Cabinet, but in my heart. I shall never forget that terrible hour; I felt that, for me, the end of the world had come. I tried to speak about them, next day in Parliament. It was difficult for me, and for all of us. In the whole history of government in Australia, this was the most devastating tragedy. Frankly, I don't believe that what happened later (I will come to it), my rejection and, as I felt it at the time, my humiliation, would have happened if these three men had lived. I still mourn for them and carry them in my memory. But I have other things to say about my ultimate defeat about which I will have something more, and something reflective, to add.

But, on that dreadful day, I was sad beyond the powers of description; some of my greatest friends had gone.

One dramatic result was unexpectedly produced. The Country Party, from the leadership of which Page had resigned, and was then led by A. G. Cameron, agreed to form a Coalition Government. Crippled as we were, we were no longer in a minority.

However, my government had encountered great difficulties, both political and personal. And so, when the normal General Election came around in September 1940, fortune deserted us. When all the returns were in, we had, out of seventy-four seats in the House of Representatives, thirty-six. Labour, including a splinter Labour group called the non-Communist Labour Party, had thirty-six. There were two Independents, one, Arthur Coles (later Sir Arthur), who had been elected by Government supporters, the other, Wilson, elected as an Independent Country Party man.

The position was obviously most precarious.

Looking back over the campaign, and recalling that before much more than a year had gone Labour would be in office with a full-blooded programme of war-time restrictions and rationing—with none of which would I disagree—it is not without its grim humour to recall that the Automobile Industry, speaking for the petrol and motor-trading interests, campaigned vigorously and expensively to defeat my government on the slogan 'An All-in War Effort is impossible on Rationed Petrol'. The irony of this is that through most of my political life I have been accused of being the servant of the big business interests!

It is worth recording that Labour's gains were almost entirely in New South Wales, where the bitter hostility of the *Sydney Morning Herald* to me had done great harm to the Government.

However, in spite of the precarious nature of our political tenure, we carried on. Coles, before long, had applied for and had been granted admission to my own party room. Wilson remained an enigmatic figure, but usually voted for us.

We continued to deal with great war-time problems. One of them in particular was deeply concerning me. Was there not a real risk that Japan might take the opportunity of coming in on the side of the enemy?

3. *I go abroad. The Far East*

Late in November 1940 I decided to pay a visit to the Middle East and to England. Seeing that I had been reduced to a majority consisting of two Independents, this was no doubt a risky venture. Indeed my wife, with feminine realism, said to me, 'If you feel you must go, you will go. But you will be out of office within six weeks of your return.' In the event, she was not a mile out!

But I knew that I had to go, and for good reasons. Later on, when Labour had come into office and Japan had entered the war, it was fashionable among some Labour propagandists in Australia to allege that my Government was unaware of the Japanese threat, and unprepared to meet it. (This legend did not prevent the notorious

'Eddie' Ward from concocting a story, months later, that we had prepared plans to base Australia's defence against Japan on a so-called 'Brisbane Line', which appeared to assert that we were well aware of the Japanese threat, and that we were prepared to retreat before it to the extent of surrendering the northern part of Australia!)

Having maintained silence for many years, on the sensible ground that a politician who is engaged in the active affairs which go to the making of history should not take time off to write history, I have now decided, in my retirement, to set the record straight.

On 25 November, I informed the Advisory War Council of my decision. I referred to the alarming position in regard to the defence of Singapore, revealed by the report of a recent Singapore Conference, and the probability that a request would be made to Australia for the dispatch of a Brigade Group, together with certain essential supplies of munitions.

I stated that this and other matters which I had in mind indicated the necessity for the Head of the Government to visit London for a discussion with the Prime Minister of the United Kingdom. The idea met with general approval.

The whole reason why I went to England was to discuss the Japanese menace and to urge the strengthening of the defences of Singapore!

Our own military advices were that while Singapore was a well-equipped British naval base, it had no capital ships or carriers, and grossly inadequate air defence. Figuratively, and perhaps literally, its guns pointed in the wrong direction. The whole establishment was unfitted to repel a Japanese attack, either amphibiously or by land.

I am not in the habit of keeping a diary, but on this journey I broke my rule, and kept one. It will serve to make my narrative more vivid if I make some occasional references to it.

My chief lieutenants on the journey were F. G. Shedden (now Sir Frederick Shedden) Secretary of the Defence Department, and John Storey (later Sir John Storey), a noted industrial engineer, who had taken over the production of aircraft. They were a great pair, full of energy and enthusiasm, and we were all close friends.

We left Sydney on 24 January 1941, by Quantas Empire Flying Boat, a slow but comfortable craft. There were a few other passengers, including three small boys from Simla in India. I report with

unaffected pride that when, on request, I gave the eldest boy my auto-
graph, he assured me, with grave courtesy, that it was 'the next best I
have, after Rudyard Kipling's'.

At Batavia (now Djakarta) I conferred with the Dutch Governor-
General, a very clear-headed and impressive man. He was pessimistic
about Japan. He told me that if Japan struck, the Dutch would resist;
but that they were short of arms, aircraft, and ammunition. He thought
that joint staff talks among the allies should occur. He went on to say
that in his opinion there should be a joint declaration by the Netherlands East Indies, Great Britain, the United States, and Australia; but
that perhaps the time was not ripe. A declaration, he thought, must not
be premature and provocative, but it should not be made so late that
Japan could be already committed.

This conversation, as will appear, was much in my mind when I
came to have my discussions in London.

In Singapore on 29 January I conferred with the Governor, Sir
Shenton Thomas, a brisk and, I judged, efficient man. Among those
present were the new Commander-in-Chief Far East, Air Chief
Marshal Brooke-Popham. I was intrigued by him. I noted afterwards
that 'he has borne the white man's burden in many places from Kenya
to Canada, and it has left his shoulders a little stooped. His hair and
moustache are both sandy and wispy and a little indeterminate.'

The other military people present were imprecise and unhelpful; I
got no impression that they were aware of the realities of their position.

Before I went to bed, I made a note of my conclusions, which I think
I should now record.

I make the record less reluctantly because I put my conclusions
before a meeting at the Foreign Office in London on 26 February.

My note was as follows:

(1) We are, in the Far East, grievously short of aircraft. Three squadrons of
    fighters, even Gladiators, would have a great deterrent effect upon Japan.
(2) The army problem is principally one of material, though a turned-over
    Australian Brigade Group would be 'most helpful'.
(3) The absence of naval craft must encourage the Japanese.
(4) If Japan is to take over Thailand and moves down the Malay Peninsula,
    we should push forward to a point already selected, even if it does mean a
    breach of neutrality.

(5) This Far Eastern problem must be taken seriously and urgently. I have sent instructions to Australia that three cornered staff talks should occur in Singapore at once, so that results may be cabled to us in London.

(6) Brooke-Popham is, I gather, active and a disciplinarian. He must ginger up these other people, who have a mere garrison outlook. Why the devil these generals and people should be ignorant of and not interested in the broad principles of international strategy I cannot understand.

(7) We must as soon as possible tell Japan 'where she gets off'. Appeasement is no good. The peg must be driven in somewhere. I must make a great effort in London to clarify this position. Why cannot *one* squadron of fighters be sent out from North Africa? Why cannot some positive commitment be entered into regarding naval reinforcement of Singapore? At this stage, misty generalizations will please and sustain the Japanese, and nobody else.

Note that this was ten months before Pearl Harbor!

4. *The Middle East*

I arrived in the Middle East, where a magnificent Australian Division was operating, when, on Sunday, 2 February, the flying boat landed on the Sea of Galilee, Lake Tiberias. I had never been there before; but I had been well schooled in the Bible, and was excited at all I saw. I was received by General Blamey, and Sir Harold MacMichael, the British High Commissioner for Palestine, then under Mandate.

I was driven down to Jerusalem with MacMichael, who was, in the old phrase, 'a scholar and a gentleman'. He was sceptical of Jewish politicians, but just and admiring about the superb Jewish work in reclamation and the improvements of agriculture. He had no illusions about the Arabs, but he liked their handsome appearance and good manners! This was superbly English!

On the way down to Jerusalem, we talked much of the classics, of which he knew much more than I did, of poetry, and of the laws of economics, the existence of which, to my intense amusement, MacMichael vigorously denied.

On the following day I went into the old City of Jerusalem with the Chief Administrator (of Jerusalem) of MacMichael's staff, a delightful man named Keith-Roach. I will never forget it. He explained the rules to me. And they are complicated rules, since Jerusalem is not only the Holy City for both Christian and Jew, but is also one of the three holy cities of the Mohammedans.

Keith-Roach spoke Arabic with dignity and ease, and explained to me the curious mystique of 'The Wailing Wall'. It appeared that, for example, a Jewish stockbroker in New York would pay an annual sum to a Jerusalem Rabbi to say prayers for him at the Wailing Wall. Keith-Roach said a marvellous thing to me—marvellous in the sense that it was so illuminating—as we drove into the old City. At intervals, along the bare hillsides, I would see something that looked like a low cairn of stones. 'What are they?' I asked. 'Ah,' said my guide, 'they are just little places where an Arab, with a long-barrelled rifle, can take a pot-shot at you as you drive along!' 'Really,' I said, 'that sounds pretty disagreeable!' 'Not at all,' he rejoined, 'you see, I like them. Except when they are politicians, the Jews are wonderful, they work hard and you can always take their word. The Arab is different; he will do you down if he can, and shoot you if a chance offers. But, my dear Sir, he is a gentleman, and it's a pleasure to do business with him.'

My little time in Palestine, or Israel, etched itself into my memory. I saw strange husbandry; ploughing by a camel and a bullock hitched to a plough that was practically a bent stick with an iron point on it!

There was an obvious problem, of reconciling Arab and Jew, a problem which, as I noted at the time, would become active again after the war.

After Palestine, in which I saw and reviewed many Australian troops and renewed my pride in my country, I went on to Cairo, where I was the guest of Sir Miles Lampson, the British Ambassador, and his mischievously witty and entertaining wife. The new Egyptian Prime Minister, Sirry Pasha, delighted me. We found that political problems are the same the wide world over, and laughed about them. Our victories in Libya had improved the Egyptian morale, normally, at that time, fairly brittle. I soon discovered that King Farouk was a focus of danger. Self-willed, flattered, and with no mental discipline, he was, at the age of twenty-one, a problem. I soon found that he disliked the company of diplomats or thinkers; his instincts took him to the 'servants' hall'.

The great pity was that so good a Prime Minister had to serve under so poor a King. Sirry Pasha was an irrigation engineer of standing, a good administrator, and completely honest. He had a healthy dislike of demagogues (who could always hire an audience or a mob of demonstrators quite cheaply). Egypt's financial position was healthy. She was enjoying the proceeds of a bulk sale of the cotton harvest, and about £2m. a month was being spent by British and Dominion soldiers.

On 7 February I went down to Alexandria, to see the fleet. I mention this, for two purposes. One is to say that I met and moved around with that very remarkable man, Admiral Cunningham—slim, red-faced, blue-eyed, radiating optimism and faith in his ships and his men. He took me aboard two of the 'scrap-iron flotilla', *Stuart* under the famous Captain Waller, who was not to survive the war, and *Voyager,* and also the cruiser *Perth.*

Cunningham loved the Australian ships and men. He had a degree of personal magnetism which I have known to be surpassed only by Lloyd George and Winston Churchill. As we went ashore at the end of the day, Shedden said, discreetly, 'What did you think of him?' 'Well, Shedden,' I said, 'I can only be glad that he did not ask me to stay with him for the rest of the war; because if he had, Shedden, you would now be sending for a new Prime Minister!'

I managed to reach Benghazi, and spent a night in the Italia Hotel after dining sketchily with the Army leaders.

It is odd how trifles occasionally remain in the memory. One of them concerning that dinner is that, being indebted to the Italians, we drank a crude white Chianti by way of an *aperitif,* and an equally crude red Chianti with our main course, which was, I seem to recall, tinned spaghetti! The other is that 'Ned' Herring, then C.R.A. of the Sixth Division, later to command an Army Corps, and who became, after the war, Chief Justice of Victoria and Lieutenant-Governor; a very remarkable man; apologetically offered me a thin and twisted cigar. 'Ned,' I said, 'when this war is over, and we meet in Melbourne, I will give you the best Havana that money can buy!'

I kept my promise; but alas! he had given up smoking.

General Richard O'Connor made an enormous impression upon me, an impression which was fortified by the unanimous opinion of those officers who served under him. He was a small, alert, refined man, of immense charm. He had been the real organizer of the incredibly successful drive to the West, in which the Italians had been outmatched, in spite of their numerical superiority, and had surrendered in droves. Some time afterwards, he was captured himself, and his active career was thus seriously interrupted. But for that misfortune, I have no doubt that he would have been one of the greatest military names in the history of the war.

All of the events in the Libyan campaigns have been faithfully recorded by objective and informed writers, and I have nothing to add except a few things, absolutely unrelated, about several quite different people.

One was Captain Frank Hurley, the celebrated war (and polar) photographer, who flew back in the same plane with me from Barce to Cairo, via El Adem, just out of Tobruk. We had gone to Benghazi, only the day before, in a fairly fast plane escorted by two Hurricanes. We had, at the Hotel Italia, felt the concussion of some 'last moment' Italian bombs.

But when we left Barce, we left in an old, lumbering 'Valencia' with a top speed of eighty-five miles per hour, and we had no escort. As soon as we made height, the warped old windows admitted so much cold air that we began to freeze. I soon found that three copies of London Punch, tucked inside the trousers, had a certain insulating effect; but welcomed the arrival of a few blankets provided by the crew. The captain came back to look at us. I asked him to tell us as a matter of interest why, only twenty-four hours before, we had been thought to need a fighter escort, while today we had none. He grinned broadly, 'Well, you see, this plane flies so slowly that no Italian fighter plane could get down to a pace at which it could hit us!' I must say that this sounded reasonable enough. When we arrived at El Adem we got out to stretch our legs, which, speaking for myself, were almost destitute of feeling. After me emerged Frank Hurley, in even worse shape than me. 'How does this come about?' I asked. 'Quite simple,' said Hurley, 'when the boy came along to offer me a blanket, I was about to grab two when my eyes caught the white polar ribbons on my tunic, and vulgar pride overtook me. No thank you, I said, on the whole I find the plane rather stuffy!'

It was a great honour to know Frank Hurley.

My second personality was General Iven Mackay, the brilliant commanding officer of the Australian 6th Division. Like O'Connor, he did not look what he was. There is more nonsense than enough spoken about that curiously misleading thing, physiognomy. I have known people with prognathous jaws and a grim gleam in the eye who didn't have the courage of a louse. And I have known mild and meek-looking men, with no hint of aggression in them, like O'Connor and Mackay, who combined the wisdom of the serpent with the courage of the lion.

Behind the whole of the operations, there was Sir Archibald Wavell, who was Commander-in-Chief in the Middle East at a time when reinforcements were scarce and supplies dangerously interrupted, but whose record in that period will survive. I don't think that Winston Churchill ever fully appreciated Wavell's stature; indeed, at the last, he was something less than just to him. Admittedly, Wavell was not an easy man, as I was to discover in Cairo. Admittedly, he later made miscalculations at the time of the Greek campaign. He could, as we all know, write like an angel. But he did not follow Goldsmith by talking 'like poor Poll'. He simply did not talk at all. He appeared to be blind in one eye, and this meant that when I sat next to him at table he would swivel his head right round, ninety degrees, fix me with the good eye, and say either 'I see', or 'Maybe', or 'Um', or nothing. I wanted to put all sorts of things to him, and thought that I had some right to do so, since Australian troops were no small part of the forces under his command. For example, I asked him whether he thought that the German forces might counter-attack to and through Benghazi; for this might have a bearing elsewhere. His only reply was to the effect that it was 'very difficult'. I left Egypt on my way to London with a depressing feeling that Wavell didn't trust me, only to find, in London, that he had reported on me quite favourably!

In London, I was to learn that his lack of oral fluency was more than counter-balanced by his astonishing facility on paper. In the next few months I saw many of Churchill's dispatches to Wavell, colloquial, sometimes imperious and even abrupt. But I also saw Wavell's replies, which proved him to be a good match for Winston on his own ground.

There were many splendid Australian soldiers in the Middle East. To make a casual reference to them would be inadequate and unjust;

they have their honoured place in our military history. But I must make particular mention of two of them.

General Blamey was in Cairo, as Commanding Officer of the Second Australian Imperial Force. In the First World War, he had, when little more than thirty, reached General rank and become the Chief of Staff to the First A.I.F.

Between the two wars, he had left the army to take up the post of Chief Commissioner of Police in Victoria, which he held for eleven years.

He was nothing if not positive; he seldom spared anybody's feelings; and so he became a controversial figure. He had plenty of critics, and not a few detractors. I was never very close to him, but we had some good friends in common. Although I had reason to know that he had a poor opinion of me, I had, and retained until the end of his life, a very high opinion of him.

When the Second World War came, and we set about raising the Second A.I.F., none of us in my War Cabinet had any doubt that, in spite of his long absence from the army, Blamey was the man to command it.

And so, there he was in and around Egypt in February 1941. I saw a good deal of him, and was glad that we had appointed him. The morale of the Australian forces was very high, with great victories at Bardia and Tobruk. I noted at the time that in the Libyan campaign no less than ten Italian divisions had been defeated by one armoured and one infantry division, our own.

We had at the outset asserted the rule established in the First War that the Australian force should operate under Australian command, with direct access to the Australian Government.

On 10 February, in a conference I had with him, Wavell said that while he thought the 'aggregation' principle for the A.I.F. was good, it should not be too rigidly applied; it was not always possible to find a front which would occupy an entire Corps. (By that time we had in the Middle East not only the 6th Division, but also the 7th Division under Lavarack, while the 9th Division was being assembled under Morshead.)

The following day I conveyed this to Blamey, whose comment was clear and characteristic. 'Australian forces must be regarded as national, under national command. This does not exclude the use of smaller units in special places, but all must be subject to the consent of the G.O.C., A.I.F.' This, I thought, was reasonably in line with what Wavell had said. But Blamey then added the Blamey touch—a vigorous Australianism, determined to maintain the Australian identity and to bristle in its defence. 'If you give these British Generals an inch, they'll take an ell!'

I left the Middle East to go on to London confirmed in my belief that we had the right man in the right place. I had a hand in two later events in Blamey's military career which, though it breaks whatever sequence there is in these memoirs, I will at this stage put on the record.

On Friday, 19 April, in London, I received my 'red box', and read of the proposed postings to various commands in the Middle East. I saw no reference to Blamey. So, rightly or wrongly, I got in touch with Sir John Dill, who was then C.I.G.S. He came to Australia House. I told him that if he had any generals in that area who were as good as Blamey, they must be very good indeed. Surely, I said, Blamey should have a command, and Wavell's staff should contain a senior Australian officer. I suggested that Dill should get a quick opinion from Wavell himself before finally determining the postings. I added, for good measure, that if the Australian public learned that Blamey, whose troops had played and were playing a major part in the Middle East campaign, had been overlooked, there would be a very strong reaction. Dill, a man of very high perception, said that he would get an urgent report from Wavell.

The reply came back promptly. In the Greek campaign, by that time clearly unsuccessful and about to be ended by evacuation, Wavell reported that Blamey had shown qualities which 'fitted him for the highest commands'. So Dill appointed Blamey Deputy Commander-in-Chief, Middle East. I was pleased. I was never sure that Tom Blamey was; he liked his own Australian Force; but I had done what I thought to be my best.

The third event occurred in 1950. Blamey had long since retired to private and business life. I had just come back into office as a result of the General Election of December 1949. I conceived the idea that Australia, which had played so great a military part in two world wars, should have a Field-Marshal, and that Blamey was the obvious man. I sent a dispatch to London, pointing out, as the simple fact was, that the only notable soldier on our side who had gone right through both wars as a senior officer was Blamey, and that an appointment as Field-Marshal would be an appropriate recognition of both the Australian Military forces and Blamey himself. My first answer was a dusty one; it was not the practice to appoint to this distinguished rank a retired officer. I retorted by making a reference to Field-Marshal Smuts, but without success. But, I thought, if retirement is the bar, I will re-post Blamey to the Active List. So I rang him up. He was in Queensland, and knew nothing of what I had in mind. Our telephone conversation was quite brief. 'Tom, I am proposing to restore you to the Active List, for reasons which seem to me to be good. Ask no questions, but say that you agree.' To which he replied, 'You do what you like. I'm just going out to sea, to fish!'

And so it was that, in the Royal Birthday Honours of 1950, he was created a Field-Marshal.

While I was in the Middle East I renewed my friendship with Leslie Morshead, then commanding the 18th Brigade (which had been to England).

He was born in Ballarat, and when I was a schoolboy in that old mining city his family was well-known. He had been a school-teacher; he had won a D.S.O. in 1917, in the First World War; he had been engaged thereafter for many years in shipping, but had returned to active service when the Second War broke out.

On 29 January 1941, he was appointed to command the 9th Australian Division. By April he was assigned to command the defence of Tobruk with his Division, some British artillery regiments, and some other units.

His magnificent leadership at Tobruk, and the courage and skill of those who served under him, make up one of the noblest events in the war. Morshead was certainly one of the greatest soldiers in Australian history.

When Tobruk was being heavily invested, beating back an armoured attack by Rommel's divisions and doing it under great disabilities of terrain, I sent Morshead, from London, a message of pride and gratitude. Years after the war, he would produce it and show it to me with pleasure.

I found, in London, that Churchill, though he understood perfectly the tactical significance of Tobruk ('We must keep it as a sally-port from which to attack the enemy's flank') had an inadequate conception of what was needed to defeat and destroy a tank attack. I remember him saying, early in April, when Morshead and his 'rats' were to fight it out against odds, 'If stout-hearted men with rifles and machine guns cannot hold these people until the guns come up, I must revise my ideas of war!'

5. *England: The problem of Japan*

On 26 February 1941, I attended a conference in Mr R. A. Butler's room at the Foreign Office in London. 'Rab' was then a Minister under Anthony Eden, who had gone to the Middle East, on an investigation which led to the expedition into Greece.

Somewhat to my surprise, the chair was taken by Sir Alexander Cadogan, the permanent head of the Foreign Office. Lord Cranborne (now Salisbury) was present. I was accompanied by Bruce (then of course Australia's High Commissioner) and Shedden.

I at once raised the question of the tendencies and probabilities of Japanese action.

Cadogan at once was quite frank about the matter. The Japanese had engaged in a drive in which they had obtained a footing in Indo-China and to some extent in Thailand, with the apparent object of by-passing Singapore. They had their eyes on the Netherlands East Indies and, he agreed, constituted a menace to Australia and New Zealand. Recent indications had convinced the Foreign Office that Japan had some arrangement with Germany for a simultaneous development of trouble in Europe and the Far East. The United States knew of these indications. Japan had been informed of this knowledge and the general feeling was that the developments had been postponed.

It became clear that the Foreign Office thought that the getting of Japanese air-bases in Indo-China or the west coast of Thailand would be dangerous.

Reinforced by my talk with the Governor-General of the Netherlands East Indies, I persisted in inquiring whether these were regarded as vital.

I put the view that the Japanese were opportunists, and might be careful. But they could well get into a position where they could not retreat without loss of face. Where should we draw the line? I conceded, of course, that it would be difficult for Great Britain or the rest of us to know whether we could nail our colours to the mast without knowing the United States' attitude. But there was nothing more dangerous than drift.

My main point was that diplomacy and military provision or action could not exist in water-tight compartments; and therefore the reinforcement of Singapore was the most important diplomatic move that could be made. I made special mention of the need for munitions and aircraft. Two or three squadrons of fighters sent to Singapore could have an effect out of all proportion to their intrinsic significance. If the Japanese were to establish themselves in the Netherlands East Indies the whole Australian defence policy and plans would have had to be recast.

These propositions were, I thought, generally accepted around the table, but there were obvious (and understandable) reservations on two points.

The first, of course, was that British and Commonwealth resources, in men and particularly in aircraft, were already fully stretched, and, at a time when German bombing raids occurred every night, a substantial diversion of fighter aircraft could have been regarded as taking a risk with an existing war in order to guard against a possible one.

The second was that a war in South-East Asia against Japan could not be willingly contemplated unless there was a near certainty of American intervention. Mr Butler felt that the immediate need was to make as solid a front as possible between ourselves, the United States, and the Dutch, and to extend that front to events in Thailand.

We thus had much common ground; it was clear that London understood the dangers of Japan, but equally clear that advance warnings to Japan would not be entertained in the absence of American support. I wrote down a note that night, which reads—'Drift seems to be the policy of the Foreign Office. Why should we allow an atmosphere of inevitability to drift into our relations with Japan? We need firmness, definition, and friendliness, and they are not impossible.'

Naturally, I kept coming back to this matter during the rest of my stay in England, but without material success.

2*

Looking back at later events, I still cannot understand why, in the light of the diplomatic exchanges which related to the problem of Japan, and the grave apprehensions of Great Britain, Australia and New Zealand, and the Dutch, all well-known to the United States authorities, Pearl Harbor, in the following December, should have come as such a surprise and caught the defenders so flat-footed.

In the long run, as history will record, Great Britain sent two capital ships to Singapore, a powerful naval reinforcement, but because they had no adequate fighter aircraft cover, they and their gallant officers and crews were lost.

I have failed to convey my meaning if I have not made it clear that it was the Japanese threat which engaged my attention in Singapore, and which had taken me to the Foreign Office in London.

But, early in March 1941, I made a speech in London which, following the modern technique of 'slanting' the news, was recorded in a section of the Australian press as 'appeasement' of Japan! This, no doubt, arose from one statement of mine that 'it would be a blunder to resign ourselves to the inevitability of hostilities with Japan'.

What I in fact said, as I had said at the Foreign Office, was that a policy of drift was disastrous; that frank discussions should occur; that Australia's attitude was that she would resent and resist aggression; that it would be a mistake for any power to believe that Australia was not prepared to fight for those things she regarded as vital. I added, for good measure, that our foreign policy was not the product of fear, but just the opposite. If possible, while keeping up our diplomatic bridges with Japan, we should, with those who were prepared to stand with us, tell Japan exactly where the limits of tolerance would be drawn.

I reiterated my statement for the benefit of the Australian people, and the 'false alarm' died down.

In all of these matters, my acting Prime Minister had carried the torch most faithfully, and conducted the business of Government (never easy if the Leader is absent) with skill and fidelity.

6. *The Greek intervention*

The very first matter to come before the War Cabinet after my arrival in London was military assistance to Greece. Churchill outlined his proposals to me on 23 February at Chequers.

There is an admirably documented and clearly stated account of the whole matter in Anthony Eden's *The Reckoning* (Cassell), and I have neither desire nor qualification to edit it.

All I want to do is to record a few personal memories.

I had just been in the Middle East, where I had seen the evidence of how successful a relatively small force could be against numerical odds, when the enemy was Italy. Wavell had decided not to advance westerly beyond Benghazi. True, the Germans had a fair crossing over the Straits of Pantellaria, in which British naval action was made acutely dangerous because of the enemy's air superiority in those narrow waters. But I had gathered the impression from Wavell in Cairo that he did not anticipate a major German offensive around the Gulf of Sirte to Benghazi.

The proposals which I had to consider on behalf of Australia, both with Churchill and in War Cabinet, involved the use of a substantial Australian force as part of a substantial total.

This presented me with a real problem. I would not have it thought that Australian troops, who had fought so magnificently from Bardia to Benghazi, would wish to be excused a share in a dangerous enterprise. We were not in a war of local defence, but in a world war, the chances of which might take us into strange places.

On the other hand, I was in War Cabinet in London, where the broad strategy would be determined, and therefore had a duty to my country to satisfy myself about the validity of any strategical conception which involved Australia. More than this, my colleagues in Australia must be satisfied. Having these considerations in mind, I first made it clear that there could be no question about our spirit, but that the case for intervention in Greece at a time when the position in Egypt and Cyrenaica, though currently satisfactory, was in its nature precarious, must be established. Moreover, though my Australian colleagues and I were willing to be bold, we also wanted to be as prudent as possible. By 26 February, I had received a message from the War Cabinet, concurring in the proposed use of Australian troops in the forces to Greece. They recognized, as I did, that the adventure was risky. True, our military advices in London were that there was a reasonable chance of success; but much, of course, would depend upon the co-operation of the Greeks and the attitude of Yugoslavia and Turkey.

My colleagues stipulated, and I said in London, that our troops should not be allocated the proposed task unless equipped on the maximum establishment scale. Further, we made it clear that our participation must be regarded as conditional upon plans having been completed to ensure, if necessary, a successful evacuation, with shipping and other services being available for that purpose. I emphasized that we were prudent; many lives would be affected by the event; but we were in no way disposed to refuse to accept risks. The whole Australian record in war had been built on the acceptance of risks, and of fighting against odds. I would therefore wish to have an up-to-date appreciation from Wavell, and a clear statement from the Foreign Secretary (then in the Middle East) and from Mr Churchill himself as to the broad objectives of an obviously difficult military intervention in Greece.

Wavell's reports, which in the event proved over-optimistic, were favourable. It is clear that his intelligence had, not for the first or last time, underestimated the German skill and strength and equipment. In the result, we were, by early April, learning of Rommel's offensive and its success.

But the important thing, from my point of view and that of my Cabinet in Australia, was that the military advice we received from Cairo advised that the diversion of troops to Greece would not diminish our capacity to hold the position in the Western Desert. Yet, by 7 April, I found myself speaking very freely at Downing Street about the way in which the speed and power of the German attack at Benghazi had been underestimated and that in the result the need to meet this attack would involve some weakening of the forces for the Greek campaign.

In one sense, therefore, the story is one of military miscalculation in Egypt.

By 17 April, when the forecast about the possibility of effective German attack in Cyrenaica had been falsified, and Yugoslavia had collapsed, my Australian colleagues still adhered to their (and my) belief that the decision to send our troops to Greece was strategically correct. But we had all become properly concerned about the prospects and practicability of the withdrawal of the intervening forces.

But the other aspect of the matter, not tactical but in the highest international sense strategic, must be mentioned by me; for, in spite of our prudent requirement of an appreciation from Wavell, it was the question dominant. Should Greece be left to its fate?

Twenty-five years after the event, and with sad memories of the failure of the enterprise and its consequences for many of my fellow-countrymen, I must still say that the decision was right. I supported it, after advising my colleagues in Australia of the arguments this way and that, and securing their approval. It would be quite wrong to say that it was a happy decision to make, for them or for me, for the whole operation was chancy. But, as I wrote early on to my colleagues, the foundation of the decision was to be found in 'the overwhelming moral and political repercussions of abandoning Greece'.

The Greeks had, with very limited equipment, been fighting and beating the Italians in Albania. Yugoslavia had not yet succumbed to Hitler and, encouraged by a demonstration of strength, might come our way. Turkey could become an active resister. In short, the whole position in the Balkans was at stake at a time when Western Europe was in Hitler's hands.

Behind all this, there was the fact that in April 1939, only two years before, Great Britain had given a guarantee to Greece. To dishonour this guarantee, without any effort to perform it, would have had disastrous moral repercussions around the world, and not least in the United States, where Roosevelt was engaged in moving American opinion into a state of rather more than benevolent neutrality.

Having all these considerations in mind, I had summed them up to my colleagues on 29 March in these words:

The view here is that while the adventure is hazardous, it has reasonable chances of success. These are improved if Yugoslavia goes as well as Churchill anticipates and Turkey is stimulated by her example. Personally, I feel that no chance to form a Balkan Front should be neglected, and that our aid to Greece may prove the decisive factor in stiffening resistance.

In the result, as we know, the expedition failed; there was an evacuation with serious losses, and much discontent.

But all the entries were not on the debit side.

After reading such records as I can, I firmly believe that the resistance of Greece, and our support of that resistance, upset Hitler's time-table for his proposed, but unadvertised invasion of Russia.

It must be remembered that late in March a *coup d'état* took place in Yugoslavia, King Peter being proclaimed. This event was encouraged by the British presence in Greece. Hitler decided to attack Yugoslavia. This delayed his Russian plans for about five weeks. This delay proved costly to Germany, and may have been crucial.

7. *The Irish problem*

It is, of course, quite obvious that the neutrality of Ireland (other than Northern Ireland) was a great cause of danger, and shipping losses, and bitterness. Relations between the two countries had never been worse.

On 9 March, Colonel Donovan, of the U.S.A., a sort of ambassador-at-large, whom I had met in Cairo, came to see me at Chequers, and we had a long and fruitful talk. He was a good man, easy, composed, comfortable looking, with a good blue eye. I thought that I could very readily accept his opinion on men or affairs. He had just made a quick visit to Dublin, and encouraged me to make one; which I did, as will appear. He thought that the core of the problem was the pressure of the Roman Catholic minority in Ulster. He thought that De Valera was troubled in his conscience for not having made clear to his own people the real moral issues of the war. This was in a sense a curious criticism, for the moral issues in the war touched and concerned Donovan's own country just as much as they did Ireland, yet America was, like Ireland, neutral. This, however, is a mere debating point, for Donovan was himself enthusiastically and whole-heartedly on our side.

He went on to make three suggestions.

First, that there should be an avenue of personal contact between De Valera and Churchill (I later made a not unrelated proposal, with the result I shall recite a little later).

Second, that there should be some encouraging words spoken in high quarters to Irish Catholics who thought as J. M. Dillon thought.

Third, that some attempt should be made to get rid of any pin-pricks against Catholics in the North.

He thought, in the broad, that the Irish farmer was beginning to discover that neutrality was not profitable, and that he (Donovan) thought the position not hopeless. The real trouble was mutual ignorance, which leaders were not adequately attempting to dispel.

I was glad to have this talk, for I had already decided to visit Ireland and spy out the land for myself.

Unlike England, Australia's population is, to the extent of roughly one-fifth, derived from Irish ancestry. It tends to have a colourful political outlook, it is for the most part devoutly Catholic, but it has never been remarkable for neutrality. Its people come of fighting stock. So I thought I should try to discover why there was neutrality in Ireland when there was none to be found among 'Irish-Australians'.

It seemed characteristic of Churchill that he never lacked gratitude to his friends, but never forgot an enemy. That was, no doubt, one of the inner springs of his vigorous and undaunted war leadership. His dislike of Irish neutrality, his well-founded belief that it placed in-tolerable obstacles in the way of success in the great and constant battle of the Western Approaches, embodies itself in his detestation of De Valera.

On the Sunday before my journey to Ireland, he asked me, amiably at Chequers, what I would be doing later in the week. I said I proposed a visit to Ireland. 'Ah, of course,' said he, 'you will be going to see Andrews in Belfast!' I told him that I was proposing to see Andrews, then the Prime Minister of Northern Ireland, and that I wanted to see something of the great ship-building works of Harland and Woolf, and the operations of Short and Harland, who were making Stirling bombers. 'But I will then go down to Dublin to see De Valera and his Cabinet.' He flared up, 'Never with my approval will you visit that wicked man.' I had to tell him that I should have liked his blessing, but that I must go without it. There was a large and loyal Irish or Irish-derived community in Australia. I was their Prime Minister, and I was anxious to investigate at first hand the attitude of the Irish Government on a matter which was the concern not only of Great Britain, though she was the immediate sufferer, but of Australia, a most active ally, whose fate was involved with that of Great Britain.

So, on the Thursday, 3 April, I flew off to Belfast in a small R.A.F. plane, got well-frozen *en route,* saw Andrews, visited the works proposed, made a speech at the Ulster Reform Club, was given an honorary degree at the hands of the Chancellor, Lord Londonderry, at the Queen's University, and returned to dine and spend the night at Government House as the guest of the then Duke and Duchess of Abercorn. They were marvellous and full-hearted people, but the Duchess soon put me through my paces. 'Is Churchill going to sell us out to the South?' You can imagine my feelings of surprise. I told her of my little controversy with Winston about my projected visit to Dublin. This, I think, mollified her a little, though I thought she still had some mental reservations!

Even in a few hours, it was made quite clear that the Ulster feelings about Eire were strong, and indeed bitter. Protestant and Presbyterian as I am, I long since learned that there are some Protestants whose protestantism is an expression of hostility rather than of faith. This reflection is not entirely irrelevant to what I observed in Ulster. But there were deep elements in the prevailing temper.

I found among responsible leaders a strong feeling that conscription should have been extended to Ulster and that the refusal to extend it was dictated by a tenderness for the feelings of the Roman Catholic minority. (Strangely enough, at that time, there came from the neutral and predominantly Roman Catholic South not less than 650 men a month, to enlist in the British Army!)

Local recruiting in Ulster was lagging, partly, I was told, because of the feeling about conscription, and partly because of the abnormally high unemployment, which at the time of my visit stood at 45,000. This could clearly have a depressing effect on recruiting if the view became current that the employed man who enlisted would, after the war, find his occupation gone. There was even a fear that the recruit's civil job would be taken by 'somebody coming into Ulster from the South'.

The chief cause of unemployment was a slackening of business at the linen mills. I was told that the position could be greatly eased if the British Government would make more use of Ulster's munition manufacturing potential.

I formed a very strong impression that Ulster would be much

stimulated if two things were done; the introduction of conscription side by side with a law protecting the conscript in relation to his civil employment; and an investigation made by the British Ministry of Supply of Ulster's industrial resources. I ventured to suggest these two steps on my return to London, but without much success.

On one matter there was complete unanimity among the political leaders. The unification of Ireland would be forcibly resisted by Ulster, for three principal reasons.

The first, of course, was that Ulster would not forego its allegiance to the Crown.

The second was that the inevitable consequence of unification would be that the whole island would be voted into neutrality by the Roman Catholic majority in the South.

The third, much less precise and more speculative, was that Ulstermen feared that their industrial establishments would be weakened and perhaps destroyed by the fiscal policies of a United Irish Parliament.

I was confirmed in my belief that the whole Irish problem was bedevilled by deep-seated emotions in three capitals, and that some effort should be made to promote contacts and understanding. It was with this in mind that I took a train, next day, through lovely rolling countryside, to Dublin, to a neutral state in a war-torn area.

I was met at the Railway Station by Eamon De Valera himself. He was a striking figure, tall and spare and ascetic. Indeed, with his long dark frieze overcoat and broad-brimmed black hat, he looked positively saturnine. Within an hour or two, I was in conference with him. I was of course familiar with the story of J. H. Thomas's negotiations with him some years before; for 'Jimmy' recounted it to me with some satisfaction. 'Why didn't you get somewhere with Dev., Jimmy?' asked his colleagues. 'Well,' came the reply, 'I 'ad two days with 'im, and at the end of that time, 'e 'ad only got up to Brian Boru!'

So I was not entirely unprepared for a personal experience of the retrospectivity of the Irish mind. At the end of my first two hours with De Valera, he had brought his historical review up to the Norman Conquest!

But I still found the Irish leader vastly interesting. He was a scholar, and in a quiet way, passionately sincere. I thought that I perceived, in a mind of the most acute intelligence, blind spots occasioned by prejudice and bitter personal experience and sometimes by a failure to realize the facts of life, as life existed in the very crisis of a great war. I was soon to discover that he had a large and devoted following in Dublin. He was 'the chief'. The very clerks in the offices stood promptly and rigidly to attention as he strode past. His Ministers, most or all of whom had been confined in British prisons, but in whom a great sense of humour had survived, spoke with freedom—but with no disloyalty—in his absence, but were restrained and obedient in his presence. But in my talks I thought that some of them had minds more flexible, and from my point of view more realistic than his.

But, as my discussions with him went on, he grew on me. My prejudices (because I arrived with some myself!) began to fade. I liked him, and occasionally evoked from him a sort of wintry humour which was not without charm. I thought him, in spite of his devotion to maps, charts, and records, not incapable of being affected by the right kind of personal and human approach.

But, in April 1941, this kind of approach was conspicuously absent. For example, when I mentioned Andrews, the Ulster Prime Minister, De Valera spoke pleasantly about him. I asked whether he saw him frequently. The reply was, 'I have never met him!'

And yet Dublin and Belfast are separated by about ninety miles!

What contact did he have with London? None. To me it was ludicrous to realize that I, who had travelled many thousands of miles to Great Britain, had had more conversations with De Valera than any British Minister had had since the war began!

As a result of our talks, I formed a few impressions, I hope accurately, about De Valera's point of view. I now record them, because they do have some relationship to a problem as yet unsolved, but which ought to be solved if prejudice is not, in the long run, to overthrow reason and good sense.

Here are my impressions; they were mine, and bind nobody else.

(1) I thought that 'Dev' was of opinion that Britain's cause in the war was a just one, and that the war was forced upon her.

(2) I felt that he would like Britain to win. He gave me to understand that eighty per cent of his people, though by accumulated instinct distrustful of the British, would like a British victory.

(3) His only grievance against Great Britain was that Ireland was still a divided country. He thought the Churchill Government hostile and unsympathetic. At the same time, when brought face to face with the fact, he recognized that Great Britain could not possibly throw Ulster into Eire if that meant that Ulster was also to become neutral and that Great Britain was to be deprived of even those bases which she then had. In effect, the campaign for union could not usefully or sensibly be pursued during the war, assuming the neutrality of Eire.

So far as that neutrality was concerned, I found it difficult to convince him that the results, for Great Britain, were disastrous. He would stand in front of the map and puzzle as to why bases in Eire could be of the slightest importance. I waxed eloquent on the vital battle of the Western Approaches, and on the immense importance of air bases for fighter aircraft if the hellish combination of the Focke-Wulf and the German U-boat were to be defeated. But I spoke in vain; these considerations were alien to his mind.

He had two great justifications for Irish neutrality.

One was that, as he put it to me, there was, in the Irish heart, a 'passion for neutrality'. I thought this a strange and unusual passion; I had never observed it in my own country or among my own Irish-Australian friends; but I accepted it.

But his other justification was that Ireland was virtually defenceless; practically no anti-aircraft guns or air force, and an army without modern equipment. He would step across to the window, and gaze out, and say, 'My beautiful Dublin could be destroyed.' It was clear to me that his neutrality policy was founded not simply on a traditional distrust of Great Britain, but upon a fear of German attack, particularly from the air. I confess that I was left with the feeling that, as the fear of attack seemed to be the principal factor, the possibility of removing it by some material assistance on the aircraft and munitions side should be explored.

But even here I came up against an obstacle. For he told me with great earnestness that with modern arms Eire could protect herself and 'therefore protect Britain's flank'. But when I pointed out that the British flank was on the western and north-western seas, and that these could not be protected by a neutral, but only by belligerent ships and aircraft, I got the impression that this platitude came to him almost as a new idea.

You may well say that there is disclosed, in this narrative, a certain *naïveté* on my part. Perhaps so; but I repeat that I did not find De Valera an impossible person, as London had expected. I thought he had fine qualities, and that his fixed ideas, like those of his own or any other people, could not be dislodged by either aloofness or force.

On the morning of Saturday, 5 April, I was to lunch with De Valera and his Ministers, but in the meantime he was engaged. Very kindly, knowing that this was my first visit to Dublin, he sent round a car and a driver, and a young man from his Foreign Office to act as guide and adviser.

It was one of those mornings where a little broken and dispersing ground mist promises a lovely day. I was, for once, all agog for sight-seeing, I little knew what errors I was to make before the morning was out.

The car moved into a broad street, and was halted. Mr X (as I will call him, for he is still going strong in the service of his country) said, 'This street is called O'Connell Street, after the Liberator. And' (opening the window and pointing up) 'that is a statue of the Liberator himself.' I made a suitable response. So far, all was well. But then I made my first error quite unintentionally, though Mr X, I fear, thought it deliberate. 'Where is Sackville Street?' said I. Mr X, who was a black-browed bigot, but a patriot, turned on me with a withering blast. 'This street, named O'Connell Street, after the Liberator, was once called Sack-ville Street; and you may tell a man's politics in this country if he still calls it Sackville Street.'

'I'm very sorry,' I mildly explained, 'but when I was at school a long time ago there were some photographs at the back of the school atlas, and one of them was of Sackville Street, Dublin. It is because of this that I have always wanted to see it!' 'Um,' said Mr X.

But though I was faint, I was pursuing. 'But wasn't it your Irishman Oliver St John Gogarty who not so many years ago wrote that fascinating book *As I Was Walking Down Sackville Street?*' To which Mr X rejoined, 'And that's exactly what we would expect him to do!'

As will be seen, I was learning that prejudice could be as obdurate in Dublin as in London. But 'hope springs eternal', and so I proceeded to my doom. Further down the street, I could see a tall column emerging from one of the banks of mist; and I asked what it was. 'Sir,' said X, 'that is the Nelson Monument, and I'll not need to tell you that many of us think that it should have been removed.' This seemed to me to be going so much too far that I inquired, rather sharply, 'And what did Nelson ever do to you, except save you from Napoleon, in common with all the rest of us?' His reply was splendid, complete, and crushing. 'Sir, he was not an Irishman!'

(Not long before I sat down to write these memoirs, I read that some partisans had blown up the Nelson Monument, so no doubt Mr X sleeps more quietly in his bed.) We drove on, turned into the Phoenix Park Road, and approached the Park. And there, alongside the road, was an equestrian statue of Wellington. Over-eager to recover some of my lost ground, I said 'Ah! There is Wellington! You can't say he wasn't an Irishman, my dear X, for, dammit, he was born on the premises!' That proved to be my swan-song. For Mr X had the last word. 'And wasn't it Wellington himself who said that to be born in a stable didn't argue that you were a horse?'

We drove on around the Bay, silent for the most part, and all contention stilled.

I returned to England, somewhat adventurously, in a chartered Dragon Rapide, piloted by a celebrated civil pilot, Captain Olley. I will recount the story, for it provides a little light relief in a serious narrative.

I had with me two members of my staff. 'Dev' escorted me to the plane. Olley arrived, wearing the *tenue de ville* of London, a short black coat, striped trousers, a black Homburg, and a folded umbrella. He had a somewhat pimply youth as navigator or wireless man. We set out across the Irish Sea, with a strong easterly headwind.

Half-way across, Olley began to look back over his shoulder, and soon went down to a few hundred feet above the white horses of the sea.

I mildly inquired why? Very nonchalantly he replied, 'there was a strange plane out on my tail, and in these days you never know! So I put down so that he would lose sight of me against the rough sea!'

We landed just outside Liverpool, refuelled, and set out for London. The wireless went 'on the blink', as they say; we were *incommunicado;* and Olley flew by landmarks, roads, and railway lines, on a rather murky day. As we neared Hendon, the pilot would peer out of his window, say 'Ah!' and then bank and turn and dip in what to me was a bewildering fashion. And so we landed. Out came the Air Officer Commanding, demanding to know what the devil we meant by coming into an airport which had, for reasons of weather conditions, been closed for an hour.

The immaculate Olley emerged, all aplomb, and said, 'We've been off the air. This is the Prime Minister of Australia.' The A.O.C. was all apologies. 'Sorry, Sir, we sent your car back to London an hour ago.' Peace having been restored (I ended up by getting a lift with a Sergeant), I said to Olley, 'You seemed to be following a pretty erratic course in the last half-hour!' Olley: 'I certainly was; I was dodging barrage balloons!' All I could say was 'with what loving care they treat Dominion Prime Ministers in England'.

I reported to my colleagues in London my impressions formed in Ireland. I even suggested that a Minister should go to Dublin and Belfast, that De Valera and a couple of his Ministers should be invited to London. I thought that such a meeting would be welcomed by some members at least of the Irish Cabinet, who were, I thought, beginning to realize that neutrality had its defeats no less renowned than war.

But I failed. Winston had the last word!

8. The people of Britain in 1941

Except on two journeys abroad, I have never kept a diary. A private diary, kept as a reminder of past error, may serve a useful human purpose. A diary probably designed for publication some day can be a great source of entertainment, as witness the great names of Pepys, Evelyn, and Greville. But we are not all collectors of that order. A diary which records events and conversations with objectivity can be of great use to the ultimate historian (if there ever will be such a divine creature!) But when a man heavily engaged in affairs sits down, at the end of a long and arduous day, or even next morning, when he has the great advantage of *'l'esprit d'escalier'*, he tends to be either hasty or defensive. He will tend to condemn others and to justify himself.

These reflections have been much in my mind as I have consulted my daily notes from 24 January to 24 May 1941. I was, of course, many years younger than I am now, and consequently more prone to intolerance and hasty judgements. 'My salad days, When I was green in judgment.' My executors will do me a good service if they use the incinerator freely.

I remember what happened when, a few years ago, the Alanbrooke Diaries were published. Extracts from them were syndicated in many newspapers. His criticisms of Winston Churchill had headlines; I frequently had to learn the context and the later modifications only when I read the full text. In my own small way, I can sympathize with the feelings of that great soldier, for I cannot read this limited 1941 diary of my own without blushing for my readiness to make snap judgements and to resort to easy epigram.

Thus, if I may be quite frank, my first impressions of notable men like Attlee, Ernest Bevin, 'Bobbety' Salisbury, and Oliver Lyttelton were both superficial and wrong.

Clem Attlee, whom I have come to regard as a very great Englishman and a most astute manager of men, first impressed me as a man 'who should be a Sunday School Superintendent'. In my folly, I discounted Bevin, who was rendering and would continue to render such magnificent and courageous service to his country and was to be a really powerful Foreign Secretary in the Attlee Government. I was to learn in due course that he had a strong and far-ranging mind, and that he was a much better man that I would ever be.

Salisbury (then Cranborne) had a capacity for silence when he agreed that misled me into thinking of him as a 'Yes-man'. I apologize to this great and wise man, with an inherited and improved capacity for dissent, for ever having made such a false start.

As for Oliver Lyttelton (now Lord Chandos), all I can say is that his then comparative unawareness of the hard facts of political life temporarily blinded me to his remarkable and practical talents, with which I was to become familiar in later years.

As for Winston Churchill I will, since they tell me that 'open confession is good for the soul', record in my chapter about him how my feelings about him changed and strengthened in the months of our war-time association.

It is increasingly difficult for a new generation to feel as well as read about the remarkable spirit and cold, deliberate courage of those days.

In the western and central London blitz which occurred when I was there, a parachute mine, floating down on its evil mission, got its ropes entangled in the high crosspiece of the temporary Waterloo Bridge. The mine, built to explode on contact, hung precariously between the crosspiece and the roadway.

Before long, there arrived a bomb-disposal group, with a motor truck which had a long flat tray. With the greatest aplomb (or so it seemed), they backed the tray under the mine and proceeded to disentangle the mine and place it quietly—gently, gently—on the tray. Then they drove off with it to the Hackney Marshes, where they detonated it by remote control; and the danger had ended.

It sounds simple, doesn't it? The men who did this thing would have casually disowned any claim to heroism; but they were the embodiment of a national spirit, of willingness to sacrifice for the general safety and defence of the realm, which characterized the England o those critical and dangerous times. Dangerous for the free world, I add, for many countries which received no such attacks at home owe an everlasting debt to the English of that period, without whom the whole history of the modern world might well have been darkened.

Not long afterwards, we had a severe bombing raid on the centre and west of London. On the following day I went for a walk to see the damage by daylight. As usual, there were roped-off areas marked 'Unexploded bomb'. It was a miracle to me how they pinpointed them, but they did. Over in Hyde Park, close behind the Hyde Park Hotel, several of these bomb-disposal heroes were at work. The man in charge was a Sergeant, grimy but cheerful. I put a most fatuous question to him—'How do you like this kind of work?' His cheerful reply was: 'Oh, it's very interesting, but promotion comes quick. You see, I haven't been at it very long, but I'm a sergeant already!'

I went down to Swansea to be given the Freedom. This meant flying to Cardiff and then going by road. A few hours before we arrived at Cardiff, the enemy had dropped on it a group of parachute mines. One of them exploded in the middle of a block of two-storeyed terraced cottages; right in the middle, where the back gardens were. It blew the insides out of every house, leaving the side walls standing. Smoke was rising from the rubble when I visited the scene. Knots of people were standing on the footpaths, while others were investigating the debris. I asked whether there had been many people killed. The spokesman of the little crowd piped up and said: 'Only one, mister, and you couldn't rightly say that he was killed; he died of heart failure!'

Later, I went down to Bristol to receive a degree at the hands of the Chancellor, who was Winston Churchill. My fellow honorary graduate was J. G. Winant, the then American Ambassador. During the previous evening, Bristol was bombed. The Great Hall of the University was destroyed. When we arrived, the ruins were smoking; several churches were ablaze; there was wreckage everywhere. The ceremony occurred in the Senate Room. The members of the faculties arrived, wearing their academic robes over their smoke-stained 'battle-dress'. It was an unforgettable picture. It represented the triumph of learning and the sense of academic continuity over temporary disaster. When we went out, robed, to the steps of the University, the smoke still rose; the battered citizens cheered Winston; he gave the victory signal, and with a fine gesture of defiance, lit a fresh cigar.

It would be easy to yield to the temptation to think of Winston Churchill as the one and only; bearing the whole country on his shoulders, unaided.

That temptation must be resisted. Of course he was something unique; there was never anybody like him; but his great genius was that he evoked courage; he did not and could not create it. He kindled fires in his people, because he reached into their hearts and homes and found that they, simple and obscure, were great people also.

The heroism, the humour, the endurance of the British people under attack, were common knowledge in 1941. But memories fade; a new generation arises. I could write many pages of my own experiences in a brief three months. I will content myself with one more typical example.

I spoke at the great Bristol Aircraft Factory to a Shop Manager. The shop covered acres of floor space. There were many hundreds of people at work, and a sustained buzz of machinery and men.

I said to the Manager: 'You've apparently been lucky here.' I knew, of course, that there had been bombing of factories everywhere every night for months; but I saw no signs of damage in that particular shop.

'Well,' said the Manager, 'you can't just give it away when you're bombed. If they bomb the roof off, we just put it on again. If they blow a hole in the wall, we plug up the hole. Not long ago, they came along and put down some of their largest bombs slap into the middle of this shop and almost blew every machine in it into little pieces. But' (and he got the reflected Churchill gleam in his eye) 'in three weeks we had increased our production by twenty per cent!!'

9. *My return in May 1941 and my fall from office*

I returned to Australia with a lively sense of the gravity of our position, and proceeded to prepare what I called a 'blue print' for our future organization and efforts. Much of this work had to be done by me personally, for I was increasingly conscious of the fact that I had been absent too long, and that there had been some erosion of the authority I had earlier possessed.

I will summarize my plans and moves. I announced them in a National Broadcast on 17 June 1941, from which I first quote a few key passages.

I am the last to underrate what Australia has so far done. If I do not dwell upon it, it is not because I am not proud of it and thankful for it. But the truth is that, so far, our national structure has been, with some modification, largely that of peace.

It is clear that our national organization must become primarily one for war. War industry must no longer be what we can carve out of civil industry. Civil industry must become that which we can afford out of the total organization of a country which is at war.

What the private citizen pays for war must be no longer what he thinks he can afford after spending what he chooses on the amenities of life. . . . For the winning of this war, your Government will completely disregard all sectional interests.

I then announced, in concrete terms, that there would be a special Minister for Aircraft Production, a Minister for Transport, a Minister for the War Organization of Industry, a Minister for Home Security, and a Minister for External Territories.

Each of these departments was created on 26 June 1941, under J. W.

Leckie, H. L. Anthony, E. S. Spooner, J. P. Abbott, and A. McK. McDonald respectively.

Up to this time, Philip McBride had for eight months been both Minister for Supply and Minister for Munitions. I appointed a separate Minister for Supply, a department with many ramifications, and assigned McBride entirely to Munitions.

I announced further restrictions on petrol consumption, to reduce monthly consumption from a pre-war 30,000,000 gallons to 12,000,000.

I dealt with the shipping problem, saying that the Government must have absolute authority over the use and movement of merchant ships:

Accordingly, the ships by which the essential coastal trade of Australia is carried on will at once be requisitioned. This means that they will be taken over upon compulsory charters from the shipowners by the Government.

Further, I announced plans for the more effective national control of Railways (normally, a State matter) and of Road Transport. Hence the new Ministry of Transport.

The important Coal Industry was brought under review. 'We propose to establish a small Commission to control and direct the production, distribution, supply and consumption of coal.'

Industrial trouble was still too prevalent.

The time has passed for merely protesting against strikes or lock-outs in war and allied industries. We propose to prohibit them, and to accompany that prohibition by giving to the Courts full powers to take the most vigorous action against those who counsel or encourage them and against the funds and property of any organization which is so unwise as to participate in them.

The creation of a Ministry of War Organization of Industry was to prove of crucial importance. As my friend and political opponent, John Dedman, was to discover when Labour came in, it could not be popular; but it was, in war, essential.

This blueprint, or 'prospectus' was, as I have said, announced on 17 June. The necessary formalities to create the new Departments were completed, and Ministers appointed by 26 June. The important programme I had announced, and which I think it desirable to put on record, was, I thought, well received by the public. But within a few weeks I was out. Their inevitable failure to operate *at once* provoked scorching attacks from my more habitual newspaper critics, who seemed to think (or at least they said) that a new Department can be created one day, and be producing tangible results next day. It was this kind of criticism which alienated the support of many of my colleagues and led, shortly afterwards, to my resignation.

Meanwhile, impressed by the urgency of securing a united national effort, I had made a specific offer to Mr Curtin. It was regarded as a generous offer by even the most doubting of my colleagues. I had seen a National Government working harmoniously in the common cause in Great Britain, and thought that in our own circumstances at home we would be wise to establish one ourselves. If my leadership and characteristics stood in the way, I should clearly efface myself.

My offer to Mr Curtin was, therefore, that if the Labour Party would join in a National, all-party, Government, I would resign, advise that Mr Curtin be commissioned as Prime Minister, and be willing, should he desire it, to serve under him in the Cabinet.

My desire for a National Government was no last-moment thought. I had mentioned it to Curtin before I went overseas.

On 22 April 1941, I had sent from London a cable to Curtin as follows:

In the present emergency which can be overcome but which will need all we have, my mind is once more running on the possibilities of a united front in Australia. You may treat my offer on this matter as still standing. My experience here, which has been extremely trying, has emphasized what difficulties a Prime Minister has when he can speak for only half of his people. This is not to say that I fail to appreciate your courtesy or the helpfulness of your party, but political debates always threaten to break out, and I cannot effectively take part in them from a distance. Kind regards.

I have no record of any direct reply, but I do know that on 27 April, Curtin made a press statement:

There never has been, nor should there be any doubt about Australia. I say that the workers of this country are determined to give their all in the war that has been forced upon us. I say that the Labour Movement of Australia will be unflinching and unyielding to the end, for we have a common interest and a common fate in resisting any aggression. Finally, I say to the world, friends or foes, that there is no political disunity in Australia in regard to the prosecution of the war.

When this was cabled to me, I thought it a robust statement, all the more so because only a week before I had received a cable from my Acting Prime Minister, Fadden, advising me to stay in Britain for another fortnight, and saying that he had consulted Curtin, who concurred in his advice. And then, early in May, I was delighted to receive a message from my colleagues in Australia, congratulating me on what I had done in England, saying that they felt that I had made a valuable contribution to the combined war effort, and that they were very happy about the results.

This was a cheering message. I had visited the battlefields of Cyrenaica and the bombed cities of England. I had discussed with political and military and production leaders, every day, great problems which concerned Australia. Literally, as I realized recently after looking through the files, I exchanged hundreds of cables with Australia, and had been made to understand that I was speaking and negotiating authentically for my country.

It will be seen from this that when I returned, and immersed myself in the formulation of new war plans largely based on my experience abroad, I had a reasonable 'expectation of life', politically speaking.

But the fates willed otherwise, as I shall show.

On 24 May 1941, shortly after my return from abroad, I spoke to a packed meeting at the Sydney Town Hall. Several of my Labour Parliamentary opponents honoured me by their presence on the platform. Drawing on my experience in London, and persuaded more than ever before of the gravity of the crisis, I made a special appeal for unity.

It is our great privilege to be governed under a system of Parliament. It is a characteristic of our parliamentary life that there should be parties and party debates. I am the last man to say cheap things about the party system or about party debates; but I say this, that at this solemn hour in our history, this fateful hour in our history, it is for us if we be intelligent men to make Parliament an instrument of war and not an instrument of dissension.

I have never had any lack of understanding of the point of view honestly held and candidly expressed by my friend, Mr Curtin. In my absence for four months I believe that I owe a great deal of stability to his understanding; but you will

understand my utter astonishment coming back from the scenes I have witnessed, coming back here from this magnificent unity of purpose and of
function and of organization that exists in Great Britain, to find that men
sitting on the Opposition benches, men like Mr Curtin, Mr Forde, Dr Evatt,
Mr Beasley and Mr Makin, those men who sit on the Advisory War Council,
should have no executive function in the direction of the war and should be
compelled to stand off and become the critics of an effort to which they might
easily be powerful contributors.

I had no doubt that things had gone reasonably peacefully during
my absence. My own visit to England had clearly been well received.
My wife's prophecy had receded in my memory.

But, until after my return, I had not fully realized what had gone on.
No sooner, had I, after immeasurable individual labour, announced my
war 'prospectus' and reconstructed my government, than the wind
began to blow. I found some dissension in my own party; not based
upon some belief that my 'prospectus' was wrong, for they all supported
it; but based upon a loss of confidence in me. To some of my *ci-devant*
friends, I had become a liability. Some of the largest newspapers,
though they approved of the programme, disapproved of me.

On 14 August 1941, the Advisory War Council met, to discuss
particularly, as it is now interesting to recall, the position in the Far
East. I told the Council that my Cabinet had requested me to go back
to London, to represent Australia in the British War Cabinet. John
Curtin was prepared to have a favourable look at this, but his colleagues
differed. Evatt, who was a seething mass of frustrated ambitions, took
the sinister view that the object of the exercise was to hamper the
Opposition during my absence.

Under all the circumstances, I announced that I would not go
abroad except with the approval of all Parties.

In my statement, I took occasion to refer to the position in the 'Far
East' (or, as I said on another occasion, the 'Near North'). What I said
was that 'the occupation of French Indo-China, coupled with the
subsequent discussions between Japan and Thailand, are clearly of
first-class importance to Singapore and Australia, to say nothing of the
Netherlands East Indies. Both matters, taken together, raise questions
as to the disposition, maintenance, and equipment of Australian overseas armies.'

It was after this that I made my offer to the Labour Party for an all-party Government. Clearly, this was not to stifle Opposition criticism, or to hamper it in its proper constitutional work. For, if accepted, it would have made the Leader of the Opposition Prime Minister, with a Cabinet equally representing both sides of the House.

When this generous offer was rejected (I have never believed with Curtin's concurrence) we had conclusive evidence that, seeing a chance of overthrowing me, a large section of the Opposition came down in favour of seizing power and leaving the prospective Opposition to its own resources.

That offer was made on 22 August. In it, I said that I was prepared to serve under Curtin or anybody else who might be chosen.

Perhaps I might be permitted to believe that this was not the most ignoble action of my public life.

It may be that Labour, seeing the state of affairs in my own camp, was developing high hopes. Anyhow, they had a meeting, and rejected my offer out of hand. (From a purely party point of view, they were no doubt right; because within a couple of months they had defeated the Fadden Government which followed my resignation, and had gone into office in their own right.)

My offer to the Labour Leader and Party having been rejected, I called an afternoon Cabinet Meeting on 28 August 1941, and invited my colleagues to speak their minds freely on what should be the next step.

Within half an hour, I had my answer, not from all (I am happy to remember) but from enough. I will mention no names. There are some things that it is good to forget. Indeed, I have lived long enough to learn that it is a great part of wisdom to know what to forget.

There was a strong view that, having regard to our precarious Parliamentary position, my unpopularity with the leading newspapers was a threat to the survival of the Government. It followed that, although they had a warm appreciation of what I had done as Prime Minister, a change in the leadership was called for.

I said that I would adjourn Cabinet until after dinner; that I must consider what I should do. Clearly, if we were not at war, I should feel entitled to accept the resignation of my critics and fill the vacancies. But we were at war, and other considerations might apply.

I went back to the Lodge, went for a walk with my wife around the adjacent fields, and then rang up Melbourne and spoke to a hastily assembled 'family' conference. We established complete unanimity of decision.

When Cabinet reassembled, I said that I had decided to resign the Prime Ministership and advised the Governor-General to send for the man they would choose. I said that I was following this course because I was not prepared to divide the ranks of the Government at a time of crisis.

This was accepted, not without opposition from some of my friends. A party meeting was urgently convened, and I made my announcement.

Arthur Fadden, the leader of the Country Party, was chosen, and I went home, and went to bed, if not to sleep.

Two things happened.

One was that Eric (now Sir Eric) Harrison, who had been absent from Cabinet—he was attending his wife's funeral—arrived in a fine rage; but it was too late.

The second was that Arthur Coles, one of the two original 'independents', but who had joined my party and attended Government party meetings, spoke up. When I informed the Party meeting of my decision, Coles leapt up and said, 'This is not a resignation; it is a lynching', and left the Party. From that moment, the fate of the new Government, not yet actually born, was sealed.

I had already made a press statement, with as much calm as I could command. I set out its terms in full; after all, it represented one of the great turning points in my life:

In my recent offer to the Opposition, I indicated that to secure an all-party administration I was prepared to vacate the Prime Ministership. The offer was rejected. It follows that the next task is to get the greatest possible stability and cohesion on the Government side of the House.

A frank discussion with my colleagues in the Cabinet has shown that, while they have personal goodwill towards me, many of them feel that I am unpopular with large sections of the press and the people, that this unpopularity handicaps the effectiveness of the Government by giving rise to misrepresentation and misunderstanding of its activities, and that there are divisions of opinion in the Government parties themselves which would not, or might not, exist under another leader.

It is not for me to be the judge of these matters, except to this extent, that I do believe that my relinquishing of the leadership will offer a real prospect of unity in the ranks of the Government parties. Under these circumstances, and having regard to the grave emergencies of war, my own feelings must be set aside.

I therefore invited the two parties to select another leader. They have unanimously chosen Mr Fadden. Accordingly, tomorrow I shall resign the Prime Ministership, and advise His Excellency to commission Mr Fadden.

The only stipulation I made was this, that every man in both parties must be prepared to give his wholehearted support, as I shall, to the new leader. This was accepted with one accord. But for it, my own resignation would have been futile, and the vital interests of our country would not have been faithfully served. I am prepared to set an example in this matter of loyal service by accepting Cabinet office under Mr Fadden, if he so desires. I earnestly hope that my present action may help to enable the Government to be carried on without discord at a time when the nation urgently needs harmony in its own ranks.

I lay down the Prime Ministership with natural regret. For years I have given of my best to the service of the country, and especially during the two years of war. Foundations have been laid and a national effort achieved, in which, I hope, I shall be permitted to take a proper pride.

On 6 October 1941, the Fadden Government, a little over five weeks old, was voted out. Coles had reverted to his Independent status. Wilson, the other Independent, was a former Country Party member from Victoria. On a vital opposition amendment to the Budget, both Independents voted with Labour, and the government was defeated.

In the circumstances, the Governor-General, assurances of support having been obtained by Curtin from the two Independents, commissioned Curtin to form a Government, and a period of eight years' Labour rule began.

At this time, and indeed throughout my long period of membership of the Commonwealth Parliament, my party heavily outnumbered the Country Party. We were and are separate parties. In substance, we have the same political philosophy; over the years, we have, with a little give and take, succeeded in presenting common policies to the electors. The Country Party has, as the name indicates, a particular association with rural interests; though this is not exclusive, since many of my own party members represent country seats. Under these circumstances, there can be local contests, and occasionally some friction. But in effect the association between the two parties had been sustained and fruitful.

3

However, at the time of which I am writing, in October 1941, and at the first meeting of my own party shortly afterwards, I raised the question of 'who was to lead the Opposition; the leader of the smaller party, or the leader of the larger party, following the usual practice.'

My party, by a majority, took the view that as Fadden, leader of the Country Party, had just been Prime Minister, he should become Leader of the Opposition. In what, I suppose, could have been regarded as a high-handed manner (but it must be remembered that, after my still recent experiences, I was in a very exacerbated state of mind), I said, 'Well, a party of our numbers which is not prepared to lead is not worth leading.'

I thereupon resigned the leadership of my party, and until after the, for us, disastrous general election of 1943, sat in a back seat on the Opposition side of the House as a private member.

Hughes was politically resurrected as Leader of the United Australia Party. During the next two years, he convened only one Party meeting. As a party, we were completely in eclipse.

It would be stupid to pretend that these events did not constitute a bitter blow to my pride, and even to my self-respect. In a very great crisis in my country's history, I had been weighed in the balance and found wanting. And yet I felt that I had done a great deal. I had not spared myself; I had worked seven days a week for at least twelve hours a day. This was, perhaps, an error, for it so absorbed my mind that I soon appeared to be aloof from my supporters in Parliament and to be lacking in human relations. But when the blow fell, it was like the stroke of doom; everything was at an end.

But today, thinking and writing about it more than a quarter of a century later, I see the whole matter more philosophically. I begin to think that, on balance, my humiliation of 1941 turned out to be a good thing for my country.

This may seem so much like 'making the best of a bad job' that I think it would be useful to explain it, quite frankly.

In 1939, when I first became Prime Minister, I had enjoyed a very rapid rise to the top position. Within six weeks of entering the Victorian Parliament I had been appointed a Minister. Three years later in 1932 I became Deputy Premier of Victoria. In October 1934, under the circumstances which I will later describe, I became Attorney-General of Australia. In the next two years, under Lyons, I had become Deputy Leader of the United Australia Party and one of the King's Privy Councillors. And then, in April 1939, Prime Minister at the age of forty-four. There was not much precedent for this kind of advancement, and perhaps some resentment of it. True, I worked hard, though some of the press commentators promoted the usual legend that I was a 'brilliant idler'. But I have worked hard all my life, much harder, I feel sure, than any of the critics.

But with so much to do officially, I do not doubt that my knowledge of people, and how to get along with them and persuade them, lagged behind. I was still in that state of mind in which to be logical is to be right, and to be right is its own justification. I had yet to acquire the common touch, to learn that human beings are delightfully illogical but mostly honest, and to realize that all-black and all-white are not the only hues in the spectrum.

I now know that a long period in Opposition, first with no official responsibility and then as Leader, did me personally a lot of good. I acquired a closer and more human Parliamentary knowledge. I learned a great deal about the handling of Parliamentary debates and an understanding of those for whom or against whom I was debating. I had a great opportunity, which I was determined to use to the full, to evolve an alternative and constructive policy. I may claim to have learned the great lesson of Opposition, which is always to remember that you are the alternative Government, and must therefore never attack beyond your capacity to perform should the electors decide in your favour.

On top of all this, my fall from office under circumstances which enabled quite a few people to write my political obituary had a special effect on a man of contentious capacity and healthy ambition. I refused to accept defeat as permanent. True, for years there were observers who would say to my party and my friends, 'You'll never win with Menzies!' But when such slogans reached my ears, I treated them as a great challenge. My unspoken response was that of the small boy—'I'll show them!'

So far, I have been writing rather subjectively, inevitably and, I hope, pardonably.

[57]

But there is another aspect of the matter which is more objective and historical. Quite plainly, if I had still been Prime Minister in December 1941, when Japan entered the war by its devastating attack on Pearl Harbor, and began its spectacular southward movement in South-East Asia, any disposition in Australia to promote political dissension would have tended to disappear; my Government could well have remained in office for the duration! And then, before long, we would have been relieved of power, as the Labour Government was in 1949, and Labour would have come in, as we did in 1949, and could quite possibly have remained in office for a long time, in the highly significant post-war period.

The fact was that the military and material foundations of Australia's remarkable war effort had been laid in the time of my own first Government. But certain further and essential things had to be done when the Japanese threat became imminent. And John Curtin, with great human relations, an unquestioned authority in his own party, and the wide backing of the Trade Union movement, was willing and able to do them without dividing the country. I hope and believe that I would have done them, but they would not have secured the same degree of public acceptance. Two great articles of faith in the Labour and Trade Union movements had to be abandoned. One was the traditional opposition to conscription for service outside Australia; an opposition which had split the Labour Party under Hughes in 1916, and which gave rise to such passionate feelings that, as recently as the Australian General Election of November 1966, senior Labour leaders were still expressing them with undiminished, if somewhat antiquated vigour. Curtin propounded a law for compulsory military *service* outside Australia and in a limited (but still extensive) area of the south-west Pacific, and got it accepted by his own people. This policy, it is true, was made practicable by our re-introduction of compulsory military *training* in 1939. But the step he took was a big one, and the country was not divided.

The other great article of faith was that there must never be conscription of Labour. The right to strike, to accept or refuse employment was bred in the bones of the unions. A 'conservative' or 'non-Labour', (or as we were frequently charged 'anti-Labour') government would have been fought tooth-and-nail had it undertaken to organize and direct labour, with no choice and by decree. But Curtin did it; the Unions accepted it; and the country was not divided.

So much for the actual war period of the Labour Government. But right after the war another remarkable development occurred. I have mentioned two traditional Labour Party articles of faith which Curtin was able to set aside without national division. But there was a third one. It had for many years been the settled attitude of the Trade Union Movement that there should be no assisted migration into Australia so long as there was any unemployment in Australia. For some reason which I was never able to understand, the Government feared that peace would be followed by a depression, and that great efforts would be needed to find employment for those coming out of the forces.

It was in the face of these difficulties that Arthur Calwell convinced not only his colleagues but also the Trade Unions that a large immigration programme should be taken in hand. This was a bold and courageous action. It could have been taken successfully only by a Minister who was known as a life-time Labour man of the strictest orthodoxy, and was both well-known and extremely popular at the centres of unionism, the Trades Halls.

The very large immigration which was then begun, and continues to this day, has been a great factor in Australia's national development and the enrichment of her social life. My own party enthusiastically favours it. But I doubt whether it could have got off to such a good start so soon after the war had it been compelled to encounter trade union resistance.

The accession to office of the Labour Party in 1941 had, therefore, some valuable results as it turned out; though I confess I did not foresee them at the time. But after the war, and when Curtin's rather broad and pragmatic mind had been removed from the scene, the Labour Party began to return to its normal and traditional objectives. The most explosive evidence of this was their ill-fated attempt to nationalize banking, a move which, if it had not been invalidated by the Courts and subsequently soundly rejected by the electors, could have had damaging results in the years which were to follow. The period since 1949, a period of unexampled national progress and of encouraged and rewarded private enterprise, with high employment, financial stability, and energetic private and public investment and a world-wide high credit rating, was beyond question assisted by non-Labour government policy. In addition to this, we set out successfully to rebuild our bridges with the United States. Labour had already shown signs of relapsing into the kind of isolationism which had marked it before the war; we took an active part in the negotiating of ANZUS and SEATO, which have had profound effects on Australia's foreign policy and international position.

The political disasters, as they seemed to us, of 1941 and 1943, can be seen in better perspective if we recall the subsequent and perhaps historically inevitable events of the last eighteen years.

10. *A postscript*

So long as one does not become too autobiographical, a fragment of autobiography may not come amiss; or even two fragments.

The first concerns the Far East. I had gone out of office, under the circumstances I have described. The Japanese had come into the War, and the position of Singapore was under threat. Churchill sent Duff Cooper on a roving mission to spy out the land. He arrived in Melbourne, and was a guest at State Government House. He asked me to come and see him. I was well out of office, a private member, and wondering what I should do next. Duff at once said to me, 'Would you be willing to become our Minister of State in South-East Asia. Winston would like it. I suppose it would mean leaving your Parliament; but we would like you to say "Yes".'

My reply was that, so far as I could see then, I had shot my bolt in my own country and would be more than happy to serve some useful purpose somewhere. Duff Cooper said 'Good! I will convey this to Winston. He will be pleased.'

However, it was not to happen that way; for Singapore fell, and the Japanese were in New Guinea. I remained as a Member of the Australian Parliament.

My second fragment concerns the events of March 1942, six months after my fall, and three months after the Japanese attack. Casey, now Lord Casey, our first, and very successful, Minister to the United States —(our post was then a Legation)—had accepted an invitation from Churchill to become Minister of State at Cairo. Curtin spoke to me.

He said that Winston had, in the very act of taking Casey away, offered a view that as 'Menzies had done well in Great Britain and in the United States', he, Curtin, might consider sending him to Washington. I replied, 'Well, John, if you want me to consider it, I shall. But for heaven's sake don't tell your Cabinet that Winston has suggested it, because that will finish it with Evatt and Beasley!'

Some rumours began to circulate. On 23 March, I sent a message to Curtin as follows:

As I gather from certain quarters that there may be a misunderstanding about my position, I should make it clear to you that if I were offered the American post, I would give the offer the fullest consideration. This message is not intended to be an application, or an embarrassment to you in a difficult choice, but is merely sent to make my own position clear.

This had been a difficult matter for me. To go to Washington as a diplomat would involve resigning from Parliament and therefore abandoning any Australian political future, such as it might be. But, on reflection, I was prepared to go.

As it happened, Curtin's Ministers were shown Churchill's message and at once reacted as might have been expected. 'What? Is Churchill telling us what we are to do?'

So I was not invited, but Owen Dixon, the greatest lawyer on the High Court Bench, was, to the great advantage of both countries, appointed.

It will be seen, from this simple narrative, not hitherto recorded, that the resolution of two chances against me kept me in my political occupations at Canberra and, in the long run, for better or for worse, made me Australian Prime Minister for sixteen years.

CHAPTER FOUR

CHURCHILL

I FIRST MET WINSTON CHURCHILL on 26 May 1935. My wife and I were week-ending in Surrey with Maurice Hankey, that courteous but effective Prince of Cabinet Secretaries. After lunch he suggested a walk across to Chartwell. I learned a great deal from him in the course of it. I made a note that night about Hankey and, unlike many of my contemporary notes, it still stands. 'What a wise and well-informed man Hankey is. When one recalls his presence and influence at almost every war- and peace-time conference of the last twenty years, one does not wonder that more than one observer considers that some day he may be regarded as one of the greatest Englishmen of the day. But it is part of his technique to be self-effacing—to be in the background—and perhaps History does not take too kindly to that sort of man.'

Mrs Churchill, as she then was, received us very pleasantly, but explained at once that 'Winston' was in the swimming pool, and that we should go out to see him. It was a splendid sight. The pool was large and of irregular shape and had, we were told, been built by Churchill himself. It was, as I later learned, heated. In the middle of the pool was a jutting form rather reminiscent of the Rock of Gibraltar. 'Clemmie', as I was later to know her, called out across the pool—'Winston, you have visitors.' Nothing happened. She called again. The rock moved. It produced two hands, which plucked two lumps of cotton-wool from two ears as the rock stood up. The message was repeated, and the rock came ashore, glowering at us as severely as Gibraltar ever did at La Linea. I felt that though I had come, and had seen, I had not conquered.

Sir Ian Hamilton arrived for tea, and I found myself, involuntarily, to be a good listener. But I confessed to some disappointment. I made a note at about that time that there seemed to be a little more of 'I told them so' in Winston's conversation than I would have expected. This impression I later found to be false, because I got to know better how almost single-handed had been his battle to alert the nation, and how bitterly frustrated he was at the euphoria which had overtaken his country, bemused by the 'Peace Ballot' and what we now know to have been a childlike belief that the League of Nations and its Covenant were an effective guarantee of peace, and that national rearmament was therefore not only unimportant, but would show a serious lack of faith! The general attitude was that Churchill was brilliant but erratic, an object of affectionate regret to the Conservatives, and a 'war-monger' to the pacifist wing of the Labour Party.

However, on that opening day at Chartwell, I thought I did rather better with Mrs Churchill. She showed me some brick walls ('by Winston') and a charming red brick cottage, built by Winston *et alios*. I can remember as if it were yesterday her whimsical remark that 'this cottage is let for £100 a year, and is the only really economic job of brick-work Winston has done!'

I was interested to discover how he had gone about the production of his great life of his ancestor Marlborough (the first volume of which he had published two years before), and how he could achieve its vivid description of events, and in particular of the great battle victories of that amazing soldier. She took me into a large room where there was a huge relief map set out on an equally huge table. Winston, she told me, having, with the help of experts, assembled his historical material, would stand by the table, literally 'view the landscape o'er', Blenheim, Oudenarde, Ramillies, or Malplaquet, as the case might be, and dictate his story as if he were an eye-witness of the events, moving the troops about in his mind's eye, noting the position of the sun and the features of the ground, and dictating his story with life and enthusiasm.

I was later to see much of his methods of work and of the way in which he prepared the first drafts of speeches and broadcasts. But that first glimpse, in 1935, explained a great deal to me. The years were to come when he would move many millions of people right round the world. He had, in his years of rejection—and dejection—learned the great truth that to move other people, the speaker, the leader, must first move himself; all must be vivid in his mind.

Later on in 1935, I was to make two other observations. The first concerned his methods in the House of Commons. He was speaking from the front row, below the gangway, and was, with some relish, attacking Ramsay MacDonald, who was then Prime Minister. To my

3*

astonishment, Churchill was reading his speech, the pages of which he had assembled into the covers of a book which he held before him. I was in the gallery just above, and watched the whole operation with fascinated interest. I was to learn in due course that most speeches in the House of Commons are read. Most of the best speeches in the House of Representatives at Canberra are spoken, and not over-encumbered by notes. Now, Churchill was making a critical, indeed an attacking speech; and I wondered how one could read a speech of this kind. I soon learned the answer. He was a master of timing; he used the pause, that most eloquent element in any speech worth hearing, to perfection. And he laced his pauses with a deep and syncopated chuckle later to become so familiar in my ears. 'That, Mr Speaker, was the occasion when I permitted myself to describe the Right Honourable Gentleman as—um, um, chuckle, chuckle—the boneless wonder!'

In short, Winston Churchill was one of the very few who could read a speech as if he were thinking it out on the spot. His carefully prepared asides emerged as the most dazzling impromptus. He held his audience; which is the immediate purpose of a speech. He read a carefully prepared piece of literature; which is the privilege of a man who feels that he is also speaking to posterity.

My second observation was a depressing one. It was sad to see a man of such talent and fire sitting in the rooms at Westminster attended by a small group of rather adulatory followers, denied the audience which great office would have given him, feeling, as he must have felt, that his political life was petering out in the sands. The possibilities of ultimate command seemed so remote as to be invisible.

I therefore looked forward, in 1941, to seeing him in command, at the height of his now fully-employed powers, and to studying at close quarters his personality and his methods.

It is now amusing for me to read, in my notes made that night, my opening comment on my first weekend at Chequers, Saturday 22 February. Here is what I wrote:

In the evening with snow falling across the purplish smudges of the Chiltern Woods, to Chequers for the weekend. The entrance drive and circle have been grassed over; they were too much of a landmark from the air. The House is closely guarded. In the Long Gallery (much more lived in and attractive) I meet once more Mrs Churchill, who is in good form and prepared to disagree with the great man, and Mary Churchill, aged 17, the freshest and best-looking young woman I have seen for years. Winston 'enters', wearing what is called a 'Siren suit', a dull-blue woollen overall with a zip-fastener down the front. 'As worn', I believe, for the sudden alarm and retreat to the basement. As a form of pre-prandial costume it mystified me, for he later appeared at dinner in the white shirt of convention, and forgot all about air-raids until 2 a.m.!

This note amuses me now, for I was soon to discover that Winston Churchill's interest in air-raid shelters was purely impersonal.

But that weekend, my most vivid impressions were of the dominating personality of the Prime Minister. Somebody may have said 'No' at some stage to something; I could not tell, for Winston was in full cry. I wrote down, 'What a tempestuous creature he is; pacing up and down the room, always as if about to dart out of it, and then suddenly returning; oratorical even in conversation.'

Before I went to bed, I made a note of two conclusions. One was that 'Winston is completely certain of America's full help, of her participation in a Japanese war, and of Roosevelt's passionate determination to stamp out the Nazi menace from the earth.'

The other, which I had good reason to modify later on, was: 'If the P.M. were a better listener, and less disposed to dispense with all expert opinion, I might feel a little easier about it. But there's no doubt about it; he's a holy terror!'

A week later I was down at Chequers again. This time Diana Churchill, then Mrs Duncan Sandys, was added to the party. I was able to observe the family at close quarters. I will again quote my own contemporary note:

This is really the most amazing family. They all admire each other. A visitor can easily get by if his manners are inconspicuous and his capacity for intelligent listening reasonable. The P.M. in a conversation will steep himself (and you) in gloom on some grim aspect of the war (e.g. tonight, shipping losses by Focke-Wulf planes and U-boats), only to proceed to fight his way out until he is pacing the floor with the light of battle in his eyes. In every conversation, he ultimately reaches a point where he positively enjoys the war.

It is interesting to me to recall that quite soon my first impressions were being corrected. Thus, by 3 March, I was able to write down:

Churchill grows on me. He has an astonishing grasp of detail and, by daily contact with the Service Headquarters, knows of dispositions and establishments quite accurately. But I still fear that (though experience of Supreme Office has clearly improved and steadied him) his real tyrant is the glittering phrase. But this is the defect of his quality. Reasoning to a pre-determined conclusion is mere advocacy; but it becomes something much better when the conclusion is that you are going to win a war, and that you're damned if anything will stand in your way. Churchill's course is set. There is no defeat in his heart.

I attended the War Cabinet meetings. Churchill's procedures were most striking. He would begin each meeting with a short but impressive statement on the current war position, which sometimes ended with words like these—'We have the singular honour of having great responsibilities, at a time of great peril, for the fate of our country. We shall proceed with the business.'

Every matter came up on a printed paper put forward by some Minister. The papers had all gone round, in their red boxes, to Ministers, wherever they might be, and had all been read and pondered before Cabinet met.

In the result, discussions were very brief. Those who concurred said so, and nothing more. Those who dissented were encouraged to be concise.

(In my later terms of office in Australia, we were never able to achieve such conciseness. One reason was that busy politicians are not avid students of documents. All too frequently I have known long submissions read out in full in the Cabinet Room. This was undoubtedly a fault of discipline on my part.)

It was on one of my earlier weekends at Chequers, when General de Gaulle was also present, that I first heard Churchill in reply to an almost blood-curdling proposal (not from de Gaulle) that Germany should be wiped out, propound his famous maxim: 'In war, resolution; in defeat, defiance; in victory, magnanimity; in peace, goodwill.'

It was on that same night that, in the manner that he had (and which Harold Macmillan alone later surpassed) of bringing out ancient instances, he reminded us of the Greek story of the conquered who were spared—'These men were spared, not because they were men, but because of the nature of man!'

Later, I sat in on a discussion between Churchill and de Gaulle about North Africa, to which I shall return.

I was soon to discover another aspect of the great man. I heard him cross-examining the experts. He proved a marvellous master of all sorts of war-like detail, but, contrary to my first impression, did not dictate to the experts. But he always insisted on action. He was quite willing to confess that he did not understand financial problems (though he had been Chancellor of the Exchequer many years before!), and was content to leave them to others. He concentrated his energies on the main business, which was the war. He did not see either the press or his constituents. He called conferences of Ministers and officials, dictated memoranda, issued 'directives', prepared and made great speeches and broadcasts.

It was no doubt this utter absorption in the task of winning the war that helped, by a cruel irony, to persuade an unexpected majority of the electors, in the General Election of 1945, that he should not be entrusted with the domestic, economic and financial tasks which would be the product of victory and peace.

Years afterwards, in 1948, I made a remark to Winston, after dinner at Chartwell which, for a moment, appeared to take him aback a little. 'You realize,' I said, 'that five years after your death, an event which I hope and believe will be long postponed, clever young men from Oxford or Cambridge or some other seat of learning will be writing books explaining that you were never right about anything!' 'Oh,' he said, in a friendly grumble, 'you think so, do you?' I retorted that, as he himself was an historian who had felt called upon to restore the reputation of the great Marlborough, he knew that such things could and would happen. 'But,' I added, 'not many years later, the clever young men will have been forgotten and your name will be seen clearly at the pinnacle.'

I repeat this conversation because I notice that the process has already begun. It is, therefore, I think, proper that I should record something of the spirit of that great man, as I saw it aflame in the first months of 1941, when Hitler was astride Europe, when the Soviet Union had a pact of non-aggression with Germany, when the United States was neutral, and when there was no 'Second Front' except those on which British and Commonwealth forces were fighting.

[67]

Nobody who did not live, adult and responsible, through that period, now a quarter of a century behind us, can possibly understand the quality or vital significance of Churchill's leadership. At a time when the cold reason of scholars would have heavily discounted the chances of victory, he never doubted it. He would walk into the Cabinet Room at 10 Downing Street, his cigar (probably unlit) jutting from his mouth, and would begin by dealing with the state of the war. He had, as I had observed at Chequers, a fascinating habit of posing the current problems in their darkest hues. He would create an atmosphere of almost 'inspissated gloom'. He understated no difficulty, and shirked no uncomfortable fact. And, having done this, he would, almost literally, tear away at the problems, until the light shone through, and we all found ourselves sitting straighter, and feeling braver, and confident of victory.

As I said in speaking about him on the day of his funeral, it should not be forgotten that 'there were, in 1940, defeatists, who felt that prudence required submission on such terms as might be had. There were others who, while not accepting the inevitability of defeat, thought that victory was impossible.'

The inspiration of a man is not easily ascertained by a subsequent cold analysis of the official documents; but it was Churchill's great genius and service which will be remembered, and which no critic can efface.

Our weekends at Chequers were, for me, unforgettable.

On practically every occasion his wife and his young daughter, Mary, were present. Each of them deserves a special chapter in any man's book. But for my present purpose all I will say is that the wise and witty and understanding wife and the sweet and sympathetic daughter combined to give an interval of light and sanity which fortified him mightily for his dealings with an insane world.

The weekends were the highlights, for I was able to see the great man at close quarters. He ate well at dinner, drank champagne (which I dislike) and brandy, and after dinner destroyed, rather than smoked, several noble Havana cigars, which he chewed and re-lit until they were offensive and were dismissed.

He had no love of social dinner-table conversation. (I remember, many years later, my daughter Heather, who, bless her, is not incapable of self-expression, sitting next to Winston at a meal, receiving none of the small change of table-talk, and coming away wondering how she had erred!) At Chequers, he usually had a few people with whom he wanted to discuss war problems; de Gaulle, or a Minister, or one of the Chiefs of Staff. His conversation during and after dinner was directed to them. Discussion waxed (it never waned) late into the night.

I remember the weekend of de Gaulle's visit, and a long Churchill-de Gaulle debate which occurred as the evening wore on. De Gaulle spoke French, and no English. Churchill spoke French, with a masterly disregard of grammar and syntax, but with a large vocabulary. I did my best to look intelligent. In fact, I made a rather wicked intervention. Churchill and I had had some faintly acid cabled exchanges over Dakar, so I invited de Gaulle to give us his views. He certainly did, but he failed to convert his adversary.

It is a fascinating pictorial memory. Churchill, the embodiment of John Bull, British of the British; de Gaulle, the very opposite of a typical Frenchman of fiction at any rate, very tall, lugubrious of manner, scornful of wit. There is no doubt that at that time, and for years afterwards, Churchill found de Gaulle prickly and difficult, disposed to over-simplify the problems of politics, of which at that time he knew but little. A strange man, but a great man and a great patriot, destined to give the new France stability of government and to give the Frenchman back his pride, but also destined, in the last year or two, to prove once more a difficult ally.

Having exhausted the other guests, who had to be off to London on Sunday night, and finding me entranced but durable, my host would not 'call it a day' until about 2.30 a.m. But, before going to bed, he would slip into the small study off the entrance lobby of Chequers, and pick up in turn his direct telephones to Bomber Command and Fighter Command, for the night reports. Praise, satisfaction, rebuke, and encouragement poured forth. Then, with a gleam in his eye, he would go to bed.

The next morning (this is hearsay, for I have never been able to reconcile late nights with early rising) he would sit up in bed at 7.30, with coffee and a fresh cigar, and read the newspapers, which he thoroughly devoured, and the dispatches and reports which had come by box during the night. He then summoned his stenographer and proceeded to dictate dispatches and 'directives' to Ministers. By 10.30 or 11 a.m., he would have done, for an ordinary mortal, a day's work. Half an hour later, if it was Monday, he went by armoured car to London. After lunch, he recruited his strength by going right into bed—into 'naked bed', as he once described it to me; 'none of this lounging on a chair or couch'—and would emerge into Cabinet at 5 p.m.

Cabinet would be through by 8 o'clock. After dinner, Winston ensconced himself in the Downing Street 'extension', walking up and down (his unspoken motto was *solvitur ambulando*), evolving ideas, pausing only to take a sip from his brandy balloon. Then, not in-frequently, his voice rang out—'Pug!' Out came 'Pug' Ismay, General Ismay, his trusted friend and adviser. 'Pug. Get hold of the Chiefs of Staff; I must see them at once!'

So, at about 10.30 or even 11 p.m., the hard-worked Chiefs, who no doubt needed a night's rest, would retreat from their beds and arrive at Downing Street. Winston would greet them with a great military idea he had worked up. If the Chiefs didn't like it, they had a couple of hours' work in front of them before they were dismissed with a grumbling reference to 'defeatism'.

I knew from my talks with them that they were up betimes in the morning, for they were never sure that they would not receive another imperative summons by 11 a.m., and have another battle.

Now, the knowledge of this kind of procedure has encouraged some latter-day critics to concentrate on his bad ideas. But the truth is that he had ten times as many ideas as other people. He lived with the problems of the nation. He made them *his* problems, and let his power-ful imagination loose around them. *All* his ideas could not be right. But he was so fertile in ideas that he could afford a high rate of wastage and still be in credit.

But as I saw him at that time, this fertility in ideas had its greatest effect on the attitude and activity of others. Even when he might have a bad plan, he galvanized others into producing a good plan.

He appeared to be a bad 'listener', and was reputed to dislike opposition. In a superficial sense, that was true. Most people in his Cabinet were wary of crossing him, and, looking back on it, I cannot blame them. Winston's force of personality was almost tangible; you felt it like a physical blow.

Only twice did I find myself bound to disagree with him on matters affecting Australia. The first concerned my visit to Ireland to learn, if I could, the basis of Irish neutrality, a matter of intense interest in Australia, where about twenty per cent of our people were of Irish descent and, in any vigorous controversy, not noted for passive neutrality! I have already described the episode. All I need now say, for purposes of my picture of Churchill, is that I went to Northern Ireland with his warm approval, and on to Southern Ireland with his violent disapproval. On my return, I wrote a paper for Cabinet setting out what I thought to be some constructive proposals. The old master had the last word. 'I find it eminently readable. I entirely disagree with it!'

The second occasion arose in this way. Naturally preoccupied, as we all were at that time, with the appalling losses at sea in the Western Approaches, Churchill had, I was informed, sent out a message to the United States proposing that British naval units in the Pacific were to be moved to the Atlantic. When this came to my knowledge, which it did quite promptly, I challenged it on the grounds that there was a possible threat from Japan (a threat which materialized dramatically only six months later) and that the security of Australia could be impaired by too great a weakening of British naval strength in the south-west Pacific, the United States then being neutral.

It was a tough battle, for I well understood the grave problems of the Western Approaches; yet I had my own duty. I almost passed out when he said, in that lovely grumble of his, 'So you want me to withdraw that message, do you?' 'Yes,' said I. 'Well,' said he, 'I will!'

When I got back to my hotel that evening, I inspected the insides of my knees, and was relieved to find no bruises.

There are, of course, other methods of controversy. On a Sunday night at Chequers, Winston exposed to me a great plan for dealing with the all too efficient co-operation of the U-boats and the Focke-Wulf aircraft in the Western Approaches. Briefly, the plan was that ships in convoy should each carry a fighter aircraft, with a catapult mechanism. When I asked what the fighter-pilot was to do after his attack aloft, Winston's reply was that he would ditch his plane as near as possible to a ship, and hope to be rescued. This dashing manœuvre was, of course, in the true Churchill tradition. Next day, Winston, in my hearing, put it to that very remarkable man, Sir Dudley Pound, the First Sea Lord. Pound added to a genial countenance the priceless advantage of deafness. So what was his reply to Churchill? 'I'm deaf, you know, Sir, and I've missed practically all that has been said. But I did hear a rumour yesterday that there was a proposal to catapult fighters off vessels in convoy and thereafter let them take their chance. Now I don't need to tell you, Sir, *as an old Admiralty man,* that such a proposal would be nonsense!'

Winston gave what I would describe as a good twinkling chuckle, and the incident was concluded. Winston had listened.

I have another memory which confirms my belief that my first impression, that Winston was a bad listener, was a superficial one. One weekend, I went down to Bristol, to see the great aircraft works. At that time, the Germans used to pinpoint the target area for their bombers by intersecting wireless beams. I had just arrived at Bristol, at the home of the Chairman, Sir Stanley White, when a message came through from Downing Street, on behalf of Churchill, to tell me that Bristol was the danger area, and that I should go to Plymouth. My reply was that nature had not designed me to be a physically fast mover, that I would stay the night, and go to Plymouth next day. I was not to know that the Germans had changed their plan and had decided to bomb Plymouth instead. And so it happened that, hurtling down through Devonshire with Sir William Rootes (as he then was), behind a driver who passionately believed in speed, we arrived at Plymouth to be the guests of Lady Astor, only to find that her house on the Hoe was something of a wreck, that a good portion of Plymouth was burning, and that nothing was more certain than that there would be another bombing attack that night, on a fire-illuminated target. So Nancy Astor led us off to the residence of the Admiral, Admiral Sir Martin Dunbar-Nasmith, a holder of the Victoria Cross, and therefore a source of moral strength for all of us.

In the best tradition, we dressed for dinner and thereafter, the air-raid sirens having sounded, adjourned to a room downstairs, the windows of which were partly, but only partly, below ground level. When the bombs were falling, 'Billy' Rootes improved my education by taking me outside (contrary to orders from Downing Street) to 'see the sights'. We had our 'tin' hats on, and needed them, for the fragments were whistling by. A little later, the Admiral took me down into the middle of the devasted city. Dinner jackets and all, he and I walked in the middle of the streets, because, although the 'all clear' had sounded, explosions were still occurring, and walls were collapsing. It was an unforgettable experience; but it was much more terrible for thousands than it was for me.

The next day I visited the Australian Flying Boat Squadron and had a warm reception. Somebody had given me a clump of wattle blossom, which I wore in the button-hole of my overcoat. Each man I spoke to would lean forward, and pluck a tiny morsel from it, until there was none left. It was a message from home. Following the unwritten rules under which politicians operate, I made a speech from the steps of the barracks. As usual, there was an interjector, and a humorous one. After a few minutes, I said: 'Would that man take two paces forward?' He did. I said: 'What are you?' 'A sergeant, Sir,' he said. 'Are you interested in politics?' 'Yes, Sir,' he said, with a grin. 'On what side?' I said. 'Yours, Sir.' Loud shouts from his colleagues. 'You'll get on!' So I wound up by saying, 'If you go on like this, you won't be a sergeant; you'll be a Senator!'

Years later, in Australia, I found, in conversation with a few airmen, that he was known as 'Senator' thereafter.

But this is a mere aside. I must come back to my proposition that Churchill was not as bad a listener as some say. I also visited the Naval Dockyards at Devonport. It was a Saturday morning. A light cruiser, heavily damaged in the fore part, was in dock and under repair. But no work was being done. I was taken through the engineering workshop, where hundreds of men were at work. An Engineer-Admiral in-charge escorted me. I have always felt sure that he had a telescope under his arm; but memory can be a treacherous thing. Each time we paused at a bench or lathe, the operative stood to attention, and his work was interrupted.

I went across to Portsmouth after the Plymouth Blitz; I had lunch with the Admiral, the famous Admiral James, 'Bubbles' James. Afterwards, he took me to a doorway looking into a small walled courtyard. Over near one of the walls (I took a moving picture of the scene) was an excavation at which a quite small man was digging industriously. Said the Admiral, 'That man is digging out an unexploded bomb. He was recently given the George Medal for this kind of exercise. Would you like to meet him?' Of course I would. So he was called across, and we met. He was a cheerful and literally disarming man; told me what he was doing; and then in a genial way he said, 'Would you like to come and see it, Sir!' Well, what else could I do? I went. We squatted by the hole. I looked down. The vanes of the bomb, quite a large one, were already uncovered. In as calm a voice as I could produce, I said: 'Is this thing liable to explode, even now?' His reply was wonderful. 'Well, probably not, Sir. But don't worry. If it does explode, neither you nor I will ever know about it!'

I walked back to the door with as much deliberation as I could muster. The journey was only about fifteen yards, but it seemed like a mile. But he went on digging!

On Sunday evening, I was back at Chequers. Winston wanted to know everything that happened. He listened with such interest that I was emboldened to tell him that I was disappointed with Devonport. So I said: 'Particularly now, when the heat is on, why do you have what are essentially industrial tasks conducted by Admirals? Why don't you get hold of some hard-faced chap from Yorkshire or the Midlands to come down and run the business as if it were his own; with drive and toughness?'

I thought the ancient roof would fall in. He began to pace up and down the Hall, with me trying hard to hang on to his arm. 'Don't you know that you are laying impious hands on the Ark of the Covenant? Don't you know that this Naval system has existed since Nelson? Who are you to criticize it?' Well, he had me there, but I managed to say that if Nelson had been with us at that time, in 1941, he would have been on my side! Well, the debate went on until, somewhat battered and worn, I was dismissed from the presence.

On the Monday, we went up to Downing Street. Winston, with quite a friendly smile, gave me a cigar. Before long, to my amazement, I heard Winston putting to A. V. Alexander, the First Sea Lord of the Admiralty, all the criticism which had fallen from my hapless lips at Chequers, and requiring investigation and satisfaction. I knew then that even when Winston refused to listen, he listened.

But for the willingness of the Labour members to serve under him—and under no other Conservative—Winston could not have become Prime Minister in 1940 and presided over an all-party National Government. In my own mind, I have always given Attlee much credit for this. That quiet little man has not yet been done justice by contemporary history. He had immense patriotism, which persuaded him that, with Hitler's successes in Europe, the crisis was at hand, and that England must, at all costs, win. He had great imagination and human understanding, and saw clearly that Churchill's hitherto unsuccessfully employed talents were just those elements which were needed in a life-and-death struggle.

So they all came in behind Winston. In a long day that I put in with him at his home in Churt in about April 1941, Lloyd George told me that Winston had too many 'Yes-men' in his Cabinet. When I queried this by asking about L G's own War Cabinet, he retorted that he had the company of several men of the highest distinction. There was, I thought, something to be said for Lloyd George's view, though I am sure he under-estimated the crushing impact of the Churchill personality.

Indeed, and as I warned you in my opening chapter, I will be discursive and say the common secret of these two great war leaders was the strength of their personal impact. Under these circumstances, neither was likely fully to appreciate the other!

Right back before the war, in 1935, I had the advantage of some talks with Lloyd George. His son Gwilym (later Lord Tenby) had me to lunch at one of the clubs off Pall Mall. He said that he understood I had been seeing something of his father, and asked me what I thought of him. This, I thought and said, was a tough question which I would much prefer not to answer. Gwilym smilingly persisted, and so I said: 'Your father has a magnetic power beyond my experience. Since the war [that is, the First World War] he has uttered no political view with which I have not completely disagreed. Yet, if he thought it desirable to make me his disciple, and worked on me, at the end of an hour I would leave all my ideas behind me, and follow him!' And I meant it.

Winston's War Cabinet contained men who were by no means commonplace; among others, there were Attlee, wise, practical, un-demonstrative, a quiet man of character; Anthony Eden, a really great

Foreign Secretary, whose fame has now been a little obscured by the Suez incident, of which I will state my own version later; Ernest Bevin, a sturdy British Union leader, who never failed to speak his mind, and to whom Winston always listened with respect; Herbert Morrison, a superb Cockney with a sort of cockatoo's crest of unruly hair, a good administrator and the embodiment of the London spirit; John Anderson, the most notable civil servant of the century, who was in charge of the close organization of the Invasion Area of south-east England.

They were a great group; but nobody doubted who was in charge. Once the war was on, Winston had a passion for it. He thought of nothing else. He spoke of nothing else. I would never hope to see a greater or more exclusive concentration of natural genius. He expected everybody else to be the same. He sought no leisure for himself, and could not understand why other people should want it. Early in May 1941, John Anderson, proposed in my hearing, that senior and responsible civil departmental men, who had not been relieved by any break for months, should be rostered out for a short holiday. Otherwise, he said, he could not answer for the consequences. Winston was quite taken aback. He respected Anderson as a first-class administrator, but he could not understand why anybody should want leave. And so I heard him say—'I cannot understand how any man, having the privilege of serving his country at a time like this, should want to be absent even for one day from the post of duty. But if you say so, it must be done!'

When I resumed my contact with Churchill in 1948, the war was over and won, and he and I were both in Opposition. I became Prime Minister of Australia again in December 1949, and continued in that office for the next sixteen years. I visited England at least once a year, and saw a good deal of him, either in London, or Chartwell, or Chequers, on each occasion.

But when I was with him in 1948, he was still feeling the wounds of his electoral defeat of 1945. He hung on as Leader of the Opposition, though many of its duties irked him, because he wanted to win an election. Nothing else would do. I rallied him about this. I said, 'I am Leader of the Opposition too. I hope and intend to win the general election of 1949. It means a great deal to me, for I was rejected during the war. This was a wretched experience, and I long since determined that I would fight my way back. But what does winning an election mean to you, who, more than any other man, won the war?' But nothing would move him. So he stayed, and won.

A few years later, when I was Prime Minister, I was in London. The Australian Club, as usual, gave me a great dinner at the Savoy. Clem Attlee was Prime Minister; but at the previous election his majority had been reduced to about six. Attlee proposed my health in his usual compact and un-rhetorical way; Winston supported it. He was in great form. He spoke generously about our association 'in difficult times'. 'History will say—or at least that history which I write myself in my memoirs——' He recalled that for a time I had been Prime Minister of Australia with a majority of one. (He was wrong here; in 1940-41 I had a majority, if that word is appropriate, of two Independents!) Then came the inevitable chuckle—'I hope he will not betray the secret to Mr Attlee!'

Apart from his deep feeling of injustice at his dismissal in 1945, Churchill had mellowed, and showed me the warmest of friendship. As the years proceeded, I could, of course, see changes in him. One did not need to be his medical adviser to perceive them. Age was beginning to come upon him. His light did not burn with a constant flame; but he continued to have the most astonishing capacity for recovery. I will illustrate this by one example which he afforded at a time when Harold Macmillan had become Prime Minister on Anthony Eden's retirement. My wife and I were at Chartwell at the weekend. Sunday's luncheon was a family affair, and Winston and I conducted a dialogue of our own, while the others had general conversation.

His deafness had increased; so I spoke up 'loud and clear'. I liked to talk to him about current problems, for I sensed that he felt out of things, while, in my own sphere, I was still immersed in them. When I spoke, his light-blue eyes for a while would seem opaque and unreceptive. Then, just as I was about to despair of getting across, his eyes would flash, and back would come his answer, clear and right on the spot. I concluded that the machine of his mind was still strong, but that, in the modern engineering term, his revolutions had slowed down. This depressed me. I feared that I was witnessing the beginning of the end.

But, a fortnight later, the Australian Club in London gave me a dinner at the Dorchester. There were over seven hundred men present, mostly Australians or Englishmen with Australian interests. As they filed in, I shook hands with all of them, until my fingers were crushed and my throat, I confess, parched. All the more parched because by this time I could see them addressing themselves to pre-prandial drinks inside.

Finally, I beckoned across one of the hotel servants, and said, 'Where are the Duke of Gloucester—who was Chairman—and the other official guests? I have not seen them.' He knew the answer, and led me around the corridors to a room in which I found them all, refreshing themselves for the labours of the evening. I just had time to greet them; the Duke, the Prime Minister, Harold Macmillan, Clem Attlee, Winston; when the red-coated Master of Ceremonies in a clear voice announced that dinner was served.

I found myself seated between the Duke and Winston, and promptly ordered myself a whisky and soda. So recruited, I had some talk with the Duke, and then turned to Winston, wondering whether I would have a repetition of my Chartwell experience and would have a rather wearing preparation for the speech which I knew I was to make after dinner. I could have spared my pains. The old man at once said, in a clear, strong, and teasing voice, as if he were five years younger, 'I'm sorry, my dear boy, to see you drinking whisky and soda. The champagne, oddly enough, is very good!' I retorted that I did not like champagne, and had drunk it with him in 1941 only because he liked it and I was afraid to refuse! 'Anyhow,' I said, 'you taught me to drink whisky and soda, and over the years we must have absorbed a considerable quantity of it. Why should you now reprove me?' He conceded the point, repeating, as if surprised at the fact, that the champagne was very good. Well, all I can say is that for the next fifteen minutes he was at the top of his form. The years had rolled away. He was crisp, clear, and witty, with no hint of old age. When he turned to his other neighbour, the American Ambassador, Mr Whitney, I caught echoes of debate about race-horses, and much laughter!

My gloomy prophecies were dispelled!

It was quite an experience for me to see how the great man went about preparing a speech.

One night at Chequers, in March 1941, I walked into the small corner study near the entrance door and found myself interrupting a dictation. I apologized and turned to leave. To my surprise (for personally I don't like dictating in the presence of a third person) Winston told me to stay, and gave me a cigar. He probably added some brandy. So I settled down, to watch and to learn.

There sat the stenographer with her silent typewriter. *Here* stood, or wandered, Winston. The rules soon became clear. While he was playing around with what might be called the 'first draft' of a sentence, trying each word for weight and simplicity, he spoke in a low voice, almost a whisper. When he arrived at the final version, he spoke up, and down went the sentence into type. Thus (and I do not profess to be accurate about the words), I would just hear 'And so the struggle will continue, continue? until victory—has been achieved . . . no, no—' and then out it came: 'And so we will fight on until the day has come!'

How many of us think in words of one syllable, only to succumb, when we speak, to the debased modern passion for long words and turgid sentences. Winston reversed the process.

His speeches had two purposes. First, he knew that he had an immediate and world-wide audience which he must arrest and hold and stimulate. He knew that the simpler the language the wider and more comprehending the audience would be, and the better would it be for all. Knowing this, he used to rehearse a broadcast speech with loving care, getting the timing and the pauses right, until art had concealed art and the words came out as if newly minted in the mind. I record this with warm admiration. He knew how important he was to hundreds of millions of people; he would have been strangely unaware if he had not. He felt that he owed the world his best; as near perfection as possible. And so he must give it his best; not some hastily assembled ideas and sentences, but the finished product. How right he was, the crucial years of the war will attest.

But second, Winston was by wide reading, which had so enriched his vocabulary, and by an inborn feeling for words, a great writer. He believed that his speeches would be published and read for years, and he wanted them to be a contribution to English literature. They must therefore have in them that nervous and vivid quality which enables the written word to endure. It took a remarkable man to reconcile these two elements in the one speech, so that the beat of his personality and emotions could be felt by the immediate audience with no conciousness on their part of art or artifice, while at the same time the work of art went on the record. That is why a newer generation, who never heard him, can read his great speeches, and be moved.

Among other things, let it be remembered, Churchill proved the immense significance of *speech* in persuasion and command. This fact is not as widely understood by dry scholars, but in the course of great events it is instinctively responded to by 'ordinary' people. For, without the great art of communication, even the greatest ideas may pass, as Bacon said, 'in smother'. It may be for entertainment; and if so there are no rules; a man who makes an after-dinner speech according to rules he has worked out is the kind of fellow who knows that at least three times he must say 'That reminds me of a good story I heard . . .' In effect, he is a bore. Churchill never was!

But the greatest function of communication is for information and persuasion. If it is aimed at neither, and is not, for compensation, amusing, speech is a mere tedious waste of time.

Now, a speaker cannot inform his audience unless he has first taken pains to *know*. He therefore 'has something to say', which is the essential element. Nor can a speaker persuade, if that is his purpose, unless he 'has something to say' which he wants his audience to accept.

A 'clever' speech may for the moment conceal its barrenness of real ideas; but a 'great' speech must be compact of ideas. There can be no great speech without substance; there can be no great speaker, in the true sense, who is not also a man of high intelligence.

So the having of 'something to say' is of the essence. But the second requirement is that it should be said as well as possible, with the most careful selection of words, and, if possible, in a voice which not only arrests attention but also holds it. It is by these processes that speech becomes an art.

And Churchill had that art, to perfection. He indulged himself in no verbal gymnastics, which weary and do not persuade, nor did he much care for the 'wise-crack' which has some currency elsewhere. He was characteristically English. His speech had no affectations or acquired accents. His humour ranged between the subtle ironies of the Home Counties and the deep chuckling 'stomach' laugh of the provinces.

After the war, and when he was in the, to him, chilling shadows of Opposition, I asked him, down at Chartwell, how he managed to interest himself in Europe, do a lot of painting at the Mediterranean, attend the House of Commons, and still produce, almost every year, a tall volume of his War Memoirs. 'I will tell you,' he said. 'Right through my term I thought the people would not deny me the privilege of having all my speeches, dispatches and directives printed in chronological order, on sheets of paper of uniform size. So when I want to deal with the events of a particular period, I take out the sheets in their order and dictate my narrative, inserting my own recorded words in their appropriate places. As I have never kept a diary, the task would have been overwhelming but for the printed and filed papers.'

I have in my library a splendidly gay seascape, painted at Antibes by Winston Churchill. It is, I think, one of two paintings of his in Australia. The story of how I got mine may be worth telling. My wife got the other, under the circumstances I shall describe.

In 1935, when I first visited Chartwell, I saw a few pictures, and was interested in this proof of versatility. In 1941, we discussed everything except painting.

But in 1948, once more at Chartwell, I conceived a great ambition. It cannot be said that in 1941 I was *persona gratissima* with Winston. There were times when I fell below the required standard.

But such matters were mere passing events in a period of some ten weeks, which the inspiration of his courage and leadership made unforgettable.

By 1948, he was out of office, and so was I. I spent a day with him at Chartwell in a warm atmosphere of friendship and fascinating reminiscence. He showed me his gold-fish, his swans and his pigs. Above all, he showed me scores of his own paintings. But my broad hints fell on deaf ears; he had an artist's pride, not only in achievement but in possession. For many years after 1948 I visited England, and had great talks to Winston about many things. But I failed to get a picture. I must say that I had offered to buy or borrow. Lady Churchill, I know, pressed my 'claims'. So did Mary (Soames). But it was in vain until

1955, not long before Winston's retirement from office. This is how it happened. Just before leaving London for Australia, I invited myself to lunch at Chartwell on a Saturday, and the invitation was approved. Arriving at about 12.40, I was taken upstairs by the butler through the study in which so much superb writing has been done, and into the great man's bedroom. The spectacle was unforgettable. A bright sun shone through a broad window. A budgerigar chirped merrily in its cage. 'Rufus', the French poodle, jumped up and down stiffly but amiably. In the bed reclined W.S.C., a bunch of papers in one hand, a noble cigar in the other, a medicinal draught of whisky and soda on a side table. We exchanged warm greetings. I perched on the foot of the bed. Winston handed me the papers, asked me to read them, and said he would like to discuss them later. With a broad grin, I inquired, 'Are you getting up for lunch, or will I have a tray up here?' With a much broader grin and a mischievous chuckle (for he loved to do a little debunking), he said, 'Of course I'm getting up for lunch! We have a very important guest!' (Menzies looks pleased.) 'We have the President of the Royal Academy coming for lunch, and he's going to select six of my pictures for the next exhibition!'

This reminder of my Great Campaign was almost too much. The butler, who had, on command, brought me a medicinal draught also, had just left the room when the miracle occurred. I was just walking slowly out, when Winston said—'By the way, you must have one of my pictures.' I spun round more nimbly than I had done for years. 'You should select three, of which I will give you one!'

Out in the corridor, I ran into Mary. 'Mary,' I said, 'you are the best family judge of your father's paintings. I know that, because you have some of his best in your own house. I'll leave it to you to pick out three, of which I am to have one, while I read these papers.'

Well, Winston appeared, we had some talk about the papers, and the P.R.A. arrived. We had lunch. We adjourned to the studio. On the walls hung many framed and signed works. Along one wall there leaned the six unframed pictures chosen by the P.R.A. Near to them leaned my three; one a lively sea picture, one a painting of 'Cranborne', and one a rather dark (and I thought early) picture of trees.

Winston moved along the line, with the P.R.A. in attendance. He stopped, and said, 'No! No! That one is a copy!' The P.R.A. made a quick recovery, and said, 'Of course. Well, I will take that one' (pointing to my sea picture). I then nominated the Cranborne picture. Winston —'Oh no! I intend that one for Bobbety' (Lord Salisbury). At this stage I fear that I cast a cold eye on the dark trees. Mary's husband, Christopher Soames, whose intelligence some people underrated at that time, at once said (catching the look in my eye), 'But that is not good enough for your old friend. What about one of these on the wall?'

He pointed to the Antibes picture. I at once expressed warm approval.

Soames (to a gangling youth brought down by the P.R.A. for packing and dispatch), 'Take that one down, wrap it up, and put it in Mr Menzies's car at the front door.' *Winston* (grumblingly): 'But that is one of my best. Kelly says it is my best.' *Soames:* 'Well, you wouldn't like your old friend to have your worst, would you? Boy, pack it up and take it down to the car!'

This helpful observation, though open to question as an exercise in pure logic, won the day. I quickly embraced the family, and departed with remarkable speed! When I got into the car, I said to the driver, 'Drive as fast as you decently can for half an hour!' There were no signs of pursuit. I had the picture. I still have it, and am living with it most happily.

Years later, my wife and I were lunching at Chartwell. She was in the first flush of ownership of a new and good camera. Now Pat (that's my wife's name), though Winston always treated her with affection, was nervous about asking him for permission to 'take his picture'. He was not very mobile at that time, and was seated deep in an armchair, after lunch.

She said, 'May I take your picture?' To her and my astonishment, he replied—'That's all right. Clemmie has it ready!'

Pat explained that she wanted to take a photograph. Winston, who had become rather deaf, repeated his, to us, cryptic answer. In the result, she took the photograph, and walked out with one of Winston's paintings, already crated up for delivery.

That is the simple tale of how it took me years of manœuvre to get my Churchill, while my wife got hers without effort, indeed without trying. And yet they say that women represent the weaker sex!

There has been in the last few years some arguments about 'Prof'

Lindemann and his undoubted influence on Winston. All I know, at first hand, about the 'Prof' (later Lord Cherwell) can be briefly stated. I first met him in early 1941, at Chequers. It was a sort of 'Thimble and the Pea' act. At one moment he was not there; at the next, he was in the room, as if an ectoplasm had emerged. Always quiet, and, unlike some of his modern opponents, a little diffident, he obviously had Winston's ear. And, after all, why not? The facts on which Winston had, in the thirties, founded his prophecies and his defeats, the facts about German re-armament, particularly in the air, were assembled for Winston by Lindemann, colloquial in German and mathematical in attainment. I met Lord Cherwell long after the war, and was still impressed.

In 1945, Winston broke up the National Government and called an election, the first since before the war. The election was lost, and Winston found himself out of office. I may be doing Beaverbrook an injustice, but I have always thought that he persuaded Winston that if he went to the people as a Conservative leader and denounced, as Socialists not to be trusted, his war-time Labour Ministers, all of whom, as I got to know in 1941, had an immense admiration and respect for him, he would win! Now, Beaverbrook's political judgement was not very good. He produced his newspapers for the quite uncritical reader, who wanted his news in snappy paragraphs, who enjoyed Low's cartoons for their astringency and wit, and, for the most part, ignored the leading articles. Which reminds me, for some reason or other, of the first time I ever met Beaverbrook, in 1935, at a reception at St James's Palace.

Bruce was present, a former Prime Minister and then High Commissioner, and properly a man of accepted standing in London. I looked across a crowded room, and saw Bruce beckoning to me. I weaved my way across to him. A short man was standing next to him.

'Ah, Menzies,' said Bruce, 'I want to introduce you to Lord Beaverbrook.' We shook hands. 'I am interested to meet you,' said Beaverbrook. 'I have been most interested to read your speeches in London on Commonwealth and Empire matters!' This was too much for me, for though I had read Beaverbrook's fervid Leaders on Empire Free Trade, I had not failed to notice that in his papers Empire news was conspicuous by its absence. So I replied, most tactlessly. 'Yes, Lord Beaverbrook, but not in your own newspapers!' It was not until 1941, when I sat with him in the War Cabinet, that I recovered any of my lost ground.

I shall always believe that if Winston, in 1945, had decided upon a general election but had avoided an attack upon his war-time Labour colleagues, the result might have been different. Suppose he had said, as only he could have said, 'My friends, we have been through difficult and dangerous years together. We have won the war in Europe, but Japan is undefeated, and we have much to do together. Let us press on to the final victory.' I have sometimes thought he might have won.

I may well be wrong, for the heat had gone off England. The troops wanted to come home, and were already thinking of the new world in which they wanted to live; a world of employment and social services and economic security in which their great war leader was reputed to be very little interested. They were not very much disposed to accept attacks upon men like Attlee and Ernest Bevin and Herbert Morrison, whose services in the war crisis had been outstanding. So probably they would have voted Labour in any event; not feeling that they were voting so much against Winston as for the people and the things they wanted in the post-war 'new world'.

In 1935, when I was Attorney-General of Australia and had been appearing before the Judicial Committee of the Privy Council, I had the singular fortune to be elected as Honorary Bencher of Gray's Inn. Over the years I have spent many happy hours within its walls and have enjoyed much friendship and true comradeship. Winston was also a Bencher. In June 1952 it happened that he and I were both Prime Ministers. The Inn therefore decided to give a House Dinner to both of us; a unique honour. The Treasurer (the head of an Inn of Court is the Treasurer) was Mr Justice (later Lord Justice) Sellers, to whom I was personally much attached. One day, quite early in June, he spoke to me and told me, with bitter disappointment, that 'Master' Churchill had declined the invitation. Could I do anything about it? I thought that I could, 'with a little bit of luck'.

Winston had gone down to Chartwell, so I rang him up. As this was one of my rare successes, I will as far as possible reproduce the conversation.

M. 'Winston, Fred Sellers tells me you are not going to attend the Gray's Inn House Dinner.'

C. 'I think that is so. It is not convenient, and anyhow I am not a lawyer and am not at home with them, as you are.'

M. 'You disappoint me. Here are you, a man with a great feeling for history. Don't you realize that this is an ancient Inn, that Queen Elizabeth was its first great patron, that Francis Bacon was its most famous early Treasurer, and that, centuries later, your friend Birkenhead was its pride and joy? And, moreover, this would be the first time in its history when two Benchers, each a serving Prime Minister, were its guests and speakers on the one occasion. I appeal to your sense of history.' There was a pause, and then he said: 'I see. What is the date? I'll be there!'

So he was. It was a great night, still, I have reason to believe, memorable in the ancient Hall.

What was the real virtue of his leadership? The very word 'leadership' is hard to define. It is something to be felt, rather than analysed. I have known some great leaders in my time, not the least of them being Field-Marshal Slim, who was for some years Governor-General of Australia, and who, if I may venture to say so without fear of reprisals, wrote the most honest book *(Defeat into Victory,* Cassell) produced by any military Commander in the Second World War. Yet I could not tell you much more than the simple fact that, as Prime Minister of Australia, and therefore his principal Constitutional adviser, whose advice he was under some obligation to accept, I never went into his presence without feeling nervous. Which was right and proper. He was (and is) a great and rare man.

But what was Churchill's particular quality? Let it be conceded that he had never been at home with the financial or economic or social problems which make up the normal stuff of politics. Even as a war leader he was not the best picker of men, nor was he always just to them in adversity. The names of Auchinleck, Ritchie and Wavell come readily to mind. He was fascinated by military history, and had vivid memories of his own soldiering days; yet, on matters of military technique and armaments, he was in some ways quite out of date and would be put right by the experts. Why, then, did he, in the crisis, bestride the world like a Colossus?

To me, the answer is clear, and it will remain clear when the critics have made their criticisms. He had 'a fire in his belly'; he would never contemplate defeat. He denied its very possibility. And, more than that, he saw and believed in victory even when quite a few people doubted it.

It was this element which enabled him to dominate most of his Cabinet, which made even sturdy and independent men like Ernest Bevin, himself strong and dominant, respect him and follow him, and which, being understood by the people at large, elicited from millions that spirit, that 'will to win', which was, in the last analysis, the chief instrument of victory. It was Napoleon who wrote: '*A la guerre, les trois quarts sont des affaires morales; la balance des forces réelles n'est que pour un autre quart.*'

If this needed proof, Churchill provided it. For he built up the morale of the free world as no other leader could have done. His immortality on earth is of the spirit.

But though this is, as I believe, the simple truth, I am not claiming for this great hero a species of perfection. He was, in many ways, a 'mere mortal', with great qualities and some of the defects of those qualities, with limitations of mind which even a vastly inferior mind like my own could perceive, and with his fair share of prejudice as well as pride.

A plaster saint may properly occupy a niche in a cathedral; but it will not stir multitudes to action. Human beings respond to their own kind; they rather like to observe a few oddities, and, if they perceive defects, well, so much the better; it induces a sense of brotherhood and understanding.

I will record some further particulars of what is involved in these general reflections.

Before the war, he had been the voice of a minority, if not despised, at least rejected. When the crisis came in 1940, all parties turned to him. He was the man to lead in a conflict which he had foreseen, and against which he had uttered warning after warning in vain. It is therefore not to be wondered at that he had a confidence in his own opinion which

4

engendered a form of intolerance. It made him frequently unkind and sometimes less than just to those who had thought differently, in particular those who had been senior members of the Chamberlain government at the time of Munich. Because they had been, as he saw it, ruinously wrong over Hitler, he had a disposition to deny them any virtue at all. Some of these men were my personal friends, and I used to speak to Churchill about their qualities. But his mind was closed. Now, this seemed to me to be a defect; a streak of littleness in a great man. But it was the defect of his supreme quality, which was that his whole mind and spirit were concentrated on one great and vital task. Like one of his great predecessors, he could have said—to himself—'I know that I can save England, and that nobody else can!' In short, his hostility to Chamberlain (and Baldwin) was based on his single-minded concentration on the war; his unspoken motto was, like that of his twin spirit, Henry V:

> He which hath no stomach to this fight,
> Let him depart.

He had a considerable knowledge of European history. It was not as broad, vivid, and detailed as that of Harold Macmillan, whose conversation was and is garnished with analogies from the European past, and who, had he not chosen the more arduous paths of political service, would have made a Professor of Modern History whose classes would have been thronged with delighted students. Winston Churchill's European history was essentially that of wars and war-leaders. An acute friend in England, like me a great admirer, said to me in 1941:

You know, Winston was made for war. He knows all about the wars of the past, and has written some marvellous books about them. He is now running this war as nobody else could. And when it is over, he will write a history of it. If, having done that, he has time and the desire, he will speculate about the next one!

I am a great advocate of Universities, and was fortunate enough to play a significant part in their post-war development in Australia. In my retirement, I have paid the penalty for this by becoming Chancellor of my own University, Melbourne.

But it was, I think, fortunate for us that Winston Churchill was no normal or orthodox product of one of the seats of higher learning. He was never an 'intellectual' in the narrow and false meaning attached to that word, nowadays, by some supposed scholars who air their superficial views on politics. Nor was he a model of objectivity, as a true intellectual should be. As so many of us have learned, the cold analysis of 'both sides of the question' can sometimes inhibit decision and action. The most classical example of this in modern times was Sir John Simon, a great lawyer, an admirable character, but a disastrous Foreign Secretary.

But Winston Churchill was something much greater. He was intelligent, brave and resolute, eloquent, and commanding. And he knew that the first 'war objective' is to win, not to pronounce a balanced judgement.

There is another aspect of the great man which should not be overlooked. He had a great sense of what is now called (sonorously) 'public relations'.

He held no press conferences, and would therefore never have done in the United States. But he had a great sense of publicity. He knew, as Montgomery was to demonstrate in North Africa, that he must have 'an image'—though that phrase had not become current at that time—and so he adopted what are now called 'gimmicks'. I became familiar with them. One was the 'siren suit'. Another was the cigar, jutting forward defiantly from the mouth. I have said something about each. But the third was the hat. He loved dressing up, and he loved funny hats. If only his people could see him, as they frequently did, wearing an old-fashioned square-topped hard hat, with a cigar beneath it, and the Victory sign displayed by his out-thrust hand, they knew that all was well. 'Good old Winnie,' they said, and returned to their work and their duty.

Long after the war, I was at Chartwell for a weekend. A considerable group of sightseers had gathered at the entrance gates. Looking out and seeing them, I said, 'There are some of your supporters here, Winston. You should go out and wave to them.' 'Certainly,' he said, 'and you come with me.' In the entrance hall at Chartwell was a table. On the table was an old felt hat, holes cut in it for ventilation, and ordinary fowl's feathers stuck in the band! He clapped it on his head, stepped outside, was received with a burst of applause, gave his V for Victory signal, gestured towards me, whom they did not know but received kindly as his friend, and the reception was over. There's no doubt about it; he was a great showman. I have never been very good at this kind of thing myself; but it is a special talent never more splendidly or usefully employed than by Winston Churchill, Franklin Roosevelt, and Field-Marshal Montgomery. But such things are superficial. Their impact would not last long unless there was substance behind them.

What then were his secret springs of action? Why did Winston Churchill make a contribution which friend and foe alike admit to be unique? Why, indeed, did the impact of his deeds and personality so effectively cross the Atlantic that the Congress of the United States later on voted him into 'honorary citizenship' of that great country?

First, he was the British Lion, with what some now think to be old-fashioned prides and beliefs. He was on familiar ground. He was fighting a rear-guard action, at which the British have always excelled. He had no rival, for his possible rivals had been rejected. It was a new war, but the old qualities would count. A descendant of the Great Duke of Marlborough would not fail.

Second, he had a passionate belief in the continuity and permanence of British history. The Napoleonic threat was fresh in his nostrils. He thought of Pitt, and Nelson, and Wellington as if they were men of yesterday. Why should he fail? Why should England be defeated?

Third, he had a dynamic personality. He was both terrifying (as I admit) and attractive. His light-blue eye, in repose, was opaque and unresponsive; his face, projected forward by hunched shoulders, could be grim and forbidding. In the mood, he could make one feel as small as a pebble. But when the light came, it was a glorious awakening. The face became that of a cheerful schoolboy. The eye became deep and lambent. A man who had seemed incapable of any emotion save that of grim and hostile determination suddenly became all human and affectionate. A warm word would bring tears to his face. I know that I can be accused of a sort of hero-worship; and if so I will plead guilty. For I never in my life saw anything like him before or since.

Fourth, he had, as I have pointed out, a great loyalty to those who had been his friends in his years of political exile. This is an element of character frequently sneered at by superficial press commentators. They dispose of it as 'nepotism'. What they do not realize is that loyalty operates both ways; that loyalty breeds loyalty, and produces a quality of team-work which no amount of intellectual detachment and dry objectivity could ever secure.

Fifth, he had a rare faculty, not widely known, for laughing at himself, though this was, not unnaturally, more perceptible after the war than during it.

Fortunately, I can illustrate this at first hand. Years after the war, I had gone down into Sussex to spend a day or so with Anthony Eden. Now, Anthony, about whose later policies and actions over Suez I will have much to say in 'My Suez Story', had been and was Winston's most faithful lieutenant. But he gave me a broad hint that in Winston's war volumes, the 'old man' set out in full what he had said or written to others, but seldom, if ever, recounted the reply. When I left Anthony, I went on to Chartwell to spend an evening with Winston. After dinner, the great man said to me, 'You remember that we had some cabled differences of opinion about Dakar?' Of course I remembered, for, as I have recounted, I had wickedly, at Chequers, in 1941, promoted a Churchill-de Gaulle debate on this vexed matter. 'Would you be agreeable to my including my messages to you in my next volume?' This gave me my opening. 'Look,' I said, 'you sent several dispatches to me on a variety of matters, both official and unofficial. To save you from having to make special requests in future, I can tell you at once that you may publish all or any of them; but on one condition. If I ever had the nerve to send a reply, you must agree to include it in the record.' He chuckled appreciatively, agreed, and acted on it!

Winston Churchill's imagination was, like that of most of us, limited by his eyes and his personal experience.

America? Yes. His mother was an American, and his broad strategic conception of the war always included the United States as a potential and almost certain ally. He never lost sight of his Western horizon.

Europe, of course. For here was the nursery of wars, and, dominating it after the fall of France, was the sinister figure of Hitler. There was something powerfully anthropomorphic about Winston. It was a good thing to fight against evil, but a more comprehensible task to fight against Hitler; it was a sort of hand-to-hand battle, reminiscent of the days of the lists. But he never lost sight of Europe, and, in the darkest days, thought much of how and where an attack might be driven through it.

India came within the sweep of his eye, for he had been there in his early years as a Lancer. It is probable that he did not understand India; for that matter, what Occidental does? Before the war, he fought a forlorn, and, in the light of subsequent history, misguided battle against the India Bill. Yet he lived long enough to acquire a marked respect for Nehru, and, in Prime Ministers' Conferences, treated him with courtesy.

The Middle East existed vividly for him. He had been in the famous charge at Omdurman.

South Africa was well in his sights. He had sustained remarkable experiences in the Boer War, had learned to respect the then enemy, and later found in the celebrated J. C. Smuts a brilliant and distinguished companion and colleague.

But of the Far East he knew nothing, and could not imagine it. Australia was a very distant country which produced great fighting men, and some black swans for the pond at Chartwell, but it cannot be said that it otherwise excited his imagination or his interest. I sometimes think that he regarded the Japanese attack in the south-west Pacific as a rather tiresome intrusion, distracting attention from the great task of defeating Hitler.

Yet these matters, though to many Australians they indicate some of his limitations, are not powerfully critical. He believed that unless and until Hitler was overthrown, the war against Japan could not be won; that when Hitler was disposed of by victory in Europe, the concentration of power against Japan would bring victory in the Pacific. My experiences in London in the early months of 1941 had shown that the danger in the Far East was underestimated, and that there would be no subtraction of forces from the European task.

Australian though I am, I am not prepared to sit in judgement. Who am I to say that Churchill was wrong to concentrate his genius and his leadership upon the immediate and urgent task of defeating the first and greatest attacker, without whose destruction there could be no peace or freedom for the world?

I will vary the menu with a reminiscence which, I fear, will be criticized as 'blasphemous'. But, just as beauty is in the eye of the beholder, so does blasphemy cease to be blasphemy when it comes from an innate sense of courtesy. This, I know, is an obscure remark, so I will proceed with my story. Well after the war, we (the Commonwealth Prime Ministers) had dined with The Queen, and had been photographed with her. The then Prime Minister of Pakistan, Nazimmuddin, was present. He was an agreeable man, short, quiet, and a devout Muslim. When we emerged into one of the drawing-rooms at Buckingham Palace, Winston, who observed no rules save those he had made himself, ensconced himself (what a nice pompous word is 'ensconced'!) at one end of a couch. The Queen and the Royal Family were moving around among the guests. Winston looked about him, caught the eye of Nazimmuddin, miraculously remembered who he was, and called him to sit at the other end of the couch. Winston, having thus physically captured his audience, began to expound the principles of the defence of the Middle East, in which Pakistan held one of the flanks.

At the end of fifteen minutes of monologue (for Nazim was not a talkative man), Winston grew a little 'drouthy', as the Scots would say, arrested the attention of a passing footman bearing a tray of drinks, and demanded a whisky and soda. Looking towards Nazim, he said, 'Will you have a whisky and soda, Mr Prime Minister of Pakistan?' Nazim was horrified, and said, 'No, thank you!'

Winston, whose hearing was even then either not acute or highly selective, said 'What's that?'

N. 'No, thank you.'

C. 'Why?'

N. 'I'm a teetotaller, Mr Prime Minister.'

C. 'What's that?'

N. 'I'm a teetotaller!'

C. 'A teetotaller. Christ! I mean God! I mean ALLAH!'

As soon as this surprising event came to my ears, further down the room, I found my way to The Queen, and started to tell her about it. She stopped me almost at once, saying, 'You're too late. Tommy Lascelles' [Sir Alan Lascelles was then her Private Secretary] 'has told me about it. And Tommy says that as the footman, in his astonishment, dropped the tray and caught it before it reached the carpet, without spilling a drop, he ought to be put into the English cricket team, where the slip-fielding needs improving!'

A great voice rolling around the world; a great spirit informing the voice; a great courage warming the listener's ears and causing their hearts to throb; a wonderful feeling that we were all at the gates of destiny. For my generation, these need no memorial. But for my grandchildren, they need to be recorded. For if, as I hope and believe, they live and work in a free country, they will owe their freedom and their enjoyable industry to one man above all; the great man who expressed the genius of his mind and the indomitable courage of his heart through the power of speech unrivalled for a hundred years.

Let the clever critics come on; let them explain Winston's 'errors', and, by implication, show how much wiser they would have been. I recall reading, many years ago, a splendid essay on France by Chesterton. Among other things, he said to his fellow-countrymen who had acquired superficial, stage, ideas about the French, 'You have not died on the barricades!'

And so I say to my successors, who will know Churchill only through the pages of books, critical as many of them will be, 'You have not lived on the barricades of a great war, or been sustained and brought to victory by the greatest man of the century.'

That, for whoever may care to read it, is, so far as it concerns Winston Churchill, my last will and testament.

CHAPTER FIVE

THREE BRITISH PRIME MINISTERS

Y OU MAY SAY TO ME, 'Why three?' since I have personally known
nine. I should answer this at once.

Ramsay MacDonald I knew but little, and then in his declining
days when he was, I suppose, over-devoted to words, the old fires
having burned low. I could not, in a few words, and most of those at
second-hand, expect to do him justice. But that, by bringing Labour
into power, with its responsibilities, he made a great contribution to
what was then the future, I do not doubt.

To Winston Churchill I have devoted a special chapter.

I have not ventured to write a sketch of Anthony Eden; but, in a
later chapter, I set out my appreciation of the great concluding crisis of
his Prime Ministership, the Suez Canal incident. It is necessary only to
add that I have such an old and intimate friendship with Anthony,
going back for well over thirty years, that I might properly be suspected of bias.

In this book, there are some references to Harold Macmillan; but I
have not attempted to paint a portrait of him. Many of the notable
events in which he was concerned, and in which on occasion I played
some small part, are as yet not concluded. At present, it would not be
possible for me to write with sufficient detachment about a man who
has honoured me with his friendship, and whose services to the nation
are not, for the moment perhaps, as fully understood as they undoubtedly will be.

For obvious reasons, I have written no more than glancing references
to Sir Alec Douglas-Home, whose retirement from the leadership of
the Conservative Party was, in my opinion, a great misfortune for
that party, or the present Prime Minister, Mr Harold Wilson, whose
tasks are difficult enough, though his talents are obviously great,
without any intervention on my part. I am not setting out, in this book,
to be a commentator on current party politics; to do so would be an
impertinence.

I therefore confine myself, in this brief sketch, to some observations

4*

about Baldwin, Chamberlain, and Attlee, made with proper apologies for the inadequacy and imperfections of my assessments.

1. STANLEY BALDWIN

When we arrived in England in 1935, Ramsay MacDonald was Prime Minister of the Coalition Government. It had been formed after the financial crisis of 1931. Shortly afterwards, there was a General Election, an appeal to the country.

Stanley Baldwin, whose reputation has since been tampered with by the critics, was a man of character. So he said to the electors:*

Here am I, the leader of the Conservative Party, who took my political life in my hands nine years ago to escape from a Coalition, asking you to support a Government led by a Socialist Prime Minister, and to enter myself under him in another Coalition. I think, if any proof that there is a crisis is necessary, that is sufficient answer. There are greater things than loyalty to one's party. I am an Englishman first.

The Socialists who had not followed Ramsay MacDonald into the Coalition were heavily defeated; the Conservatives came back, with a very large majority. But Baldwin, Leader of his triumphant party, served under MacDonald with conspicuous loyalty.

For not only was he 'an Englishman'; he was a great Englishman.

He succeeded MacDonald, whose powers were obviously failing, in 1935. It was in that year that I met him. By the end of 1936 I had (as I have recently discovered) written a 'piece' about him, which I now reproduce as a pre-war estimate, set down with enthusiasm and affection.

Future historians will no doubt quarrel about Stanley Baldwin, and un-imaginative research students will, with all the dogmatism of the very young, find in him the proof of the mediocrity of statesmanship after the World War. I met a bright young political gossip-column writer at dinner in Mayfair one night, and his contempt for his Prime Minister was complete. I forget his name.

The average newspaper reporter, who yawns over the difficult things of public policy and the intricacies of administration, waiting for an odd member of Parliament to call another a liar and so provide material for an account of the

*Arthur Bryant: *Stanley Baldwin*, page 173.

day's debate, cannot understand Baldwin, because he thinks there is nothing to understand. The political cartoonist, trafficking in externals, thanks God for his pipe and his pigs, but would naturally prefer Jimmy Maxton any day. They are both wrong. It has been my privilege to meet Stanley Baldwin on many occasions, in official conferences and in informal private discussions. I have breakfasted with him at Downing Street; I have sat with him at an Empire Ministerial conference in the Cabinet room at No. 10, with Walpole's portrait over the fireplace, gazing with mild surprise (or did I imagine it?) at the statesmen of a British world of which he never dreamed. I have sat in the gallery of the House of Commons while four hundred members of every shade of political opinion hung silently on every honest English word falling from the lips of the grave-faced man at the dispatch box.

On 4 July 1935, there was a great luncheon for the Empire Parliamentary Association, as it then was, in Westminster Hall; the most historic place in London. I found myself sitting at table with the Speaker, Baldwin, the Earl of Athlone, Ramsay MacDonald, Neville Chamberlain, S. M. Bruce, and Sir John Simon. The reason for this promotion was that I had been selected to speak on behalf of the Dominions in reply to the toast, to be proposed by Baldwin. It promised to be a great ordeal; for some helpful person whispered to me that I was the first Dominions Minister ever to speak in that place. I had for once written out a speech, so that I would not collapse or stumble in the shades of Burke and Fox. Baldwin spoke magnificently, with a ring in his voice, and poetry in his prose. He had vigour, eloquence, a rich historical imagination, and a great prestige. He dealt with the topic I had selected for myself; the deep roots of English history; the day when many centuries before Westminster Abbey had stood, white and beautiful, across the way; of the centuries in which the rule of law had been established in and around Westminster. '*Lex est rex, caveat rex.*'

So I put my notes away, and prayed for help, and, Heaven be praised, had some success.

Now, that was an exciting day in my life; but my chief reason for writing about it is that it made me understand two of the great qualities of Baldwin; his deep love of England and the history of the English, and his remarkable capacity for expressing it in simple but moving words.

They will tell you that he is indolent and disposed to postpone his problems. Men who work easily and without heat will always encounter this allegation. They will tell you that he lacks the dynamic qualities for a great crisis. But every crisis of his career, the Great Strike, the financial crisis of 1931, the Abdication, has found him rising to the noblest heights of unselfish statesmanship. They will tell you that he is dull and unimaginative. But his speeches reveal not only a rare literary quality, but the acutest and most sympathetic understanding of his people and of the countryside which has nurtured them. They will tell you that he is matter of fact and unspiritual. But no statesman of my time has been so great a Christian in the sense that he has felt it his duty to do something to establish the Kingdom of God on earth, to 'build Jerusalem in England's green and pleasant land'.

The truth is, I think, that the genius of Baldwin lies in his English-ness. We chide Baldwin for procrastination when it has been part of the English genius for affairs that they have sometimes postponed difficulties out of existence altogether. Your hasty fellow, who prides himself on deciding everything today, is best kept at a small job. Why count it against Baldwin that he does not plan ahead when he leads a nation which in its heart regards planning as a transatlantic eccentricity and reminds itself from time to time that while it has rarely won a battle it has never lost a war? Why be contemptuous of the alleged vacillations and hesitations of British foreign policy under Baldwin's Prime Ministership when the truth is that Baldwin is a great democrat, and only dictators can afford to outrun public opinion? Perhaps it is this last observation which gives us the key to Baldwin's eminence. He is a great leader, because on every great occasion he has expressed most perfectly the mind and instinctive judgement of a fundamentally grave and sensitive people. He has never played down to the worst in his audience; cheap demagogy, the evocation of selfish passion or cruel prejudice, are abhorrent to him. He aims higher than that. He knows, what so many political leaders forget, that in a British country the appeal to the best in man, his unselfishness, his chivalry, his sense of obligation for the destiny of his race, his instinct for beauty and harmony and justice, is never made in vain. He has 'never sold the truth to serve the hour'. Such men are rarely spectacular. But they keep the nation sane and tolerant, and are the real trustees for the British heritage of the future.

It was always interesting to be in the gallery when Baldwin was at the dispatch box. He used copious notes, at which he peered from time to time. He stood stockily, with a sort of well-planted countryman's quality about his legs, his arms outstretched to the two ends of the box. His voice, with a masculine music in it, revealed a cultivated simplicity. He used the arts of oratory—the pause, the sudden emphasis—but sparingly. No single sentence might seem beyond the thought or utterance of any of his listeners, and yet, it seemed, so informed was his speech by a sort of moral grandeur and earnestness, he had his listeners, as the old phrase has it, 'where he wanted them'.

He understands the temper of the House of Commons perfectly. And the essence of that temper is that it is a good temper. On one occasion in 1936, Lloyd George, returning to the House after an indisposition, launched a brilliant but vitriolic and unfair attack on the Government and on Baldwin in particular. The House, while it no longer believes in Lloyd George, admires his powers of invective and is ready enough to roar at the pungency of his witty rhetoric. Baldwin rose in reply. With the utmost mildness, he began by saying 'how glad he was to see the Right Honourable Member for Caernarvon Boroughs back in his place, and, judging by his speech, in such admirable health and spirits'. What can you do with a man like that?

I was once taking part in an election campaign in Tasmania. Everywhere the hoardings were thick with posters announcing the superior merits of the various candidates. One of these posters arrested my attention. It contained the photograph of a respectable looking man with a button-hole in the Austen Chamberlain manner, and a legend which said 'Vote for Jones, who has mixed in all grades of society, from Royalty to the slums.' Unfortunately, this undoubted catholicity of taste did not avail him, and Canberra is still without him. But in a less fantastic way, Baldwin, in experience, has something in common with that of the gentleman from Tasmania. He was for years a private employer in the steel industry, meeting his employees, thrashing out their problems, adjusting differences, getting to know them, to sympathize with them, and to understand their point of view. Later, he was a silent back-bench Member of Parliament, with an inevitable appreciation of how the business of government looks to a private member who can rarely hope to catch the Speaker's eye; and then a Minister, Prime Minister, with the world's problems at his doorstep, with Kings and Queens and the great ones of the world for his associates. And all the time, he has escaped as occasion offered into the country, into his beloved Worcestershire, to the county with its beech and oak and elm, and the song of the lark at heaven's gate, and the slow smoke of a wood fire mounting to the sky—and, yes, if you like—the savage grunts of pigs at feeding time.

It is in this varied and intimate contact with life that we can find the explanation of Stanley Baldwin's wisdom and understanding.

There is one other aspect of Baldwin which must be mentioned in any account written by a Minister from a far-off Dominion. He has an entirely modern outlook on the British Empire. We have progressed a long way from the days when angry colonial parliaments and executives could and did quarrel about 'dictatorship from Downing Street'. But even today, one may find traces, not a hundred miles from Westminster, of the notion that Dominions are placed whose useful but unspectacular function it is to grow food and produce raw materials for the inhabitants of the U.K., who will in turn supply them with manufactured products. Today the younger men at Whitehall clearly understand that this simply won't do: that a secure British world requires Dominions developed to the utmost in point of population, production, manufacture, and all the resources of civilization. Among the older men, I found Baldwin easily the most lucid in his understanding of and ambitions for this new British world, with a distributed strength but a concentrated moral and political force. It was said of the elder Pitt that nobody could come out of his presence without feeling a better and stronger man. It can certainly be said that I never came out of the presence of Baldwin, that most English of the Englishmen, without feeling a better and a stronger Australian; that there was work to do, and I had better set about the doing of it.

Those were my feelings about the man as I knew him during his Prime Ministership.

I have now lived long enough to know that he became a controversial figure in his own party. He tended to irritate Neville Chamberlain, whose precise habits of mind disliked imprecision.

He may very well, as responsible writers tell us, have been unattracted by detail and slow to decision; not disposed to master the hard facts of new problems; somewhat given to procrastination. I can well believe that from time to time he puzzled and disappointed those whose talents were different. But I shall continue to believe that his great contribution to history is that he understood the English countryside and the English people, and on the crucial events with which he had to deal, gave them a sense of unity. Because of his capacity for postponement, a capacity not uncharacteristic of the race, his spiritual home, as some critic has said, was 'in the last ditch'.

And, so it was that, in that precarious place, he displayed understanding, skill and resource.

No doubt Baldwin could be seen as a provincial Englishman, with very little knowledge of Europe (though he used to take a 'cure' at Aix) and no very great interest in it. His democracy was of a kind which disposed him to understand and follow public opinion rather than take great political risks to create it.

Winston Churchill himself used to have sharp things to say about Baldwin's failure to heed warnings, and rearm while there was yet time. But Baldwin believed that a full-blooded and costly rearmament programme, presented to a nation which had just voted overwhelmingly for a foolish and dangerous 'peace ballot', would result in his defeat and the coming to power of a Labour Party so bemused by the notions of the League of Nations and the Covenant of the League that it was all for national disarmament—a policy which J. L. Garvin was to describe as 'the ecstasy of suicide'.

It was, indeed, a grim choice for Baldwin to have to make. True, he began to do some things about rearmament; but, as it turned out, too little. In the result, he left Britain inadequately prepared for war; almost certainly because he did not clearly see the dangers looming up in Europe. He was, let us remember, not the only one. At that time, one became conscious of a current of opinion in England that the Germans should be our natural allies, and that war with Germany was unthinkable!

As to the then attitude of the Labour Party, I recall that, in 1936, when we were both engaged, on opposite sides, before the Judicial Committee of the Privy Council, my friend and political opponent, Stafford Cripps, said to me at lunch, 'Menzies, what do you think of my Party's defence policy?' I was bold enough to reply: 'Well, until recently, I did not know that you had one. But I now observe that you are all for sanctions imposed by the League of Nations; that you will most fully support them; and that if this leads to hostilities you will wage war with bows and arrows!'

But, since no judgement on these matters can be either final or dogmatic, I will, with retrospective wisdom, assume that Baldwin followed the politically prudent but wrong course.

Yet he did make a contribution to our ultimate survival. For, as I once said on another occasion, 'The superb national unity with which Great Britain went to war in 1939 owed not a little to the man who had nurtured it in the deep and simple pride of his people.'

2. NEVILLE CHAMBERLAIN

It falls to the lot of few men to be praised to the skies (as Neville Chamberlain was at the time of Munich in 1938) and, within eighteen months, to be denounced and supplanted.

Was he, at Munich, so deceived that he really thought that he had secured 'Peace with honour', and that peace would endure, or was he buying time?

I offer no dogmatic answer to these questions; but I think it proper to recall some of the facts. I was, as Attorney-General of Australia, in England in 1938, and learned something of the state of the national defences. The anti-aircraft defences were quite nominal; the air force itself, though high quality was beginning to emerge in the fighter force, was numerically vastly inferior to the Luftwaffe. Churchill, with Lindemann's statistics before him, was almost a lone voice. He was 'suspect'; he 'spoke too much of war'; his 'judgement had always been poor'.

In recalling these matters, one must pay some attention to public opinion, which has great influence in a democracy. Most political leaders respect it, as indeed they must. Perhaps the average political leader bows to it as if it had some enduring validity. A leader of long experience comes to know that, in the short run, when the tides of emotion are in flood, the people can easily be wrong, and not infrequently are; but that in the long run, with time to be informed and reflect, they are, in true democracies, almost always right.

Chamberlain became Prime Minister in succession to Baldwin. He inherited from Baldwin a people proud of their inheritance, and with a consciousness of unity. But those same people were still tired of war, and bemused by the idea that the League of Nations, the Covenant of the League, and the Kellogg Pact afforded in themselves some guarantee of security; 'collective security'.

It is easy, in the light of later and terrible events, to condemn both Baldwin and Chamberlain for not having gone out to arrest and convert public opinion. But public opinion, reflected in Parliament, has its own force. Baldwin and Chamberlain were essentially men of peace. Baldwin, let it be conceded, was a typical English countryman, with no real knowledge or understanding of Europe, but with a deep and almost poetic faith in his own country. He might have exemplified the old proverb that 'for the English, the negroes begin at Calais'. Chamberlain was essentially a man of affairs. Of slim build and features, he looked as one would expect a chartered accountant to look; his hair dark with grey at the temples; a study in black and white. He constantly wore the orthodox garments of the London business and official classes, the black Homburg hat, the short black coat and striped trousers, the rolled black umbrella.

After his fall from office, some people (most of whom had applauded him at the time) affected to make fun of him taking his umbrella with him to Munich. They should have known that there were many thousands of men in London at that time, and there still are, who would never move without that habitual part of their street wear, the rolled umbrella! With unfeigned joy, I once saw two learned clerks in Whitehall walking through a sharp shower of rain, the umbrellas still furled!

So far, one may appear to remember Chamberlain as in essence conventional. But, like some other noted Englishmen I have known, he was something of a paradox. One year he had, as I discovered when we were both at Swinton, in the West Riding of Yorkshire, taken over for Whitsun the home of Philip Cunliffe-Lister, as he then was.

It is a considerable estate, but in the course of an afternoon Chamberlain could identify every tree or shrub or plant with botanical accuracy. The songs of birds were familiar in his ears. Here was the intelligent and informed countryman who had left the city behind him!

When he was Chancellor of the Exchequer, I heard him deliver two budget speeches, each of them a model of lucidity and clear economic thinking. It was a pleasure to discuss a practical problem with him, for he would always make a decision. I will give an example. I was in London as Attorney-General when I was requested to see the then Chancellor of the Exchequer about a matter affecting the important Australian sugar industry. I studied the documents which accompanied the request, sought an appointment with Chamberlain at the Treasury, and in due course saw him. He had an official with him to record the discussion.

I put the case as I understood it. I had, of course, no first-hand knowledge of the facts presented to me, but on those facts I thought we had a strong case for the arrangement we were seeking. When I had finished, Chamberlain said, 'If your facts can be supported, you seem to me to be on strong ground. But my people may not agree about the facts, in which case a different issue would arise. Do you mind us critically examining your material?' Of course I said that I was more than willing, and the interview ended.

Two days later I was asked to see him again, and did so. He said, 'Your statement of the facts is confirmed, and therefore the arrangement you sought will be accepted.' 'Thank you,' said I. 'Give my kind regards to your wife,' said he. 'Thank you very much,' said I. The whole interview was over.

But he knew little or nothing of the European mind. It was a tragic blunder on his part when he went over the head of the superbly well-informed Anthony Eden, to engage in negotiations himself with Mussolini, and so find himself receiving Eden's resignation.

Chamberlain's 'appeasement' at Munich was an appeasement from military weakness. He believed that Britain was not capable of a major war, and, in short, that the best must be made of a bad job. I have never been able to convince myself, though I know that better men have disagreed, that if Chamberlain had thrown down the gage at Munich, we would have won the ensuing war.

The real test is—what happened to British armament between Munich and September 1939? Winston Churchill made no secret of his belief that Hitler gained more strength from that fateful year than we did; that his taking over of Czechoslovakia gave him enormous resources of a military kind. On the other hand, there can be little doubt that British equipment in fighter aircraft—the development and production of the Hurricane and the Spitfire—grew rapidly under the energetic and imaginative administration of Philip Swinton.

I have not the slightest qualification to decide the issue. If Chamberlain believed not that he had secured a lasting accommodation with Hitler but that he had time to prepare, and if he acted vigorously in the gained period, then the later judgement that he was gulled and quiescent must be revised. Meanwhile, it must be recognized that when war came, and France fell, the House of Commons had no doubts, and rejected Chamberlain, and turned to Churchill. This historic event is itself evidence against Chamberlain, who was in any event never designed by nature to be a war leader. But, after all, Churchills come only once or twice in a century. When they come, they are supreme, but they do not make more ordinary mortals contemptible.

3. CLEMENT RICHARD ATTLEE (now Earl Attlee) is beyond question one of the great Englishmen of our time. By personal background, he might have been expected to be a Conservative. But by conviction and early experience he was a Socialist of a practical and humane kind. He was the victim of no theories; a social reformer rather than a doctrinaire. If I write of him in the past, it is simply because he has largely withdrawn from politics, and has become an elder, and much respected, Statesman.

I am not concerned to sketch his biography; that is a task that will be better performed by others. All I want to do is to set down some personal memories of a man whom I got to know fairly well in 1941, when he was Churchill's principal lieutenant in the War Cabinet, and with whom I had many contacts in the post-war years, particularly when he became Prime Minister himself.

His personality and methods were in remarkable contrast to those of Churchill, though it must be remembered that when Neville Chamberlain fell, in 1940, it was Attlee, speaking for the Labour opposition, who said that his party would serve under Churchill in a War Government, and under nobody else. It was a fruitful partnership, of crucial historic importance. Attlee, as he has frequently said, and rightly, regarded Winston as a great war leader. He brought with him, into the Government, some remarkable men; the shrewd and experienced 'cockney' administrator Herbert Morrison, the powerful and wise Ernest Bevin, the greatest trade union leader of his time. One of the foundations of Britain's survival and success was a remarkable degree of unity at home, the existence of a clear national spirit. For this, these three men must be given a full share of credit. If any of them had played party politics, the nation's fate might have been different. They helped materially to enable Winston Churchill to concentrate his genius on the conduct of the war, and to employ his unmatched fire and eloquence on the expression of a united and resolute national spirit. Winston was the British bulldog personified. He was a showman, addicted to curious clothes and antiquated hats and 'property' cigars, but he had great goods to sell. His personality, as I have said elsewhere, had an impact compared to which a blow from a steam-roller was no more than a gentle caress. Attlee was smaller, orthodox in appearance, and unaddicted to rhetoric. Churchill, the Conservative, always looked and sounded like a crusader. Attlee, the Socialist, always looked and sounded like a company director.

I can best illustrate what I am trying to say by three personal reminiscences.

In March, April, and May of 1941, the War Cabinet met, normally, on Monday afternoons. For that period, I was, by courtesy, a member of it. The rest of us would meet in the ante-room at No. 10, and then go into our allotted places in the Cabinet Room. After a short interval, Winston would make an entrance, 'siren suit' and cigar complete. We would rise to greet him. He would then make a short speech about the state of the war, grim and yet strangely moving, and the business would begin. We were all experienced politicians, with relatively dry and sceptical minds, but we were moved by a deep sense of history.

Years afterwards, when Attlee was Prime Minister, I attended a Cabinet meeting, with Attlee presiding. We all sat down together. The Prime Minister moved at once into the business. He had several

Ministers of a highly individualistic order; Stafford Cripps, Ernest Bevin, Herbert Morrison, Aneurin Bevan, Hugh Dalton. Here, indeed, was a difficult orchestra to conduct. All Ministers were treated as having read the Cabinet papers. Nobody was encouraged to speak too long. Then would come the still small voice from the chair—'I think the general view would be "A".' And 'A' it was.

When Winston came back into office, he convened a Prime Ministers' Conference in London. I took two of my senior Cabinet colleagues with me to the opening session. As it happened, neither of them had ever seen or heard Churchill. He made his famous entrance, as of old, a cigar in mouth. With a schoolboy grin, he said, 'There is a rule against smoking in this room. Do I take it that you accept this?' He looked at me, whom he knew to be an inveterate cigar smoker, and I blandly nodded. 'Good,' he said, 'and now that we have done proper obeisance to the rule, Anthony, pass the cigars!'

He then looked around the table, and made a perfectly Churchillian speech. Looking at each of us in turn, he recalled the past, he glowed with his memories, he made each of us feel that we were in that historic room on an historic occasion. My colleagues were delighted. I said to them later that they had witnessed a little bit of vintage Churchill. They went off with an enduring memory.

How different it was with Clem Attlee, at another Prime Ministers' Conference. 'Well, gentlemen,' (looking out over his steel-rimmed spectacles) 'I am glad to see you. I hope you all have suitable accommodation. I will ask the Foreign Secretary to speak first.'

'Clem' Attlee has a prominent place in Constitutional history. He was British Prime Minister from 1945 to 1951.

He had been an active member of the Simon Committee on India in 1927-8, and had developed strong views about the inevitability of independence. As Prime Minister, he set out to deal with the problem. He sent out a Cabinet Mission, consisting of Cripps, Pethick-Lawrence, and A. V. Alexander, in 1946. It came back without a solution, though, as Attlee himself says in his characteristic book *As It Happened* (Heinemann), it accomplished much in the creation of good relations.

He was very conscious of the most difficult aspect of the problem. Should there be a partition into two States—Hindu and Moslem— leaving a perceptible minority in each State? If this were done, could a

Moslem Pakistan divided into two parts, East and West, separated by many hundreds of miles, survive? He met this problem by sending out Mountbatten as Viceroy in the place of Wavell. His first task was to find out whether a single government for the whole of the sub-continent was acceptable. It was not. So partition was decided upon.

Attlee introduced the India Independence Bill in July 1947, and by 15 August India and Pakistan became members of the (at that time) British Commonwealth of Nations.

India then chose to become a Republic, and, during the period of Attlee's Prime Ministership, was authorized to remain in what then became 'The Commonwealth'. I will have something to say about this in a subsequent chapter.

My immediate purpose has been to show something of the sweep of Attlee's mind, and the mark which it made.

CHAPTER SIX

SIX AUSTRALIAN PRIME MINISTERS

WHEN I WRITE of each of six Australian Prime Ministers, I am not undertaking to do more than record the man, as I knew him and in some cases worked with him. I shall not attempt to deal elaborately with the details of the problems or controversies in which he was involved.

1. WILLIAM MORRIS HUGHES

The first in point of time is William Morris Hughes, the young Cockney of Welsh blood who came to Australia, followed a variety of occupations, teacher, locksmith, umbrella repairer, stage supernumerary, waterside worker, until he became the founder and leader of the Waterside Workers' Union, went into State Parliament and then Commonwealth, and became in turn Labour Minister and Labour Prime Minister. His *Case for Labour,* now being republished, remains a masterpiece of political polemics. Somewhere along the line he attended lectures and was admitted to legal practice in New South Wales. But I am bound to say that in my later direct experience of him, he struck me as being singularly unaffected by any known legal consideration.

His story has been written, and is known in Australia. During the First World War, in which he showed notable leadership, he fell out with the Labour Party over the issue of conscription, crossed the floor of the House, formed a coalition with his traditional opponents, and ruled as Prime Minister and leader of the newly formed 'Nationalist' party until he was relieved of office early in 1923 and was succeeded by S. M. Bruce.

All I knew about him in this period was as a Melbourne University student who wrote verses about him, of a highly laudatory character.

I first met him in October 1934, when I had gone to Canberra as Latham's successor in Kooyong and as Commonwealth Attorney-General. From the time, in 1929, when he had been the most fiery of those members who brought about the defeat of the Bruce Government, with the consequent crushing defeat of that Government at a general election, Hughes had been a private member, rich in anecdotes but with a markedly diminished public influence. When the Scullin Labour Government, which was swept into office by the Nationalist débâcle of 1929, was drastically defeated after two years of difficult Depression life, J. A. Lyons had become Prime Minister. For three years, Hughes remained in the shadows. Then as, after the 1934 General Election I found myself Attorney-General, Lyons, to my surprise, 'recalled' Hughes, like Dr Manette, 'to life', and made him a Minister. I still think this was a mistake, for Hughes gave us all some anxieties thereafter. But it was a mistake made by a man of warm humanity, eager to do some honour to one who had done the nation great service in his time. As I will point out later, he was a marvellous parliamentarian, tolerant and understanding, whose judgement was entitled to respect.

Now, writing for myself with the panorama of Australian politics unrolling behind me, I cannot profess to paint a balanced portrait of this unique little man 'Billy' Hughes. His great days were behind him when I first knew him personally. And they were undoubtedly great days. He had fire, magnetism, an intense Australianism, all backed by a somewhat florid Welsh eloquence. It was not for nothing that in those days and years he was frequently compared with David Lloyd George. My late uncle, Sydney Sampson, Member for Wimmera, used to speak to me about him, his majestic command at Party meetings, and the near impossibility of effectively answering him. His successful battle at the Versailles Conference for Australian control of Papua (New Guinea) won him great and proper acclaim.

But by the end of 1934, in the Lyons Government, he had become primarily reminiscent.

> Old men forget; yet all shall be forgot,
> But he'll remember with advantages
> What feats he did that day . . .

He had a malicious but devastating wit. In my time, his contributions to discussion in Cabinet were almost invariably destructive. He was very deaf, and in either the Cabinet Room or in Party meetings or in the House he was compassed about by a great cloud of hearing devices.

In those days there was no official Cabinet Secretary. If a Minister brought up a Submission, the decision of the Cabinet was endorsed by the Prime Minister on the document, and appropriate action in the Department concerned was hoped for. I remember Hughes presenting a Submission one day. It was discussed, and was disapproved by all the rest of us. Half-way through, Hughes, seeing how it was going, disconnected his hearing aid. At the finish, he passed his submission to the Prime Minister with the bland observation, 'Well, I take it my proposal is approved!' But it wasn't!

In the Lyons Government, from 1934, Hughes became Minister for Health and Repatriation. For a while I enjoyed his grace and favour. It was during this early period that Australia was visited by the distinguished Canadian, Arthur Meighen, who had been Canadian Prime Minister for part of the period of Hughes's Prime Ministership of Australia. Meighen, who was to be the Government guest at Canberra, arrived in Sydney. Lyons, with characteristic thoughtfulness, invited Hughes to meet Meighen in Sydney. The little man accepted the invitation and was duly photographed at the Hotel Australia, greeting his old contemporary. At Canberra, there was to be a Cabinet Luncheon for the guest. 'Billy' called for me and took my arm as we walked across to the dining-room. On the way, I ventured to make some observation to the effect that Meighen must be a very considerable man. Hughes at once dissented violently. 'You're quite wrong. He's no good. I can't stand him.' I do not attempt to reproduce his colourful language. Taken aback by this, I decided that something must be done to improve the atmosphere. Finding myself sitting next to Meighen, I told him that a reference to Hughes would be well received.

When Meighen rose to make as eloquent a speech as I ever heard at such a gathering, he came to a point at which he said, 'My pleasure at your reception is increased by the fact that here I see the famous William Morris Hughes, a man whose name and fame are known wherever the English language is spoken!' I glanced at Hughes and found him nodding his approval. Clearly, all was not lost. As Hughes and I walked back together, I looked down at him and said, 'Well, whatever you may say, I was tremendously impressed!' The reply came pat. 'Brother, you say most peculiar things. "Whatever you may say." Well, I'll tell you. That man is a great judge of values. He's a great man, and I'm having dinner with him tonight!'

In November 1935, Lyons asked for Hughes's resignation, for a reason that has more than a little contemporary interest. Italy was invading Abyssinia, without justification. Mussolini was beginning those overseas exercises which he clearly thought would give him and his country glory but which, as we now see, both in relation to Abyssinia and Albania, were the beginning of the end. The League of Nations called upon its member nations to impose economic sanctions. Australia did so, the Minister appointed by the Cabinet to prepare and introduce the legislation being myself, as Attorney-General.

We were having quite a battle in Parliament, though a successful one, when Hughes, choosing his timing strangely, published a book the theme song of which was that 'Sanctions mean War'. Lyons took great exception to this, regarding it as an attack on Government policy, and called for and obtained his resignation on 6 November 1935. By 26 February 1936, sanctions not having proved very effective, Hughes was back in the Government. For some reason or other (or for no reason), Hughes thought that I had persuaded Lyons to force him out. After his return, Lyons, hearing of his belief, told him that I had not sought to influence the event at all. This was generously spoken, and true in fact. The immediate result was that one afternoon, at tea, Hughes came to the table where I was sitting and, to my surprise (for he had not spoken to me for over three months), sat down opposite and addressed me. The dialogue, if I may so describe it, should be recounted, though his inimitable intonation cannot be reproduced in print. It was pure vintage Hughes.

H. 'Are you a fisherman? I don't mean a poor amateur, but a professor of the piscatorial art?'

M. 'No, I fear not.'

H. 'Then I'll tell you a story. Years ago I was out fishing on Pitt Water with some friends. We were using prawns for bait. We lowered our lines into the sea. Nothing happened. The waves rolled on, and we grew weary of failure. Then I had a bright idea. I asked my host for the whisky, poured some into a mug, drew up my line, and dipped the unsuccessful prawn into the whisky. Well, brother, *the effect of the alcoholic absorption on the crustacean was dynamic.* I lowered the line. At once there came a strong tug on the line. I hauled it in, and there, at the end of the line, was the prawn, *grasping an enormous fish firmly by the back of the neck!*'

In April 1939, Mr Lyons died. After a brief period of nineteen days when Earle Page, as Deputy Prime Minister to Lyons, was sworn in as Prime Minister, I was elected by my party and (somewhat to Page's annoyance) became Prime Minister on 26 April. Hughes was Attorney-General and Minister for Industry until October 1940, and thereafter, until my resignation on 29 August 1941, added the portfolio of Minister for the Navy. The Second World War began on 3 September 1939, and was clearly threatening for months before then. Now, I would have expected that Hughes, as the legendary war-horse of the First War, would have been the constant advocate of action. But his fires had burned low. I cannot recall one major defence decision to which he was not opposed.

The first thing I wanted to do by way of war preparation was to re-introduce compulsory military training, which had been abandoned nine years before. Opinions in Cabinet were divided. I had a great deal of support, but not enough, having regard to the nature and con-tentiousness of the proposal. After a few weeks I secured virtual unanimity, with Hughes dissenting. He told me with heat and emphasis that my proposal would 'split the nation from stem to stern'. He was still thinking of the failure of his Conscription Referendum during the First War. Anyhow, our decision was promptly announced and, no doubt to Hughes's surprise, was well received by press and people, and only very faintly challenged by our opponents. By the end of the day I was fascinated to learn that Hughes was being given credit for the decision!

When the war broke out, we had a somewhat similar experience. We decided to recruit for a Second A.I.F., and the recruits poured in. Again the dissenter was Hughes. The man who had twice, as Prime Minister, asked the people to vote for conscription for overseas service had now developed a belief that no Australian military force should leave the country; they were all needed at home. (This was, of course, two years before Japan's entry into the war.) For similar reasons he was against dispatching the Second A.I.F. to the Middle East. And finally, when the Chief of the Naval Staff wanted to send the now famous 'scrap iron' flotilla from Sydney to Singapore—the first phase of its famous career—he had to by-pass his Ministers and come to me for approval.

As I look back on these events, I am still surprised at his attitude. I think the truth is that he had with advancing years developed an exaggerated fear of public opinion and a much reduced capacity for judging it.

He had a great talent for phrase-making. We were still in Opposition after the General Election of August 1943, in which Philip McBride (now Sir Philip), then a Senator, was defeated, though he still remained a Senator under the Constitutional rules until 30 June 1944.

We were having an Opposition Party Meeting, in the course of which McBride, who held strong views to which he adhered almost (we sometimes thought) to the point of obstinacy, offered some pungent remarks with which Hughes disagreed. He expressed his disagreement in characteristic manner—'Ah! My friend McBride speaks! He is shortly to leave us! It follows that he speaks *with a falling inflection!*' But at that time, hopelessly out-numbered in the House, we needed all our resources to be effectively deployed in debate. We might have expected some material contribution from a man of Hughes's vast experience and verbal talents.

I was a private member from 1941 to 1943, having resigned from the leadership of my party in October 1941. Hughes succeeded me as leader; quite nominally, as it turned out, for he did not convene party meetings, and organized no debates. After the electoral disaster of 1943, I was invited by the party to resume the leadership. I accepted the invitation under the circumstances I describe in a later chapter on the 'Revival of Liberalism'.

I will, I think, show how imperative it was that if we were to fight our way back into political power we must have a sense of common purpose, a genuine zeal, and team-work with each doing his best.

All the help we could get from Hughes in our party discussions was the oft-repeated and cynical remark, 'Well, you may decide to do what is proposed to you; all I can say is that whichever way you decide you will before long wish you had done the opposite!' If we had acted on this advice, we would have done nothing and remained permanently in Opposition.

2. STANLEY MELBOURNE BRUCE

I have hesitated to write about this Prime Minister. He is, I am happy to say, 'alive and kicking', and there could be nothing more embarrassing than to be praising or criticizing a living contemporary.

Therefore what I write about Lord Bruce (as he now is) is not to be regarded as complete, or as a sort of premature obituary.

But I have decided to say something about him, and for a very good reason. Of all the Australian Prime Ministers of my time Bruce has been the most underestimated; and I want to make a small contribution to the scales, to make the balance right.

Stanley Melbourne Bruce was born the son of a partner in the great Flinders Lane firm of Paterson Laing and Bruce. He was prominent at the Melbourne Grammar School, went to Cambridge, was a notable oarsman in the Cambridge boat, and was called to the Bar at Lincoln's Inn. The first great war came along. He served in it with distinction, was wounded, and returned to Australia in 1918 with a feeling in him that he would like to do some further public service.

Now it turned out that, just at that time, Sir William Irvine who was the Federal Member for Flinders, in the State of Victoria, who had been Premier of Victoria, and then Attorney-General of Australia, was appointed Chief Justice of Victoria, and Flinders stood vacant as a good non-Labour seat.

Among the contestants for pre-selection in the party interests were Sir Edward Mitchell K.C., a leader of the bar, prolix, ponderous, without humour but with much prestige; the favoured candidate; and the young Captain Bruce, handsome, dark-haired, rich (as he perhaps then was), with the aura of notable and honoured war service about him, but, as he would have been the first to admit, little knowledge of the local political scene. Bruce was chosen, won the seat, and within three years was a Minister; in fact, Treasurer!

He had been appointed Australian Delegate to the League of Nations, returned to Australia, broke the then existing records by making a full and fascinating report in Parliament, and became a man marked for promotion.

I may say at once, at the risk of offending him (though I know him to be a very realistic person) that Bruce had no aspirations to what is called oratory. His vocabulary was, I thought, somewhat limited. I got the impression that he was not a wide reader. His unspoken motto was, in Mark Anthony's words:

> I am no orator, as Brutus is;
> But, as you know me all, a plain blunt man

But as Mark Antony was effective, so was Bruce. His star was rising.

At the General Election of 1922, Hughes's star, as Prime Minister, was setting. His flamboyant characteristics had begun to pall. True, his government won the election with some losses; but a new party, the Country Party, had arisen, led by Earle Page, a noted surgeon and a skilled political operator (as he was to prove). The Hughes Government could not survive without Page and his Country Party. They made it clear to Hughes that they would not support him, but that they would support young Bruce. And so the Bruce-Page Government began, and ruled for the better part of seven years.

That Government did great and enduring things for Australia, both in development and finance. But by 1929 it was to encounter the wintry blast of the great World Depression, with the overseas loan market closing up, and the prices of Australia's primary exports plummeting downwards.

It was then that Bruce made a political tactical error. He had been greatly impressed by the confusion in Australia's industrial laws, with the Federal Court and State industrial tribunals overlapping, and the great Trade Unions taking advantage of both. Advised by John Latham, his Attorney-General and a most experienced and logical lawyer, Bruce reached the conclusion that if one tribunal could be played off against another, great wage inflation could occur, and that this would be financially disastrous.

He convened a Premiers' Conference, which I attended as a junior Minister in the McPherson Government in the State of Victoria, and put the choice. Either the States could, under the Commonwealth Constitution, refer full industrial power to the Commonwealth, or the Commonwealth itself could vacate the field. These proposals reflected all of Latham's logical exactitude, but they had no relation to some very important facts of industrial life.

The States rejected the proposal for reference of State Powers, whereupon the Bruce Government brought in legislation to repeal, in effect, the Commonwealth Conciliation and Arbitration Laws.

This was, I repeat, a tactical error, for three reasons. The first was that pure logic has no popular appeal. The trade unions which had secured awards from the Commonwealth Arbitration Court saw that they were going to lose them. Certainly, they could have recourse to the State tribunals, but this was to convert a reality into a contingency. The second was that, for some reason I have never understood, the Commonwealth Bill was brought down, *as an urgent measure*, just before the Report of a Commonwealth-appointed Committee on Constitutional Reform was due to be received and tabled. The Government's opponents in the Federal Parliament properly made a great feature of this. The third reason was very human. Hughes, who had been a great pioneer in Union affairs, who had been rejected summarily and had been replaced by Bruce, was not a man to forget his grievances. He had bided his time and his time had now come. All he needed was a handful of supporters, and the Bruce-Page Government would be out. He got his supporters, and the Government fell. Parliament was dissolved, and the Government was heavily defeated at the ensuing election. Bruce lost his own 'blue ribbon' seat of Flinders, and appeared to be out of public life.

Pausing there, I would say that the great services Bruce's government had rendered to Australian development and the proper organizing of her finances faded from sight in the clamour of 1929. With the inevitable exaggerations which occur in a hotly contested election, Bruce had been represented as 'opposed to a fair deal for the worker', 'an English toff who was not a true Australian'. He was even ridiculed for wearing spats, as I myself have been ridiculed by the more sartorially modern for wearing double-breasted coats!

When the Scullin Government fell, Bruce, though abroad at the time, came back as Member for Flinders with a record majority. He was very amusing about this. 'I have learned that to be well beaten you must be present at the campaign. To win handsomely you must stay away!'

Later on, Bruce accepted from Lyons the post of High Commissioner for Australia in London. Here, of course, he did not lack his critics among Australians visiting London. This, I must add, is a not uncommon experience at Australia House, where officials become accustomed to urgent and sometimes unmannerly demands, and where a High Commissioner is sometimes thought by visiting Australians to be a man with largely social responsibilities.

Some visitors who reached his office professed to find him cold and remote. True, he was no back-slapper; but he was an unsurpassed High Commissioner, who gave great prestige to Australia, who was profoundly respected both in The City and Whitehall, who had the easiest of access to Ministers from the Prime Minister down, and whose skill in close negotiation I have never seen excelled, or, for that matter, equalled. He was, if he will permit a smaller successor to say so, an even greater Australian in London than he was in Australia itself.

In London, he had one country to serve, his own. He never permitted himself to forget it. In terms of finance and trade, he did great things for us. He was, of all the notable men I have been associated with, the most down-to-earth and practical, and the least concerned with either theory or rhetoric.

3. JAMES HENRY SCULLIN

In my political life-time there were three Labour Prime Ministers of Australia. I shall write something about each of them.

The three, James Henry Scullin (1929–32), John Curtin (1941–5) and Joseph Benedict Chifley (1945–9) were, of course, all different. Yet, if taken as a group, they typified the nature and characteristics of the Australian Labour Movement in the most remarkable fashion. Not one of them was what is now called an 'intellectual', or even the product of a University; Labour in Australia has tended to distrust such people, preferring to base itself on the Trade Union movement, which has provided a powerful foundation for party membership and electoral finance.

It is, indeed, one of the many interesting and important differences between Australia and the United States that in the latter the great unions are not in their nature aligned with some political party. There is, in the United States, no Labour Party except in the most fleeting and nominal sense. The two great parties, Republican and Democratic, each contains and expresses a bewildering variety of views. In the case of the Republicans, these range from the extreme conservatism of the Goldwaterites to the more realistic adaptation of private enterprise to broad social responsibilities and modern conditions which I have encountered in New York—what I might call the 'Rockefeller' view, while the Democratic Party includes an even more bewildering variety, from the 'New Dealers', the radical social reformers and the liberally-minded thinkers to the almost reactionary 'Dixiecrats' of the Deep South. Despite its reverses at the mid-term elections of November 1966, it is a powerful party, but its internal bond of union sometimes consists less of a community of ideas than of hostility to a common enemy.

In the result, a Presidential Election tends to be a conflict, not between pre-determined or doctrinal bodies of ideas, but between leaders who propound ideas and policies, conduct very lengthy personal campaigns, and in the result are voted for or against as people. After some months of residence in the United States a year ago, I still found American politics quite anthropomorphic. Under these circumstances, the great Trade Union organizations have found it advantageous to swing their support to the Presidential candidate whose personality and policies are most nearly acceptable to them at the time.

I have set down these observations in order to point out, particularly to American readers, the special and significant fact that in Australia there is a permanent association between the Trade Union movement and the Political Labour Party. This is not to say that in Australia all members of Unions automatically support Labour candidates. Many hundreds of thousands of them have no doubt supported Conservative candidates; but in general, union support is a vital element in Labour politics.

For the most part, Labour Members of Parliament in Australia come up *via* union office into party-organization office and then into political selection. They have a tough training, which tends to make them ready debaters. When they achieve prominence and personal influence, they do not readily forget their origins; they keep up their contacts with their Unions, which they rightly regard as the continuing bases of their political existence.

James Henry Scullin achieved the leadership of the Australian Labour Party by a combination of characteristics developed by this kind of experience. He was a man of less than the average size and physique. In my time he had a silver crest of hair, fluency and occasionally elegance of speech, and a marked devotion to duty. He had competed for oratory prizes at the famous 'South Street' Ballarat competitions. This gave him a taste for the rounded phrases, now somewhat out-of-date. But he was an effective public speaker, particularly to an audience of enthusiastic believers.

He worked hard in Parliament. He achieved, for example, a considerable grasp of such a complex and difficult matter as Taxation.

After he became Prime Minister in 1929, there were not lacking people who, for their own reasons, were willing to make whispered imputations against him—this is the common lot of political leaders—but I must insist that, beyond question, his integrity was absolute and his personal standards high.

As an eloquent Labour Prime Minister in normal times (if there are such), he could have enjoyed success. Economic tranquillity would have helped his performance. His record could have looked better, and he would have lived longer. But his luck was out. The cup of success, put into his naturally excited hands in 1929, was dashed away by the great blasts of the Depression. Overseas borrowing, which had done so much for national economic growth during the Bruce régime, became quickly impossible. Unemployment rose sharply. The state of the Budget forebade the increase of social benefits. The anticipated Socialist Sun came under eclipse. This was a bitter prospect for a man who had, after thirteen years of opposition, led his party to success at the polls. He found himself compelled by circumstance and public opinion into a severe policy—the 'Premier's Plan'—of retrenchment, a retrenchment which involved the reduction of such established payments as the Old Age Pension. This really broke Scullin's heart. The reason is not far to seek. Scullin was no revolutionary. His was the Socialism of social betterment, of a better deal for the 'under-dog'. To him, and indeed to many of his political successors, the answer to most problems was to be found in higher pay, shorter working hours, and larger social benefits. Frankly, I do not think that he ever wasted much of his nervous energy on the 'socialist objective' of the then Labour platform—'nationalization of the means of production distribution and exchange'. This is not to say that he did not believe in it. He did. But his unspoken political policy was, in Cardinal Newman's famous lines—'I do not ask to see the distant scene, one step enough for me'. Viewed as a Labour man, he had an orthodox mind. With no practical experience of public administration (he had never held political office), he found himself confronted by a state of emergency in which the old doctrines were to be questioned and the old landmarks, if not actually removed, obscured by the dust of the economic whirlwind. His mind lacked both the experience and the flexibility needed to deal with Depression problems. It is not without significance that in 1930, when he attended what was then called an Imperial Conference in London, he regarded as his great mission the securing of a Prime Ministerial decision that the appointment of a Governor-General was to be on the nomination of the government of the Commonwealth nation concerned. It followed from this that the new Governor-General of Australia must be his sole nominee, Sir Isaac Isaacs. In each of these objectives he succeeded. But neither of them had any relevance to the economic storms which blew in Australia. Back home, he found himself unable to swim strongly in troubled waters. His Treasurer, the celebrated E. G. Theodore, formerly Premier of Queensland, rejected the idea, then predominant, of a balanced Budget as a vital element in recovery, and propounded proposals for a fiduciary note issue to take up any Budget deficit. This created great differences in the Government itself. It led to the crossing of the floor of the House by Joseph Lyons and several others. The party itself began to break up in 1931. A section was led by J. A. Beasley, and made life difficult for Scullin. In the result, the Government was defeated on a procedural motion, and an election ensued, in which the Labour defeat was as dramatic as had been its victory two years before. Lyons became the Prime Minister as leader of a new coalition party, and Scullin became Leader of the Opposition.

Looking back on it all, it would be easy to say that there was a strong economic case for deficit-budgeting in a period of depression; we have all come to accept this. But the truth is that there was, in those two years, a crisis of confidence in Australia. The Government was widely suspected of not facing up to the realities of the situation. The business world was uneasy; it shortened sail; capital investment for future development faded away; and so unemployment grew apace.

Thus it was that a term of Labour office which had begun with such enthusiastic promise ended with defeat and, in a sense, humiliation.

Scullin never recovered either his spirit or his health. As I have said, he became Leader of the Opposition. A few years later, when I had myself gone to Canberra, he resigned this office, and John Curtin was chosen to succeed him. Walking away from the House one day, I ventured to ask him why he had resigned. His answer was most illuminating. 'Well, I have come to believe that a man who has been Prime Minister suffers a handicap as Leader of the Opposition. He is expected to press the Government in every possible way; to insist upon statements on sensitive international matters; to call loudly for the tabling of international communications. But I know how delicate such matters can be, and how obliged a government may be to be, for some time at least, silent. Another leader would feel more free.'

I tell this story, not as one who later followed his advice (for under the circumstances of years later, I did not), but to illustrate Scullin's sensitivity and sensibility of mind, and the high standards by which he guided his own life.

It may be said, I hope without offence, that Scullin failed and fell because he was neither temperamentally nor intellectually equipped to deal with the fundamentally complex problems of a novel world crisis. But he failed with honour, and preserved his self-respect. I am glad that I knew him, and shall always remember him with admiration and affection.

4. JOSEPH ALOYSIUS LYONS

Joseph Aloysius Lyons was Prime Minister from 1932 to 1939. He had a remarkable career, beginning as a school-teacher in Tasmania, the smallest of the Australian States, going into the Tasmanian Parliament as a Labour member, and then becoming Premier of Tasmania. In the landslide election of 1929 he went into the Federal Parliament and became a Minister in the Scullin Government.

In a Socialist setting, he was never quite at home. He was more of a reformist than a dedicated doctrinaire. He was, above all things, a humanist. He could never achieve the habit of regarding people as statistical units. He had a warm feeling for them as individuals with whose problems he had an unaffected sympathy. Above all, he had impeccable honesty, and had literally no interest in clever moves or soulless political manœuvre.

The tragedy of the great Depression moved him profoundly. He quickly came to understand that the failure of investment and the slackness in business and employment were the products of a crisis of confidence; and that the prime duty of Government was to restore confidence by sound administration and financial stability.

He is vivid in my mind's eye as I recall and write about him. His hair and his face reminded the cartoonists, not unreasonably, of that agreeable Australian the Koala Bear. It is not to be wondered at that before long people developed a great affection for him. He had, of course, a remarkable and talented and beautiful wife; and that, as I have reason to know in my own case, is no small matter. But he was no secondary person. He was shrewd, and spoke easily with a rare combination of dignity and simplicity. As I was to learn when, in October 1934, I became one of his Ministers, he was a really brilliant Parliamentarian, with a real command in the House; a command which owed nothing to rhetoric or repartee, but was the product of a well-recognized sincerity and genial courtesy.

But before I pursue this, I must go back to the events of 1930 and 1931, in which years I first got to know him. The Scullin Government, through E. G. Theodore, propounded, as I have said, a scheme for a fiduciary note issue to supplement the public purchasing power, which the depression had considerably reduced. If this proposal had formed part of a constructive economic policy, it would have had much to commend it. But, taken by itself, it over-simplified the problem. It seemed to offer the easy way out at a time when a national effort was needed to restore the confidence of investor and entrepreneur alike. It was, as Lyons and many of us considered, an inflationary measure which would impair the restoration of the loan market and therefore inhibit a much-needed revival of investment.

When Scullin went to England in 1930, Lyons, who was Postmaster-General, became Acting Treasurer. He was a close believer in 'balancing the Budget', opposed inflationary proposals, and became increasingly the voice of a minority in his party.

Before long, it became clear that some accommodation between the 'right wing' Labour man, for whom Lyons spoke, and the Opposition, led by Latham, would need to be found. Lyons's resistance to inflation or repudiation of debts had made him prominent; his personality was engaging; at a time of manœuvre and counter-manœuvre his clear integrity had a great appeal.

There was, however, considerable disarray among the organizations which had come into existence. The Government was confused and divided. It became clear to a group of men in Melbourne, of whom I was one (being at that time an Opposition member of the Victorian Parliament), that we needed a combined organization and a leader with popular appeal.

Latham, who had led the Opposition with marked ability, had a coldly logical public personality. Great lawyer and patriot though he was, he lacked something of warmth and magnetism. Lyons, his intellectual inferior, could supply both. He had a growing public, and a great opportunity. For, if the normal party lines were preserved, the Labour Government would sail on, almost rudderless, and Australia would suffer. It was a period of crisis. As a practising politician, I knew that at the General Election which would come normally at the end of 1932 (then a long way in the future), Latham might well win and become Prime Minister. But could the country wait?

It seemed clear to many of us that Lyons was the man who could, in an early election, win. We did a great deal of work on policy and organization, including the creation of a new Party.

On 31 March 1931, Lyons, who had resigned from the Cabinet on 29 January, voted against the Scullin Government, and thus expelled himself from his party. On 17 April, Latham, behaving with great character and generosity, gave up the leadership of the Opposition; a post to which Lyons was elected, as leader of the new United Australia Party. Several of Lyons's fellow members followed him across the floor of the House.

The Scullin Government, thus weakened, found itself, in 1931, in grave trouble with a vocal and energetic group of its supporters, led by J. A. Beasley. It was beaten on a procedural matter, saw that it had lost control of the House, and resigned. The political atmosphere had been clouded for Labour by the astonishing policies and actions of the celebrated J. T. Lang, who had become the Premier of the Senior State, New South Wales. He was all for repudiation of overseas debt obligations, and was dealing shattering blows at Australia's reputation abroad. He had nothing in common with Scullin, whose risk of defeat he converted into a certainty.

Now, in this book, I am not writing a political history. For the most part, I am writing about people. I served under Lyons for over four years as his Attorney-General, and for more than half that time as his Party Deputy-Leader. He was responsible for my resignation of the office of Deputy Premier of the State of Victoria and my transfer to Canberra. The story of how this happened is simple and human.

I had got to know Lyons very well in the course of the talks which accompanied the moves which made him the Leader of the Opposition and created the United Australia Party. John Latham, in 1934, told Lyons that he wanted to go back to the Bar, of which he had been a notable leader, and that he would not re-contest the Victorian Federal seat of Kooyong, in which I lived. Lyons sent for me, said that he would like me at Canberra, and that if I succeeded Latham in Kooyong he, Lyons, would appoint me Attorney-General! I had a young family. My two sons would probably have to go to boarding school, and I would tend to lose the normal close contact with them.

More importantly, since I would be in Canberra only for part of my time, our home in Melbourne would have to be kept on, and, with a very small daughter to be looked after, my wife could not be expected to go to Canberra except on rare occasions.

In addition, I was very happy at the Bar, a good deal of my work at which I could maintain so long as I lived in Melbourne. To spend a great deal of my time in Canberra seemed like exile to me, and a substantial separation from family life. So I thanked him for a great compliment and said No.

When I got home I told my wife about it, saying for a start, with I hope not inexcusable vanity, that I had been offered the Attorney-Generalship of Australia, the official pinnacle of the Bar, and had refused.

My wife at once said, 'Why on earth did you do that?' I replied that my main reason was that I did not want to be cut adrift from her and the children. Whereupon she said, with measured clarity, 'In what place can you give the greatest service to the country; here, or in the National Parliament?' Well, there could be only one honest answer to that question and I gave it. 'Right,' said my indomitable wife, 'you'd better ring Mr Lyons up right away, and say that you have changed your mind!'

And that's how it all happened, and how I came to serve under a man who commanded my admiration and affection in an uncommon degree.

As Prime Minister, Lyons did not fall into the error of seeking to propound exciting new measures in a hurry. In spite of his uncommon talents, or perhaps because of them, he was essentially a man of the people. He understood ordinary men and women, and they understood him. He was a family man with many children. He was a comparatively poor man, with no silly social pretensions. The instinctive feeling he evoked from the public was that he could be trusted to do his best for the unfortunate, and for households grievously afflicted by the Depression.

He knew that there were some critics who said that he should do more and experiment more. But, having a high degree of wisdom and a balanced sense of responsibility, he acted on the principle I have already referred to. What the people needed was a revived confidence in the future; a steady increase in the volume of employment, an improved business investment induced by an optimism which had been so disastrously shaken.

He succeeded in his task. In his own undemonstrative way, he illustrated the moral force of leadership.

5. JOHN CURTIN

John Curtin, though he also had those qualities which evoke affection, was a quite different personality.

In his earlier years, he had been a journalist. He carried the marks of that training into his later years. He was, therefore, as one could say, more at home in the general than the particular. He had a philosophical mind which ranged over many problems and ideas. He loved nothing more than a personal discussion which had no particular relationship to the 'business before the House'.

Right through the years of our political opposition to each other, we had a regular practice of personal meetings and conversation. I have in an earlier chapter referred to our personal relations, but these personal contacts did not prevent him from being a formidable debater in the House.

He was a good and effective speaker; not, perhaps, a great one. He had something of a passion for abstract nouns, and I thought his speech was marred by a love of rolling Latin endings. In his mouth, 'war' or 'the battlefield' became 'the theatre of disputation'.

It is some evidence of the fallacy of reliance upon physiognomy that Curtin did not look like a great man, though he undoubtedly became one. His head tapered towards the top, and lacked massiveness. One eye was defective, and needed a special glass. He had, as was well known, passed through a period of drinking to excess, and this had kept him from the front places of his party. By a remarkable demonstration of character, he completely overcame this weakness. In fact, in all the years in which I had dealings with him, he took no alcoholic liquor of any kind.

He became the Leader of the Opposition in October 1935, and achieved great authority among its members. In the same way he was, years later, as Prime Minister, to show a marked capacity for securing the confidence of the Australian public, a confidence which, as Prime Minister from 1939-41, I had lost (if I ever had it) in the face of the hostility of some of the large newspapers and the feeling, which I have described, in my own Cabinet that a change of leadership would be of advantage to the Government.

Two personal reminiscences will illustrate my relations with Curtin; each of them will show how uncommon those relations were in the tough world of politics.

When, under the circumstances I have described in an earlier chapter—and it was a wretchedly unhappy period for me—the Opposition decided to attack and defeated the Fadden Government which had succeeded mine and in which I occupied a post, John Curtin spoke to me. I was out, and discredited, and the Government was out. What he said was, 'You know, old man, I was quite happy about you as Prime Minister. So were my fellows. Had you continued as you were going, we would have taken no steps to defeat you. But when your own people rejected you, my people decided to attack, and nothing could hold them!'

Those incidents occurred in 1941. In 1943 a General Election was due. I had become a private member of the Opposition, for when I resigned the Prime Ministership I also resigned the leadership of my own party, for the most obvious reasons. One of my oldest and most faithful colleagues told me in 1943 that he had been approached by a man who professed (I suppose wrongly) to speak on behalf of a very prominent member of the Government. The proposal made by this person was that this Minister and some followers should cross the floor of the House, that the Minister should become Leader of the Opposition, and that the Curtin Government should be voted out. My colleague was, for understandable party reasons, attracted by the idea. My reply was quite unequivocal—'I am a private member, and the least of God's creatures. But I must have a few personal supporters left. If that man crosses the floor and, as an Opposition Leader, moves a vote of no-confidence in Curtin, I will vote for Curtin. And, if even a few of my friends vote with me, the "sacrifice" will have been all in vain!' In the result, nothing happened. Either the Minister's name had been quoted improperly—something that does happen in politics—or the word had gone back. Subsequently, I told Curtin about this; he was not tremendously surprised!

As Prime Minister during the succeeding years of the war, Curtin rose to his greatest heights. He led his party out of a species of pacifism and isolationism which had marked it for many years into strong courses of a war-like kind. He showed a clear patriotism 'in the crunch'. He developed a capacity for inspiring confidence. True, the second Australian Imperial Force had been raised and dispatched abroad by my own Government, had fought splendidly at Bardia and Tobruk and in Syria and in the crucial battle of El Alamein. We had created the Department under that great executive man, Essington Lewis of the Broken Hill Proprietary, and industrially the country was on a war footing. Departments had been created for Supply and the War Organization of Industry, with a wide charter. Compulsory military training had been re-established as far back as 1939.

Curtin realized and appreciated these facts. With a great sense of responsibility, he decided to build upon these foundations, and to secure public support for his measures. His party had a long-standing hostility to conscription in any form; he persuaded it to accept it for the south-west Pacific area. He established the closest relations with General Douglas MacArthur, who led the newly-arrived American forces. He introduced manpower control—'industrial conscription' as it would otherwise have been styled—and imposed the ancillary restrictions. These were notable achievements. I have said something about them. They made heavy inroads on his health, for he did not lack domestic political problems, and had some difficult political colleagues.

We had, in the nature of things, many differences. But it is not my purpose, nor is this the occasion, to write a political history. My immediate task has been to explain how and why John Curtin became one of the very greatest Labour leaders of my time, and why it is that I respect his memory.

6. JOSEPH BENEDICT CHIFLEY

Joseph Benedict ('Ben') Chifley was Curtin's Treasurer and most trusted colleague. It is one of the engaging ironies of history for me to recall how I first met him. He had been for a time a Member of the Commonwealth Parliament, for the electorate of Macquarie, and had been defeated by a member of my own party, my close friend the late John Lawson. When, after the fall of France in 1940, I had the good fortune to enlist the services of Essington Lewis as Director-General of Munitions, we discussed the names of able men who could be brought in to help him. We needed somebody to take charge of Trade Union problems. Lewis suggested Chifley, whom I then proceeded to interview and appoint. I little thought that the day would come when this quiet man would be Prime Minister of the country.

Many years before, Chifley had been an engine-driver in the New South Wales Railways. He had no more than an elementary education. He was a devoted unionist. He was, as an engine-driver, accustomed to driving straight ahead, on a narrow and fixed track. In later years, this faculty remained with him. I came to know, when he was in office, how powerful he was within his limits. As Treasurer, he mastered the techniques of public finance and achieved the habits of command. As Prime Minister after Curtin's death, he retained the portfolio of the Treasury, and was the master of his Cabinet. Yet throughout he was the Trade Unionist. He not only subscribed to union authority, but believed in it with all his heart. It is one of the engaging paradoxes of his life that while he was a masterful man, he believed in the discipline of the organization. In my opinion, he was the most authentic Labour leader in Australian political history. To him, the preservation of the unity of his party was paramount. To him, the actions of Hughes in 1916 and of Lyons in 1931 were not only unpardonable; they were inexplicable!

For him, the 'socialist objective' was more than a slogan; it was a principle of action.

Two instances will prove this.

He decided that the airlines of Australia, like the railways, should be publicly owned and controlled. He therefore put through Parliament a Bill to create an Australian Airlines Commission (to be known as T.A.A.) which, pursuant to the Commonwealth's powers over inter-state trade and commerce, was to have a monopoly of inter-state air services. This would have put out of business the pioneer private airline known as A.N.A. The scheme was tested in the Courts, which found that although the Commonwealth could validly create its own inter-state airline, it could not, in face of Section 92 of the Constitution, guaranteeing the freedom of inter-state trade commerce and intercourse, prohibit private enterprise inter-state air services. So, although the Government airline so established has proved very successful, Chifley's first great attempt to nationalize an industry failed.

But his desires were not yet exhausted. Labour stood for the Socialist objective, and he stood for Labour. He had, in 1945, put through Parliament a Banking Act which, *inter alia,* provided that States and State instrumentalities should conduct their banking business only with a bank approved by the Commonwealth Treasurer—which, of course, was to be the Commonwealth Bank, the Government's bank.

The Melbourne City Council, voting to adhere to its own long-standing private trading bank arrangements, challenged this law in the High Court, and secured its invalidation as a discriminatory law.

For the only time in my experience of him, Chifley, learning of the decision, lost his temper. The Socialist objective, his 'light on the hill' must not be blotted out or obscured in this way. And so, after a brief Cabinet meeting, he announced curtly that the Commonwealth would nationalize all the banks under its Banking power, and then proceeded to pass the necessary legislation. This was in 1947. The High Court, affirmed by the Privy Council on appeal, found the act invalid.

Concurrently, a great campaign arose in the country, and a massive opposition developed.

The issue of Socialism, for years thought to be a rather academic topic for the debating societies, became a burning one in practical politics. It was the dominant issue in the General Election of 1949, and the Labour Government was overwhelmingly defeated. Labour has remained defeated at every election since.

This short narrative throws some light on Chifley, his strength and his weakness. Politics is partly a science. It has principles, and evolves a system. A political leader who lives from day to day, who has tactics but no strategy, can succeed in the short term, but he will leave little behind him. A political leader to whom certain principles have become mere dogma will soon become detached from public opinion and lose public support. The business of politics is both science and art. The political leader is not to be a cynic, without intellectual or emotional roots, but he must be pragmatic in action, moving from event to event, from case to case, like the historic processes of the Common Law.

John Curtin, confronted by a practical and difficult world, grafted a pragmatic approach on to the historic dogmas of his party, and so made a fine place in Australian history.

Ben Chifley, the urgent and vitally practical problems of the war being over, reverted to type. By upholding the principles of his party, he paradoxically helped to destroy his party. For one who has his own strong political principles, this is a fearsome thing to say. But the point that I make is that if one's ideas are so rigid that they will not bend, the chances are that they will break. The *ignis fatuus* of socialization led Chifley to defeat.

I looked at him across the table for years, and never failed to be ascinated by him. He was not a tall man; he was lean and by nature dark-haired. Much out-of-doors speaking in his early days had left him with a gravelly voice. He aspired to none of the arts of oratory. He cast himself for the role of 'the village blacksmith' of literary legend. But, quite frankly, I always thought that he had a sort of naïve vanity; that he hoped to be underestimated, with advantage.

Of his character, there can be no question. He was a man of integrity, even though he occasionally made a virtue of a species of adopted humility. He was an opponent never to be taken lightly.

There is another side to his attainments which I should wish to record. He had, like other men I have known, left school early, but he had read widely and deeply. For some years, we were fellow-members of the Commonwealth Literary Fund, a Committee to aid writers to write and to publish. Every now and then, we met the members of an Advisory Board and received their expert advice. On these occasions, Chifley was superb. He knew the works of the contemporary writers, and he had his own standards, which were admirably high. I shall never forget one meeting at which some new poet, of the school which has substituted words for meaning and elusive incoherency for rhythm, was highly commended. One of his poems was read out. I turned to Chifley with an interrogative eye-brow. He looked across the table to a distinguished Australian authoress and said, 'Miss . . . , I hope you will forgive me. But I think it is all bloody nonsense.' I was grateful to him, for I thought him dead right.

CHAPTER SEVEN

THREE AMERICAN PRESIDENTS

I. PRESIDENT ROOSEVELT

WHEN WINSTON CHURCHILL published his *Great Contem-poraries,* he wrote about those who had gone. This was to be expected. And if it was right for him, how much more right is it for me. For to discuss my own living contemporaries, except in so far as they emerge in my record of great events, would argue a degree of assurance and judgement to which I cannot pretend.

Yet it would be somewhat odd to observe the rule too strictly. Take the American Presidents of my time.

Franklin Delano Roosevelt would be 'eligible' for description and comment. But President Truman is still alive, and, so far as I can gather, in great shape, though no longer politically engaged; under the rule I have mentioned, he would be 'ineligible'. But I shall write something about him. President Eisenhower is still an active political force, and I shall therefore not write about him, except in so far as he comes into my 'Suez Story'. Nor do I write about President Johnson, who is in the very centre of the current American political storm; though I feel bound to record that his policies in relation to South-East Asia command my admiration and, as is well-known, my whole-hearted support.

My personal contact with President Roosevelt was relatively limited, but stimulating. I first met him when I passed through America in 1935 as Attorney-General of Australia, when most of the influential newspapers were against him; yet I had no doubt that he would win in 1936. He was clearly a master-politician.

It was a tremendously interesting period in American and world history. President Hoover, in spite of his massive abilities, had found himself blamed for the Great Depression, for which, in truth, no government was to blame. So he went out. Roosevelt came in, full of ideas and resolution. Stern measures were taken; the New Deal emerged, with its enormous increase in Government activity; a species of American socialism. It would be absurd to pretend that Roosevelt was not referred to in the high centres of business and finance as 'that man', and was even regarded as a traitor to 'his class'. As I have said, most of the influential newspapers were against him. He was one of the few statesmen I have known who saw that this was not necessarily a disadvantage. It is, if I may say so as a democrat with a small 'd', a mistake to think that the people are easily gulled, or disposed to take orders from newspaper proprietors. It is, indeed, one of the benefits of broadcasting and television that the influence of the press has waned.

Roosevelt was the first American President to see this. He made his 'fireside chats' direct to the people, and as his voice came pleasantly and persuasively to the ear, he had a nation-wide audience that no newspaper could have given him. His personal influence became enormous. He was a sort of symbol of courage; only a rare man could have survived a great illness and found himself a cripple and gone straight on as if nothing had happened; only a man of immense inner grace of character could have won to his side men of superlative intellect; but he did.

In May, 1941, on my way back from sitting in the War Cabinet in London, I had exciting talks with him. I had been in close association with Winston Churchill for ten weeks, and I acquired from him some of his magnificent and confident belief that Roosevelt was with us, and that in due course the United States would be: part of Churchill's courage and spirit, in the very dark days of early 1941, derived from his almost clairvoyant belief in what Roosevelt would lead the United States to do. This was a tribute to Churchill's insight; it was also a tribute to the personality of Roosevelt.

I was with Churchill and witnessed his delight when he received from Roosevelt the famous excerpt from Longfellow:

> . . . sail on, O Ship of State!
> Sail on, O Union, strong and great!
> Humanity with all its fears,
> With all the hopes of future years,
> Is hanging breathless on thy fate!

Winston Churchill never wavered in his confidence in Roosevelt's friendship, understanding, and ultimate partnership. Being the kind of man he was, Winston, in the old phrase, 'egged' Roosevelt on. He knew his man. He knew that generous emotions should be encouraged, and that it does no harm to make your friend know that you rely on him.

Some of you may remember that broadcast of Winston's when he was beginning to see the pale hues of American neutrality suffused with the first rosy colour of intervention. I was with him at Chequers when, one night after dinner, he gave his inimitable schoolboy chuckle, and declaimed the famous words:

> And not by eastern windows only,
> When daylight comes, comes in the light,
> In front the sun climbs slow, how slowly,
> But westward, look, the land is bright.

'Do you know who wrote those words?' With simple vanity, I said: 'Of course, Arthur Hugh Clough! But don't be discouraged by this shred of unexpected Antipodean learning. Put it in the broadcast. It will ring a bell right round the world!' And he did; and it did. He was, of course, excited about Roosevelt. He knew that the day must come. It is to the immortal credit of Roosevelt that, while he performed the difficult task of leading his people out of neutrality, he had the imagination to renew the fires in the great leader of Britain at a time when there was no 'second front' except those manned by British and Commonwealth troops. At this time he was leading the United States through a period of benevolent neutrality into a period of active assistance to Great Britain which stopped just short of armed intervention. The perfidious Japanese blow at Pearl Harbor was six months in the future.

As I travelled back through the United States at that time, I formed some impressions which I noted down. I thought that general American sentiment was on our side, but that the current slogan—'Help Britain'—was wrong; it should have been 'Help Ourselves!' My own theme, in speeches in New York, Washington, and Chicago, had been 'This is *your* struggle as well as ours'. I thought that the key of the door was in Roosevelt's hand; that, whatever he did, the people would back him.

When I saw the President, he was in bed, recovering from a touch of gastritis. He was looking older, and tired; but my hour with him was most vigorous. I pleaded for realities about Singapore and the Netherlands East Indies. He, and Cordell Hull a day before, agreed that we all ought to tell Japan 'where she gets off!' But each of them stopped short of actually instructing the U.S.A. Ambassador to do so. Nevertheless, I was left in no doubt—though there were no actual words of commitment—that America would not stand by and see Australia attacked.

I thought that Hull and other senior Ministers were for war. But President Roosevelt, like Woodrow Wilson before him, seemed to me to be waiting for an incident which would in one blow get the United States into the war and get the President out of his election pledge that 'I will keep you out of war!'

I am not writing these words with the benefit of a knowledge of later events. I recorded them at the time.

Franklin Delano Roosevelt was a handsome man, of great personality. His lack of physical activity, due to the causes I have mentioned, seemed to compensate itself by a remarkable enlargement of the mind and the spirit.

He did not become Winston Churchill's colleague and friend *ex officio*. They were in many ways 'two of a kind'. Each was a patriot. Each had a touch of flamboyancy, of showmanship. Each had the great art of communication, and reached the innermost feelings of his fellow-countrymen by the most direct route; as they now say, 'person to person'.

Great men who become dominating figures in great events tend to cast deep shadows. For they are in the middle of the stage, and the footlights are fierce. It is difficult for a new generation, which inherits results and sometimes takes them for granted, to see and understand these men in their setting.

But the merest tyro in the study of modern history must know that President Roosevelt was the Chief Executive and unquestioned leader of his nation in two great crises of two entirely different natures.

He first became President in 1932, when the World Economic Depression was blowing its bitter blasts over the lives and employment of hundreds of millions of people. Orthodoxy had been tried and, in the opinion of many, had been found wanting. It was, as Roosevelt saw it, a time not only for decision, but for swift and radical action. I have already made some reference to it. His supporters were relieved and happy; his business opponents were aghast. The 'States' righters', still numerous, were repelled by the growth or assumption of central power. Some, no doubt, thought (and perhaps rightly) that Alexander Hamilton had come back from the dead, and had converted the Democrats.

But the medicine worked. I did not ever think that Roosevelt was in any way a doctrinaire. He saw the problems as they arose, and dealt with them pragmatically. He carried the people with him.

He fell out with the Supreme Court, for his conception of Federal powers was new and unorthodox. His moves to 'pack' the Supreme Court shocked me at the time. They shock me a little less now, in retrospect, because I have lived long enough to know that, of all the final courts in the English-speaking world, the Supreme Court of the United States is, by the very nature of the 'Bill of Rights' amendments to its Constitution, and the nature of the issues which they throw up, the most affected by political considerations.

It is the fate of many public men to write their names on water. The tide turns, and the names disappear. But what Roosevelt did in the economic field largely survives. The radical departures of those early years are, for the most part, now regarded as commonplace.

His second crisis came with the second great war. Here his political craftsmanship showed itself to a marvel. That he should see quickly that the war against Hitler was a war to defend human freedom, including the freedom of Americans, is not to be wondered at, for his intelligence was lambent and far-reaching. He saw very early the true indivisibility of liberty. But he was the leader of a country which had, after the passing of Woodrow Wilson and America's abstention from the League of Nations, developed a strongly isolationist tendency. Even today, in 1967, one can see many traces of it still. But Roosevelt, in his heyday, knew that the time must come when the United States would be in. His nursing of public opinion, his steady and imaginative conversation of strict neutrality into benevolent neutrality into all aid short of actual war, has given us one of the great chapters of modern political and international history.

It is not by accident that Roosevelt has become, in a true sense, a great figure in British history. His statue stands in Grosvenor Square, in London. He is no 'foreigner' to the British people.

Would the United States have remained technically neutral but for the perfidy and tragedy of Pearl Harbor? The question is now academic, but interesting. My own guess is that if the V_1 and V_2 bombs had begun to achieve success against Britain, and a real public fear had arisen in the United States that Hitler might win, Roosevelt would have brought his country in. But the Japanese answered that question in their own way.

2. PRESIDENT TRUMAN

There is a town named Colac, in the Western District of Victoria. It is a market town in a rich pastoral area, its boundaries lapped by the waters of Lake Corangamite. Periodically I used to visit it to make political speeches to quiet audiences. There was nothing sensational about the atmosphere. Yet, as it turned out, Colac has provided me with three vivid memories.

At the beginning of September 1939, I was booked to speak there, in the Victoria Hall, as Prime Minister. Tension with Hitler was at its height; anything could happen at any time. I dined with a friend before the meeting. During dinner I was called to the telephone from Melbourne, and told that Hitler had invaded Poland. I went round to the hall, to find a large and expectant audience. My speech was brief. 'I have just heard that Hitler has invaded Poland. You all know what that means for Britain and for us. I must return to my office at once, for great decisions must be made without delay.' As I walked to my car, a man stopped me, and said, 'That's a remarkable coincidence. It was in this very hall that Andrew Fisher, in August 1914, made his famous statement that Australia, in the war then beginning, would be behind Britain "to the last man and the last shilling".' Within thirty-six hours I had announced to the nation that we were once again at war.

In December 1941 my first Prime Ministership had abruptly ended, though I remained a member of the Advisory War Council. My younger brother and I decided on a walking tour south through the Otway Ranges; I had taken no holiday of any kind for two and a half years. We took a train to Colac, there to begin our long walk. The Station Master came to me and told me that Japan had attacked Pearl Harbor, and that he had been instructed to give me the news. When the news was confirmed a few hours later, a meeting of the Advisory War Council was called and the walking tour was cancelled.

Years later, when I was Leader of the Opposition, I went further down into the Western District for a meeting. On my way back to

Melbourne, through Colac, a police officer hailed me and said, 'I have been told to advise you that President Roosevelt is dead!' I can remember that, as we drove on, I said to myself, as many thousands of other people did—'What a disaster; this great man gone, and a little man has become President!' From the point of view of the outside world, and certainly that of Australia, his background was unknown; he was an obscure businessman from the Middle West; had a respectable record in Congress; and now he was suddenly succeeding a famous President who had become during his life a legendary figure. 'Oh, what a fall was there, my countrymen.'

There was a feeling of depression, a feeling based, as it turned out, upon ignorance. It is a pleasing fiction, which affects us all, that great men never come in succession. For, as a man's greatness becomes recognized, he tends to become more of an institution and less of a human being. He is thought to be unique, and therefore, by implication, irreplaceable.

How wrong we were proved to be. Nobody, as I said at the outset, can ever anticipate or rely upon the 'verdict of history', for historians have their full share of fallibility and prejudice. But my own verdict would be that Harry Truman proved to be one of the very great Presidents, taking momentous decisions that his ailing and ageing predecessor, the later Roosevelt, might not have taken.

It is always interesting to look at the world's big people, even from afar, and to speculate about the reasons for their greatness. The scholar observer will be tempted, I imagine, to make an intellectual assessment; and so he will need to be reminded that very few pure intellectuals have risen to the top places in practical affairs. Perhaps the last American President to be in this category was Woodrow Wilson, and in his great effort, the creation of a League of Nations with United States membership, he failed.

Mr Truman (happily still with us in the appropriately-named city of Independence) would give a good Missouri chuckle if charged with intellectualism. He had a normal basic education; by some chance he read history extensively, and remembers it with accuracy. No man ever entered the White House with fewer pretensions to academic scholarship, but with more native intelligence. He proved, over the years, to have the supreme basic elements of leadership. These elements can be added to and decorated by pure scholarship, but they are not the product of scholarship. There is no substitute for them. What are they? I will try to answer that question in my own way.

First, a national leader must strive to know the facts. This will involve much hard labour, a great deal of which must (since the clock is inexorable) be done by trusted assistants. When the point for decision arises, the facts must have been clarified to the highest possible degree of certainty. The truth will not be absolute; it never is. But its aspects must be honestly sought, and fairly expounded.

The relevant facts having been thus assembled, the question to be answered will emerge. At this stage, an able and competently served leader (in the United States the President, the Chief Executive) will need to have the penetration of mind to see the nature of the issue, and the firmness of mind to decide it. He is looked to, as all practical men of affairs must be, not for his doubts but for his judgements. It was in these aspects that the true stature of President Truman manifested itself. He was not afraid to make decisions. He made them. Some of them altered the course of history, and are still the subject of controversy. The Hiroshima Bomb. The Korean War. The Marshall Plan; though it is not controversial. The man from Missouri had a simple and direct courage. Lincoln would have approved of him.

But decision must be followed by action, and action must to an enormous extent be the action of subordinates. The leader must command their loyalty and their convinced enthusiasm. To command this spirit, he must be as loyal to them as they are to him. For loyalty is reciprocal. In his capacity for giving and evoking loyalty, Truman exhibited the second element of greatness. If any proof of this were needed, his staunch backing of that great man, Dean Acheson, against vicious and unprincipled attack would supply it.

The third great element is resoluteness in adhering to a decision once made. I have reason to believe that President Truman suffered no nightmares about Public Opinion Polls. He saw them proved fantastically wrong in the Presidential Election of 1948. As a great leader should, he believed in himself and in the ultimate judgement of the people who, in countries like our own, may be distracted and even misled in the short run, but tend to be right in the long run.

I visited America in 1948, to witness a Presidential election at first hand. I was Leader of the Opposition in Australia, had grossly over-worked, and went on a health journey by sea to Great Britain with my wife and daughter. In the then state of the international currencies, dollars were scarce. Mr Chifley, who was Prime Minister and Treasurer, kindly allowed me to buy enough dollars to take me from London to America to see the Presidential election for myself, while my wife and daughter explored Ireland. At Indianapolis, I met and heard Mr Truman. His speech, at a great outdoors rally, was unimpressive; he seemed to have few of the arts of oratory. But my talk with him impressed me enormously. All the polls were against him. The news-papers were busy foolishly explaining who would be in the Dewey administration and, in a nation which does not have compulsory voting, lulling Republican supporters into a false certainty of victory. But when I asked him at his hotel what he thought of his prospects, he smiled and said, 'I shall win!' It was clear to me, as an old campaigner, that he was not just whistling to keep up his courage, but that he meant it, and believed it.

Governor Dewey, whom I heard at Syracuse and visited at Albany, was a far more impressive speaker, with a great background of ex-perience and courage. I liked him, and have enjoyed his friendship ever since. But Truman went on his way, speaking to one local group after another in homely terms, making them all feel that he was one of them; that the goods in the shop window were not all that attractive, but that the stock behind the counter was what they wanted.

And so, to the surprise of most people except himself, he won.

Truman was (and is), as everyone knows, a very human being. Where his personal affections were involved—as, for example, when the music critic lambasted Margaret Truman's singing, President Truman broke all the orthodox rules of restraint. If he had been a different sort of man, deprecatory noises at his outburst would have been heard right across the continent. But the actual comment, widely heard, was 'Good luck to him. He's her father, after all!'

I am prepared to believe that Truman, like most of us, could be small in small matters. Indeed, I hope so. For, if he were not, I suspect that he would have become an intolerable bore. Pomposity is the last state of the perennially correct!

One way or another, I have seen a good deal of him. I came to know something of him as a man; a warm and friendly man whose smile was lit from within and not just switched on from without. He could get to the point as quickly as any man I ever met. One example, an important one for my own country, will suffice.

In 1950, a few months after we had come back into office, I told my Cabinet colleagues that a careful examination of the Treasury and Trade documents had satisfied me that we could not properly perform our policies for the active development of Australia without a large supply of American dollars. Heavy equipment was at that time available only from dollar sources. Yet the view expressed by the former Treasurer was that we could not borrow dollars in America. We earned some on current account, of course, by our exports to the United States, but these went into the sterling-dollar pool in London. What were we to do?

My colleagues, no doubt in that agreeable state of euphoria which follows victory after many years of defeat, said smilingly, with one voice, 'Quite clearly, P.M., you are the man to raise the money. Go abroad and get it!' It was a touching vote of confidence, but a forlorn sort of assignment. However, I went to London for a few days, saw Stafford Cripps, then Chancellor of the Exchequer, and got his generous agreement that if I raised a loan, about which he offered no encouragement, the proceeds were not to go into the sterling-dollar pool, but were to be entirely to Australia's credit.

At this stage, I did not know very clearly to whom to apply—the Export-Import Bank, the International Monetary Fund, or the International Bank for Reconstruction and Development ('the World Bank'). It was useless to seek a direct Government to Government loan; such transactions had a poor history.

Under these circumstances, I decided to go to the top man first; it is a practice, if you can get away with it, which has much to commend it. Mr Truman made this procedure easy, and the order of events assisted. I found on my arrival that I was to be his guest at an official luncheon at Blair House, and that it had been arranged that I should address both the Senate and the House of Representatives during the following week.

Reinforced by these friendly facts, I sought a personal meeting with the President at the White House to explain our developmental needs

[141]

and, if possible, enlist his support. He gave me a long interview, put me completely at ease, quickly saw the human interests involved. Before long, he had me standing with him before a map of Australia and explaining in what areas what things were needed. He sent for Averell Harriman—a happy omen this, for Averell and I had become close friends in England in 1940—and said 'We must do what we can', Averell, for this is a good country and a good friend!' The word went down the line, as such things do at the White House.

Before long, I found my footsteps directed to the World Bank, and to Eugene Black, then its President. My Treasury experts waited in an ante-room for half an hour while Black and I fell into conversation, not about money, but about poetic drama, from Beaumont and Fletcher to Christopher Fry! Two results followed. Eugene Black and I have been friends ever since, and, only a few weeks after the financial discussions which ensued, we got a loan of £150 m. on favourable terms!

In subsequent years, we came back for more, until we became, for a time, the largest borrower from the Bank. Passing through Washington on one occasion, I went to the Bank to sign the latest Loan Agreement, and was given by Black a most precious souvenir. It was two volumes of the Variorum Edition of Shakespeare inscribed 'To R. G. Menzies, my largest debtor, and my smallest worry—Eugene Black.'

But I have never forgotten that the *causa sine qua non* of this success was the quick initial understanding and prompt decision of President Truman. He was, and is, a warm-hearted human being; something which cannot always be said about the great, but can and must be said about him.

3. PRESIDENT JOHN KENNEDY

I recently spent a few months in the United States of America. So far as I could judge, the most popular literary pastime (and a well-paid pastime it must be) is to write and publish a book on how John F. Kennedy died. The horrible crime of his assassination still provokes a morbid interest. One bullet, or two; one assassin, or two; an individual effort, or a concerted plot. Much would have been learned through the usual legal processes of prosecution of Lee Harvey Oswald, who had quite quickly been arrested, but for the fact that the Texas police who astonishingly arranged the passage of the prisoner from one place to another at a time convenient to the press and television, created a state of affairs, in time and place, which enabled Oswald himself to be murdered in the presence of onlookers and the television cameras which made eye-witnesses of many millions of others. A powerful Committee was appointed, under the respected Chief Justice, Earl Warren, to investigate the circumstances of President Kennedy's death. It was highly authoritative. It made a long and careful examination of witnesses. It made an elaborate report. But already, half a dozen profitable books have been written to explain either that the Warren Committee was wrong in method, though conceivably right in result; or that it was right in method, but wrong in the interpretation of the facts; or that some of the witnesses were not clearly understood; or, in short, that the writer would have made a better job of the investigation. So far as I have been able to observe, none of these critics is really in a position to produce fresh evidence of a material kind, such as would induce a normal court in a criminal matter to grant a new trial. But the 'good work' goes on. An outsider finds it all nauseating.

To me, all this morbid controversy obscures the great question about John Kennedy, which is 'How did he live?' and not 'How did he die?' For I have no doubt that President Kennedy had the stuff of greatness in him, a stuff which had yet to be woven into its full fabric. His brutal murder was a terrible thing for the world and for his country. It terminated the exercise of his qualities; it did not endow him with new ones.

It is because I believe that these recent controversies are diverting attention from the living Kennedy, the young and ardent President, that I venture to set down a necessarily limited sketch of the man as I had the honour to know him. Limited, indeed, since my own dealings with him as Prime Minister of my own country were limited. But, for me, they were unforgettable.

Let me begin by saying that it would have been difficult for any American President to start, before I knew him, further back in my estimation than John Fitzgerald Kennedy. This was not his fault. I had been in England during the dark and difficult days of March, April and

May of 1941. Practically every night, there was a German bombing raid. Each day the sun rose on great areas of smoking ruins, and more hundreds of dead citizens. J. G. Winant was the American Ambassador; by instinct and training a man of peace; a reserved man whose very voice puzzled me (it seemed to come from so far back in his throat); he was dark-haired, dark-eyed, and intense. But for his instincts of peace, he could have been one of Cromwell's Ironsides.

I am proud to say that we became close friends; I spent many memorable hours with him at the Embassy in Grosvenor Square and at my own hotel.

He proved to be, under the hammering of the times, a great realist. He attached increasing importance, not to the avoidance of defeat, but to positive victory. His predecessor, Joseph Kennedy, the 'founding father' of the family, had, as I soon discovered, been badly regarded by a beleaguered Britain. He was, rightly or wrongly, thought to be a defeatist; and this in a country which had never been defeated since the Norman Conquest, which had resisted and defeated Napoleon and the armies of the Kaiser, and was not disposed to concede anything to Hitler.

Now, the feeling about Ambassador Kennedy may well have lacked foundation; I am not qualified to judge, for my knowledge of the facts is at best second-hand. I rather suspect that opinion in Whitehall in 1940-41 was distorted by Irish neutrality, of which I have said something elsewhere in this book. The only point I am concerned to make is that when I first met J. F. Kennedy, any prejudice I had was not in his favour. It would have been a foolish prejudice in any case, for I have now lived long enough to learn to judge people on their own merit and not in the light of either gossip or propaganda.

My first discussions with President Kennedy at the White House concerned the problems of South-East Asia, and in particular of New Guinea. I was at once struck by the extraordinary youthfulness and alertness of his mind. In spite of a back injury which he had suffered during the war in the south-west Pacific, his uprightness of carriage—he was a much taller man than the press photographs had suggested—and his physical activity were impressive.

I had had a considerable experience of the courtesies of international talks; the polite question put, and the answer all too frequently ignored.

But when President Kennedy put a question, he put it because he wanted to know the answer, and followed it up with other questions. And, as I learned later, he remembered the answers. This could, of course, be cynically dismissed as a harmless piece of flattery for the benefit of the head of a much less significant government. But it was much more than that. He was young and eager; but his total experience of large matters was of necessity relatively small. He was that rare creature, a man called to the most important office in the world without great experience, and he was desperately anxious to learn as soon as possible all that there was to be learned from whatever source.

He was to demonstrate this dramatically in the case of Cuba. The 'Bay of Pigs' incident exposed him to bitter criticism. All the critics knew where he or his Administration had gone wrong. And they *had* gone wrong, grievously wrong. But he learned, and remembered. And thus it was that when he confronted Khrushchev over the Cuban missile bases he acted with courage and speed, and delivered the most powerful blow against Soviet expansionism that has been struck in post-war history. If, as I firmly believe, the tension between the Soviet Union and the Western World has lessened to a remarkable degree, the reason may be found not only in the successful Berlin air-lift, in the existence of the Nuclear Deterrent, and N.A.T.O., and the slow growth of an intellectual *bourgeoisie* in Russia, tremendously important as they were and are, but in Kennedy's *coup* over Cuba.

For some years, I had a belief which I used to impose upon my more patient friends. 'The historic moment of truth will come when the Soviet Chairman is confronted by a democratic leader who has the power and the personality to say "You go no further", *and who is believed*. And the only man who can say this, and be believed, is a President of the United States.'

And therefore I want to think of the living Kennedy, and mourn the fact that the assassin's bullet abruptly ended what had only just begun—a career which could have turned out to be of enduring value to mankind.

I have never quite known what 'an intellectual' is, for most of those who claim this distinction seem to me, in their public utterances and behaviour, to be governed unduly by their emotions, and to lack the objective judgement demanded of true scholars. But John Kennedy was a highly educated man with wide intellectual and artistic interests. His talents were not narrow; his mind quested in a wide field. But he did not lose sight of his immediate responsibilities. He never lost sight of the domestic problems of his nation, and showed courage in his treatment of them. But above all, he made himself an active force in world affairs.

On the international economic front, he was deeply concerned with the future of the European Economic Community and its relation to Great Britain, the British Commonwealth, and the United States; and with the problems of South-East Asia. On my way to a conference on these and other matters in London, in 1962, I had a long and valuable discussion with him at the White House. We very quickly found that our two countries had a great deal in common. We shared a fear that if the European Community developed too strongly in the direction of self-sufficiency, and particularly if Great Britain joined in, the effect on world trade might turn out to be adverse. An enlarged domestic market for European (including British) manufacturers could increase their overseas selling capacity. But if their agricultural and pastoral policies tended to limit or exclude imports, both the United States and Australia could suffer. Self-sufficiency was not a good world policy. And, since imports have to be paid for by the customer's exports, the European Community itself could suffer.

After our discussions, we issued a brief joint statement dated 20 June 1962, which I will quote, since it exhibits the mind and promise of President Kennedy in a clear way. It deserves to be on record.

The President and the Prime Minister expressed gratification at the opportunity presented by the Prime Minister's visit for furthering their personal as well as official friendship symbolizing the cordiality of relations between the American and Australian people.

The President and the Prime Minister discussed the question of peace in South-East Asia. The President noted with satisfaction Australia's active interest in supporting the struggle of the Government of Vietnam against subversion and aggression organized and directed from abroad. Both leaders looked forward to the effective realization of the Geneva Accords assuring the independence and neutrality of Laos.

The President and the Prime Minister agreed that a peaceful solution of the West New Guinea dispute would be in the best interests of all concerned, and they recognized that the efforts of the Acting Secretary General of the United

Nations, U Thant, and his representative, Ambassador Ellsworth Bunker, had provided the atmosphere for the achievement of a significant contribution to the cause of peaceful settlement of international disputes.

Both the President and the Prime Minister agreed on the desirability of maintaining the excellent record of Australian-American security consultation and co-ordination through the ANZUS and SEATO Treaties.

President Kennedy expressed his strong belief in the importance of the Commonwealth as a source of stability and strength for the Free World. At the same time, both leaders recognized that European unity could contribute substantially to the strength of the Free World.

They reviewed therefore the implications for the trade of their two nations of the possible accession of the United Kingdom to the European Economic Community.

It was agreed that in this event the United States and Australia would, as great suppliers to Britain and Europe, face problems in endeavouring to maintain and expand access for their goods.

The Prime Minister offered the view that it would be a grave misfortune if, after the negotiations, it turned out that the conditions laid down for Britain's entry were unacceptable to Commonwealth countries on the ground that they damaged Commonwealth Trade and expansion.

The President and Prime Minister took note of the fact that with respect to certain articles and commodities Australia's historic terms of access are different from those of the United States. They recognized, however, that Australia competed with the United States in the United Kingdom market with respect to only a relatively small number of these items—though the items themselves are by no means of small importance. They agreed that with respect to these items technical discussions would be held between the two Governments in an effort to reconcile the trading interests of both nations.

With respect to the great bulk of articles and commodities they noted that, as non-members of the European Economic Community, their countries faced essentially the same problems, and they joined in hoping that the Community would pursue liberal trading policies. President Kennedy pointed out that under the Trade Expansion legislation now pending before the Congress the United States Government might be able, through reciprocal agreements, to bring about a general reduction of trade barriers for the benefit of all. Moreover, both leaders agreed that, with respect to a number of key primary products, the problems raised by the expansion of the Common Market might best be solved through international arrangements.

During the course of their interviews the President expressed his warm interest in Australia and his understanding of Australian needs in terms of development and growth, recognizing the problems of particular regions as well as industries. Both he and the Prime Minister were agreed that the problems arising out of Britain's proposed entry should be approached not on any basis of theory or the use of particular words but upon a practical basis examining commodities one by one, having in mind the protection of the interests of both countries.

This, from the point of view of my country, was an important meeting.

It is well to note particularly the reference to 'international arrangements', i.e. on commodities. This remains an unsolved problem, but President Kennedy was one of the few statesmen of the great industrial nations who seemed to me to understand it with clarity.

The problem arises in this way. Massive financial and technical aid has been and is being given to new or 'emergent' nations; new in political independence, frequently primitive in production and living standards; properly anxious to complement their political freedom by economic independence. Yet, when the aid they receive has been put to work, and they produce for export (without which they cannot secure the capital needed for future growth), they find, all too frequently, that their exports, principally of primary products, are met, in the older and economically larger and richer countries, by tariff barriers or quotas which deprive them of an adequate market at prices which will be remunerative to reasonably efficient producers. In the result, the gap between the standards in the richer and older countries and those in the new tends to grow wider. Fair international commodity arrangements are indeed urgent. For there can be no enduring basis of peace in the world so long as this grievance continues. My Australian colleague, John McEwen, the notable Australian Trade Minister, has been an able and persistent pioneer in this field.

If President Kennedy had lived, there would have been a powerful ally in the contest, and much might have been achieved. No doubt it still will be. But it is not common to encounter a Head of Government of a rich and powerful country who combines national pride with a profound sense of national responsibility. It is a good thing for the world that the United States has continued to produce such men.

CHAPTER EIGHT

MY SUEZ STORY

The mission of mediation to Nasser at the time of Suez; he virtually volunteered for this job, which gave him the world limelight he sought, but he did his country some harm in the doing of it. (*Extract from an article in the London Sunday Telegraph of 23 January 1966, arising out of my retirement from office.*)

THE AUTHOR OF THE ARTICLE has no particular significance for me and could be safely ignored but for the fact that his erroneous account of events had already enjoyed some currency in Australia, where it became fashionable among some of my political opponents to treat my acceptance of the Chairmanship of the Suez Committee of the eighteen nations who formed the great majority at the London Conference in 1956 as a prime blunder on my part, and even as bringing discredit to my country. Now that I am no longer in office, with its myriad preoccupations, I will set the record straight. I am not writing a documented history of the whole incident. That has been done by others. There were later aspects of it with which I had no contact. All that I want to do is to confine myself to events in which I actually participated and of which, therefore, I had first-hand knowledge.

I had been in England on a political errand in July 1956. I was on my way back to Australia *via* Canada and the United States when President Nasser of Egypt made his dramatic declaration that Egypt was nationalizing, or taking over, the Suez Canal. It had been promptly proposed that there should be an international conference in London to discuss the matter. I rang through to Canberra, and sought the opinion of my colleagues as to whether I should return to London (which I was not anxious to do), or whether Mr Casey (now Lord Casey) (then Minister for External Affairs) should take my place. The answer was that, as the future of the Canal was of vital importance to Australia, I should return to London, and that Casey would come over. I agreed with this view; it would have surprised most Australians if any other decision had been made.

On 31 July 1956, I saw the British Ambassador in Washington (Sir Roger Makins) and, in the absence of John Foster Dulles then in

London, Mr Hoover. I told the Ambassador that I would doubt the efficacy of a threat of force unless it had the support of the United States. But I made it clear that in my opinion Nasser's action was illegal.

On 4 August, Dulles was back from London, and I had a long talk with him. He said that he regarded the crisis over the Suez Canal as the gravest incident since the Second War. Fresh from his discussions in London, he greatly interested me when he said that while the United Kingdom and France had agreed to the convening of a conference, they were in no mood to allow Nasser to get away with any favourable settlement. Unless his prestige could be materially diminished, they would be exposed to trouble after trouble in the Middle East.

He made it clear to me that both the United Kingdom and France would not hesitate to use military force should that become necessary. He had questioned the wisdom of this, and had pointed out the dangers of provoking a large war.

So far as I could tell, little if any thought had been given to the possibility of economic sanctions.

On 5 August, I forwarded to my colleagues in Canberra my own opinion that it would be vastly important to be able to show the world that all means short of war had been resorted to. I discouraged public talk about force, saying that it would merely deter Nasser from attending the proposed London Conference, a conference which I thought it most important he should attend. I added that it might also discourage Nehru from attending, which would be a misfortune. In the result, neither attended, but Nehru was represented, as I think unhappily, by Krishna Menon.

On 15 August, the acting Prime Minister of Australia, Sir Arthur Fadden, made a press statement as follows:

After considering the latest cabled advices on the Suez Canal issue and conferring with those Ministers now in Canberra, I have cabled the Prime Minister recommending that, having regard to the valuable influence he can continue to exert from London, he remain on until there is a clearer picture of conference developments.

On arriving back in London, I had lunch with Eden and Selwyn Lloyd. By this time I had read in sections of the British press (and I had read the same kind of thing in America) statements to the effect that Nasser's 'nationalization' of the Canal was legally valid, and that in consequence we must just make the best of it.

I told Eden and Lloyd that I disagreed with this, and indicated my reasons. They were deeply interested, because, as the effect of Sir John Simon's famous speech at the time of the General Strike had shown, the British public has an innate respect for the law, and would rather be with it than against it.

Would I be prepared to go on to television and state my opinion? I said I would, and did so on 13 August. The full text of that statement has been published in my earlier book *Speech is of Time,* and I will not reproduce it here.

But a brief summary of the main points is essential to an understanding of my position at this historic period.

I pointed out that the Canal, though on Egyptian territory, was not built by Egypt. 'It was the product of the bold vision and engineering genius of a Frenchman, de Lesseps, and the financial resources of a company whose shareholding was and is (subject to Nasser's action) international.'

The then Government of Egypt granted to the Company a concession expressed to endure until 1968. The Suez Canal Convention of 1888, by which Egypt was bound, contained an express recital that it was desired to establish 'a definite system designed to guarantee at all times, and for all the powers, the full use of the Suez Maritime Canal'.

The validity of the Concession and of the Convention had never been challenged by Egypt. On the contrary, the Convention was expressly upheld by the Anglo-Egyptian Treaty of 1954, only two years before; while the Egyptian Government as recently as June 1956 had, in its latest financial agreement with the Company, acknowledged the duration and the international character of the Concession.

I said that, on these clear facts, Nasser had violated the first principle of international law by using what would be a normal domestic power (to nationalize an industry) to violate what was a clear international obligation.

I referred to an analogous case which concerned the United States. The Panama Canal was constructed by the United States on land belonging to the Republic of Panama, a perpetual lease of the land being granted to the United States. Could Panama, by unilateral action, terminate the perpetual lease, take over the Panama Canal, and collect the dues?

It is very interesting to me now to recall that Professor A. L. Goodhart, a most eminent authority on such matters, discussed the matter in an article published in 1957.

With his permission, I will quote some material passages from his opinion.

It is obvious that every country is entitled to nationalize any company or undertaking within its territory unless there is some special reason which prevents such a step. Thus, to take certain examples which have been frequently cited, Great Britain has nationalized its coal mines, its railways, and its electricity companies, but it has never been suggested that this was contrary to international law, although foreigners undoubtedly owned shares in these companies. Why then was there such a strong protest when Egypt nationalized the Suez Canal Company?

It is important to note that the protest was not limited to Great Britain and France. The United States, although opposed to any threat of force, made it clear that it regarded this step as illegal. Moreover, the sudden and violent seizure of the offices and other establishments of the Canal Company by Egypt suggests that that country was not prepared to assert its alleged right in the usual and orderly manner, but preferred to rely on a *fait accompli*.

It has been frequently emphasized that the Statutes of the Universal Suez Canal Company, January 5, 1956, provide in Article 3 that 'the company has its seat at Alexandria and its administrative domicile in Paris', but this does not mean that the company is not an Egyptian one. The existence of a company does not depend upon its domicile, and therefore, Egypt, having created the company, had the legal power to bring it to an end, unless there was some special ground negativing the exercise of this power.

It is submitted that such a ground can be found in Article 4 of the Statutes which provides that 'the duration of the company shall be equal to the duration of the Concession.' The only possible purpose of this provision could be to prevent the control of the Company from being seized by the Egyptian Government while the Concession was still in force. As the Concession was to last for 99 years from the date of the opening of the Canal in 1869, the Egyptian Government was under an obligation not to bring the company to an end before 1968. The claim that nationalization of a company does not bring it to an end, but merely shifts the control, is clearly nothing more than a legal quibble. . . .

. . . The fact that the Suez Canal Company is technically an Egyptian company does not negative its essentially international character. . . .

. . . It is not suggested that Egypt would not have been entitled as the sovereign state to nationalize the company and seize the canal if there had been supervening necessity for such a step. This police power must exist even when a concession is made in absolute terms, because no government has the right to surrender the power to maintain order. But the Egyptian Government did not allege, and it could not have alleged, that the seizure of the Canal was based on this ground. Colonel Nasser made it clear that the sole purpose of the nationalization was to obtain financial benefits for Egypt. . . .

And, on this matter, he concluded by reflecting that:

Although in the past the basic principle of international law was thought to be *pacta sunt servanda,* every country may now regard itself to be free to repudiate its solemn covenants on the ground of national sovereignty. The validity of every concession will in the future depend solely on the will of the promisor. . . .

The London Conference met on 16 August 1956, at Lancaster House. Representatives of twenty-two nations attended. After a brief opening by Eden, Selwyn Lloyd, as Foreign Secretary of Britain, took the chair. John Foster Dulles represented the United States.

Proposals had been worked out between Britain, the United States, and France. They had the clear mark of Dulles upon them. In fact, Dulles was *the* man of the Conference, clear, eloquent, moderate but grave.

As carried by eighteen nations, the proposals were as follows:

The Governments approving this Statement, being participants in the London Conference on the Suez Canal:

Concerned by the grave situation regarding the Suez Canal:

Recognizing that an adequate solution must, on the one hand, respect the sovereign rights of Egypt, including its rights to just and fair compensation for the use of the Canal, and, on the other hand, safeguard the Suez Canal as an international waterway in accordance with the Suez Canal Convention of 29 October 1888;

Assuming for the purposes of this statement that just and fair compensation will be paid to the Universal Company of the Suez Maritime Canal, and that the necessary arrangements for such compensation, including a provision for arbitration in the event of disagreement, will be covered by the final settlement contemplated below.

Join in this expression of their views.

1. They affirm that, as stated in the Preamble of the Convention of 1888, there should be established 'a definite system destined to guarantee at all times, and for all the Powers, the free use of the Suez Maritime Canal'.

2. Such a system, which would be established with due regard to the sovereign rights of Egypt, should assure:

   (a) Efficient and dependable operation, maintenance and development of the Canal as a free, open and secure international waterway in accordance with the principles of the Convention of 1888.

   (b) Insulation of the operation of the Canal from the influence of the politics of any nation.

   (c) A return to Egypt for the use of the Suez Canal which will be fair and equitable and increasing with enlargements of its capacity and greater use.

   (d) Canal tolls as low as is consistent with the foregoing requirements and, except for (c) above, no profit.

3. To achieve these results on a permanent and reliable basis there should be established by a Convention to be negotiated with Egypt:

   (a) Institutional arrangements for co-operation between Egypt and other interested nations in the operation, maintenance and development of the Canal, and for harmonizing and safeguarding their respective interests in the Canal. To this end, operating, maintaining and developing the Canal and enlarging it so as to increase the volume of traffic in the interest of the world trade and of Egypt, would be the responsibility of a Suez Canal Board. Egypt would grant this Board all rights and facilities appropriate to its functioning as here outlined. The status of the Board would be defined in the above-mentioned Convention.

   The members of the Board, in addition to Egypt, would be other States chosen in a manner to be agreed upon from among the States parties to the Convention with due regard to use, pattern of trade and geographical distribution; the composition of the Board to be such as to assure that its responsibilities would be discharged solely with a view to achieving the best possible operating results without political motivation in favour of, or in prejudice against, any user of the Canal.

   The Board would make periodic reports to the United Nations.

(b) An Arbitral Commission to settle any disputes as to the equitable return to Egypt or other matters arising in the operation of the Canal.

(c) Effective sanctions for any violation of the Convention by any party to it, or any other nation, including provisions for treating any use or threat of force to interfere with the use or operation of the Canal as a threat to the peace and a violation of the purposes and principles of the United Nations Charter.

(d) Provisions for appropriate association with the United Nations and for review as may be necessary.

It was ultimately decided that a Committee should be chosen by the Conference to approach the Government of Egypt to place before it the views of the eighteen governments, to explain their purposes and objectives, and to find out if Egypt would agree to negotiate a Convention on the basis of those views.

The Committee was ultimately chosen unanimously, without the necessity of either candidature or election. The chosen representatives were those of Australia, Ethiopia, Iran, Sweden, and the United States, with myself designated by name as Chairman. It was clear that we were not to negotiate a treaty but only to secure such agreement in broad principle as would enable later negotiations for a treaty to proceed.

In view of the quotation which stands at the head of this chapter, I must recount how I came to be appointed Member and Chairman. For, so far from being a volunteer, I was, to use Foster Dulles's expression, 'drafted'.

It happened in this way. On 18 August, I had spoken at some length in the Conference in support of the Dulles proposals, and had been listened to. I spoke with conviction of the justice of the proposals, which I still think were fair, indeed, generous. At the same time, I don't think any of us was optimistic. Nasser was deeply committed, and it was obvious that he would regard his whole prestige in the Middle East, in the Arab world, as being at stake. Nevertheless, we felt that the joint opinion of the eighteen nations, representing an enormous aggregation of power and of world influence, could have some effect if we presented an unbroken front. In a word, it was worth trying, for not to try was to surrender.

On 21 August, as the Conference neared its conclusion, the Soviet representative made a long and inflammatory propaganda speech, containing the usual clichés about colonialism, and designed to induce Egypt to say 'No'. Dulles was very angry about some of the more offensive statements, but rightly felt that *he* should not answer or rebuke them, because (as I have myself frequently pointed out) it is a constant Communist device to line up all world political issues as issues between the Communist nations and the United States, with the rest of us as innocent bystanders. Foster Dulles therefore sent around a note to me asking me to reply if I felt so disposed. I did so, pointing out that inflammatory statements addressed to Egypt were a grave disservice to peace. I was to remember those words later on.

At that time the general idea in the Conference was that the document finally emerging should be presented to President Nasser with an indication that, say, three representatives of the Conference would be willing to meet him for discussion in some neutral place. It was thought, as I recall after reading my cable report to Canberra, that the three spokesmen would be Dulles himself, somebody from the British Commonwealth, and one other. The United Kingdom, as a direct disputant, should not be in the talks.

I returned to my hotel, feeling that the business had almost ended, and that I could soon resume my interrupted and much delayed return to pressing duties and problems at home.

And so, with some contentment, I went to bed and promptly to sleep. At about 2 a.m., the telephone rang, and woke me up. On the line was Winthrop Aldrich, the American Ambassador, with whom I was on terms of friendship. He said: 'I want you to come up to my house (in Regent's Park).' 'When?' I asked. 'Right away. Anthony, Selwyn and Foster are here, with some others. They want to discuss a matter with you!' I protested, and asked whether it would not keep till the morning. He said that it would not, and that he would send a car down to the Savoy at once. I got up, dressed, and arrived at the Residence at about 2.30 a.m.

They explained that they were now contemplating a Committee of five, to get a properly balanced result. Anthony Eden then said to me, 'We all want you to be a member of the Committee.' Dulles interjected, 'No, Anthony, not a member, Chairman. We want him as our chief spokesman, because he knows how to put a case!'

I at once demurred. I was long overdue in Australia; we had introduced some financial measures—a 'little Budget'—only a few months
before, and were in consequence suffering some unpopularity. I should
be at my post in Australia. They kept at me. I suggested some other
names, but they would not have them. 'If you say "No", we will
re-think the whole matter of the Committee.'

Finally, at I suppose 4 a.m., I said that I would give no answer until
I had consulted my colleagues at home, and that I would then advise
them.

'And so to bed', for the second time. A few hours later, I sent a cable
to my Deputy Prime Minister, Arthur Fadden, explaining the Committee proposals and saying that I was under very great personal
pressure from Eden and Dulles. I said that I had explained to both of
them my own political problem and had said that I could not delay my
return unless they had genuinely strong views which satisfied my
colleagues and were presented in terms which could be made public.
I said this because I wanted the Australian public to know that this
engagement, if I entered into it, was not one of my own seeking.

Fadden promptly replied that he and our colleagues realized the
problems but would await the anticipated messages from Eden and
Dulles. These arrived in a few hours.

Eden's message was as follows:

The help, experience and counsel which your Prime Minister has brought to
our proceedings during these anxious days has proved quite invaluable. All my
colleagues would join with me in gratitude to him and to you for making this
possible.

It looks now as though we are about to embark on the second stage of the
work of the Conference, the first having had most encouraging progress so
far. The seventeen nations are likely to want three or four from among them
to present the outcome of their work to Egypt and to give if need be explanation in reply. We are most anxious that this small Committee should be as
strong in personalities as possible. This is also the view of all the delegates to
whom I and the Foreign Secretary have had the opportunity to speak. I know
that the Scandinavians, as well as the Americans and other Europeans and
ourselves would like to see your Prime Minister available for it. For your most
confidential information, we hope that the other members will be drawn from
the United States, Scandinavia and a Middle Eastern power. Thus the four
corners of the world would be represented.

I truly feel that the Commonwealth of Australia would be rendering a signal service to the solution of this vexed problem if you and your colleagues could spare your Prime Minister for a few more days to give his personal help.

Foster Dulles sent a message which was brief but clear.

We are drafting Bob Menzies to serve on, and be Chairman of, the Committee to be set up by this Suez Conference to make contact with the Egyptian Government.

This is a task of supreme importance. I hope myself to give some personal service to that task. I trust you and your colleagues will acquiesce in your Prime Minister thus serving in this work which is so vital to the peace and well-being of so much of the world.

Fadden's reply—all these messages were in the space of twelve hours—was that, having had messages from Eden and Dulles, he had replied to each saying that, in the circumstances described by them, he and our colleagues were in full agreement that I should be available for the Committee.

My colleagues were, as I now know, delighted. They regarded the appointment as a compliment to Australia, though they (and I) fully understood the immense risks, perhaps the certainty, of failure. They and I have lived long enough to learn that, in the opinion, or prejudice, of many critics, no man should undertake a public task without either a guarantee or reasonable probability of success, if he desires to avoid obloquy.

And so the 'Suez Committee' was established. As the events (though they have now faded a little in the public memory) are of historic interest, I think I should, without impertinence, record my impressions of those who served on it.

John Foster Dulles, who was, I think unfortunately, not able to go to Cairo with us, but who attended the earlier Committee meetings, was a controversial figure; after all, he was Secretary of the State Department—a species of Prime Minister!—and a man of remarkable individuality. Over the years, I got to know him very well.

He had a constructive mind. His contribution to the London Suez Conference demonstrated that. The proposals adopted were in a real sense his. He was a man of deep religious faith in an age when scepticism prevails. He had high character. He has been accused of two rather incompatible things—vacillation and 'brinkmanship'. 'Brink-manship', or, as it might be said, 'skating on thin ice' can be the technique of a somewhat dangerous skill, but vacillation certainly cannot be. His reputation for vacillation was so widespread that, years after Suez, I presumed on our close personal association to tell him how I thought he had acquired a reputation for inconsistency. 'Foster,' I said, 'there is no mystery about it. You love press interviews, sudden or organized, as much as I dislike them. But when I have an interview, and know that I am going to be asked about some particular matter of policy, I make up my mind before I invite the press in. This is perhaps because in our system of government Cabinet makes policy; whereas in the United States policy seems to emerge from a sort of public debate.

'In your case, Foster, you go into a press conference, and, not having a fixed conclusion, you proceed to think aloud. The gentleman from "A" asks you about the problem of, say, Ruritania. You reply, "Well, of course, an answer to that problem could be 'X'."

'This solution suits the "A" newspaper, so off goes its representative, and around the world's news services goes your "policy" on Ruritania. But hardly has the representative of "A" got out of the room when you are saying "On the other hand, the correct solution may be 'Y'", and are proceeding to give your reasons. And so on. And all around the world earnest people are saying "Why can't Dulles stick to one policy?"'

He was disposed to admit this soft impeachment. He liked 'thinking aloud', which was, let's face it, sometimes embarrassing but infinitely better than not thinking at all.

His 'brinkmanship', on the other hand, was a by-product of his legal habits of mind. I thought that he rather enjoyed defining a position with what was, in his mind, precision, recognizing, as he must have, that the position might be distorted or misunderstood, but remaining convinced of the logical correctness of the position itself.

Upon reflection, I think that John Foster Dulles suffered very much from the defects of his own qualities. He had ability, patriotism, and honesty; all great elements. If he had the advocate's gift for persuading himself, and it is one of the first attributes of advocacy, this was not really inconsistent with his innate honesty of mind. For he had truly convinced his own mind.

6*

Years after the Suez incident had created deep differences of opinion between us, I had a talk with him in Canberra which illustrates some of these reflections. I will come to it later in my narrative.

But in late August and early September of 1956, when he attended the first meetings of the 'Suez Committee', he was the devoted expositor of the principles which he had himself presented and explained to the London Conference.

His alternate, *Loy Henderson*, who succeeded him on the Committee and went to Cairo, was a calm, level-headed, career diplomat with wide experience in the Middle East. He had good and cautious judgement, and was an excellent corrective to my own occasional impetuosity.

I noted, before we were through, that Henderson was 'somewhat cluttered up with a number of expert advisers. The American expert adviser is of a race apart. He loves sitting in committees to draft documents. . . . He exercises considerable ingenuity in the elaboration of proposals; the elaboration sometimes departing considerably from the main theme. Whenever Henderson has come to a committee meeting after a long session with his experts, the marks are heavy upon him. When he speaks for himself without such well-meaning help, his views are wise, clear, and experienced.' At the same time, Henderson had a capacity for healthy indignation which emerged during our discussions with President Nasser, of which more anon. His presence, and his contributions to our work, did much to construct our remarkable unanimity of approach in a matter in which a common front was so important.

Dr Ardalan, the Foreign Minister of Iran (Persia) had geniality and aplomb; he was a good colleague and an agreeable companion; very conscious of the particular problems of the Middle East; firm without being doctrinaire. He has a warm place in my own memory.

Ato Aklilou Hapte-wold, Foreign Minister of Ethiopia, interested me very much. He had aquiline features, a very dark ebony skin, and an engaging sense of humour. He spoke French, but understood some English. I spoke English (or what I believe is regarded as its Australian equivalent) and understood some French. So we got on well. So well that I permitted myself once at Cairo, where the heat was intense, to say to him (in some language or other!) that no doubt, as an Ethiopian, he did not mind the heat at all. He replied, 'You are quite wrong. I come from Addis Ababa, which is 7,000 feet above sea level, and where the climate is remarkably temperate!' 'Then,' said I, 'how does it come about that you are easily the most sunburnt man on this Committee?'

Osten Unden, Foreign Minister of Sweden, was a man of immense learning in international relations. He constantly recalled us to the legalities of our position, but was always constructive. His voice had somewhat mournful intonations—and I don't think any one of us was very optimistic—but he had an engagingly dry wit.

In short, I was fortunate in the Conference's choice. No chairman could ever have had a better Committee. It was not its fault that we failed.

On 24 August, we transmitted to President Nasser, through the Egyptian Ambassador in London, our request to meet the President and to explain to him the proposals of the eighteen nations. We suggested a meeting at Geneva. The reply was that 'the President proposes to meet with the Committee in Cairo on Monday, September 3rd.' We agreed. We decided that, to avoid all difficulties, we would acquiesce and interview him on his own ground and among his own people. We had no desire that our talks would fail on some point of pride. We then had a number of meetings in London to hear evidence from experts on shipping and trade, so that we might be well informed on the practical aspects of canal operation. (As it turned out, this was 'love's labour lost', since in the result we were met and rejected on a broad front.)

Then we went to Cairo by chartered plane, on Sunday, 2 September. I recall that at Rome, where we refuelled, Clare Boothe Luce came out to see us and helped me with her advice to buy an Italian scarf for my wife!

We arrived at the Cairo airport—then not so grand as it is now—in the dusk. There seemed to be hundreds of reporters, broadcasting men, and photographers with flashlights. They had all been allowed to swarm on to the field. Half-blinded by the lights, interrogated loudly by scores of half-seen people, I battled my way through to where I could discern the tall shape of the Australian Minister to Egypt, Mr Roden Cutler, v.c. (now Sir Roden Cutler, Governor of New South Wales). We hopped into his car and escaped in good order to the city and to the Australian Legation, where I was to live and where the Committee was to meet.

Next day, Monday, 3 September, we had a first meeting with the President. We moved in through a barrage of photographers, whose craft and presence seem to be rather more important to dictators than to elected people; and that is saying a good deal. Our meeting was purely preliminary, designed to establish personal contact and arrange procedures. When we met, I asked the President whether he would prefer our case to be put in some language other than English, in which case an interpreter should be engaged.

He said that English would be satisfactory; and indeed throughout our subsequent discussions he appeared to understand and speak it very well. I asked him to make it clear to me if, at any time, he did not fully understand me, for it was most important that there should, on a matter of great world interest, be no confusion. He willingly agreed. He had with him Wing-Commander Aly Sabry, a trusted Minister who had been an Air Force officer and who had been in London at the time of the Lancaster House Conference, though not actually present at the Conference itself; and Mr Fawzi, an old Egyptian Foreign Office hand, quiet, moderate, and, I felt, wise. We left with the President—and it is important to remember this—an *aide-memoire* which we had prepared in London. I set out its terms in full, because they clearly exhibit the spirit in which we were making our approach.

We have been authorized by 18 nations, which are the major users of the Suez Canal, to approach the Egyptian Government on their behalf, to present to it certain proposals relating to the future operation of the Canal, and to explain to the Egyptian Government the nature and objectives of such proposals. The text of these proposals is attached hereto.

It will be readily understood that the nations for whom we speak regard their vital economic interests as being deeply affected by the future of the Canal. They have a clear belief that, if the Canal is to be maintained and developed as a waterway open to the use of vessels of all nations, it should be detached from politics, and the management of its operations should be placed on such a basis as to secure the maximum of international confidence and co-operation.

At the same time, we wish to make it clear that those whom we represent have not approached this problem in any spirit of hostility. There is a long history of friendly relations with Egypt. In two great wars, several of the nations we represent have had a direct and mutually helpful association with

Egypt. We have all welcomed Egypt's attainment of complete self-govern-ment and we would desire that anything done or proposed now should be regarded as containing no derogation from Egypt's sovereignty and national dignity. These two points of view were indeed clearly illustrated by the whole temper and tone of the discussions at the London Conference.

It is our deep conviction that the negotiation of a convention along the lines suggested in our proposals would be for the benefit of Egypt and of all nations and individuals using the Canal and would certainly help to restore the kind of peaceful international atmosphere which the world at present so desperately needs.

In case it should be thought that what we are proposing conflicts with the sovereign rights of Egypt with regard to the Canal, which flows through Egyptian territory, we should at the outset of our discussions make it clear that we do not believe that the Convention of 1888 and a Convention of the kind we are suggesting supplementary to that of 1888 affect Egypt's sovereign rights at all. It is, indeed, the existence of those sovereign rights and their continued recognition which afford the whole basis of our proposals. It is our desire and need that there should be a definite system for the operation, maintenance and development of the Canal which, while it recognizes Egyptian sovereignty, will serve dependably, for a long time to come, the manifest interests not only of Egypt but of all users of this most important waterway.

We trust that our discussions will proceed amicably on this basis. Though superficially it may be thought by some that there is on this matter an irrecon-cilable difference of principle, we do not believe this to be so. It would be a grave misfortune for the world if it were so. It is because we are confident that that there is a basis of principle for the negotiations of an agreement which will properly protect the interests of all that we have come to Egypt, have sought conference with the Government of Egypt, and will in a reasoned way do our best to secure a peaceful settlement upon a basis of justice to both sides, and such a consolidation of future of the Canal as will take it out of the area of political conflict and so enable it to serve the peaceful purposes of many millions of people all over the world.

The text of the proposals was attached; I have already quoted them.

The next day, late in the afternoon, we met for business. I presented the case on behalf of the Committee. That case was subsequently reduced to writing. This letter and President Nasser's reply are reprin-ted as an appendix on p. 363. I did not read an essay. I used no notes except the bare forms of the proposals. I was listened to with attention and complete courtesy. In spite of some irritating mannerisms—and I suppose we all have some—I got the impression that we were dealing with a patriotic Egyptian who had a strong sense of responsibility and of the gravity of the issue. Nasser was a man of imposing physique and presence; obviously the master of his Government, of much intelligence, but with some marks of immaturity and inevitable lack of experience. But he was impressive and clearly courageous. I was heard at length; a few questions were put to clarify points, but no answers were made. We did not expect to get them that day.

But I had noticed in the local press that, a day before we met, he had addressed his military leaders, and had assured them that the announced Franco-British mobilization moves were 'all bluff' and could be disregarded. I decided, therefore, to do something which was not within my terms of reference. I asked whether, when our meeting adjourned, I could have a private talk with him. He agreed. I told my colleagues I would see them later at the Legation, and report to them.

I will now set down, from memory of course, but the memory is vivid, our conversation.

Menzies: Nothing I now say is to be regarded as a threat. I have no authority to make one, and I have no desire to make one. But there is one thing I really should say to you with all frankness. You are the trusted leader of your country, and are entitled to be treated with candour. I notice that yesterday you described certain British and French military mobilizations as 'all bluff'. Now, I have just come from London, and I know something of the state of opinion there. I know something of the French state of mind. There seems to be a general assumption in the Egyptian press that the London Conference decided against force. This is not so. The London Conference did not discuss that matter at all; it devoted itself to securing a peaceful settlement by working out fair and constructive proposals. It would, in my opinion, which I offer in the friendliest way and in no sense as an agent, be a mistake for you to exclude the possible use of force from your reckoning. I repeat: the members of my Committee and I are not talking force, or contemplating that it should become either necessary or adopted. But I don't want you to be misled about the state of opinion in London or Paris. No representative of the United Kingdom Government could say this to you without giving you a strong feeling that you were being threatened. But I am certainly not making any threats; I am merely saying to you, in a friendly way, that I believe that it would be a mistake to eliminate the possibility of force altogether from your mind. This is a completely spontaneous and individual observation by me, and I hope you will understand it in the spirit in which it is made.

I added that the Australian Government had given no thought to force;

it would regard any such consideration as not appropriate at a time when its own Prime Minister was busily engaged, on behalf of eighteen nations, in trying to secure a peaceful settlement.

Nasser: I do not at all resent what you have said, nor do I regard it as a threat. I have a great sense of responsibility for my country and its people, and will carefully consider all that has been put to me tonight.

We parted in a most amicable way, and I reported the conversation to my colleagues. As I put it to them, I thought the odds against success had 'shortened from 1,000 to 1 to perhaps 100 to 1'. But next morning, when I read the newspapers, I knew that it was all over. President Eisenhower had spoken.

Both the French and English language newspapers in Cairo carried flaring headlines. They had picked up reports of statements made by President Eisenhower to the American press. Questioned about the possible use of force, he rejected it completely and unconditionally. Asked what would happen next if the eighteen-nation proposals (the 'Dulles' proposals) were rejected, he made it clear that as the United States was committed to a peaceful solution, further proposals would have to be worked out.

His actual words were:

For ourselves, we are determined to exhaust every possible, every feasible method of peaceful settlement . . . and we believe it can be done, and I am not going to comment on what other people are doing. I am very hopeful that this particular proposal will be accepted but, in any event, not to give up, even if we do run into other obstacles.

We are committed to a peaceful settlement of this dispute, *nothing else.*

This, of course, was, though well and honestly meant by the President, all the encouragement Nasser needed. By expressly and unconditionally excluding force, President Eisenhower, who, after all, had played a notable part in the use of force as the *ultima ratio* in a great world conflict, gave the final power into the hands of Nasser, so far as the United States, the greatest military power in the world, was concerned.

As I said in a message to Canberra, 'it is all very well for people to denounce the idea of force, but in a negotiation of this kind, it is good sense to keep the other man guessing.'

For if force was unconditionally excluded, what had Nasser to do except sit tight, reject the Dulles proposals, reject any watered-down proposals that might be made, and continue the process until he had, in the homely phrase, 'written his own ticket'? Meanwhile, his practical grasp of the Canal would be consolidated, and the *fait* would be completely *accompli*.

With unfeigned respect, I cannot regard it as an element in statesmanship to relieve one's opponent of anxiety. In great matters, nations do not commonly commit themselves in advance, in absolute terms, to anything.

But one of the phenomena in American public life, if my many good American friends will forgive me for saying so, is the new dominance of Press, Radio, and Television. These 'media', as they are now called, demand audience and demand answers; and, I regret to say, many American politicians defer to them.

And therefore, at a time when silence would have been golden, the President of the United States, by speaking, relieved us of whatever chance—and a very slim chance it was—we had of success.

Dulles himself had already created an atmosphere in Washington on 28 August. Instead of saying that there were negotiations by a Committee representing the 18-power proposals, that those proposals stood, and 'no comment', he said: 'That is not a matter which is primarily of U.S. concern but primarily of concern to the many countries whose economics are vitally dependent on the Canal.'

The President's intervention meant two things to Nasser. The first was that my friendly warning of the previous evening about the possibilities of force could be ignored, since he would naturally assume that force would not be employed against the will of the United States.

The second was that he could safely reject our proposals, knowing that if he rejected them quite strongly America would be casting about for new proposals which, if they were to have any chance of acceptance, would need to be more favourable to Egypt.

So, when we met in the evening, it was at once clear—one had only to see Nasser's face to know it—that we were finished. Why should he give way, or even make a concession?

Putting on one side the slogans and other rhetorical expressions which ornamented President Nasser's oral arguments, it became quite clear that he had been advised that his action had complete legal authority. He was not alone in this, for, as I had noticed before making my televised speech in London, his views were shared by several English newspapers, and later had considerable currency in America.

In his letter to me of 9 September 1956, answering the one signed by me on behalf of the Committee on 7 September, he went to this point at once.

The starting point of the present crisis was July 26th, 1956, where, in the exercise of one of its prerogatives, the Government of Egypt nationalised the Company which bore the name of 'The Universal Maritime Company of the Suez Canal'. That the Government of Egypt was fully entitled to nationalise that Egyptian Company cannot be seriously contested.

Here, Nasser thought he had a great advantage, and was not slow to make capital of it. If what he had done was lawful, if the Canal belonged to Egypt free of any contractual obligations, then all that the eighteen powers were doing was to ask him graciously to make concessions at his own will.

I had, as I have shown, strong views to the contrary; but, having regard to the proceedings in London, all my Committee could say, in our letter of 7 September, was:

The 18 nations have not attempted to arrive at any joint opinion as to the validity or otherwise of Egypt's nationalisation decree. The London Conference felt that to have a debate on this point would be fruitless, since the conference possessed no authority to make any judicial determination.

This was a position of weakness.

I should add at this stage that after I had returned, with my colleagues, to London to report the failure of our mission, I returned to Australia *via* Washington. I wanted to see President Eisenhower, and he most courteously facilitated a meeting. He said that he had received very favourable reports of my conduct of matters at Cairo. I thanked him, but went on to say (as I thought I should) that whatever faint hope we had of success had completely disappeared when the Egyptian papers, the morning after I had put the case, carried headlines and reports of what he, Eisenhower, had said at a press conference. His statements meant that Nasser could probably get more favourable terms if he rejected the Dulles proposals—for Dulles, I reminded him, had propounded them in London—and that the war-like threats which were then in the air could be disregarded. I felt very nervous about making such statements to an American President for whom I had, and have, such an affectionate personal respect, but he took it very fairly. 'When a press conference is held, the democratic process requires that questions should be answered.'

I said that, as a pretty experienced politician myself, I doubted that proposition. 'Surely,' I said, 'it is always possible to say "no comment", or, better still, to say "there is a trusted Committee handling this difficult matter in Cairo, and I will say nothing".' I added that in London and even in Paris there had been silence. But the President came back to the 'democratic processes', and there was nothing more to be said.

The salient fact was that Nasser had been left in possession of the field, that there was no room left for negotiation, except at a disadvantage, and that France and England were left with a grim choice between surrender, or force.

So, that evening, with a broad and cheerful smile, President Nasser took our proposals apart, tore them up, and metaphorically consigned them to the wastepaper basket. He had frequent recourse to slogans, the principal one of which was that what we were suggesting was 'colonialism in the canal'. He kept repeating this, as a sort of operative phrase. Finally, I said that I for one took no exception to this rather abusive remark, since I had been born a colonial and had become the Prime Minister of what had then become an independent nation. The problem, I said, would never be solved by attaching tags either to people or proposals. I invited my colleagues to say what they would wish to say on this matter. The results were extraordinarily interesting. Loy Henderson, a staunch American, reminded Nasser that the United States could not be accused of colonialism, for it had been a twentieth-century leader in getting rid of the colonial system. He spoke with obvious sincerity and understandable warmth.

Ardalan said, briefly, that had our proposals had any element of colonialism in them, he would not be present, and his Government would never have supported those proposals. Aklilou, of Ethiopia, ventured the observation that anybody who thought that his country favoured colonialism in any form must have a singularly deficient knowledge of modern history. This was a good thrust. And finally Unden, with an almost melancholy touch of humour, said, 'My country had a colony in America. That was many, many years ago. It did not last very long!'

Strange things sometimes befall us in strange countries. Cairo for me was not to prove an exception.

Normally I ate at the Australian Legation with the Cutlers. All vegetables were carefully treated before being cooked; a wise precaution in these romantic but insanitary areas.

After discussion with the Committee, it had been agreed that we were up against a complete rejection; that further conferences would be fruitless; but that it was essential that we should set down in writing what we had been putting to the President, so that it could be on undisputed record for the information of the world.

I undertook the task of drafting this letter, of some thousands of words. I devoted a day to this task. That night, Cutler and I accepted an invitation to dinner at a restaurant. There (I think I must have been over-excited by the discussions) I made the elementary blunder of eating some prawns! Next morning the Committee met, went through the draft and, with one or two verbal amendments, approved of it.

To their surprise, I got up at once—the aftermath of the prawns was making itself known to me—and said, 'There will be no more meetings for thirty-six hours, gentlemen. I will sign this letter when it is ready. But my immediate purpose is to go smartly upstairs, and thereafter divide my time between my bedroom and my bathroom.' They all knew what I meant, but I could not wait for their sympathy.

I looked rather haggard afterwards, and the story got out. Professor Herman Finer, in *Dulles over Suez* (Heinemann) sums it up neatly (on p. 200):

Thus the Menzies mission departed from its visit to Cairo with nothing except a flea in the ear and dysentery!

While we were in Cairo and later, attempts were made to spread a story that there were acute differences of opinion in the Committee, and some unpleasantness.

This was quite untrue. In our many meetings in London we had carefully worked out how the case was to be put, and how prospective arguments should be answered. I was made to feel throughout that, just as the nations they represented had unanimously requested me to take the chairmanship, so did they, as individuals, have confidence in me.

When we presented our report in London, we said, by way of summary:

We should add that we performed our functions of presenting and explaining the London proposals with the complete co-operation of the President. On the substance of those proposals, however, we encountered with regret an immovable resistance to any control or management of the operations and development of the Canal by anybody other than the Government of Egypt itself. In spite of our best and most patient efforts, we constantly came up against such phrases as 'collective colonialism', 'domination' and 'seizure' and what seemed to us to be an unwillingness to meet reason with reason. In the result, therefore, the central proposals of the Eighteen Powers were completely rejected.

I was also able to say, quite accurately, in a short supplement:

One remarkable fact about our discussions both inside the Committee and with the Government of Egypt has been that representatives of five nations from five different continents have been able to work together in such harmony and with such unanimity. I am greatly indebted to my colleagues who have brought this about. Their energy and steadfastness have been a great strength for me upon whom a good deal of the oral argument devolved. From first to last we were all sustained by the belief in the justice and fairness of our proposals.

And my colleagues sent me this letter:

9th September, 1956.

Dear Mr Prime Minister:

We cannot take our leave without expressing to you our deep gratitude and admiration for the high quality of leadership you have displayed as Chairman of our Committee.

Your unfailing courtesy, thoughtfulness, and good humour have leavened our task and made our association one the memory of which we shall always cherish. Your wide experience and knowledge have been of inestimable value in our work. Our unity of purpose could not have been translated into unity of action without you.

Faithfully yours,
(Sgd.) O. UNDEN—Sweden
A. G. ARDALAN—Iran
A. AKLILOU—Ethiopia
L. W. HENDERSON—United States

Rt. Hon. R. G. Menzies, C.H., Q.C.
Prime Minister of Australia.

I hope I may be forgiven for referring to a broadcast made by M. Mollet, the French Prime Minister, in the course of which he said— 'I met Mr Menzies in London. I want to tell him again publicly and to tell the other Members of the Committee of the gratitude of the French Government for the competence and tact with which they have fulfilled their mission.'

Clearly, although we had failed, we were not discredited.

It has been said by some of his critics that Dulles should have gone to the Cairo encounter himself; that if he had done so he would not have been heard later to say that the Canal was not a matter of primary interest for the United States; that the most powerful politician in America would have carried more weight than any of us.

These comments are true enough within their limits. But I well understand why he did not go.

He could hardly have been expected to serve under me; it would have been necessary for him to be chairman and chief spokesman. This I would have most willingly accepted. But it would have put the United States into a position when it would appear as a direct partisan. Of course it was in substance a partisan, for Dulles was the first and true inventor of the proposals we carried with us, but no doubt he did not want to put his country too far out on the limb. And, in any event, Loy Henderson, his alternate, was a splendid and co-operative colleague. But, conceding all this, Dulles's absence from Cairo and his return to Washington had certain effects, as I would judge, on his own state of mind. His physical remoteness induced a sort of intellectual remoteness. He tended to revert to legalism at home; became much less the party, and much more the censor.

I was not personally involved in the later proceedings in the United Nations. They are all matters of record, and I need not recite them. But, from the remote fastnesses of Canberra, I found myself puzzling about how it came about that the Dulles of the first London Conference, clearly convinced of the injustice of Nasser's actions, could have moved into a position in which, as several commentators have said, he became, for the United Nations, the prosecutor of Great Britain and France, and *ipso facto* (though I am sure he did not think of it in this sense) the defender of Nasser. For, in the long run, it was the attitude of Dulles which dominated the General Assembly.

It is clear, it was made quite clear to us in Cairo, that Nasser, particularly after President Eisenhower's press interview, but perhaps clearly enough before it, felt that, even assuming that his proclamation was invalid, he was the man in possession, and that possession was nine points of the law. It was the United Nations which later gave him the tenth point, and made his title absolute. For to push Great Britain and France out of the Canal Zone under threat of sanctions was to confirm Nasser's actions, which eighteen nations, led by the United States, had condemned in London.

The only man who can look back on it all with satisfaction is President Nasser himself. For he got the Canal; he humbled two of the world's great powers; he spread his prestige and his authority over a great part of the Arab world. He had defied the United Nations over the Israeli shipping issue; he got its backing over the Canal; and had profited from both. The whole series of events, disastrous though they have been for the Western World, were a tribute to Nasser's talent, boldness, and force of character.

When I got back to Australia, it was quite clear that the use of force was becoming a very dangerous issue between Great Britain and France and the United States administration. I therefore decided that, in making my report to the Australian Parliament, after very close consultation with Cabinet, I should say something about this sensitive issue which might prove to be a contribution to thought on both sides of the Atlantic. It should constantly be remembered that the proposals put to Nasser were introduced and expounded to the London Conference by the United States Secretary of State with, one is bound to assume, the full backing of President Eisenhower. If the only idea was that they should be presented to Nasser, and that if he rejected them the incident should be treated as closed, then some of us, duly entrusted with the task, were clearly wasting our time and nervous energy, for the odds against acceptance were prohibitive. I for one thought, and I understood Foster Dulles to agree, that perhaps the prime purpose of the exercise was to demonstrate to the world the utter fairness and reasonableness of the eighteen-nation proposals, to establish the record, so to speak, and to make it clear that on these matters the United States, Great Britain, and sixteen other nations in Europe, Asia, and Africa were of one mind. I did not regard myself as going to Cairo to conduct a debating-society exercise.

Speaking to my own Parliament on 25 September 1956, with the backing of my own Government, I narrated the course of events. I set out my reasons (to which I have referred earlier) for the view that Nasser's action had been a breach of international law.

I pointed out that the reaction in Great Britain had been very strong. I reminded the House at Canberra that, on 2 August, Sir Anthony Eden had said:

In these circumstances, and in view of the uncertain situation created by the action of the Egyptian Government, Her Majesty's Government have thought it necessary ... to take certain precautionary measures of a military nature ... to strengthen our position in the Eastern Mediterranean and our ability to deal with any situation that may arise.

To this Mr Gaitskell, then Leader of the Labour Party, had said:
'I do not myself object to the precautionary steps announced by the Prime Minister; I think that any Government would have to do that,' while Herbert Morrison, who had served under Churchill and had a great native faculty for direct speech, thought it wrong to exclude the use of force should other measures fail.

When, in the course of my own Parliamentary statement, I came to this problem myself, I made an analysis which I think I should now repeat. I do so because it was, before many months, to become the fashion both in Great Britain and the United States to decry the Anglo-French military operation and to heap obloquy upon the theretofore honoured name of Anthony Eden himself.

What I said was this—and with all the advantages or disadvantages of hind-sight I shall adhere to it:

The question of force calls for a cool and clear answer. There has been a great variety of vocal opinion, ranging between what I call two extreme views.

One view is that force should at once have been used to defeat a confiscation by force. This view is out of harmony with modern thinking; at any rate, this side of the iron curtain.

The other is that force can never be employed (except presumably in self-defence) except by and pursuant to a decision of the United Nations Security Council. This I would regard as a suicidal doctrine for, having regard to the existence of the veto, it would mean that no force could ever be exercised against any friend of the Soviet Union except with the approval of the Soviet Union, which is absurd. The public exponents of this view have been much heard during the weeks of the Canal negotiations. Their opinions have enjoyed great prominence in Egypt, and profoundly and obviously influenced the current of our conferences with Colonel Nasser in Cairo. They ended by convincing the Egyptian Government (which was quite willing to be convinced) that there was no danger in rejecting our proposals; that, force being absolutely out, Egypt could afford to sit back, agree to nothing, carry off the spoils of victory, and further build up its prestige.

Each of these extreme views must, I believe, be rejected.

The truth is that, in a world not based on academic principles, a world deeply affected by enlightened self-interest and the instinct of survival, but nevertheless a world struggling to make an organization for peace effective, force (except for self-defence) is never to be the first resort, but the right to employ it cannot be completely abandoned or made subject to impossible conditions.

Let me say, quite plainly, that the whole lively and evolving history of the British Empire and the British Commonwealth of Nations was not the product of any theory. It has been, from first to last, a practical matter, an inductive process, like the slow creation of the Common Law and of all the great instruments of self-government. It would be a sad day if it allowed itself to be theorized out of existence. We need not get into a timid state of mind in which the very mention of the word 'force' becomes forbidden. There is no community of nations which can say, with a clearer conscience, that it has set a great twentieth-century example of using force only when forced into it, and then not for conquest but for resistance to aggression.

But does this mean that we are to be helpless in the presence of an accomplished threat to our industrial and economic future? I believe not. Is our task to 'patch up' peace and no more? Surely our task is not merely to prevent hostilities but to build up a firm order of law and decency, in which 'smash and grab' tactics do not pay. We must avoid the use of force if we can. But we should not, by theoretical reasoning in advance of the facts and circumstances, contract ourselves out of its use *whatever those facts and circumstances may be.*

It should be recalled that before I spoke in Parliament, the Second London Conference had constituted a Suez Canal Users' Association which was designed to promote Canal traffic and to hold and disburse revenues. Quite clearly, the Association was still-born, for by then Nasser was in command; and the position of the United States was becoming equivocal. I thought and wrote at the time that the scheme seemed to me to be about as workable as trying to run two different sets of railway managers on one set of railway lines. And so I came to the final analysis:

Should the United Nations, by reason of the veto, prove unable to direct any active course of positive action, we may find ourselves confronted by a choice which we cannot avoid making. I state the choice in stark terms:

(a) We can organise a full-blooded programme of economic sanctions against Egypt, or

(b) we can use force to restore international control of the Canal, or

(c) we can have further negotiation, provided we do not abandon vital principles, or

(d) we can 'call it a day', leave Egypt in command of the Canal, and resign ourselves to the total collapse of our position and interests in the Middle East, with all the implications for the economic strength and industrial prosperity of nations whose well-being is vital to ours.

It is, I suppose, unwise to be too positive about that strange *mélange* of disunited nations known as the United Nations. But clearly, so far as the Suez Canal was concerned, no favourable action by the Security Council, with the Soviet Union, Nasser's most vocal backer, possessing the veto, could be expected, while the General Assembly, though notoriously disposed to arrogate to itself a sort of executive authority since the 'Uniting for Peace' Resolutions, has not been noted for giving support to any 'old colonial' power. In fact, when the time came, it clearly relished the opportunity of coming down in favour of Nasser.

So I must say to my readers—'What would you have done had you been the Governments in London and Paris?'

Further negotiation, except in the form of a thinly disguised capitulation, was impossible. International action by way of economic sanctions could not be secured. So, would your answer have been 'Look the other way, and do nothing?'

Such policies of retreat from vital principles have been tried before, and still have their advocates. But they breed nothing but disaster, and ultimately lead to war at a disadvantage.

I had spoken plainly about this matter on my return to Australia on 18 September 1956.

The truth of the matter is that the President of Egypt has not been exercising a legal right. He produced this crisis by repudiating the concession granted to the Suez Canal Company. Indeed, it is very well worth noting that as recently as June of this year, he executed with the Company a periodical agreement with relation to charges and such matters for the duration of the balance of the concession. That is to say until 1968. Yet within six weeks, he had repudiated the concession giving as the reason that he wanted the money that was earned in the Canal to help to pay for the Aswan Dam—a singular excuse for a grossly illegal act.

It is also overlooked by those who talk a good deal about force, either for it or against it, that this repudiation by the President of Egypt was committed without notice, without consent, and in fact, by force, because he took over the property and tackle of the Suez Canal Company by installing armed men and taking over possession. Those things are worth remembering.

This crisis was a *crisis produced by repudiation and force.*

At the end of October, fighting having begun between Israel and Egypt, Britain and France sent their joint message to both countries. The one to Egypt was:

The Governments of the United Kingdom and France have taken note of the outbreak of hostilities between Israel and Egypt. This event threatens to disrupt the freedom of navigation through the Suez Canal, on which the economic life of many nations depends. The Governments of the United Kingdom and France are resolved to do all in their power to bring about the early cessation of hostilities and to safeguard the free passage of the Canal. They accordingly request the Government of Egypt:

(a) to stop all warlike action on land, sea and air forthwith;
(b) to withdraw all Egyptian forces to a distance of ten miles from the Canal; and
(c) in order to guarantee freedom of transit through the Canal by the ships of all nations and in order to separate the belligerents, to accept the temporary occupation of Anglo-French forces of key positions at Port Said, Ismailia and Suez.

The United Kingdom and French Governments request an answer to this communication within twelve hours. If at the expiration of that time one or both Governments have not undertaken to comply with the above requirements, United Kingdom and French forces will intervene in whatever strength may be necessary to secure compliance.

A similar document was sent to Israel.

Israel agreed. Egypt refused.

And so the great incident occurred. Great Britain and France put troops into the Canal Zone, and were ordered out by a General Assembly resolution which would have been impotent but for the support of the United States. Clearly, to me, the action taken by Great Britain and France was *police* action; the only quick and practical means of separating the belligerents and protecting the Canal.

On 3 November 1956, in Australia, I said:

If the United Nations Assembly accepts the idea of a United Nations police force in and around the Canal, and the Security Council adopts it and acts on it, the object of protection of the Canal will have been achieved. Meanwhile, it is clear that Britain and France cannot withdraw. Police action, to be effective, must be continuous while the danger exists.

And I went on to say, with some bitterness—'That the author of the Suez Canal confiscation and the promoter of anti-British and anti-Israel activities in the Middle East should now be represented as the innocent victim of unprovoked aggression is, of course, both wrong and absurd.'

This, I have been told, was not the way in which an Australian Prime Minister should have spoken. I should have been neutral, and temporizing. But Australians are not devoted to the principle of neutrality.

Five days later, I made a statement in the House of Representatives at Canberra, after a 'cease-fire' had followed an announcement by the United Nations. I reviewed the Israel-Egypt situation, and what Britain and France had done by way of military intervention. I went on to say, and I was speaking for the Australian Government, 'They have, I believe, been well justified in the result. It is *just because they took strong action that the United Nations itself has been galvanized into action.*

'I would think badly of myself, and my colleagues would think badly of themselves, if we remained silent or neutral under circumstances in which the Government of the United Kingdom has been assailed for taking action which we regard as both practical and courageous.'

So there it was; right on the line. I know that it has become fashionable to condemn Anthony Eden, to say that he ruined his great and deserved reputation as Foreign Secretary of Great Britain by his 'inept' handling of the Suez crisis.

Of all the politicians now surviving this event, I should be the last to adopt this fashion; for I still think that he was right.

A few days after the Statement I have just quoted, I made another speech to the Federal Council of the Liberal Party of Australia. I would apologize for quoting myself if it were not for the fact that I have no desire to revise the past or take refuge in a latter-day wisdom. These crucial events were hot news, and the matter of current controversy. And, as I am writing *my* Suez Story, for what it is worth, I must expose my own mind with all frankness.

In this speech, on 12 November 1956, I said:

I wonder whether there would be a United Nations force in Egypt if the British and French had stayed at home.

This question, I thought, admitted of only one answer.

But was I wrong? Suppose Britain and France had meekly accepted defeat, and had abandoned the eighteen-nation proposals as completely as Washington had abandoned them, but the Israeli forces had pressed on. There can be no doubt that they would have reached the Canal, which would at once have been littered with the wreckage of war. There can be little doubt that, in the absence of intervention by one of the great powers (the Soviet Union?) they would have defeated Nasser in Cairo itself.

What would the United Nations have done about it? And how long would it have taken for it to organize its forces and its position?

It is little wonder that these terrible and historically tragic events caused a great breach in Anglo-American relations, a breach now happily repaired.

I made a public statement about this in Australia on 30 November 1956.

If, from now on, constructive efforts are to be made to repair the breach which has occurred in Anglo-American relations, it seems quite clear that the approach should be that of realism and not that of theory. The first thing is to get the facts right. I have doubts as to whether, even now, they are as clearly understood in the United States of America as they are in Australia. It seems to me that the stark facts of the present situation in the Middle East could be put in this way. Great Britain and France have been ordered out of Egypt by the General Assembly of the United Nations. Their forces are being replaced by a fragmentary United Nations force which is pretty clearly not designed to be a fighting body. The whole operation appears to be based on the consent of Colonel Nasser and subject to whatever conditions he thinks fit to impose. This means that Egypt's military defeat having been arrested on the very threshold, Colonel Nasser remains in possession of the field and appears to be dictating terms as if he were a victor. The Soviet Union is notoriously supplying implements of war to both Egypt and Syria, and possibly to other Arab States. Israel, having been ordered out of the territory which she captured so swiftly from the Egyptians, finds herself once more hemmed in by those who are hostile to her and whose capacity to attack her is being steadily built up.

And then:

Meanwhile, Colonel Nasser, without any condemnation by a General Assembly which appears to have been so eager to divert its attention from the massacre of Hungary that it has concentrated all its fury upon Great Britain and France, has sabotaged the Canal, has directed the sinking of many vessels in it, and has put it out of action for many months. In the meantime, the current oil supplies of Great Britain and Western Europe have been terribly reduced, petrol rationing has been re-introduced, and a great deal of unemployment seems inevitable. We are thus witnessing a state of affairs in which Russian morale has been elevated; the already difficult economic situation of Great Britain aggravated; the prestige of Great Britain and France in the Middle East swept aside; and the basis of Western European defence, which includes the maintenance of defensive positions in the Middle East, gravely impaired.

It may be believed by theoretically minded people that when the British and French forces leave under orders, the Suez Canal problem will be back where it began. . . .

I would like to remind all of the 18 nations that the very essence of the proposals which my colleagues and I were sent to Cairo to present was that the character of the Suez Canal as a free international waterway must be preserved by taking the operation of the Canal out of the political control of any one nation. It is to be hoped that the 18 nations will not forget about this and that it will continue to be regarded by them as their major task to bring that result about. . . .

My voice was a small voice, and these words were no doubt spoken in vain. But, faint yet pursuing, I came back to the matter on 5 December, after a full discussion in the Australian Cabinet.

Ministers have today given very careful consideration to the current state of affairs arising from the agreed withdrawal by the United Kingdom and France of their forces from the Suez Canal.

In retrospect, the United Kingdom and France can truly say that their intervention in Egypt, however grossly it may have been misrepresented, halted the spread of hostilities in the Middle East.

The United Kingdom and France can also truly say that but for their intervention the United Nations might have been confronted by the need to pronounce upon a much graver situation than that with which the General Assembly had to deal. The United Nations might well have been called upon to send in, not a police force of limited size to operate under conditions of cease fire, but a substantial fighting force capable of separating actual combatants. Further, it can properly be said that but for Anglo-French action there is no reason to assume that the United Nations would have intervened either promptly or effectively.

In the course of subsequent discussions over the years, I have come to know that American State Department opinion tended to the view that Nasser's 'nationalization' of the Canal and its operations could not be distinguished from the British Labour Government's 'nationalization' of the British iron and steel industry. This was and is, to me, a false analogy. The iron and steel industry in Britain is a purely domestic matter. Though it may do a good deal of international business, and may, for all I know, have some foreign shareholders, it has no international status. It may be dealt with by the Parliament at Westminster as it thinks fit. Indeed, as Great Britain has no written constitution, Parliament could direct the taking over of any domestic industry on any terms it chose to declare.

There is no parallel between such a 'nationalization' and the action taken by Nasser, which, for the reasons I have set out, was a high-handed repudiation of an international contract which had the essential character of an international law.

But there can be no doubt that the great cause of what became a sometimes bitter dispute between the United States and Great Britain and France was the use of force by the latter. This was, in Washington, regarded as a blatant breach of the Charter of the United Nations, under which, the Administration felt, force must not be used without the authority of the United Nations except in direct self-defence, or within the scope of the Charter, pursuant to a regional treaty, such as NATO or SEATO, recorded with the United Nations and recognized as having been made within its structure and terms.

This state of mind has two inherent dangers.

The first is that it has persuaded some prominent Americans to believe that to take a matter to the United Nations is itself an act of policy, and that, the matter having entered that jurisdiction, whatever result may emerge will be authoritative. But surely this doctrine involves the abandonment of responsibility, and may prove to be fatal to vital national interests which no nation can safely ignore. A great nation which takes a matter to the United Nations without first working out with great care what it wishes the United Nations to do, accepts two devastating risks.

One is that in the Security Council, which still remains the only organ with direct executive powers, it will be confronted by the veto.

The other is that, under the new-found authority of the General Assembly, it will probably find itself out-voted by a growing number of relatively small nations, whose passions are easily aroused, and who for the most part lack political maturity.

I will add a little to what I said earlier about the alleged legality of Nasser's action.

A learned writer in the United States, Mr Louis Henkin, in *International Law and the Behaviour of Nations*, finds in the ultimate humiliation of Great Britain and France at the hands of the United Nations a notable 'vindication' of international law. Great Britain and France, he believes, violated that law; they should have gone to the United Nations, and acted strictly under its direction.

To me, this view is utterly unrealistic. The same writer admits that 'Nasser did not have to fear judgement. In the Security Council he could count on the protection of a Soviet veto; in the General Assembly he could command enough votes to prevent a two-thirds vote against him.'

In other words, Nasser could succeed in both Security Council and General Assembly *with a minority of the votes!* Yet Great Britain and France, each of whom had great interests at stake, are condemned for not taking these matters to so strange a tribunal!

The United Nations had already proved to be a broken reed when it came to Canal matters. Neither of these great nations had forgotten (nor had any of us concerned in these matters) that on 1 September 1951, the Security Council had passed a Resolution relating to issues which had arisen between Israel and the neighbouring Arab States, including Egypt.

It solemnly declared, overruling Egypt's submission to the contrary, that:

since the Armistice régime, which has been in existence for nearly two and a half years, is of a permanent character, neither party can reasonably assert that it is actively a belligerent or requires to exercise the right of visit, search, and seizure for any legitimate purpose of self-defence.

It concluded its Resolution with a fine flourish. It would show what it could do! So it *called* upon Egypt

to terminate the restrictions on the passage of international commercial shipping and goods through the Suez Canal wherever bound and to cease all interference with such shipping beyond that essential to the safety of shipping in the Canal itself and to the observance of the international conventions in force.

In a preceding paragraph it had identified the restrictions it was dealing with, in these words:

The restrictions on the passage of goods through the Suez Canal to Israel ports are denying to nations at no time connected with the conflict in Palestine valuable supplies required for their economic reconstruction, and these restrictions, together with sanctions applied by Egypt to certain ships which have visited Israel ports, represent unjustified interference with the rights of nations to navigate the seas and to trade freely with one another, including the Arab States and Israel.

So here the world saw a triumphant vindication of international law. But what happened? History records the answer. Nothing!

Egypt treated the Security Council with contempt, and continued to exclude Israeli shipping from the use of the Canal. Perhaps it sometimes wondered what the Security Council might do. It did nothing. It made it clear to all practical observers—including of course Israel—that while legal theory, so far as it has achieved any certainty in international affairs, pointed to the supposed authority of the United Nations, the ancient law of self-preservation in a hard and sometimes urgent world pointed away from it.

For Egypt consistently maintained its attitude that it was still 'at war' with Israel. When, in 1956, Israel decided that war was a two-sided affair, invaded Egypt, and drove the Egyptian forces into disorderly retreat, the corridors and meeting-places at the United Nations rang with indignant condemnations of Israel—not of Egypt!

But for the action of Great Britain and France in announcing that both sides must cease fire, and remain ten miles from the Canal; and that temporarily Anglo-French forces would move into key positions at Port Said, Ismalia, and Suez, there is reason to believe that the Egyptians would have continued to be beaten back. The Canal would have been blocked by the wreckage of war, but Nasser's visions of Empire would have been gravely impaired.

The truth is that John Foster Dulles, who was in effective control of United States' policies on the Suez matter, possessed a strong and legalistic mind. But he was from time to time given to moralizing about distant affairs, and admonishing distant nations.

I still wonder what would have happened if the Republic of Panama, in an angry mood, had appropriated the Panama Canal, the creation of the United States under a solemn agreement! (Some time in the future, it may do so; who knows?), I feel sure that the mood in the State Department would have been different. Foster Dulles would not have been able to say 'The Panama Canal is not a primary interest of the United States'. American public opinion would have been violently aroused. I cannot believe that a humble acceptance of whatever the United Nations might or might not do, of action or inaction, would have been felt to be a satisfactory solution of a great American national problem, in which vital American shipping and trading interests were deeply involved.

I can never forget that, in his notable speech at the first London

Conference, a speech which I listened to with close attention, and which I later supported with enthusiasm, John Foster Dulles had said some powerful things. I will quote some of them which had a particular relevance to my subsequent task:

... On 26th July, 1956, the Egyptian Government, *acting unilaterally and without any prior international consultation* of which we are aware, issued a decree purporting to nationalise the Universal Suez Canal Company, and to take over all its property and rights pertaining thereto, and to terminate its rights, affirmed by the 1888 Convention, to operate the canal until 1968. The installations of the Suez Canal Company were then physically taken over by the Egyptian Government. Its employees were prevented from leaving their work without Egyptian Government permission under penalty of imprisonment.

... *The United States does not believe the Egyptian Government had the right to wipe out that Convention* establishing the rights of the Universal Suez Company until 1968. This arrangement had the status of an international compact; many relied upon it. The operating rights and assets of that Company were impressed with an international interest. The Government of the United States questions that the Government of Egypt had the right unilaterally to take its action of July 26th last.

Some years later, Foster Dulles was at a conference in Australia, and I took the opportunity of having a talk with him about the Suez incident. I repeat it here because it served to illustrate how interwoven with Dulles's moral reflections were the legalisms which, in my experience, always attracted him.

'Foster,' I said, 'I've been wanting to ask you something about Formosa, or Taiwan, and the occasional threat we have lived through by Communist China against Quemoy and the Matsus. Suppose word came through that China was mounting an amphibious attack through these islands and towards Formosa. What would your reaction be? Would you take the matter to the United Nations, or would you order in the United States fleet?'

His reply was instant: 'Order in the fleet, of course!'

'Well,' said I, 'why did you take Great Britain and France to the United Nations in 1956? Their vital interests in the Suez Canal were not inferior to yours in Formosa. Indeed, for most of us, including them, the matters at stake were probably more significant.'

His reply was interesting: 'But we have a treaty with Formosa!'

'So,' I rejoined, 'if Great Britain and France, or I suppose either of them, had had a treaty with, say, Israel, whose ships were being denied the passage of the Canal in the very teeth of United Nations resolutions, your position would have been different.'

His reply was that the state of affairs would have required consideration.

Our difference, of course, went beyond a mere matter of semantics. As I have stated earlier, my own view was that Nasser's seizure of the Canal was a gross breach of international law, and therefore an offence against the whole purpose of the United Nations. I imagine, though I cannot be sure, that at bottom, Dulles did not agree with that view. It followed, if I am right, that in his mind, and in spite of what he had said in London, the Franco-British action lacked legal justification because Nasser's action had a valid legal foundation.

Postscript

The circumstances of book publication required that my writing should conclude as at early June 1967 just as a dramatic series of events had begun in the Middle East. For my present purpose those events lend point to my narrative in this chapter.

On page 179 I referred to a 'fragmentary United Nations force which is pretty clearly not designed to be a fighting body. The whole operation appeared to be based on the consent of Colonel Nasser'. We now know that when Nasser felt that the time had come to strike he told the United Nations to remove its Force and the United Nations meekly obeyed! It is clear to me that the United Nations' performance in 1956 built up Nasser's position and prestige, fatally damaged the regional influence of Great Britain and France and made the position of Israel desperately precarious. In brief, it increased the possibilities of aggressive war in one of the World's critical areas.

This cannot be regarded as one of its great achievements!

CHAPTER NINE

A CRITICAL EXAMINATION OF
THE MODERN COMMONWEALTH

W HEN A MAN is politically engaged, and particularly when he is a political leader, he must, in a substantial sense, speak for others. He cannot indulge in the luxury of 'going on a frolic of his own'. He is a member of a team. This is not to say that, for the sake of conformity, he will abandon fundamental beliefs which are close to his heart and inspire the convictions of his mind. I was fortunate in my Australian colleagues. On vital matters we could always formulate a joint opinion which I had no difficulty or reservations in expressing. But no leader, especially when he is Prime Minister, is 'at large'. It is not for him, while in office, to expose the innermost secrets of his own mind. I am now 'at large'. Nothing I now write can be properly imputed to others. I am writing as one who has, over many years, had some part to play in Commonwealth development, who has had many anxieties, who loves his political inheritance and would wish to preserve it, and who now, in his afternoon, proceeds to set down his thoughts, with much affection, if you like, but without fear or favour. The new Commonwealth cannot survive and be useful unless we are prepared to face the facts and do what we can to arrest wrong trends. It is in that spirit that I write this chapter, which is a mixture of autobiography, historical record, and political philosophy.

I like to think that my former political colleagues will share my beliefs in a substantial way; to say that is to express a sort of nostalgic pride in a long and happy association; but if anybody is to be criticized for the inmost thoughts which I here disclose, it is myself.

I write this to put the record straight, and not by way of apology. For if I, as one who has attended more Prime Ministers' Conferences than anyone else, and who has been involved in some of the most acute crises in Commonwealth history, cannot be expected, after his retirement from active affairs, to speak his mind, who is ever to do it?

And there is much to say, as will appear as my narrative proceeds.

In the year of my birth—1894—Queen Victoria was on the throne of the United Kingdom and Ireland and the Dominions and Colonies beyond the Seas. She presided over 'the British Empire', and was specifically the Empress of India. *Regina et Imperatrix*. For us, the maps of the world were patterned with great areas of red, at a time when red was a respectable colour.

It seemed to be a settled world, and on the whole a good one. And of all the ancient landmarks that might be moved the British Empire seemed to be the most unlikely. I have seen all of this change; and the changes have been far more than those of form.

By the time of the First World War, Australia, South Africa, and New Zealand had been added to Canada as completely self-governing 'Dominions', as they were soon to be called. Each of them participated in the First World War with unstinted patriotism and sacrifice.

In 1926 the famous, but I fear now obsolete, 'Balfour formula' was evolved, to give expression to the new status, which it was agreed had been richly earned; and the discussions which led to the Statute of Westminster began. The Prime Ministers—at that time there were but five of them—no doubt regarded the new formula as not only historic, but actually definitive. The Dominions were, by common consent, declared to be 'autonomous communities', 'in no way subordinate one to another', 'united by a common allegiance to the Crown'. These Dominions were to be 'within the British Empire', and were to constitute 'the British Commonwealth of Nations'.

So defined, this was the British Commonwealth at the time at which I became involved in politics. For many years after I went to Canberra, I could and did speak of it with emotion. For it was something in the blood; it connoted a common allegiance, and a great brotherhood. So much did I believe in the elements of the Balfour Definition (though I had never thought a formula necessary) that some years later I came to be referred to as an Empire or Commonwealth 'statesman'.

And then the changes began. If they had affected form only and had left the substance unimpaired, we could have said that when we commit the initial error of reducing the intimate and impalpable and even emotional to formal terms, we must expect verbal changes from time to time. But in 1948 and 1949, when I was Leader of the Opposition in the Australian Parliament, the first great substantial change came. It was fundamental, but because somebody thought of 'a form of words', it was hailed as a proof of the inexhaustible adaptability of the Commonwealth.

The Prime Ministers, in April 1949, approved of India remaining in the Commonwealth as a Republic. In one stroke, the common allegiance to the Crown ceased to be *the* bond of union, and the 'British Commonwealth' became 'the Commonwealth'. As a basis of agreement, India 'accepted the King as the symbol of the free association of . . . the member nations, and as such the Head of the Commonwealth'.

The precedent thus established has been followed, as it inevitably had to be, with the result that modern applications by former British colonies to be members of the Commonwealth 'as Republics' have become a commonplace, and are accepted, save in the case of South Africa, as almost matters of routine. Nkrumah of Ghana emphasized how much a matter of routine it was when he went to London, was sworn in as a Privy Councillor—and, as I know, the Privy Councillor's oath is just about the most royalist expression in the world—then promptly returned home and declared for a Republic, of which he would be the first President! After that cynical performance, it was not possible for me to have any personal respect for him; but at least he did make it clear that the old Commonwealth bond had gone. When we were all related by a common allegiance, our relationship was organic and internal; it still is for most of the older members. But for the Republicans, the relationship is in a sense functional and certainly external.

J. C. Smuts was opposed to this, and, for that matter, so was I. But neither of us was in office. The great change was made.

Now, however a monarchist might regret these events, I, for one, learned to live with them. After all, there were some elements in the association which could and should survive. Our association could still be a special one, with a special sense of relationship which could be unique in the modern world. Here we were, 'autonomous' communities, equal in all things, 'in no way subordinate one to another'.

Commonwealth Prime Ministers could still meet in conference, exchange views, agree or disagree; have no votes or resolutions, but announce to the world such concerted ideas as could be unanimously agreed upon.

But in the very latest conferences which I attended, a great change began to manifest itself. Some of the newer nations in particular displayed a keen desire to intervene in the domestic affairs of others, and to sit in judgement upon them. This came to a head in the case of South Africa, to which I will return a little later. It has been further developed in relation to Rhodesia.

Before I deal with these two cases, I think that I should set down some of my own observations on the kind of modern development which in my opinion, and I record it with sorrow, threatens to convert the Commonwealth into an organization (if something so lacking in structure can be called an 'organization') which no longer expresses unity but exists chiefly to ventilate differences, even to advertise conflicts, and to develop pressures upon individual members, frequently without reason and not infrequently for bad reasons.

The first symptoms of this modern disease appeared when certain new Prime Ministers began to equip themselves, at Prime Ministers' Conferences, with 'Public Relations' organizations, with the prime purpose of press publicity for carefully prepared speeches. Prime Ministers' conferences were always held in private, so that frankness and informality could be encouraged. This was changed in fact, though not in theory, for two reasons. The first reason is that we have many more Prime Ministers—now the better part of thirty—and the large Conference Room at Marlborough House is jammed full of people. Quiet discussion is impossible. All intimacy disappears. Each 'speech' is one made to something very like a public meeting. Political leaders, when they address a public meeting, seldom make the helpful concessions which are possible in a small and friendly conference. The second reason is that such 'public' speeches tend increasingly to be directed to the 'home' audience thousands of miles away ('Did you see how our man made them sit up?') and so I became accustomed to reading in the London afternoon press the text of a speech not yet actually delivered.

This, I think, is a deplorable development. It brings into what was the special and intimate relationship of the Commonwealth the worst techniques of the United Nations. I fear that, unless the tide turns, we will some day read of resolutions, and amendments, and votes, and 'abstentions' in Prime Ministers' Conferences, and the last shreds of cohesion will disappear.

These tendencies present a great challenge to Commonwealth political leaders. Most of them, I believe, attach value and significance to the Commonwealth. A few regard it as a platform or sounding-board. Conscious effort, and a concerted self-discipline will be needed if the Commonwealth is to survive as more than an honoured memory and a splendid name.

There is another comment which needs to be made. I have never been able to believe that, when a former colony is granted full political independence, it can be substantially endowed, by agreement or decree, with democratic institutions. If it is to have real autonomy, it must, of course, adopt its own form of government, which in many cases will assume an autocratic form, gathered around the personality of the leader of the independence movement. This is a matter for understanding, and not complaint or pressure. If the then President of Ghana, Kwame Nkrumah, chose to have a one-party state and put his leading opponents into some kind of detention, I did not think it necessary to invoke either Commonwealth debate or Commonwealth action, though clearly there was no more of a true democratic system, as we understand and practise it, in Ghana than there is in South Africa; probably much less.

But, at a series of Prime Ministers' Conferences, I became accustomed to hearing some African leaders, themselves devoted to the 'one-party' state, demanding, with tedious repetition, the adoption, by others, of 'one man, one vote'.

One afternoon, at Marlborough House I had a frank and full-blooded discussion on this fundamentally deceptive slogan. What I said was (and I admit I engaged in quite a bit of reiteration myself), 'In my country we are familiar with the principle of "one man, one vote", and have practised it for many generations. With us it means "one man, one vote, with a choice of candidates". Can all of you say that this is what you want? Of course not. Your one-party states exclude a choice of candidates. You have rejected Parliamentary democracy, which requires a choice of parties and of people. So it is really very tiresome to hear this slogan of yours pronounced as if you really wanted democracy.'

But it was all in vain; they had an admirable faculty of laughter when the arguments became pressing, and so they laughed.

Thus it came about that some of us found ourselves required to listen to demands for 'one man, one vote' in Rhodesia, when we knew perfectly well that what was being demanded by some of the advocates, not all, was that without delay the Rhodesian Constitution should be amended to put every adult person on the voters' roll—which would produce an immediate African majority, and that, this having been achieved, only one Party should be permitted, the minority (the European Rhodesians) being free, perhaps, in an economic sense, but politically voiceless.

I think I know the comment that will be made on this statement. It is that in countries like South Africa and Rhodesia the majority of people are not represented either effectively or at all and that therefore the white people are in command, and the coloured people voiceless. So why complain if the position is reversed? The point could be well taken, provided that one great condition is accepted.

The right to vote should be approximately related to the capacity to vote. In British democracies, universal suffrage and universal education go hand in hand. The recent history of the Congo should be sufficient proof that a premature grant of self-government can lead to a great community disaster. A basically uneducated community will mean a basically uneducated electorate; in which case there will be a dictator or a small oligarchy. Freedom will not result.

In considering the growth of self-government, therefore, the time-table is very important. My immediate purpose is to question the idea that the first thing to be done in a new country is to give everybody a vote. It is fascinating to observe the modern power of the slogan. It is part of the world of propaganda in which so many of the new leaders have grown up and come to power. I will have something more to say about this when I come in detail to the Rhodesian episode. Meantime, it is sufficient to say that at the modern Commonwealth meetings the differences of interpretation of what might appear to be a common vocabulary are so great that misunderstandings have become inevitable. And, under the new rules, misunderstandings are better advertised than any substance of agreement could ever hope to be.

7*

In the early part of 1960 all my thinking about the Commonwealth was brought to a head by two events. The first was that Cambridge invited me to deliver the first Smuts Memorial Lecture, and that I accepted and chose as my subject 'The Changing Commonwealth'. The second was that the shootings at Sharpeville gave rise to world-wide denunciations of South African racial policy. There was much hysteria. Those least encumbered by knowledge shouted the loudest. There were proposals, which I confess I did not then take seriously, that South Africa should be expelled from the Commonwealth! Asked in Parliament, I said that we would not intervene.

On 31 March 1960, the then new Leader of the Opposition at Canberra (Mr Calwell) moved that the circumstances of Sharpeville should be 'listed for discussion at the forthcoming Prime Ministers' Conference', and accused me of 'condoning' the attitude of the South African Government.

In the course of the debate, I pointed out that so far from 'condoning' the events in South Africa, as Mr Calwell had alleged, I had said that 'we were following a policy of non-intervention in what is, though tragic and terrible, a domestic problem for the Union of South Africa'. Having been challenged to offer my personal opinions, I said, 'One of the inhibitions that is laid upon the man who is the head of the Government of Australia is that his personal feelings are a luxury in which he cannot publicly indulge when the real problem is what political attitude the government should take and express. This is a great responsibility. It requires calm judgement and a sense of responsibility to the future as well as to the present.'

I went to some pains to point out to the Parliament that we must not, in the flurry of the moment, establish a precedent which could prove to be most damaging. 'If the domestic jurisdiction principle is abandoned in the heat of the moment, so to speak, we may live to see the day when other nations, whether in the United Nations or otherwise, will seek to discuss our aboriginal policies and claim as a precedent whatever action occurs in relation to South Africa. We hope and believe that we will never have incidents of the kind now under discussion, but all these things are matters of degree; and a point of principle, once surrendered, is not easily recaptured.' All this occurred at a time when a Prime Ministers' Conference was to meet in London in May. By the time of Sharpeville I had drafted my Smuts Memorial Lecture; before long I doubted whether it would ever be delivered except in a quite new form.

In Australia the currents of opinion ran noisily. The question of who should vote in South Africa was elevated into a moral, and even a religious issue. The greatest denunciations fell from the lips of people who, in other aspects of their labours, attacked our restrictive immigration policy and seemed anxious to create inside Australia those very racial problems which have puzzled the wit of man in South Africa and have presented the United States of America with its greatest unsolved social problem.

My own attitude, backed by the Cabinet, was perfectly clear though, in the heat of the moment, somewhat unpopular. I said, both in and out of Parliament, that *apartheid* (or 'separate development'), was a domestic matter and that we in other countries should not interfere. I felt that, in a multi-racial community, it was a matter for political judgement, upon which honest and upright men could differ, whether development should be based upon the separation of races, or upon their integration. I saw quite clearly that if the many 'busy-bodies' who are active at the United Nations had their way and threatened South Africa with reprisals, the 'domestic jurisdiction' rule enshrined in Article 2(7) of the Charter would be grievously, and perhaps fatally, damaged.*

My colleagues and I were not unconscious of the dangers to our immigration policy inherent in the propostion that a matter *normally* one of domestic jurisdiction can become one of international jurisdiction if it excites criticism and hostilities in other lands.

The whole question thus being one of immense importance for the future, judgement and foresight alike demanded that I should not get on to 'the band-wagon', and that at the Prime Ministers' Conference I should be in a position to speak impartially to and with the Prime Minister of South Africa, and be able to exercise some moderating influence in what might be, from a Commonwealth point of view, a dangerous situation.

---

* 'Nothing contained in the present Charter shall authorize the United Nations to intervene in matters which are essentially within the domestic jurisdiction of any State or shall require the Members to submit such matters to settlement under the present Charter. . . .'

There had been some loose talk of 'expelling' South Africa from the Commonwealth. I thought this idea an extremely foolish one. In London in April the opportunity arose for saying why, to a Commonwealth Parliamentary Association Meeting of British Members of Parliament at Westminster Hall. To them I pointed out that the Members of the Commonwealth are not governments but nations. Governments come and go. Policies can change. To talk of expelling South Africa because we objected to the Verwoerd Government or its policy was to punish a great section of electors who oppose the Government 'and to put out of the Commonwealth 9,000,000 Bantu whose greatest hope for the future, for all we know, is their continued inclusion in the Commonwealth'.

These were, I thought, fairly elementary ideas, but it was clear that they had novelty for some of my listeners.

The policy of restraint was abundantly justified in the result. True, Dr Verwoerd, as a result of a criminal attack, was not able to come to the 1960 Prime Ministers' Conference. He was represented by Mr Eric Louw, his Foreign Minister. I knew Louw well. I had always found him somewhat stiff and intractable, with that kind of deductive mind which proves difficult for us who are bred in the inductive and somewhat pragmatic processes of the Common Law. Yet I knew him to be courageous, honest, and devoted to what he regarded as the proper interests of his country.

When the Prime Ministers' Conference met, my friend, the Tunku Abdul Rahman, while replying to a short speech of welcome made by Mr Macmillan, took the opportunity of raising the South African problem and saying that he wished to have it debated.

Harold Macmillan and I had discussed this probability and had agreed that a debate on South Africa in what might be called 'a full meeting of Prime Ministers' could be disastrous. I therefore took the matter up by pointing out that we had never discussed such problems in the past and that in the case of Kashmir, the Conference of January 1951 had, with the full concurrence of Mr Nehru, declined to list or debate the matter even though it was one which related to a conflict between two member nations of the Commonwealth, and was therefore international in character.

The South African problem seemed to me to be an *a fortiori* case.

Much to my relief, the Conference agreed unanimously that it would not discuss this matter as a conference, but that it would accept the offer which Louw then made to have limited groups of Prime Ministers discuss the matter privately with him. A couple of private meetings subsequently occurred.

To me, the most interesting thing at that time was that Nkrumah, Ayub Khan and the Tunku all followed a most moderate line. They showed a willingness to appreciate the position of the European population in South Africa but they had sharp comments to make about the application of the South African policy, particularly as it related to the treatment in South Africa of Africans or Asians, official or unofficial, who might find themselves in that country.

These suggestions were all courteously presented and Louw undertook to convey them to his Prime Minister.

The crucial moment came when we were discussing the communiqué. I had never concealed my own view that the issuing of a communiqué after Prime Ministers' conferences is a blunder. In the very nature of such conferences, nothing could be included in the communiqué without unanimous agreement. In other words, each of us had a veto. Under these circumstances, I have thought and said that we could very well produce a communiqué which omitted any reference whatever to some of the most important matters we had been discussing. I have said repeatedly in these conferences that the object of the Conference is not to pass resolutions but to have a meeting of minds, an exchange of views and of information, to improve our personal understanding not only of each other but of our various problems; and that, under these circumstances, the issuing of a communiqué, which might be appropriate as between strangers, was ill-advised and misleading.

My voice was that of a minority, and so we got to work on the communiqué.

A paragraph was drafted with relation to the South African talks. It was, after some consideration, accepted by Louw, who had spoken by telephone to his Prime Minister. Two of the Prime Ministers, however, indicated that they thought the paragraph inadequate. They suggested a change which seemed to me to be quite rational, but which Louw regarded as outside his authority. He accordingly refused to agree, and reminded us that without his agreement the paragraph itself could not be included. Macmillan adjourned the conference for a quarter of an hour so that we might think about it. It was at this stage that my own somewhat detached attitude and the close relations that I had maintained with Louw paid a dividend. I remained behind in the Conference Room with Louw and spoke to him in pretty stringent terms. I told him that I was probably the only Prime Minister present who had lost votes over the South African issue; that I thought that his objection was not sensible; and that if he persisted in being completely intransigent on the matter, I would have to regard him as adopting an unfriendly attitude towards myself. What I had to say to him was what one can and should be able to say to another member of a Prime Ministers' Conference. He was at first shocked and then impressed by it. I left him to his deliberations. He went straight up to Macmillan who had gone upstairs. Within a minute they were both back. We reassembled and Macmillan was able to tell them that Mr Louw had agreed to the paragraph as amended. This meant that the immediate crisis was over and that we were able to conclude our meetings in a spirit of friendliness, without bitterness or recriminations.

There was, however, a matter raised in the Conference by both Nehru and Nkrumah which I felt might have serious consequences. Nkrumah, having in his own country carried a referendum in favour of a Republic, and having taken steps to establish one, applied for permission for Ghana to remain in the Commonwealth as a Republic. This was unanimously approved.

Louw then raised the question of South Africa. A little battered by the previous discussions, he had on behalf of his Prime Minister asked of the Conference whether the continued membership of South Africa 'as a Monarchy' was unwelcome. *The answer to this, after very brief discussion was 'No'*. When Nkrumah had concluded his successful application, Louw sought approval for South Africa to remain in the Commonwealth as a Republic if their referendum turned out that way, as he was sure it would. At once there were expressed reservations of opinion. The prevailing view was that put by Harold Macmillan who said, very sensibly, that, as the question must await what would no doubt be a vigorous campaign about having a Republic, it would not be appropriate for us 'to appear to intervene in the domestic affairs of

South Africa'. (Having regard to the discussion about apartheid, this was a shrewd thrust, though its effects, as we shall see, wore off.) Quite clearly there might be some people in South Africa who would normally vote against a Republic but who would be less disposed to vote against it if they felt assured that the vote would not put South Africa out of the Commonwealth. This was an intelligible argument, and Louw felt its weight. But in the course of the discussion both Nehru and Nkrumah raised the question of South-West Africa and delivered a lively attack upon the South African Government for having, they said, ignored the original mandate and defied the decisions of the United Nations. I felt alarmed by the raising of this argument and said so, somewhat to Nehru's discontent. My point was that as we had agreed that South Africa was welcome in the Commonwealth *as a Monarchy*, notwithstanding the South-West African dispute which we all had in mind, it would be strange for us to raise that known issue as a reason for refusing South Africa's continued membership '*as a Republic*'. I pointed out that we were not an agent of the United Nations to enforce the Charter, and that we must not put ourselves in the position of being a special committee of the United Nations. I also took the opportunity of repeating my views on what was involved in virtually expelling a member nation.

The matter was concluded as well as possible by recording that if and when South Africa decided to become a Republic, it should then make an application which could be dealt with by correspondence. But I was left extremely uneasy. I hoped that the nations concerned would not take the opportunity of securing a virtual expulsion by saying in their correspondence that they could not agree to continued membership unless a change of South African policy in relation to South-West Africa occurred.

In the course of the discussion, Louw pointed out, and (I thought and said) with good reason, that three years ago we had agreed in advance to Ceylon remaining in the Commonwealth as a Republic and that in point of fact, though three years had elapsed, Ceylon had not taken the necessary steps to become one. This was a clear precedent for an anticipatory decision.

It is, of course, one of the characteristics of the British Commonwealth that it has developed on no logical basis. But I thought it would be a calamity if it turned out that continued membership of the Commonwealth depended upon acceptance of the criticisms or judgements of other members in relation to either domestic politics or the relationship between a member and the United Nations. About a week later, I spoke of these matters with, as it turned out, undue optimism, in my Smuts Memorial Lecture. Here are my words, so out of line, I grieve to say, with some recent developments:

We do not meet as a tribunal, to sit in judgement upon each other, or to ventilate intra-Commonwealth issues. We are not a super-state.

During the recent tragic episodes in South Africa there were not wanting suggestions that South Africa should be expelled—presumably by majority vote—from the Commonwealth. Any such suggestion, in my opinion, misconceived the nature of our association. We do not deal with the domestic political policies of any one of us, for we know that political policies come or go with governments and that we are not concerned with governments and their policies so much as we are with nations and their peoples. If we ever thought of expelling a member nation of the Commonwealth it would, I hope, be because we believed that in the general interests of the Commonwealth that nation, as a nation, was not fit to be our associate.

The Prime Ministers' Conference would break up in disorder and the new Commonwealth would disintegrate if we affected to discuss and decide what we thought to be the proper measure of democracy in our various countries; whether particular groups should or should not have the vote; whether oppositions should be respected; whether a Parliament should control the Executive. On all such matters 'autonomous' or 'independent' nations must have the right to manage their own affairs in their own way.

How little my optimism was warranted clearly emerged as new members were admitted, and new pressures came to be exerted.

After returning to Australia, I wrote to Dr Verwoerd, who was not personally known to me, on 2 July 1960, setting out a few observations on what had happened, and offering some views of my own.

With the courteous permission of Mrs Verwoerd, I will now make public the text of our letters, omitting, as I think I should, some passages which are not relevant to an understanding of the issues involved.

Menzies to Verwoerd
My dear Colleague,

I hope that you will not take it amiss if I send you in this way a few observations on the London Conference.

As you know, I had adhered very closely to the principle of non-interference in the domestic affairs of another country. I had not condemned apartheid; I had not approved of it; I had simply said nothing about it. This line of action, though warmly approved of by my own Cabinet, exposed me to a great deal of criticism from partisans, including a considerable number of the clergy, and I think may have cost me some votes. Of course, at the back of my mind, there was, over and above the domestic jurisdiction principle, a hearty detestation of people who have an itch to talk about the policies of other lands while remaining astonishingly ignorant of the circumstances.

In London when we met, the position was that most of the Prime Ministers had announced their views, and I greatly feared that such a heated controversy would arise as might threaten the Commonwealth structure. The Tunku Abdul Rahman had actually secured a resolution of instructions from his own Parliament. . . .

. . . When the Conference met, as you know, the Tunku, in the course of replying to a little speech of welcome by Macmillan, brought up the South African question. I took the line very strongly that we should not discuss this matter in Conference. . . .

. . . Fortunately the Prime Ministers agreed that the old principle should be upheld but accepted Eric Louw's willingness to engage in private talks with limited groups. As I attended such private talks as occurred, I think it might help if I were to give you my own impressions.

First of all, Louw was of course at a disadvantage in that he was not Prime Minister and could, therefore, not speak with final authority. In spite of all this, we all thought that he showed great courage and perhaps almost too much firmness. The spectacle of one man defending a policy against the critical minds and words of almost everybody else present is one which excites respect, and I want you to know that Eric Louw secured it. But the great thing that impressed me in these talks was the moderation of Nkrumah, Ayub and the Tunku. . . .

. . . It very soon appeared that there were three matters which affected them and which they thought ought to be changed.

The first was the representation of the Cape Coloured, on which both they and I thought that, if Parliamentary representation by the Cape Coloureds themselves could be achieved, a great step forward would have been made.

The second was the representation of the Bantu. Your policy and programme for the Bantu Reserves was explained by Eric Louw and produced no adverse comment. But your policy and programme in relation to the Bantu living in what I will call the 'white' areas was regarded as inadequate in the sense that it would perpetuate within the one Province discriminations based upon race.

My own view on this, which I offer to you with all diffidence, is that the policies of education and health and so on which you are directing to the Bantu must in due course produce a more competent people, and that when they have reached a relatively high stage of training they are not likely to accept indefinitely a position which they will regard as one of inferiority. My own mind is unexcited by some of the extravaganzas that have been engaged in on moral and even religious grounds; the problem to me is one of practical statesmanship, and its solution depends upon the exercise of honest and informed judgement. You will, I am sure, accept this comment of mine as being honest, though you may well reject it as being uninformed.

To return to the London talks, I was particularly pleased to hear from both the Tunku and Ayub, with Nkrumah certainly not dissenting, that they recognized the position of the white population; that they realized that it had been responsible for the economic development of the nation; that it had created the whole structure of government and administration; and that they did not expect for one moment the immediate adoption of policies which would put the position of the white population at risk. I want you to know that they seemed to me to be entirely fair and quite moderate and indeed quite under-standing on these points. 'But,' said the Tunku, 'why can't you give the Bantu just a few seats in the Union Parliament, not enough to affect the balance of power but enough to make the Bantu feel that they are citizens of the country?' My recollection is that the Tunku suggested about half a dozen seats which might be voted for by the Bantu as separate constituencies, which is broadly what happens to the Maoris in New Zealand.

The third point which they urged was, I think, the most important one in their minds. They took great exception to personal discriminations and gave some instances of them. What rankles, for example, in the Tunku's mind is that should he visit South Africa in any capacity other than his present official one, he believes that he would be denied entrance to first-class hotels and otherwise treated differently from a white visitor. Eric Louw with great spirit asked whether any of us thought that a negro would be allowed to take a suite at the Waldorf Astoria in New York. My own reply to this was and is that should such occasion occur it would be the result of a decision of the management of the Waldorf Astoria and would be quite unrelated to any government policy.

I have mentioned these three points because they seemed to be the hub of the matter in the minds of our colleagues. Oddly enough, Sharpeville was never mentioned. This was, I think, because everybody realized that although Sharpeville had, in the modern phrase, 'triggered off' violent outbursts of opinion in other countries, it was not in itself a matter which any of us ought to affect to determine. The real question was the policy in its bearing upon other Commonwealth countries, and it was to this that the discussions were directed.

In my opinion the rules of a racial kind which you adopt are not, in the broad, matters which I feel competent to examine; nor indeed was there any very clear definition by anybody of the changes which might be made. But there was and is one aspect of the matter about which I think I should, even if impertinently, put something to you. Nkrumah was obviously hurt by the current failure to receive a High Commissioner from Ghana at Pretoria. As I understand the position, you don't receive Diplomatic Missions from what I will call the 'coloured' countries. This, I think, is regarded as disagreeable and unco-operative by our colleagues. I spoke very earnestly to Eric Louw in private about it. He said that if such Missions were received and in consequence a considerable number of Asian and African diplomats and their staffs were established in Pretoria and Cape Town, it would run counter to the policy of separateness. I said to him, as I now say to you, that since we all meet in London on terms of equality and conduct close and intimate and friendly discussions with each other, it must be impossible for these other governments to understand why similar discussions on the ordinary diplomatic level cannot occur in your own country. It is your business, and I don't presume to be positive, let alone dogmatic, about it. But I do want to tell you that my personal opinion is that if you found yourself able to invite these other Commonwealth countries to establish Diplomatic Missions in South Africa, and were able to assure them that they would be received and treated in exactly the same way as the representatives of Great Britain or Australia, a lot of the heat would be taken out of the present conflict. This is particularly the case with India, whose importance in the Afro-Asian world cannot be ignored.

In Australia, as you know, we have a very strict immigration policy, primarily because we don't wish to see created in our own country the tremendous racial problems which you have to encounter. Yet we have found no difficulty in receiving diplomats from Asian countries or in meeting them socially and otherwise on equal and friendly terms. The Tunku, to take one example, upholds our immigration policy but greatly admires the absence of discrimination in respect to Asians who come to Australia temporarily, either as diplomats or students or traders. This, unhappily, sets up in his mind, when he thinks of South Africa, a somewhat angry contrast. It is on this side of personal relations and personal treatment that he, and I think the others, becomes most critical.

You are, of course, familiar with what was done about the South African application to remain in the Commonwealth, if and when it becomes a Republic. The postponement of any discussion on this matter until after your referendum was based primarily upon the view that to give a decision in advance would be to intervene in the political campaign which will surround your referendum. I need not elaborate this. Eric Louw will have put you in possession of it. My own anxiety arises from the fact that I do not regard it as quite certain that an application by a Republic of South Africa will be accepted by all Prime Ministers. If one or two of them dissent, the well-established rule of unanimity would put you out. I am afraid in particular of what the attitude may be of Nehru and Nkrumah.

This fear arises from the fact that each of them, when the application was made, raised the question of South-West Africa and made quite pungent remarks in relation to it. I at once said that I was alarmed by these remarks since they appeared to suggest that the Prime Ministers' Conference ought to be regarded as an instrument for enforcing the Charter of the United Nations, which we are not. I also pointed out that whatever criticisms they had about South-West Africa were equally valid whether South Africa was a Monarchy or a Republic, and that to expel (in effect) South Africa from the Commonwealth as a Republic because of South-West Africa was completely illogical. I am, of course, by no means certain as to what line these people will take if South Africa becomes a Republic. All I say is that I am a little apprehensive. That perhaps is another very good reason why I would personally think it a good thing if you could establish normal diplomatic relations with them . . . .

. . . Do forgive me for writing to you at such tedious length but I thought it might be helpful if in a frank way I gave you my version of what went on and offered a few views, not only as a senior Prime Minister who ought to be able to take a detached view, but also as a friend of your country.

With kind regards,

Yours sincerely,
Robert G. Menzies

The Prime Minister's reply was delayed for very good reasons. But on 24 August he wrote to me a full explanation of his policies; which I think to be of historical importance.

My dear Colleague,

I highly appreciate your communication which I certainly do not take amiss. It is perfectly clear that you adhere to the principle of non-interference in the domestic affairs of another country, and that the observations you make in your private letter come from a friend to a friend. I wish to avail myself of this opportunity to thank you very warmly for the stand taken by you at the Prime Ministers' Conference and elsewhere when South Africa was under attack. My colleague Eric Louw always speaks in the very highest terms of you and with keen admiration, and is very emphatic on the great influence you have and brought to bear. I can only add that, apart from my own and my Government's deep sense of gratitude for such support at a time when friends are inclined to shy away, your attitude has not escaped the attention of the public of my country. You are seen by all shades of opinion as perhaps the best friend South Africa has, and the feeling of comradeship with Australia has never been better.

It is with regret that I note your attitude may have done you some harm amongst a portion of your electorate, and can only express the hope that this may change when the humanity and justice to all sections of our population, and the honesty, of our policy, becomes generally better realized overseas which we hope will be soon. Naturally we are fully aware that you too do not endorse our good neighbour policy of separate development, but that is not the point.

Perhaps it may be of value to you if I try to state my point of view with regard to the five fundamental issues in your letter: the representation of the Bantu; representation of the Coloureds; personal discriminations; diplomatic missions from non-white countries; and a South African republic and the Commonwealth.

At the outset I would wish to state unambiguously that the policy of separate development is not based on the desire to suppress any non-white group. To the contrary it is seen as the solution by means of which Whites would not dominate any of the coloured groups. On the other hand only in this way can it be ensured that the Bantu would not ultimately dominate the Whites, Coloureds or Indians by sheer weight of numbers. A method was sought to enable each group to become politically independent as nearly and as soon as possible while all would remain economically interdependent. (Here one could make some comparison with what is happening in Euromark where the states remain politically separate but are breaking down economic walls.)

It must be remembered that both the Bantu and the White are foreign to South Africa. Each settled portions of what was, fundamentally, empty land. It has been the policy of the White man throughout the centuries to preserve the black man's areas for him, and during the last fifty years to add to it at the White man's expense. It is true that in the White man's areas large numbers of Bantu have been allowed to enter, at first as refugees from black tyrants for protection, later to seek work and food in order to escape poverty and hunger through their own lack of knowledge and initiative. Their numbers were further increased in those areas by health and other services.

It is against all sense of justice and would be a form of bloodless conquest if the White man should now have to give away the political control of his country to those at present in his midst as a result of his humane and Christian treatment. Yet this would be the case if on the one hand the native territories were developed, for the Bantu's sole control, with the White man's aid, as is our policy, and in addition those in the white area were given political rights to be exercised there which would on account of their numbers also ultimately mean full control.

It is quite futile to suggest as the Tunku does that token representation by say six Bantu representatives would prove the final solution. Not only is the clamour for one man one vote already to be heard here, but in the other British areas in Africa this policy of granting a junior partnership has proved to be only the beginning of greater demands and more serious trouble. Kenya, and now Southern Rhodesia, provide clear evidence that what seems theoretically feasible becomes in practice the beginning of the end of White man's rule. Whatever may be the rights of the case elsewhere, it would be sheer injustice to the White man of South Africa if he were thus to be robbed of his rightful heritage.

It must also be remembered that if the White man gradually gave way, he would not be the only one to suffer, but the oppression of the Indian and Coloured minority groups by Bantu rulers would be equally certain. For this proof can be found in what is happening elsewhere in Africa. 500 Indian traders have already left Tanganyika. The Bantu masses too would not benefit, for dictatorship by the few is typical of the Bantu mind, of which Ghana provides an illustration.

This was our dilemma. On the one hand any form of multiracial government or partnership would become the thin end of the wedge for the ousting of the White man from what is his rightful centuries old national home. (I am leaving out what it would mean to the world, particularly in the event of a struggle against communism, or a clash between the East and the West, if the only State which is a certain friend of the West in Africa were also sacrificed.) On the other hand from no people can political rights and full opportunity and human dignity be withheld as they become educated and trained and developed, and this training the black man in South Africa receives at the hand of the White man.

The only way out was to follow the example of the development of the Commonwealth. The dependencies or colonies were never represented in the British Parliament but were helped to develop, step by step, governments of their own, until they attained full independence. This is the goal we are setting for our Bantu. They are also commencing with the forms of government which they know and can run best, but the road is wide open to any form of democracy they may find suitable.

The South African Bantu consist of several nations with own languages and are as widely different as French, German and Russian. These national groups are gradually being granted their independence as such, whether they live within the white areas or within their homelands, and they all obtain and must exercise their rights, political and other, within those homelands. Furthermore it must be remembered that the Bantu can and will, as industry and towns are developed in their areas, find it increasingly to their advantage to return there and put to account the experience and capital gained in the white areas. The fact must also be noted that not only must the black man in the white areas exercise his political rights in his own national home, but the White man in the Bantu areas similarly is not given any political rights there, but will exercise his rights only in the white area. Therefore, there is no discrimination in so far as the same principle applies to White and Black alike, however long they may have been in the other area. Voting for their government in their own area, whether they live there or in the white areas, is a just and sensible arrangement, and is in fact followed by Great Britain herself in the case of Basutoland. Not only do the Basutos in the Protectorate exercise their political rights, including the vote, there, but also the Basutos of Basutoland working and living anywhere throughout the Union of South Africa.

South Africa has chosen this system of separate development and good neighbourship in order to do justice to the White man on the one hand and to the Black man on the other. A further development is already being envisaged, and has been announced viz. that as this growth to independence progresses, there should be set up something similar to a Commonwealth relationship, including a Conference, similar to the Prime Ministers' Conference, of the leaders of these White and Black national entities on an equal basis. The Bantu authorities or governments could send representatives from urban and/or homeland areas. This proves that by providing safety and a future for each group separately, equal opportunity, co-operation, good neighbourliness and full acknowledgment of the human dignity of all will be acknowledged and practised. This would not be the case if there were any danger of the Whites being swamped, which would happen if the other policies or suggestions were followed. Then the struggle for self-preservation would sweep all other considerations aside.

Token representation for the Bantu is in fact much less progressive and of much less value than this readiness to encourage full development of their own nationhood. We also contend that this is more in line with the development of own Black States in Africa than multiracial governments which are soon after their institution rejected everywhere by the Blacks—cf. Tanganyika, Kenya, Nyasaland.

At this stage of evolving independence we are already providing in the place of the former white members of Parliament for the Bantu (who were always in opposition, even in General Smuts' time, and could achieve little in practice) direct representatives of the Government, just like High Commissioners, to each of the territories to aid in the progress towards independence and for direct consultation with the authorities of the Bantu there.

I may add that a form of local municipal authority for the Bantu in the white areas is being introduced next year which will have direct links with the authorities in the homelands. This provides urban natives with a double opportunity for looking after their own interests.

I have dealt with this at some length since the Bantu is the fundamental problem. The other issues can be discussed more briefly.

The Cape Coloured were formerly on the common roll and in rare instances one of their number succeeded in being chosen for the Cape Provincial Council. Theoretically they therefore had equal rights, and I suppose the world outside would be satisfied if this system had been retained. In practice it became a bluff and was fundamentally dishonest. Coloured voters were exploited by a political party seeking their votes and then forgetting all about them. The present Government put them on a separate roll and their White representatives are now solely dependent upon their choice and therefore really represent their needs in Parliament. A Coloured Council has also been instituted, partly appointed and partly chosen, and this is regarded as an interim arrangement which will lead to direct representation in some form. It is now only advisory but its legislative power will be gradually extended as it proves itself.

The Coloured people are gradually being trained in self-government. At this stage separate full municipal government by Coloureds in their own townships will be instituted as soon as possible and then further steps higher up will be introduced as experience is gained.

If the Coloured were to be represented by Coloured in Parliament before sufficient progress had been made towards the general acceptance of Bantu separate development as set out above, this would only be taken as an encouragement to break down that development and to agitate for Bantu representation and all the dangers of multiracial government would again have to be faced as set out above. Coloured representatives cannot be contemplated now but it is one of the possible alternatives for the future. The one principle which has been accepted is that as the Coloureds succeed in more local government their further progress will be undertaken. We cannot be hurried as the Congo was.

The problem of personal discrimination in hotels, music halls, trains, etc. must be viewed against the background of the situation here. V.I.P.'s of whatever colour from other countries cannot complain of discrimination or discourtesy but are treated well under, it is true, special arrangements by their hosts or the Government. At present it is also true that similar treatment for all people of colour who would wish to come here could not be arranged, and they will have to fall in with the customary separate facilities. It is all very well to say that in other countries this does not occur, but then in other countries such as Australia, ordinary mixing would make no difference to the general run of things. If in South Africa all non-whites from outside the country were to be dealt with as White visitors would be, then there would be no justification or possibility for dealing differently with the non-white inhabitants of the country. Due to the latter's numbers this would mean a swamping by non-whites of everything the White man has developed. Full social integration would necessarily follow and the White man would not be able to preserve anything for himself, including political control. Again this would mean giving away everything that he has built up. Here again we are dealing with a possible thin end of the wedge. It must be understood that only after sufficient success has been achieved in the direction of separate development with full opportunities for all, each among the members of his own group, can relaxations take place in the white area. It is, therefore, not a matter of human dignity but of self-preservation with full readiness to waive distinctive treatment when the danger of losing out has disappeared.

The following point in your letter was that it is regarded as disagreeable and unco-operative that diplomatic missions are not received from coloured countries and that this also affected India. This is not quite correct. We have a diplomatic mission from Egypt and there are Chinese Consular representatives. India was represented in the Union but withdrew it of its own accord. There would be no objection to India or Pakistan being represented. Japan is being considered.

You mentioned the case of Nkrumah. It must not be forgotten, however, that before there was any talk of representation, he had made known that Ghana would do everything in its power to aid Black men everywhere in Africa, including South Africa, to take over the reins of government. Apart from all other considerations, it could not be expected that we would receive a mission which could easily become the centre of agitation where those would foregather, White and non-white, who wish to create a multiracial or Bantu government here. South Africa has had such an experience with Sowjet Consular-generals and had to request the closing down of that Consulate rather than invite further trouble. It was, therefore, felt that representation by Ghana and others should be postponed until conditions of separate development in this country, less active interference by others in our domestic affairs, clear indications of goodwill by African States and worth while relations with them, had created the right atmosphere. If Ghana and the others were at all politically mature, they should have accepted as a first step the many proofs of goodwill shown and co-operation in technical matters given by the South African Government. South Africa sent a special representative and a present to Ghana when it became independent. It met several requests for specialist advisers. It wished to send its Minister of External Affairs to Ghana and knew that diplomatic courtesy and custom would demand the acceptance of a return visit by his opposite number, although this could not be agreed to, when made a condition implying distrust.

There are many other ways in which South Africa was and is prepared to establish friendly relations with the African States but consistently this has been made impossible by the unfriendly attitude these immature new states immediately take up. They all fail to fulfil the expectations of their own people on achieving independence, and cover up their failings by attacks on the White man and more spectacularly South Africa. Naturally we also have our own particular problems to consider if members of these missions from Black States moved in Government social circles. What justification would there be for the same not happening to educated Bantu here, or to the leaders of the big Bantu national groups, whose followers are almost as numerous as the population of Ghana? Yet until separate development has progressed far enough for this to be possible without endangering the whole position of the White man as described above, we have to tread warily.

It is, therefore, not a matter of not wishing to receive such missions on a non-discriminatory basis, but of having to consider all the consequences which a country with only a small non-white population would not need to face.

I have not yet mentioned a further fact viz. that nearly all these African States at times play hard and fast with the Communist countries and call themselves uncommitted and neutral in order to play off the Western nations against Russia in order to get the most they can. South Africa with a large and susceptible non-white population must keep such influences and examples as far away as possible. Who can guarantee that Moscow-educated or inspired Black men would not be on such missions? Not a disagreeable attitude towards colour, but many quite different factors compel us at this stage to prefer diplomatic action from afar, and sporadic visits, to permanently stationed missions.

Finally, you mention that South Africa might find that she would be opposed as a member of the Commonwealth if she asked to remain such on deciding to become a Republic. I accept this as a possibility and would wish to state my position in that case just as I did to Mr. Macmillan.

I believe that, in spite of no assurances or undertakings whatsoever, the United Kingdom, Australia and certain of the members would wish to retain South Africa as a member and would exert themselves to this end. In view of doubts expressed as to whether unanimous approval could be secured for the retention of South Africa's membership of the Commonwealth, as well as in view of public statements by Nkrumah and others, it was only fair that, when announcing the date of the referendum, I stated firstly that before the actual establishment of the Republic, a request will, in accordance with past practice, be made to the Commonwealth Prime Ministers for retention of South Africa's membership, but also, secondly, that in the event of continued membership being refused, the Republic will be established outside the Commonwealth. Naturally I added that it will be the policy of the Republic to continue with its present policy of maintaining cordial relations, and co-operating in all matters of common concern, with all the friendly disposed Commonwealth countries, particularly in the common cause of resisting communism.

The reason why we would proceed is that such an adverse decision would not be directed against the fact that South Africa became a republic, but would indicate that an important change in the character of the Commonwealth was taking place. It would mean interference, possibly by attempts at indirect coercion, in the domestic policies of member countries, and also the beginning of a predominating influence by the younger members. The non-white members would gradually dominate by weight of numbers or due to the fact that the others wished to appease them at all costs and for whatever reasons. This would prove a threat to South Africa and her White citizens even if she were to remain a monarchy, and the resultant conflicts at conferences would certainly be most embarrassing to her older friends in the Commonwealth, and could easily lead to estrangement from them as well. Under such circumstances a Republic outside the Commonwealth might have a better chance of retaining and cultivating friendship and co-operating wherever possible with those member states who would be willing and could then avoid taking sides in conferences which could no longer be confined to seeking common ends. Refusal would, therefore, lead to the Union accepting that the Commonwealth had so changed that it had no option but to become a Republic outside the Commonwealth.

It is clear that you believe that there is an alternative, namely that the Union should pay the price of changing its colour policy to the extent necessary to appease its attackers among the member nations. I am afraid that however delicately it is put as if we would be deciding unilaterally on such a change in order to attain a certain end, this would be generally accepted as no less than the result of criticism of and interference in the Union's domestic affairs by one or more fellow members. It would be useless deluding oneself. Everybody would realize what had happened, and similar pressure tactics would become part of Commonwealth procedure.

It must also be realized that should minor adaptations satisfy older members, but not the younger and politically less mature ones, then the latter would continue making demands in the same aggressive manner, and the former would most likely again succumb to their desire to obtain agreement from the latter. Further expectations of our changing our policies would then be forthcoming.

In addition, it may not be forgotten that in spite of opposition and misunder-standing we firmly and honestly believe that our policy of separate development, which is a good neighbour policy, is the only morally justifiable one, and will in its ultimate realization serve best the provision of human and all other rights to both white and black in South Africa. We cannot be expected to change our deepest convictions in order to remain within the Commonwealth. This is not expected of any other member whose policies we dislike or condemn.

We would co-operate loyally within the Commonwealth in all matters of common interest, including particularly the resistance to Communism, in spite of the virulent attacks made upon us by some members, and the harm they seek to do us. Being politically mature we would be willing to confer with them and work together on all points of agreement, even if it proved impossible to resolve our differences with them, and without interfering in their domestic affairs however critical we might be. We expect the same of the others.

Please forgive this lengthy exposition. I sincerely trust it will never again become necessary to inflict something similar upon you. For this once, however, it might prove useful to both of us.

Yours cordially,

H. Verwoerd.

To this I replied:

6th September, 1960.

My dear Colleague,

I have your letter of 24th August and have read it with profound interest. It is certainly a powerful exposition of your policy and point of view and will do much to inform my own mind.

I have never undertaken the role of judge on this matter for reasons which you well understand. My attitude of non-interference in your domestic affairs, so far from being weakened, is strengthened by the foolish talk which goes on and by what seems to me to be the incredibly foolish policies of boycott which are being advocated or adopted in various places. If by such economic pressures it is thought that you will be compelled to adopt policies of which you don't approve, it seems to me that some of our friends have much to learn about the South African character. If such policies are designed to help the Bantu then, as I have more than once pointed out, the last thing that ought to be under consideration is the expulsion of South Africa from the Commonwealth; since for all I know, or our other friends know, the Bantu themselves find much of their future hope in Commonwealth membership.

But without imposing on you any obligation to justify your policy to me in every particular, I would like to say that one thing that has troubled me is the future of the Bantu in what I will call the 'non-Bantu' areas; those areas in which the white man politically and economically dominates the scene but in which the Bantu themselves may form a not inconsiderable portion of the population.

Is it feasible to develop a form of self-government for the Bantu in these areas, side by side with that of the white man? To put it in another way, can two sovereignties ultimately co-exist in the one geographical area? The position seems different in the Bantu territories where your policy, I think, admits of no serious challenge. When I say that this particular point troubles me, I want to add most hastily that I am very glad that in my own country we have been able to avoid this kind of complication.

But the real matter that I want to commend to your consideration is this, assuming that South Africa decides to become a Republic. What happens next? At the London Conference it was rather assumed that, if and when you completed the Republican move, you would then write to the other Prime Ministers seeking their approval for continued membership of the Commonwealth as a Republic. I have a strong feeling that this would be a bad procedure. Writing cables or letters at a distance, it would be easy, and perhaps inevitable, for say Nkrumah or The Tunku or Nehru or all of them to say 'no'. This, of course, would give rise to another question as yet unsolved as to whether what would be a virtual expulsion could be brought about by a minority. I don't like the idea of majority and minority votes in our Commonwealth Association and would wish to avoid one on this matter. I would, therefore, like to see your application made at a time when the Republic had been substantially established but perhaps not actually proclaimed. I would like to see it made in person at a Prime Ministers' Conference. People like myself are not without some personal influence with our colleagues; that influence can be much better exercised by direct discussion than it can be by writing delivered at a distance. It would, for example, enable us to discuss in the frankest possible fashion the principles upon which and the procedure by which a membership of the Commonwealth, either new or continuing, should be determined. I would regard it as a great misfortune for all of us should South Africa find herself outside the Commonwealth. I cannot believe that people like Macmillan, and Diefenbaker and Nash would not have the same feeling. Between us all, sitting at the table, we might do some good.

Thanking you most sincerely for the food for thought which you have provided for me, and with kindest regards,

Yours sincerely,

R. G. Menzies.

Before dealing with these developments, I will, for the sake of clarity, state in summary form my account of what has happened to what I will call my 'SMUTS' propositions, just quoted.

1. South Africa was in fact expelled at the Conference of 1961.

2. The leaders of the attack on South Africa's political system were several African nations who, while they loudly demand 'one man, one vote' in South Africa and, later, Rhodesia, do not practise that principle themselves.

3. The campaign against the Government of Rhodesia in Commonwealth meetings (Rhodesia being absent and unrepresented) has built up into a violent interference with the normal authority of Great Britain to settle her own relations with one of her colonies; a matter over which the other Commonwealth Prime Ministers have no authority whatever. I will amplify this in a special section on Rhodesia.

4. In short, the old rules of non-interference which, by recognizing autonomy, gave a real cohesion to the Commonwealth, are already marked for destruction, and the whole future and fate of the Commonwealth are in the balance.

So that it will be seen that my views are neither extreme nor unwarranted, I will now make a more detailed examination.

At the next Conference, in March 1961, Dr Verwoerd was in attendance. His people had voted for a Republic. Throughout the proceedings, so fateful for him, and both in and out of Conference, he behaved with conspicuous courtesy and dignity. But he would yield no ground. Here was a man of high character, but unbending in his beliefs.

Before the Conference began, Macmillan and I had a talk about the dangers of the South African debate which was clearly to occupy the centre of the stage. We both thought that a Commonwealth Conference, conscious and proud of its multi-racial character, would be reluctant to promote a division which would appear to be on 'colour' lines, and that therefore the moderating counsels of the 'old' Commonwealth countries should be effective to avoid an actual point of crisis.

We thought that the matter should be handled in two parts. First, we should try to establish, as a matter of routine for the future, a 'Constitutional' proposition that where an existing member of the Commonwealth decides to become a republic, this should be regarded as its domestic affair, and should need only to be notified to other members. On this principle, South Africa would automatically continue its membership as a Republic.

Second, this being disposed of, there should be a debate, in full conference, on South African affairs, with South Africa as a participant and not a petitioner.

Dr Verwoerd, to whom we spoke, accepted this. He said, much to his credit, that, while preserving his attitude on jurisdiction, he would be willing to take part in the discussion.

I was soon to be disillusioned. When the Conference assembled, two things happened. One was that the 'constitutional' proposition was by-passed, and we were led into a debate in which the domestic policies of South Africa were treated as matters which should determine the right of South Africa to continue its membership of the Commonwealth. This departure from what I thought to be sound procedure proved to be fatal. For the attack upon South Africa was promptly led by Diefenbaker of Canada, who came armed with a resolution of his Parliament and presented his views with immense emotion. Not even some side-queries to him about the Red Indians and the Eskimos in Canada could deflect him from his course. Disaster, I thought, now became inevitable. The attackers moved in. I found myself virtually isolated, for Macmillan suffered the inevitable inhibitions of chairmanship, while the New Zealand Prime Minister, Keith Holyoake, though I know he agreed with me in substance, was perhaps not so openly and zealously wedded to the principle of non-interference as I was.

Frankly, I thought that there was an air of unreality about some of the attacks. It could hardly be denied, for example—and I took leave to point it out—that there were some racial discriminations in Malaya, and some problems about the Tamils in Ceylon, each of which I thought should properly be left to the respective Governments, who had popular support and were quite capable of handling their own affairs.

The form in which the matter had come up for decision is of historic interest. His referendum in South Africa having succeeded, Dr Verwoerd formally sought leave for South Africa to remain in the Commonwealth as a Republic. The very Prime Ministers who opposed leave and attacked South African policy had, at the previous Conference, agreed, as I have recorded, that South Africa was not unwelcome in the Commonwealth *as a monarchy*. Yet here they were, mostly Republics, saying with great vigour that she would be unwelcome *as a Republic!*

The 'kill' appeared to be inevitable. Yet an effort must be made. Accordingly, several of us got together to draft a statement for the communiqué. The broad idea was that we should set out, in brief terms, the views of those Prime Ministers who were strongly critical and who wanted to go on record against South Africa and her policies; that we should say that these had been conveyed to Dr Verwoerd, that he had said that he would of course give them careful consideration, but that he held out no prospect of agreement. Verwoerd, standing firmly on the ground that this was a domestic matter and should not be dealt with in a communiqué coming out of a Commonwealth Prime Ministers' Conference, disapproved. We then had a short adjournment, in the course of which Macmillan discussed the matter with Verwoerd. Thirty or forty minutes later Macmillan re-entered the Conference room looking happy, and said to me, in a low voice, 'it's all in order. Verwoerd will accept the suggested communiqué.' My pleasure was short-lived. No sooner had Verwoerd said that he would accept the draft, than Nehru was heard to say that *he* would not; that he was not prepared to temporize; that he would never let the matter rest; that not only at Prime Ministers' meetings but at every opportunity that presented itself, he would wage war on *apartheid* and the country which practised it. The attackers all followed suit. It was clear to Verwoerd that the day was lost; his application was going to be rejected. So, after the discussion, and with great dignity, he did the only thing he could do; he begged leave to withdraw his application. This, of course, meant that South Africa would cease to be a member of the Commonwealth. The decision was one of expulsion, not in form, of course; but in fact and in substance, it could have no other meaning.

I was very distressed. What to me was a vital principle of Commonwealth association had been abandoned. I made a press statement about the matter in these terms:

This is an unhappy day for those who attach value to the Commonwealth as an association of independent nations each managing its own affairs in its own way, but all co-operating for common purposes. The criticisms which we all had to make of South African policies were plainly expressed in the Conference in a debate which took place with the complete concurrence of Dr Verwoerd. The debate was of a frankness and intimacy which, in my experience, is possible only in a meeting of Prime Ministers. It is, I think, deplorable that it can never be conducted in such a forum and atmosphere again.

What the implications for the future nature of the Commonwealth may be, we do not yet know. For myself, I am deeply troubled.

It is always fascinating to recall the history of events, and how they arose. This is particularly true in the case of Rhodesia, which began in my life as 'Southern Rhodesia'. At that time, it was a self-governing colony, and its Prime Minister was Sir Godfrey Huggins (later to become Lord Malvern). How Huggins ever came to attend our meetings at No. 10 was never quite clear to me, until I had a letter from Mr Winston Field in September 1963, for Southern Rhodesia was not a completely self-governing country (defence and international affairs remained with Great Britain), and was therefore not a Member of the Commonwealth. But, every time we met, Godfrey Huggins, by tacit consent, was present. He was quiet, fairly deaf (he wore a deaf-aid in his ear) and extremely laconic. He was a surgeon by profession. As I used to say in my own irreverent way—'I envy Godfrey. He operates on the electors every morning, and governs them every afternoon. He is unbeatable!' And so he was. At our conferences he was not a thruster; his longest speech could not have exceeded three minutes. We all liked him, and enjoyed his presence and company. It is one of the oddities of political history that his country, which was in the earlier post-war years the only African country outside South Africa to be represented at Prime Ministers' conferences should now be the only one not so represented.

In brief, what happened was that the Government in London, which has created quite a few Federations but has never had to operate one, created the Federation of Rhodesia and Nyasaland, of which that sturdy man, Sir Roy Welensky, became Prime Minister. At the next Prime Ministers' Conference, Roy arrived. Though he is, like myself, addicted to plain speech, he behaved splendidly. He did not intervene in matters which did not immediately concern his own Federation.

[215]

8

In due course, the new African Prime Ministers having become more numerous, his attendance was challenged, and a hostile resolution was threatened. Finally, I am happy to recall, my own suggestion was accepted. It was that Sir Roy was clearly not present as of right, since his country was not fully independent and was therefore not a Member of the Commonwealth. But he was present in continuation of a long-standing courtesy extended for many years. He had not abused this privilege; nor had his predecessor. To become technical and rigid at this stage would be a mistake. Southern Rhodesia should be permitted to continue its attendance at our meetings. This was accepted, and he remained.

In due course, and for reasons which need not be examined for my present purpose, the Federation was dissolved. Northern Rhodesia became Zambia, and Nyasaland Malawi, and each, being granted full independence, became a Member of the Commonwealth. Rhodesia remained as a non-independent colony.

Under Winston Field's premiership, Rhodesia began to seek independence though at the same time, oddly enough, it believed that it was already a Member of the Commonwealth. In June 1963, I had the advantage of a long conversation in London with Mr Howman, Southern Rhodesian Minister of Internal Affairs, Local Government, and African Education. I had exchanged some friendly correspondence with Mr Field, in the course of which he had made a remark to the effect that 'Southern Rhodesia is and has been for many years a Member of the Commonwealth'.

I thought this to be a complete misconception; that it under-estimated the difficulties which Southern Rhodesia was confronting. As a friend of Rhodesia, I ventured to tell Mr Howman that he was in error; that Godfrey Huggins and Roy Welensky had never attended as of right; that Rhodesia was now seeking that measure of full independence which would for the first time qualify her for Commonwealth membership; that he must therefore face up to the fact that Rhodesia could not become a member except with the approval of the Commonwealth Prime Ministers' Conference; and that, in the temper of many of my new colleagues, this approval was not likely to be forthcoming so long as the Rhodesian electorate was not fully representative of the whole African population. This genuinely surprised

Howman, who had conceived the idea that as Rhodesia was already a Commonwealth member, all that the critics could do was to move for her expulsion, a course which, in spite of the South African precedent, he regarded as unlikely.

I therefore wrote to Mr Winston Field, to clarify my own view and assist his. He was good enough to send me a document which explained the basis of their belief. With his consent, I will quote it:

The basis on which Southern Rhodesia was invited to attend Imperial and later Commonwealth Conferences was determined when Southern Rhodesia was invited to participate in the Imperial Economic Conference at Ottawa in 1932. In a letter dated 3rd December, 1931, to Sir Cecil Rodwell, Governor of Southern Rhodesia, the Secretary of State for the Dominions wrote as follows:

'Since this Conference will be dealing with economic questions, and in view of the special interest which Southern Rhodesia has in these questions, the suggestion has been made that it would be appropriate if arrangements could be made for the Southern Rhodesia Government to send a representative to Ottawa who would attend the Conference as an observer, with liberty by permission of the Conference, to speak at its full meetings, and with a right to participate in the work of its Committees.'

The Secretary of State concluded by saying that it would be necessary to put forward the suggestion to the Dominions to ascertain whether it would be agreeable to them. Southern Rhodesia accepted these conditions and attended the Conference with the approval of the Dominions.

In a conversation with the Secretary of State on 26th July, 1934, Mr Huggins, on being informed that in the following year an informal meeting would take place in London between representatives of the Dominions assembled for the Jubilee celebrations, asked whether 'Rhodesia would be invited to attend such a conference in the same capacity as their representatives attended the Ottawa Conference'. The Secretary of State pointed out that the main subject to be discussed would not be of any interest to Southern Rhodesia. But he recalled the conditions under which Southern Rhodesia was represented at the Ottawa Conference and stated that he had no doubt that at the next official Conference a similar invitation would be extended to Southern Rhodesia. He thought it would be inadvisable to make any formal application for inclusion in such a Conference as it would raise the question of the status of Southern Rhodesia.

The Prime Minister of Southern Rhodesia and, subsequently of the Federation, has been invited to attend all subsequent Imperial and Commonwealth Conferences. He has not been invited to participate in discussions affecting Commonwealth membership but in all other matters has been given a free and equal voice.

The latter part of this document refers to the discussion I have already mentioned. The earlier portion is self-explanatory; but it does not record any decision to make Southern Rhodesia, as a non-independent country, a Member of a Commonwealth composed of independent nations.

Mr Field went, and Mr Ian Smith came, bringing with him unquestioned patriotism and courage, but a certain rigidity of mind, formed against the background of a body of white settlers who believe, and with reason, that they have made Rhodesia economically, that they have literally and figuratively planted their roots in the country, and are determined to resist their expulsion by a mass 'African' majority in a new State which will (on recent precedent) become a 'one-party' State in which their majority will have no effective voice.

When we were both in London for Winston Churchill's funeral, I met Smith and discussed this teasing problem with him. I liked him personally, but found him at that time virtually immovable.

My thesis can be stated quite briefly. It was this. The 1961 Rhodesia Constitution had created two electoral rolls which for some years would involve a European majority, with a minority representation of Africans. But clearly, as the people entitled to vote on the 'B' roll grew, the time would come, as economic and educational development went on, when there would be an overall African majority. I said that this was clearly contemplated by the 1961 Constitution; that it was just impossible, in the modern world, indefinitely, to perpetuate white rule in a society in which the vast majority of human beings were coloured people; and that the problem of practical statesmanship was to work towards a time-table which, after a reasonable period of years, and backed by an energetic educational campaign, would result in an African majority reasonably trained and competent to accept the responsibilities of full citizenship.

That still remains my view. I have always understood that it was, in the broad, the view of two successive British Prime Ministers, Sir Alec Douglas-Home and Mr Harold Wilson. The latter formulated 'five principles' which, in subsequent negotiations, are understood to have been accepted by Mr Smith; the ultimate, and tragic, breakdown of negotiations being due to differences in detail and in application.

The five principles, which, when he told me of them, I advised Harold Wilson were in my opinion sound and practical, were as follows:

1. The principle and intention of unimpeded progress to majority rule, already enshrined in the 1961 Constitution, would have to be maintained and guaranteed.
2. There would also have to be guarantees against retrogressive amendment of the Constitution.
3. There would have to be immediate improvement in the political status of the African population.
4. There would have to be progress towards ending racial discrimination.
5. The British Government would need to be satisfied that any basis proposed for independence was acceptable to the people of Rhodesia as a whole.

The Rhodesian question was in my time twice debated by the Prime Ministers; first in 1964 and again in 1965.

It seemed to some of us very important to get it established that the responsibility and power for the creation of complete self-government in Rhodesia belonged to Great Britain. She had achieved these results in the case of her former colonies, now full members of the Commonwealth, without outside intervention or aid. She had, in fact, got on to the road in the case of Rhodesia, with the agreed 1961 Constitution. I thought it essential that the location of the power and responsibility should be affirmed in unambiguous terms.

There was no logical or historical (or indeed legal) argument to the contrary. And so, the remarkable fact is that both conferences affirmed the power and responsibility of Great Britain *without dissent*!

But immediately the itch to give advice, to demand promises from Great Britain, to lay down and publish conditions, prevailed, and pungent debates ensued. Britain must convene a Constitutional conference. The African leaders then in prison or under restraint must be released, and should attend the Conference. The actual grant of independence should not formally be made unless and until the principle of 'one man, one vote', about which I have already made some amiable remarks, had come into operation.

I protested that, as we had agreed that it was not our business, but clearly a matter of difficult and delicate negotiation between Britain and Rhodesia, we should not embarrass the parties by what would appear to be orders given publicly by people who had no authority at all.

Having failed to avert a full debate on a matter which I thought was outside our jurisdiction, I then put up another proposition, with an equal lack of success. It was, in effect, that as we were proposing to discuss the internal government of Rhodesia and were being pressed to make very hostile findings concerning the Government of Rhodesia, the principles of natural justice which were recognized in several Commonwealth countries required that we should invite the Prime Minister of Rhodesia to be present and state his own case. This proposal was received with something approaching derision. Once more I had displayed my complete inability to understand the nature and beliefs of the new Commonwealth!

The first of these conferences, in 1964, at which Sir Alec Douglas-Home presided with admirable firmness, great tact, and almost unbelievable patience, was difficult enough, but we did end up with a communiqué which, in its relevant section, made it expressly clear that the authority and responsibility for guiding Rhodesia to independence rested with Britain. This principle was reaffirmed at the Prime Ministers' Conference of June 1965. At this conference, Mr Harold Wilson presided, also with great patience and firmness.

The final communiqué included this passage:

While the Prime Ministers re-affirmed that the authority and responsibility for leading her remaining Colonies, including Rhodesia, to independence must continue to rest with Britain, they also re-affirmed that the question of membership of the Commonwealth by an independent Rhodesia, or by any other newly independent territory, would be a matter for collective Commonwealth decision.

The second part of this paragraph merely affirmed a practice of long standing. It did not make the granting of independence to Rhodesia a matter for Commonwealth decision; that remained a matter for Britain; it dealt entirely with what would be subsequent events.

And then, in 1966, there was another Prime Ministers' Conference in

London. I was, of course, not present, having retired from office. It occurred when I was spending a term at the University of Virginia, and was out of touch. But later on, I read the communiqué. It includes one of the most momentous decisions in modern Commonwealth history; a decision which, in substance, overruled the earlier decisions which I have quoted. It reads:

Given the full support of Commonwealth representatives at the United Nations, the British Government will be prepared to join in sponsoring in the Security Council of the United Nations before the end of this year a resolution providing for effective and selective mandatory economic sanctions against Rhodesia.

Having regard to the earlier recorded decisions, for each of which I had worked hard, I am at a loss to understand why Great Britain concurred in a decision to take the problem to the United Nations, not primarily for information, as she had earlier done, but for debate and United Nations action, thus putting into the hands of people without responsibility in the matter, and with easily aroused emotions, a problem which was by earlier concession exclusively British.

What had happened? Two things. One was that a Commonwealth Conference had been called at Lagos by my late and valued friend, Abubakar, to discuss Rhodesia. It was clear to me, and to my colleagues at Canberra, that the majority of those attending (not Abubakar) would demand force. As we could never accept force, it seemed to us that all that the Lagos Conference could do was to record differences; and that there was no value in this.

So we refused the invitation. On 28 December 1965, I publicly stated our reasons for our refusal.

I pointed out that we had publicly stated that we regarded the Unilateral Declaration of Independence by the Smith Government as illegal, and went on to say:

We have refused diplomatic recognition of the new régime.
We continue to believe, and to say, that any constitutional settlement in Rhodesia must be on the basis of a steady progress towards majority rule and the removal of measures of racial discrimination.
We believe that in preparation for the achievement of an African majority

there should be an active educational programme, to which many of us might contribute.

We have strongly supported the financial and economic sanctions imposed by Britain, and have ourselves imposed sanctions covering 93% of our Rhodesian imports.

We believe that, if extensive economic measures are adopted by a sufficient number of nations, the persuasive pressure so generated will induce a return to the Conference table.

But we are deeply and publicly opposed to the proposals, made by some Commonwealth members, for the use of armed force. We are not aware of any evidence that Rhodesia contemplates any armed attack upon any other country. We would regard the assembling of non-Rhodesian forces on the frontiers of Rhodesia as needlessly provocative and dangerous.

The vital interests of Zambia, for example, can be protected only if peace is maintained.

It is necessary to ask what the purposes or likely results of a special conference would be.

The Australian Government believes that the Government of Britain has behaved with firmness, expedition, and good sense; and that its resistance to the use of arms to enforce a constitutional settlement is sound.

But several Commonwealth countries are publicly demanding that armed force be used, and by Britain. Some of these countries seem to have deeply and passionately committed themselves.

Under these circumstances, a Prime Ministers' Conference would in our view be unlikely to do more than record and emphasize differences. No unanimity of view could be achieved, and considerable bitterness would be disclosed. This would be a terrible price to pay for the convening of a conference upon a problem in relation to which, as the last Prime Ministers' Conference unanimously re-affirmed, 'the authority and responsibility for leading her remaining Colonies, including Southern Rhodesia, to independence must continue to rest with Britain'.

My Government has consistently opposed the giving of any Commonwealth orders to Britain as to how she should exercise that authority and discharge that responsibility. To have her, in effect, attacked and threatened at a special conference would be a grave departure from proper practice in a Commonwealth gathering. It would also open the door to a new era in Commonwealth relations, the abandonment of the old sound rules of non-intervention in the affairs of other Commonwealth countries, and the encouragement of those outside nations and groups which are ever ready to fish in troubled waters.

My Government does not, as it now sees the matter, wish to involve itself in a process which would prove so disastrous, not only to the Commonwealth but to Australia, which would run a grave risk of having its views distorted or misinterpreted.

The Lagos Conference offered its views, which were stated to be unanimous, in these words:

The Prime Ministers declared that any political system based on racial discrimination was intolerable. It diminished the freedom alike of those who imposed it and of those who suffered under it. They considered that the imposition of discriminatory conditions of political, social, economic and educational nature upon the majority by any minority for the benefit of a privileged few was an outrageous violation of the fundamental principles of human rights. The goal of future progress in Rhodesia should be the establishment of a just society based on equality of opportunity to which all sections of the community could contribute their full potential and from which all could enjoy the benefits due to them without discrimination or unjust impediment. To this end several principles were affirmed. The first was the determination of all present that the rebellion must be brought to an end. All those detained for purely political reasons should be released. Political activities should be constitutional and free from intimidation from any quarter. Repressive and discriminatory laws should be repealed.

Now, there is one ominous word in that report, a word, I regret to say, sometimes used by the British Government, 'rebellion'. That the Unilateral Declaration of Independence by Rhodesia was illegal, I have never doubted. My own Government at Canberra took this view, and acted upon it. But, at the very time that we said so, we publicly rejected the idea of force. So, I thought, did the Government of Great Britain.

But the word 'rebellion' is a word of ill-omen. It might have been appropriate at the time of the Revolution of the American colonies, but it is inappropriate today. For a rebellion (*re-bellum,* or war) is, according to the authoritative Oxford Dictionary, an 'organized armed resistance to the government of one's own country'. The use of the word in the communiqué suggested that the answer to force, or armed resistance, was force, to the avoidance of which both Great Britain and my own country were explicitly committed.

When Great Britain invited her Commonwealth colleagues, after Mr Smith's Unilateral Declaration of Independence, to refuse recognition of what had become an unlawful government, my own Government promptly agreed, and I said so to Parliament. When it invited us to impose economic sanctions, we gave careful and critical

[223]

thought to the proposal. My senior Ministers and I had vivid recollections of the failure of sanctions against Italy over her Abyssinian invasion. We were extremely conscious of two aspects of the matter; first, that economic sanctions could very well bear with great severity upon the African employees, and second, that sanctions can never be regarded as a measure at large; they must be imposed to secure acceptance of a policy.

And what was the policy for Rhodesia to be, having regard to the clear fact that there was a variety of policies, and no clear and agreed solution?

However, it soon became clear that, having regard to our own international problems and geographical position, Australia could not be the 'odd man out'. After all, we clearly rejected the U.D.I., and wanted to see, in due course, a recognition of majority rule in Rhodesia; so we imposed sanctions, though, as I said in the House 'with some reluctance'.

For myself (and I am setting down my personal memories, I speak for nobody else), I had a great fear of reference to the United Nations. I had three reasons for this.

The first was that several of the African Prime Ministers were demanding the use of force. This, when they proposed it, meant force by Great Britain against Rhodesia, a policy impossible to contemplate or support. War between British troops in Africa would be the ultimate disaster. The Rhodesians were brave, and had effective armed services. They had fought alongside British forces in both wars. It was, as I thought and still think, impossible to imagine that the British should make Rhodesia a battlefield on behalf of other countries, most of whom did not practise the democracy which they demanded for Rhodesia. Reason and quiet negotiation could, I thought, produce a settlement in Rhodesia, fair to both the European and the African peoples. Force, war, could produce nothing but disaster. So far from creating good race relations, it could throw the whole of Africa into a racial turmoil, and embitter race relations for ever.

My second reason for fearing a reference to the United Nations was that it would amount to a concession that what is in essence a domestic issue can be converted into an international issue if sufficient nations choose to make a point of it. The cant phrase 'constitutes a threat to the peace' is heard in the mouths of delegates to the General Assembly, in spite of the fact that the only threats of force in respect of the Rhodesian problem have come from the vocal attackers; none from Rhodesia. What an irony it would be if counsels of violence prevailed in the United Nations! We would doubtless see the creation of something euphemistically called a 'peace-keeping force', whose first function would be to destroy the peace which now exists.

The United Nations was not created to provide means by which a group of nations can without consent interfere, if necessary by arms, with the domestic affairs of another country; quite the contrary. But should this deplorable process be encouraged, we may all find ourselves and our autonomy put at risk in the presence of a well-organized 'mob' sentiment.

I will take two possible examples. Throughout its history, the Commonwealth of Australia has had—and both sides of the Parliament have supported it—a restrictive immigration policy designed in substance to build up a homogeneous population, and to avoid the creation of internal racial problems of a kind which are to be found in the United States and in South Africa, and are, indeed, beginning to emerge in Great Britain. Immigration policy has always been recognized to have a domestic character; it is one of the attributes of sovereignty that any nation may determine for itself how far and on what principles other people may enter or become citizens. This right is freely exercised in several important Asian countries. It is exercised by the United States of America and by Canada. The fact that each operates a restricted quota system is not a derogation from sovereignty over this matter; it is an expression of it.

Yet, if unfortunate modern precedents for interference are followed, those member nations of the United Nations who object to our Australian policy can, if they secure a majority of votes, say loudly that the policy constitutes a 'threat to the peace', and promote action against Australia to compel her to open her doors and so permit her future social and cultural structure to be determined by others.

And will the United States enjoy any immunity? Nobody can live for even a few months in America, as I have, and read the press, and hear the talk, without realizing that the disputes about 'integration' and 'segregation' go deep, and have a well-advertised bitterness. It will be historically interesting to see whether the United Nations decides to take a hand in the matter. The fact that it has not done so yet is understandable, for if the United States became subject to hostile attack by the U.N., and withdrew its support, the whole structure would collapse. But other smaller countries have just as good a right to the upholding of the domestic jurisdiction principle as has the U.S.A. itself. Financial power cannot be the sole determinant.

My third reason for opposing reference to the United Nations has particular relevance to the Rhodesian incident. The setting up of United Nations mandatory sanctions against Rhodesia must be assumed to have a known or knowable purpose. Is it simply designed to punish Rhodesia by inflicting grievous economic damage? If so, it is a judicial act by a body not judicially qualified. Is it, as I think it must be, intended to compel Rhodesia to accept some new constitutional structure? If so, what structure?

The original Commonwealth sanctions were designed, not to destroy Rhodesia, but to put pressure upon the Smith Government to get 'back to negotiations with Great Britain. But the United Nations sanctions are surely designed to impose a new Constitution, not worked out between Britain and Rhodesia, but, presumably, laid down by the United Nations. What will that constitution be, and how will it be formulated?

It is nothing short of a disaster that a problem which, when the 'five principles' were accepted, seemed eminently capable of solution, and which looked even nearer to a solution after the meeting aboard H.M.S. *Tiger* between Mr Wilson and Mr Smith, should now have become so apparently hopeless. It is not reasonable to believe that details do not admit of adjustment, given goodwill and common sense on both sides (which one should be able to assume) and an absence of misunderstanding. Everything I have read suggests that the *Tiger* proposals, particularly those relating to the position and powers of the Governor under the proposed Constitution, were interpreted differently in London and Salisbury. But this is all hearsay, and has no place in this book, which is essentially a personal record.

For myself, I do not defend Rhodesia's Unilateral Declaration of Independence. I think that it was unlawful, being in breach of Constitutional authority; I think it was impetuous and ill-advised; I think that the ruling party in Rhodesia errs grievously if it believes that, in this century, it can indefinitely maintain white authority in a predominantly coloured population.

But surely there could be compromise on some basis of 'gradualism'. For two facts seem to me to be beyond dispute. The first is that if U.N. mandatory sanctions are both universally applied and economically complete, Rhodesia may be economically and financially ruined, with disastrous consequences for the very Africans whom the United Nations designs to protect. There is a marked, and indeed vital, difference between sanctions aimed at exercising pressure, and far-reaching sanctions which are aimed at punishment and even destruction.

My second fact is that the chief agitators in this matter (who are not primarily Rhodesians) will not rest until they talk the United Nations Assembly into recommending force. This would mean a racial war in Africa, the effects of which could last for a century, and would certainly divide the Commonwealth beyond repair.

I am therefore among those who, like that wise and great man, Sir Alec Douglas-Home, think that it can never be too late to mend; that even now vigorous efforts should be made to clear up any misunderstanding and secure an honourable settlement. It would be a wicked tragedy in Commonwealth history if the one British African colony which was represented in London conferences for thirty years should in future find itself the only one to be shut out from the family, driven into an involuntary republicanism, and involved in utter tragedy.

Do these rather melancholy reflections mean that I think that the Commonwealth has been modernized out of existence, and that, even if not actually dead, there is no health in it? I hope not, and for two quite disparate reasons. The first is that so long as there remains a nucleus of nations who live within the common allegiance to the Crown, there will be a British Commonwealth which will need no documents to maintain it. I mention this, not because I think it either inevitable or desirable, but for a good practical reason. As I have seen the new Commonwealth develop, and as my ears have been accustomed to the language of attack and of promotion of differences, I have become increasingly conscious of danger. On the issues promoted by some of the new members, there inevitably arise differences of substance or of degree between some of the old members. This is something to be watched. If it turns out that the new Commonwealth has been called into existence to divide the basic unity of the old, we may end up with no Commonwealth at all.

This would be a world tragedy. For I still believe that a cohesive Commonwealth is of great importance to world freedom. I concede that cohesion in the sense of unanimity of outlook and policy is impossible. But I still think that there are some elements of cohesion which we should do our best to maintain and promote. We used to make lyrical after-dinner speeches about them; they now require prosaic attention. For no special association of nations, whether it is the Commonwealth, or NATO, or SEATO, can long endure unless it has more important things in common than it has in dispute. As I have repeatedly said, the Commonwealth is not a committee of the United Nations. If it becomes one, its reason for existence will come to an end. If all that is needed is a periodical platform for the ventilation of opinions, the United Nations can provide it. Indeed, that was the original purpose of the General Assembly.

But the Commonwealth is a special association, with its roots in history. It must, if it is to endure, preserve its separate and unique character. Is it too late to pause, and take stock, and concentrate upon the things that unite us?

What things have I in mind? Not Parliamentary Democracy at present, though it is one of the great British gifts to the world. For Parliamentary Democracy, as I have pointed out earlier, is not a common element in the new nations. With the passage of time and the growth of education and a demand for the rights of citizenship, it may become so.

Could the recognition of the Rule of Law, the second great creation of Great Britain, prove to be a uniting element? In Australia, in 1965, there occurred a 'Commonwealth and Empire Legal Conference', widely representative of Commonwealth countries. It was a success. It gave me great hope for the future. For the Commonwealth must stand for the ideal of a high civilization, the very basis of which is the Rule of Law and the honest administration of justice.

I also attach high value to the work and meetings of the Commonwealth Parliamentary Association, which has been happily able to develop a tradition of frankness and dignity, without divisive resolutions.

The other real nexus is, of course, the Prime Ministers' Conferences. As I have indicated, they became, for me, extremely frustrating and even puzzling; too willing to set aside what seemed to me to be important principles.

It may, of course, be retorted that, as one whose ideas on the Commonwealth go back many years, I have developed fixed ideas, and that I must move with the times.

Well, I suppose that we all must; life is never static, and our ideas cannot be. 'Why,' I am told, 'we have a genius for compromise; the whole history of the Commonwealth proves it!'

This is a self-comforting idea. No man could have had my long experience of politics without learning that politics is the art of the possible, and that compromise is inevitable. But there are certain basic articles of faith which must be inviolate. It is to these that I have directed myself in this critical study.

CHAPTER TEN

THE CROWN IN THE COMMONWEALTH

A S WE HAVE SEEN, there are today some Members of the Commonwealth who are within the direct allegiance to the Crown; there are others, consequent upon the events of 1949, who own no allegiance, but 'recognize' the Queen as the 'Head of the Commonwealth'.

Therefore, in evaluating the place of the Crown in the Commonwealth, it is no longer possible to make a single assessment.

It would, I think, be unduly naïve to imagine that the phrase 'the Head of the Commonwealth' can be expected to mean very much to the private citizens of republics. As years go on, it will mean less and less, until in due course it may evoke no more response than would be evoked by an acknowledgment that 'X' is 'recognized as President of the General Assembly of the United Nations'. This, I hasten to say, is not a disgruntled remark by an old Monarchist who is also an 'old British Commonwealth hand'. I set it down in plain English, because I believe it to be inevitable.

And why not? The best way in which to demonstrate the truth of this elementary prophecy is to say something about what the Monarch means to and in Commonwealth countries who retain the direct allegiance; not for submission, but for pride.

In my own country, the 'Royal Style and Titles Act' (in the working out of which I had taken an active part in London) declared Her Majesty to be 'Elizabeth the Second, by the grace of God, of the United Kingdom, Australia and her other Realms and Territories Queen, Head of the Commonwealth, Defender of the Faith'. 'Elizabeth the Second.' Who was the first? The instructed memory of every schoolboy and schoolgirl goes back to the first Elizabeth, to the days of Shakespeare and Raleigh. To the royalist, the whole essence is that the Crown represents the history of centuries; that it is no new invention, but something about which our history has long revolved. It gives us a focal point, a centre of gravity, without which no nation can survive.

And this feeling about Monarchy, so deep-seated as to have become instinctive, is made vivid for us in almost every public activity.

In the Australian Parliament, elected Members publicly take the Oath of Allegiance. They pass into law Acts which begin 'Be it enacted by the Queen's Most Excellent Majesty, the Senate, and the House of Representatives of the Commonwealth of Australia, as follows'.

True, the Act receives the Royal Assent in almost every case by the hand of the Governor-General. But he is, by the Constitution, 'Her Majesty's representative'. Appropriations of money by the Parliament should not be made 'unless the purpose of the appropriation has in the same session been recommended by message of the Governor-General to the House in which the proposal originated' (Section 56).

In however nominal a way—and I know that the Monarchy is a Constitutional Monarchy, that is, controlled by the Constitution—the Queen is part of the Australian legislature. She is, in that sense, as she said to us on her first Royal visit, our colleague.

She is also part of the daily administration of the law. 'Her' judges preside in court; it is 'her' writ which runs; in the criminal courts it is 'her' prosecutor who prosecutes. And, in the courts, certain senior counsel are appointed 'Queen's Counsel'.

The mail is still the 'Royal Mail'.

I could give many more examples; but these are enough to indicate that, in a Commonwealth country which remains within the direct allegiance, the Crown remains as a pervasive element. Powerless, if you like, in a substantial sense, except by the will of the democracy, but powerful in the sustaining of a sense of history and of unity.

Australia could never become a Republic except by a deliberate decision not only to eliminate the allegiance to the Crown, but to get rid of all those factors which, in our daily lives, recognize the Crown.

In countries which have become republics in the new Commonwealth, these things have been done, presumably with public approval. The Queen has lost her internal significance. She has become, not a colleague but an outsider, respected in her office but no longer part of the daily national life. I do not offer impertinent opinions on what these countries have decided to do. It is their business, and not mine. To interfere in it, even by unasked opinion, would be to challenge their independent authority.

But, having regard to certain modern tendencies which I will discuss, I think it proper to say something about the reasons why some Commonwealth Members adhere to the Crown, and why we attach real value to it. The problem is not just one of mechanics; nor is it to be solved by a sort of rearguard action.

I think I can understand how the modern movement towards Commonwealth republicanism occurred.

The creation of a republic does not make complete independence more independent. Why should people think it does? Well, in countries like India and Pakistan and the new African nations Republicanism has presented itself as the antithesis and opponent of 'Colonialism'. What is colonialism? Does it, as it should, connote a state of affairs in which a country or race is governed, against its will, by another? Or, if not literally against its will, without the opportunity of expressing its own will through representative institutions?

Frankly, I do not believe that this is the current connotation of this much used, and frequently abused, word. If it were, it would be clearly fantastic for the leader of the Soviet Union, which has converted into colonies or satellites European nations such as Poland and Hungary, and has thus become a great Imperial power, to speak glibly to countries like Indonesia about 'the struggle against colonialism and Imperialist aggression'. Nor was it rational for Sukarno of Indonesia to have invoked the passion against colonialism in order to support his claim to convert Dutch New Guinea into an Indonesian colony.

It thus seems clear that, when the word 'colonialism' is used in Asian or African countries, it connotes control of an Asian or African community by a Western or European power. So understood, the Soviet Union is innocent of colonialism; Australia is a colonial power in relation to East New Guinea and Papua; Indonesia, with control of West New Guinea, is not a colonial power at all!

I think that this simple analysis goes a good way to explain how it is that India, having been to a large extent prepared for self-government and having been granted it, turned away from that independent status under the Crown which Australia enjoys, and chose to be a republic. I have always doubted whether the republican idea had the same appeal and urgency in Pakistan. Yet, when an Indian Republic was retained in the Commonwealth, the Republic of Pakistan became inevitable. For, though a member of a Republic is no more free than a subject of the Queen, he is disposed to think that he is. He will tell his neighbours so. His neighbours will in due course come to agree with him.

In addition to this, it has, in recent years, become vulgarly fashionable to write and publish in England denigratory articles about the Crown and (for good measure) about the Royal Family. The attackers, whose names will perhaps occur to you, wear the mask of the disilusioned intellectual, a mask which conceals their own inverted snobbery. They have not wit enough to realize that to occupy much time in attacking something which they affect to despise is to reveal their own lack of any sense of perspective.

But if they wish to be rid of the Monarchy, and substitute an elected President; if they wish to convert Buckingham Palace into a White House, which will attract its own 'social circle'; if they affect to prefer the publicity which attaches to a President's family to the publicity which attaches to the Queen's family; then there are some facts to be faced. As a loyal Monarchist, I will endeavour to state some of them.

I propound a few questions.

Do we really believe that a State can exist without a Head of State? Can we conceive of a nation or State whose structure has no centre?

Do we believe that, in the modern world, there is no longer any need for a symbol of national unity?

These questions answer themselves, as I think even the critics would concede. If they do not concede, then I am lost; for they are envisaging a world of which I know nothing, and which passes my imagination; a strange, discrete, even anarchistic world.

What, then, is the significance of the Crown? In my time, I have seen many notions current, whether consciously or subconsciously.

Taking it at the lowest, there is the social idea. To have seen the Queen is something, to know somebody in her entourage is something better, to have spoken to the Queen is to enter, though unofficially, the ranks of the nobility. All this is harmless enough, but it does not have the root of the matter in it. The cheapest and most stupid of film stars and music hall crooners or weepers have their 'fans' and tumultuous 'bobby soxers'. We must go much deeper if we are to understand the significance of The Crown.

There are, therefore, several questions to be put and answered. What is the legal significance of the Crown? I have answered this question.

Is this significance nominal only, or has it structural significance?

Is loyalty to the Crown a transient emotion, or is it a true constituent in national integrity?

Should the Crown be brought 'nearer to the people', or should there remain some mystery, some aloofness, so that we think of the Crown as something beyond and above our daily lives, something *fixed* and durable in a world of social and political change and conflict, something 'above the storm'?

In my generation, and I have lived through an increasingly materialist age, we tend to measure the success of people by what they can earn, the achievement of scientists by what they can add to national power, the merit of governments by the current standards of living and social services. We are not sufficiently disposed to believe in disinterested public service. We are so little concerned with the things that really make life worth living that we half starve our clergy and expect many of our best writers and artists to live in a sort of eccentric penury.

It is not quite as bad as this, of course. I overstate the case; but there is too much truth in it for comfort.

It is just because this utilitarian philosophy has become so prevalent that so many misconceived arguments about the Crown arise. What are its uses? Does it justify the money we spend on it? Since its real powers are now vestigial, should we now get rid of it?

I am a Monarchist just because to me, and millions of others, the Crown is non-utilitarian; it represents a spiritual and emotional conception more enduring and significant than any balance sheet cast up by an accountant.

The attack on the British Monarchy begins by maintaining that it is powerless and therefore insignificant; that it is, in the old phrase, 'useless, dangerous, and therefore should be abolished'. The wheel of history is indeed to be turned. The whole process of British Constitutional history has been from absolute to constitutional monarchy.

As the powers of the people, through Parliament, have come to be paramount, so have the powers of the Crown diminished.

This, in our simple fashion, we have thought to be good. The Monarch is no longer the tyrant, but the symbol; the confidante and unofficial adviser of Ministers, no doubt, but powerless to overrule them or refuse to give effect to their decisions; inspiring loyalty and setting an example, evoking a powerful sense of allegiance and therefore of national unity, but not asserting an authority of her own.

Now, these latter-day English Republicans do not for a momen believe that the cure for Monarchy is simple abolition. Their occupation would be gone indeed. But they want a President, partly because this would (they affect to believe) get rid of Palace snobbery—meaning by that the snobbery of people who wish to be invited to the Palace, and the even more virulent snobbery of those who have not been so invited.

Well, what sort of President do they desire? On this, they have not condescended to particulars. A titular President, as in the Republic of India? If their passions are based on economic considerations, are they sure of their prospective savings? The splendid Viceroy's palace at New Delhi, so vast that, as one wit said to me when I was a guest, you need a bicycle to travel the length of a corridor, is now occupied by a President. There are still splendid-looking men in uniform, and hosts of servants. And there would be such people at Buckingham Palace, if a President took over. No people courting invitations? No rules of protocol? Forget it!

If, in Australia, we became a Republic, would Government House be closed because the Governor-General, the Queen's personal representative, had gone, and a President, a purely titular head of State, had come?

In brief, and it needs little argument, the substitution for the Crown of a titular President, splendid but powerless, would bring about no change except the substitution of election for heredity. Such a President, to put it plainly, would be a temporarily-elected Republican Monarch. Every few years there would be a Presidential Election, after a great party election campaign, which would make the President a controversial figure without adding one ounce to his power.

But if what is desired is an Executive President, as in the United

States of America, a political and powerful Head of Government, other considerations will apply. I do not criticize, in fact I think that I understand, why the American colonies, having successfully rebelled against a stupid and oppressive Government in London, having made a Declaration of Independence in noble terms which have become part of the inheritance of their now great country, chose to have as President a man who would replace both English King and English Prime Minister. He was to be the Chief Executive of a new and independent nation. And, as Chief Executive, he was to be chosen by the people, and replaced, in due course, by the people. He was not to be merely an honorific substitute for the King.

Now, the genius of the American people has made the system work; and I, for one, have no complaint to make about it. The whole world is indebted to it. But it was the product of a Revolution against a Monarchy dominated by a highly political King who still aspired to a sort of absolutism.

Those of us who have, in the nineteenth and twentieth centuries, inherited, first, a system of Responsible Government, and then a Constitutional Monarchy in the true sense, have not been forced into revolution. Our inheritance and our instincts are continuous.

A democracy needs a focal point; otherwise it is 'without form and void'. There must be a powerful centripetal force in any nation if it is to be cohesive and strong.

In a republic the focal point is the President; in a monarchy, the Crown.

If a President is designed to be non-political, then Monarchy has the superiority every time. For, as I have said, the notion of a non-political President periodically elected by popular vote, after an election campaign, is a contradiction in terms. This is, of course, the reason why Republican Executive Presidents are always party politicians backed, at each election, by the whole strength of the party machine. The President of the United States of America is the Chief Executive of the nation, with very great powers. He has always been the subject of political controversy. There have been other Presidents elsewhere with almost absolute powers; but under such circumstances there is no true democracy.

The focal point in a democratic Republic is therefore an office, occupied by a man. The office may be held in veneration, but the man may well be, and not infrequently is, as now in the United States, criticized or actually abused by half of the electors.

American Republicans like this system; they understand it; it works.

In a Monarchy like ours, the focal point is also an office, the Crown, now occupied by a woman, the Queen. Her actual powers are small; she acts upon the advice of her Ministers, whose views are, on political occasions such as the Opening of Parliament, expressed by her, but not attributed to her. She never enters the political lists. Rooted as her office is in the deep soil of history, enduring as it has proved through the great shocks of political and military and social events, it enjoys the respect of all but a handful of her people. The Queen is seen, in all the countries within her allegiance as the fountain of honour, the protector of the law, the centre of a Parliamentary system in which she makes and proclaims statutes 'by and with the advice and consent' of Parliament. True, all of these things are, if you like, a matter of form. Even the Royal prerogatives are now defined by the law and are exercised in accordance with it. But no amount of cold analysis can destroy the basic fact that the Crown remains the centre of our democracy; a fixed point in the whirl of circumstance. This great and practical truth is seen most clearly on historic occasions.

My wife and I, accompanied by our daughter, were in London in November 1948, at the time when Prince Charles was born at Buckingham Palace. We had a flat in Berkeley Street. The air was full of expectation. There were crowds outside the Palace, waiting for the news. As the day wore on the crowds grew. We were among them. They represented a broad cross-section of the people, from Privy Councillors to small boys. We had hardly returned to our flat for some sustaining refreshment when the announcement of the birth came over the wireless. At once we set down our glasses and our knives and forks and literally galloped across the Green Park to the Palace. There was the physician's bulletin, posted at the gates. The excitement was intense. We were all friends, and slapped the backs of perfect strangers with complete abandon. For sound reasons we could not call out for the Princess, but we did, most lustily and senselessly, call out for the Duke. By the end of another hour we, thousands of us, changed our quarry, and roared for the King. No result. The balconies of the

Palace were untenanted. We then put it on a family basis. We, and nobody more vociferously than the ex- and future Prime Minister of Australia, cried in unison 'we want grandfather!' Wearied by unsuccessful well-doing, we then went home.

That is a simple enough story, but it contains, if you consider it, the essential beginning of an understanding of the place of the British Crown in the hearts and minds of those who own allegiance to it. It was a democratic crowd; its cheers and exuberant goodwill were those of a democracy which saw the Crown, not as its opponent, but as its focal point; and, in those moving hours, it saw beyond the panoply of monarchy to a grandson, a daughter, a grandfather, whom it dearly loved.

I first became a Minister of State, in Victoria, in 1928; and a Minister in the Australian Commonwealth Government in 1934, retiring in 1966. Thus it was that I had the honour of serving under Kings George V, Edward VIII, George VI, and Queen Elizabeth II—four monarchs.

Mere figureheads, the sceptics, the 'clever modern men' will say. Nothing could be further from the truth. I hope I may be acquitted of presumption if I set down a few observations, made at first hand, about each of them. For I am an unrepentant monarchist; I believe in the significance of the Crown in our British system of Government; and above all I believe that in my time we have had monarchs of high character and powerful personality, who have made a notable contribution to our history, who have been real contributors to the continuity of our institutions, and whose status, both official and personal, has helped to establish that simple sense of continuity and endurance to which the world has owed so much in two great wars.

I am impatient with some recent commentators. 'Let us bring the monarchy down to earth,' they seem to say. 'Let it abandon any atmosphere of remoteness, and mix freely with us, and it will soon find its own level!'

This is, of course, mere demagoguery, based upon envy and ignorance. The monarchs they criticize, and to whom they would deny any private life of the kind they reserve to themselves, have succeeded in reconciling the necessarily 'remote' dignity of the office with a warm interest and involvement in the affairs of human beings.

Perhaps the right way in which to establish this truth is not to work out an elaborate theory, but to deal with individual cases.

As I said at Cambridge in 1960, and I crave leave to repeat it:

The great King George V came to the throne amid murmured and sometimes loudly spoken criticism. He survived both, and a great war, and grew into the hearts of his people. When the war was over, a great stirring began, which transformed the conception of Empire and produced the new Dominion Status and the Statute of Westminster. The King shrewdly saw the implications. He accommodated himself to the new democracy and the new Commonwealth. He saw vividly the technical limitations on his own official power, but with great penetration saw that his own personal influence and experience were not irrelevant. He secured the friendship of Tory and Socialist alike. He on occasion affected their conduct without assertion of prerogative. He lived to be a much loved man, with a much loved wife. He asserted few or no rights, but he was, nevertheless, the centre of constitutional government. He was, in my opinion, the first great Constitutional Monarch.

When the Ramsay MacDonald Government came in, there was wide speculation about how it would get on with the Crown. Previous governments, whether Conservative or Liberal, had to a large extent been drawn from the more highly educated classes. Court circles were, almost inevitably, thought to be predominantly Conservative. How would the Socialists, with a rich and colourful representation of Trade Unionists, be received. How would they fit in?

It at once transpired that there was no problem at all. This was due to a sense of adjustment on both sides.

It used to be one of the unfortunate traditions in the Australian Labour Party that it was 'undemocratic' to wear formal clothes, even to Government House. To do so would be a concession to the Capitalists.

The British Labour Party had no such inhibitions. There were, of course, exceptions, but they were very few. The late J. H. Thomas ('Jimmy'), who was fond of describing himself as 'the humble carriage-cleaner', conformed. He told me once, with uproarious glee, that, being Lord Privy Seal (and dealing with unemployment) he arrived at Buckingham Palace, in full court uniform, for a State dinner. By way of compromising with democracy, he arrived in a taxi driven by a typical London cabby; cloth cap, wispy moustache, old pipe, and a sardonic gleam in the eye! At the entrance in the inner courtyard, a splendiferous footman opened the door and announced to the footman at the top of the entrance-steps 'My Lord Privy Seal!' To which the cabby was heard by 'Jimmy' to add, 'Lord Privy Seal be damned. It's only Jimmy Thomas!'

Now, the purpose of this story is double-edged. The fact that Jimmy Thomas, when we had become friends, told it to me with immense gusto (and, having respect for the Lord Chamberlain, I have altered only one word) shows what a rich character Jimmy was. The fact, which I later verified at the Palace itself, that King George V had a soft spot for 'Jimmy', and usually converted a formal audience into a private conversation, shows what a character the King was!

King George V was of rather less than middle height—a feature accentuated by the facts that Queen Mary was tall, regal, and reserved, and also had a taste for tall hats known (I am credibly informed) as 'toques'. He was bearded. His eyes were prominent. His deep voice had a hint of bronchitis in it, which, in my experience, gave it a rather confidential character. He knew and had known men of all sorts; and could put as whimsical a question to me about 'that little devil, Billy Hughes', formerly a picturesque Prime Minister of Australia, as he could about people better known on the local scene.

I have ventured to describe him as the 'first great Constitutional Monarch', because I believe that he was the first to realize that, in the modern democracy, he had to deal with human beings chosen by their fellows; that he must earn their confidence and respect, that he should always be willing to proffer advice without pretending to authority; in brief, that he should bring the dignity of the Crown and the rights and responsibilities of a chosen popular government into the same room.

Queen Mary had, as the world saw her, a sort of noble but awful dignity. She was, I think, the last Queen to enforce the formidable rule that 'when you are with royalty, you speak when you are spoken to'. When I first had the honour of being presented to her, I had a *'mauvais quart d'heure'*, for the only eloquent thing was my silence. There were no such problems with the King. I was to live long enough to be given tea by Queen Mary at Marlborough House when Hitler's Germany was on the attack, and hear her say one of the most perfectly

English things I ever heard: 'Don't you think that this fellow Hitler is the most dreadful bore?'

In 1935, there came the Jubilee of King George V's accession to the throne. There were unforgettable ceremonies, and a really tremendous outpouring of public affection. ('I had no idea that I was popular,' he said to me afterwards, with considerable emotion.) The demonstrations were not just those of courtiers; they moved from people of every rank and occupation. I take leave to repeat one personal experience. The day after the great procession to St Paul's, and the Service of Thanksgiving, I went to have a haircut at a little barber's shop up an alley off the Strand. The barber was a museum piece, with a friendly manner and a fine quiff of hair falling over one side of his forehead. Naturally, he did not know me from Adam, and spoke as he thought. Brandishing the cutting implements of his trade, he said: 'Did you see the procession to St Paul's yesterday, sir?' I had. 'Did you notice what a lovely day it was?' I did. 'You can't tell me God didn't have a hand in that, sir!' I agreed. And then I said (may I be forgiven), 'Do you believe in all this royalty business?' It was a deliberately discouraging question, but the answer was superb. 'Well, you see, it's like this. When I knock off work, I go up to a pub in Holborn, and have a couple of pints with some of my friends. We argue about a lot of things, but *we're all for the King!*'

'The Crown provides a sort of raree show for the populace,' say the modern cynics, 'but it serves no useful purpose.' One has only to recall the events of 1935 to see the answer. For those events made it clear that for the British people, the Crown was the symbol of a profound national unity; a unity which, in only a few years, was to be the foundation of victory.

In brief, King George V was a great King because his people grew to know him, to see in him the simple virtues of ordinary life, and to respect him. He was in a sense remote as a King; but he was not remote as a man. There were many who knew more about books than he did; but few who knew more about men. His intellectual interests may have been limited; but he had a great compensation; there was no limit to his common sense.

He was succeeded by Edward VIII; a paradoxical man, a vastly popular Prince of Wales who, before he could be crowned, abdicated with general, though sad, approval.

Here indeed, is a puzzle; yet it can, I believe, be understood. For Edward the Prince was, as we say nowadays, 'temperamental'. Perhaps he had lived in the limelight when he was too young to achieve a perfect balance. He was undoubtedly moody. I remember that in 1936, in London, when I was Australian Attorney-General, I was at receptions given by him on two successive days. When I came up to him the first time, he was abrupt, made some off-hand remarks about Australia, and, so to say, dismissed me into outer darkness.

The next day, all was sweetness and light. The moment my turn came, he said, 'Come into the next room; I want to have a talk!' Off we went. For twenty minutes he discussed constitutional problems —with which I was professionally pretty well acquainted—with a degree of knowledge and clarity of expression which I could only envy.

I had later occasions to notice this strange duality in the personality of this gifted but emotionally disturbed man. But that he would make a fine king, uniting deep knowledge with a genuine human interest in the unfortunate and depressed, none of us doubted. The events leading up to his abdication therefore came as a great shock. I will not attempt to sit in judgement on the issues raised by him in *A King's Story*, that most moving narrative, for I have no knowledge of what passed between the King and his British Ministers at that time.

But I can, at first hand, record what happened with us in the Australian Government and Parliament.

On 28 November 1936, the then Prime Minister of Australia (Mr J. A. Lyons) received from Mr Baldwin, as he then was, Prime Minister of the United Kingdom, a secret and confidential message informing him that King Edward VIII contemplated abdicating and leaving the Duke of York to succeed to the Throne. There had been much talk, particularly in the American press, of the King's attachment to Mrs Wallis Simpson, an American lady, of whom Mr Lyons said to Parliament on 11 December, that she had been twice divorced, the first and second husbands still living. He added that 'the decree nisi for her divorce from the second of those husbands has not yet been made absolute'.

Mr Lyons reported that Mr Baldwin's message said that 'He had had conversation with His Majesty the King about Mrs Simpson; that His Majesty had stated his intention to marry Mrs Simpson; but that at the same time His Majesty had said that he appreciated that the idea of her becoming Queen and her children succeeding to the Throne was out of the question, and that consequently he contemplated abdicating'.

Mr Lyons went on to say, of Mr Baldwin's message, that 'His Majesty had subsequently asked Mr Baldwin's views on a new proposal, namely, that special legislative provision should be made for a marriage to Mrs Simpson which would not make her Queen and would not entitle her issue to succeed to the Throne. Mr Baldwin informed me that he had advised His Majesty that he did not think there was any chance of such an arrangement receiving the approval of Parliament in Great Britain; also that the assent of the Dominions would be essential to the carrying out of such an arrangement. He invited any personal views'.

Having this message before him at his hotel in Melbourne, Mr Lyons rang me and asked me to come in. I found him deeply distressed. He was a warm-hearted man of the highest principles, with, as I knew, an affectionate regard for the King, a deep regard for the significance of the Crown, and a great belief in the family. We discussed the matter and found ourselves on common ground. Mr Lyons would express his personal views, as requested; but neither of us had any doubt about what Australian public opinion would be. The cable he sent was in fact drafted by me at our meeting.

Lyons summarized this message in the House on 11 December as follows:

I then communicated with Mr Baldwin offering my personal view—since at that time the whole matter was highly secret and confidential—that the proposed marriage, if it led to Mrs Simpson becoming Queen, would invoke widespread condemnation, and that the alternative proposal or something in the nature of a specially sanctioned morganatic marriage would run counter to the best popular conception of the Royal Family.

It will be noticed that this advice went beyond the proposal for a morganatic marriage; it covered also the much more debatable possibility that the King would desire to make Mrs Simpson Queen. Baldwin had made it clear that the King himself did not propose this.

It may be that if Baldwin had given him any encouragement the King would have pressed for a Royal marriage in the full sense. If this is so, Baldwin was right in not offering any encouragement. For Lyons was right in saying that such a marriage would 'invoke widespread condemnation'. Baldwin, later much criticized for a failure to understand the growing dangers in Europe or to take strong measures to resist them, was essentially a shrewd English countryman, with a great understanding of the English character and a strong feeling for and influence over the House of Commons.

These last observations apply to Lyons in Australia.

For myself, as emerged in the course of our talks, I entirely agreed with Lyons, and for reasons which may be worth setting down.

First, a morganatic marriage might have been 'acceptable' at the end of the eighteenth century, but in 1936 it would have shocked the public and dealt a grave injury to the Monarchy. It could not be entertained. (The late John Curtin, then Leader of the Opposition, was to say in the House, 'The Australian Labour movement would not have agreed, in any circumstances, to confer upon the wife of any man, even though he should be King, a status less than that which would be the inherent right of her wifehood as the wife of her husband.')

Second, a marriage to Mrs Simpson under which she became Queen and her children in the line of succession would have had unhappy consequences. It must be remembered that the air had buzzed with rumours after the American publications. Mrs Simpson's name and marital history had been bandied about and, with the constant cruelty of rumour, not to her advantage. It was highly improbable that the people would welcome her as Queen after the dignified and impeccable Queen Mary.

Right through the sixteenth, seventeenth and eighteenth centuries, with the exception of the period of Cromwell's Commonwealth, the Monarchy as an institution commanded the public loyalty, whatever many people might think about the Monarch himself as an individual. But in modern times all institutions have come under scrutiny and even challenge. It has, in my time, been one of the strengths of the Monarchy that succeeding Monarchs have enjoyed the personal respect of the people. We have come to expect a model family life and a high example. The institution has been preserved, and as I would believe strengthened by the character and reputation of those who have worn the Crown. But the more truth there is in this belief of mine, the more the damage that could be done if public respect for Queen, or King and Queen, waned or was replaced by angry criticism and personal disrespect.

Looking back to the state of opinion in 1936, with the public attitude to divorce much more critical than it probably is today, and with a high degree of cynicism about American divorces in particular, I still believe that we were right. The growing strength of the Monarchy under George VI and his great Queen was one of the good products of the Abdication.

In the Australian Parliament on 11 December 1936, the King's Instrument of Abdication and his accompanying statement were read:

I, Edward the Eighth, of Great Britain, Ireland, and the British Dominions beyond the Seas King, Emperor of India, do hereby declare My irrevocable determination to renounce the Throne for Myself and for My descendants, and My desire that effect should be given to this Instrument of Abdication immediately.

In token whereof I have hereunto set My hand this tenth day of December, nineteen hundred and thirty-six, in the presence of the witnesses whose signatures are subscribed.

(Signed) Edward R.I.

My execution of this Instrument has been witnessed by My three brothers, Their Royal Highnesses the Duke of York, the Duke of Gloucester, and the Duke of Kent.

I deeply appreciate the spirit which has actuated the appeals which have been made to Me to take a different decision and I have, before reaching My final determination, most fully pondered over them. But My mind is made up. Moreover, further delay cannot but be most injurious to the peoples whom I have tried to serve as Prince of Wales and as King, and whose future happiness and prosperity are the constant wish of My heart. I take My leave of them in the confident hope that the course which I have thought it right to follow is that which is best for the stability of the Throne and the Empire and the happiness of My peoples. I am deeply sensible of the consideration which they have always extended to Me, both before and after My accession to the Throne, and which I know they will extend in full measure to My successor.

I am most anxious that there should be no delay of any kind in giving effect to the Instrument which I have executed and that all necessary steps should be taken immediately to secure that My lawful successor, My brother, His Royal Highness the Duke of York, should ascend the Throne.

Edward R.I.

Each House then, without a division, carried a resolution assenting to United Kingdom legislation making the alterations in the Succession Laws rendered necessary by the Abdication.

It was made clear in Mr Lyons's speech that the governments of Canada, South Africa, and New Zealand had expressed views substantially in agreement with the opinions expressed by the governments of Britain and Australia.

Nothing that I have written will, I hope, give rise to an idea that the Australian Government was in haste to be rid of the King. The contrary was the fact. Edward VIII had visited Australia in 1920 as Prince of Wales. Handsome and gay, he won all hearts. At that time, perhaps, he was seen more as a debonair youth than as a successor to great responsibilities.

Yet, long before his accession to the Throne, we had come to admire him for his serious interest in the social and industrial problems of Britain, and for his broad, but practical, concern with Commonwealth trade and constitutional structure. It was with a warm desire to avoid misfortune that Lyons, on 10 December, having been advised by Baldwin that the King's decision to abdicate was firm, sent a direct message to the King expressing the sympathetic understanding of the Australian Government, and its sincere regret, and begging, in the name of His Majesty's subjects in the Commonwealth of Australia, that he would 'reconsider his decision and continue to reign over us'.

But the King had made up his mind, and decided to abdicate. And who can criticize his decision? He had a grim decision to make. True, he was a King, and in that capacity not his own master; not an absolute Monarch, but a constitutional one with far more duties than rights. But he was also a man, with his own feelings and his own domestic desires for a life of love.

No King ever had a more grievous choice. He made his choice, as a man, not as a King. Those of us who are not Kings (and that puts us in a remarkable majority!) but are ordinary human beings, will understand his choice.

There is another aspect of the Abdication, its legal and constitutional aspect, about which I want to say something. I was Attorney-General. There was, so far as I knew, no precedent for a royal abdication in the constitutional history of the British people. True, Edward II had been deposed; Richard II executed a deed of resignation; but subsequently Parliament drew up articles against him, and he was in substance deposed.

In 1688, James II was in effect driven out of the Kingdom, and the Convention Parliament resolved that the King 'having violated the fundamental laws and withdrawn himself out of the Kingdom has abdicated the Government and the Throne is thereby vacant'.

Having recited this history, I offered the view—but with no specific precedent to guide me, and a common lawyer likes a precedent!—that the constitutional principle was that a ruler's abdication could not be properly carried out without an Act of Parliament; the basis of this view being found in the doctrine (many years before identified and explained by A. V. Dicey in his great *Law of the Constitution*) of the Sovereignty of Parliament.

This, I said, explained why the Parliament of the United Kingdom was introducing a Bill to which the Australian Parliament was being asked to give assent. The British Acts of Succession, being Statutes, could be modified only by Statute. The Deed of Abdication of itself could not bring one reign to an end and cause another to begin. I went on to say:

It is of the greatest importance, constitutionally speaking, that the force of these propositions should be admitted and recognized, since the power of the Crown today depends upon its place in a well-balanced constitutional structure, and not upon either the personal authority of the sovereign, or upon older ideas of his prerogative and rights.

Though at that time the *Statute of Westminster* 1931 had not been adopted by the Australian Parliament, I referred, I think properly, to the Second recital to that Statute as an objective statement of the Constitutional position. That recital reads:

And whereas it is meet and proper to set out by way of preamble to this act that, inasmuch as the Crown is the symbol of the free association of the members of the British Commonwealth of Nations, and as they are united by a common allegiance to the Crown, it would be in accord with the established constitutional position of all the members of the Commonwealth in relation to one another that any alteration in the law touching the Succession to the Throne or the Royal Style and Titles shall hereafter require the assent as well of the Parliaments of all the Dominions as of the Parliament of the United Kingdom.

I concluded by saying:

I have stated with some fullness the constitutional position as I see it, in remarkable and unprecedented circumstances. Although very naturally our interest is directed to, and our emotions are stirred by, the personal drama of the King's proposed marriage, our primary duty as a Parliament in a British community is to preserve the constitutional rights of both the Parliament and the people, established in their modern form 300 years ago, and brought to full power by generations of our predecessors in the responsibility of government.

I have set out, as briefly as possible in relation to a long and closely reasoned speech, the substance of the principles expounded, for one reason only. The Abdication attracted great attention all round the world. It is desirable that its constitutional implications should be understood. So far as I have been able to discover, it was in my own Parliament that they were most fully discussed. It is for this reason that I put them on the record.

Now, these events could have shaken the Crown as an institution but for the fact that it passed to the then Duke of York, who became King George VI, who had married Elizabeth Bowes-Lyon, one of the most admired women in the realm, and had two attractive children, the elder of whom is now Queen. At that time, the new King was indifferently well known; he was a little shy, and spoke with a embarrassing stammer, which he later mastered. But there never could have been a better example of what a sense of duty can do to make a man grow in office. Before he had run his course, he had become one of the greatly loved sovereigns in British history, Why? Well, partly because he was the son of his parents; partly because he had a marvellous wife; partly because he had a great sense of continuity as a British Monarch; but in particular because he was a natural human being, with the basic virtues of humanity, and no desire to pretend. He had, as it turned out, the instinct for the occasion.

When he died in February 1952, I spoke about him in the House of Representatives. I will quote my words, not because they were mine but because they are utterly true of this great man in the crisis of his life, and ours:

His Gracious Majesty King George VI, whose sudden death we mourn today, reigned over us with singular distinction, unfailing courage, and the most constant devotion. He was a Constitutional monarch in the grand tradition of his father, King George V, of happy memory. Possessed of great force of character, a most royal sense of duty, a keen perception of the movements and issues of his day, our late beloved King was in the vast and bitter crisis of the war, in which he served us all so well, ruler, and leader, and friend. His was no distant throne, for he sought no security and shared cheerfully every danger and every trial. All those who saw England under daily and nightly attack in the great battle of 1940 and 1941 were stirred by the spectacle of an embattled nation, normally not unacquainted with internal divisions and hostilities, in which there was unity, cheerfulness, courage, a common resolution which ran through factory and farm, which made the King and his humblest subject feel a deep and human brotherhood. It was that superb fusing of the common will which defeated the enemy, and did so much to save the world.

King George VI and his Queen Elizabeth were among the great architects of that brotherhood.

I will repeat a story which I told in Sydney, after my return in 1941 to Australia:

The King, who, with Her Majesty the Queen, is to be seen on every stricken field in Britain, and who grows in vigour and force as she grows in charm, was visiting an area in which bombs had fallen, in which homes had been shattered, in which loved lives had been lost. As they moved around this place with words of encouragement and sympathy to the people, one of the onlookers, one of those who had been bombed out of his home, and had seen the efforts of his life reduced to fragments around him, stretched out a friendly hand, and put it on the King's shoulder and said robustly, in a sort of Australian manner—'THANK GOD FOR A GOOD KING!'

To which the King replied, in words that deserve to be immortal, 'And thank God for a good people.'

It is an open secret that he did not want to be King; he was deeply grieved by the abdication, and his personal ambitions were modest. But he rose to the occasion; and he also will go down in history as a great Constitutional Monarch.

I have a belief that the basis for the continuity of the Monarchy in the British crown countries has changed since the eighteenth century. The early Georges did not survive by personal popularity, or for that matter by possessing characters which excited general respect. The first

George spoke no English, and therefore had no means of popular communication. The second George was not really known to his people. I was brought up on J. R. Green's *History of the English People,* and therefore remind myself of his uncompromising passage about these two monarchs.

Under the two sovereigns who followed Anne the power of the Crown lay absolutely dormant. They were strangers, to whom loyalty in its personal sense was impossible; and their character as nearly approached insignificance as it is possible for human character to approach it. Both were honest and straightforward men, who accepted the irksome position of Constitutional Kings. But neither had any qualities which could make their honesty attractive to the people at large.

George III was different. He was clearly determined to play a large part in politics, and did so, on the whole, with disastrous results. He became no more popular at home than he was in the American colonies. His mental capacities seem to have been of a fluctuating order. He opposed and sought to frustrate his greatest statesmen, such as the elder Pitt. He had, in effect, a 'King's Party', and intervened in the operations of Parliament with singular lack of scruple. Among the outside public, his actions were bitterly resented.

He became temporarily mad in 1788, and again in 1811. His son, the Prince, was given to high life and low company. And all this when what was, up to that time, the greatest crisis in Britain's battle for survival was being faced, with Nelson fighting and winning crucial battles at sea, and Wellington conducting, with unsurpassed skill and patience, the long campaigns in Europe which led to the overthrow of Napoleon.

It is open to doubt whether the British Crown could have survived these monarchs had they lived in the twentieth century. But it did survive, because the institution, and not the person who sat on the throne, held its place in the public consciousness.

Today, it may be unlikely that monarchy would survive a bad or glaring incompetent ruler. I may well be wrong, for we have a great sense of institution. But the question has not arisen, nor is it likely to do so in foreseeable history; for the accession of George VI and then of the present wise and gifted Queen, with a most distinguished husband and splendid children, has firmly established a line of succession which enjoys, in the fullest measure, not only the respect due to an historic institution, but the personal respect and affection of the people.

I have written about the Crown. For the record, and particularly in the light of Harold Nicolson's narrative of the appointment of Sir Isaac Isaacs to be Governor-General of Australia, I want to add my own contribution to Constitutional History.

The Australian Commonwealth Constitution, Section 2, provides that 'a Governor-General appointed by the Queen shall be Her Majesty's representative in the Commonwealth, and shall have and may exercise in the Commonwealth during the Queen's pleasure, but subject to this Constitution, such powers and functions of the Queen as Her Majesty may be pleased to assign to him'.

I do not propose to examine what those 'powers' and 'functions' are, or the procedures of assignment. What I want to write about is the method of appointment. This is a matter of considerable historic interest. In the Australian Commonwealth's earlier years no material question appears to have arisen. The practice was for the Prime Minister of the United Kingdom to make nominations to the King after some kind of informal discussion with the Government of Australia. This meant that the effective selection was made at the London end.

But after the 1914-18 war, a new conception of Dominion status arose. It was, in 1926, enshrined in the so-called Balfour formula. By 1930 it had led to the preliminary discussion of what was to become the Statute of Westminster 1931. Resolutions were passed by the Imperial Conference of 1930, which was attended on behalf of Australia by the then Prime Minister, J. H. Scullin. The retiring Governor-General was Lord Stonehaven. The newly elected Labour Government had come into office at the end of 1929, after a prolonged period of opposition. It contained within itself a strongly nationalist element, which was determined that any new Governor-General must be an Australian. Obviously there might be wide objection to the appointment of a practising Australian Labour politician (an objection which, as we were to see, would later on be abandoned). The Australian Government's choice therefore fell upon Sir Isaac Isaacs, who had been for many years a distinguished judge, and who was then Chief Justice of the High Court.

Harold Nicolson, in his *King George V*, has vividly described the course of events. It is sufficient for my purpose to say that two things emerged.

One was that the Imperial Conference resolved that the King, in appointing a Governor-General, should act 'on the advice of His Majesty's Ministers in the Dominion concerned'.

The other was that Scullin refused to discuss anybody other than Isaacs, insisted upon his nomination, and, to the anger of the King, won the point.

I had thought a great deal about these events which, as I will recount, became material to a decision which I had to make many years later.

The formal resolution of the Conference was not without ambiguity. The phrase 'on the advice of' may refer to the formal act of appointment, in which case it was a proper recognition of the new status of a fully self-governing dominion and of its direct relationship to the Crown. On the other hand it might refer to the substance of the procedure by which the new Governor-General was to be selected. If so, did it mean that the King had no say, that only one name was to be put forward, and that the King must therefore, at once, agree? Such a view would, in my opinion, ignore the significance of the Governor-General as the King's personal representative. That a King should have forced upon him a personal representative whom he, for example, disliked and distrusted would scarcely be conducive to good representation and would inevitably, as its implications became known, tend to weaken the vital position of the Crown in the Commonwealth. That the King should force upon a Prime Minister somebody known by the Prime Minister to be unsuitable and unacceptable would be equally damaging.

However, it was clearly assumed in 1930 that the King had no choice either in form or in substance.

The problem arose again in 1947, when the term of office, as Governor-General, of H.R.H. the Duke of Gloucester was coming to an end. J. B. Chifley was then Prime Minister. Chifley was a very much abler man than Scullin; his grasp and command of many matters were quite outstanding. He was not, however, deeply interested in external affairs which, with a wry smile, he left to the ambitious Evatt. Nor did he have the instinctive understanding of the place of Parliament and of the place of the Crown in the Commonwealth, which was possessed by the more reflective Curtin.

Chifley, in short, thought that the Governor-Generalship was a well-paid 'job' which could usefully be held by a party member, whether the King knew him or not, or liked him or not. There was no discussion with the King. One name only was put before him, and that by cable. The choice fell upon W. J. McKell, the serving Labour Premier of the State of New South Wales.

McKell, now Sir William, was well known to me. He was a lawyer and politician whom I respected, and with whom I had a personal friendship. But, when the appointment was foreshadowed, I asked Chifley, on 22 November 1946, whether he could make any announcement. He replied, oddly enough, 'As the right honourable gentleman knows, this appointment lies in the hands of His Majesty the King!' The answer was, of course, technically correct.

On 28 November, I returned to the matter, rumours about the projected appointment of McKell being in full spate. Having referred to the fact that there was 'no substantial nexus between the British Nations except the Crown', I went on to say, 'The Governor-General of Australia being the King's direct personal representative, the appointment of somebody notoriously not chosen either by, or in effective consultation with him, and whose appointment would, by reason of party political convictions, be distasteful to a large section of Australian citizens, must inevitably weaken the symbolism of the Governor-Generalship, and, therefore, of the Crown which it represents.'

I then said, to meet the argument that 'Australians need not apply'— that 'the immediate point at issue is not whether an Australian should be eligible for appointment as Governor-General, but whether an active party political leader should be transferred by his own party to a post which should, by tradition, and, indeed, necessity, be completely free of party politics'.

Later, I stated my own view of the constitutional position in words which I was later to recall as Prime Minister.

'It is true that, by modern constitutional practice, the King is bound, in the last resort, to act upon the advice of his Ministers in the exercise of his power of appointment, but it is equally true that Ministers exercising the responsibility of advice should not forget that the man appointed is to act as the trusted personal representative of the King, and not as the political representative of the Australian Government for the time being; and that, therefore, great consideration should be extended to His Majesty's wishes in the matter.' Shortly thereafter, McKell's appointment was announced. I referred to the matter in the House on 20 February 1947. I even quoted Professor Laski, not much of a royalist—'the strength of the Crown rests upon the conviction that its neutrality is, in all cases, above suspicion' and added that this must be equally true of the Crown's Governor-General.

Close observers have not failed to notice that, as the Governor-General holds office *at the Queen's pleasure,* a pleasure to be exercised on political advice, an enforced appointment of a political Governor-General, 'enforced' because the Queen had no choice, could be followed, on a change of Government, by an enforced termination. Carried to its grimmest logical conclusion, this could mean that Governors-General would go in or out with Governments, all pretence of neutrality being abandoned. I dealt with this matter myself in these words:

If all political parties in Australia took the same view as the Labour Party does about the Governor-Generalship—in other words if all parties in this House believed the Governor-Generalship was simply a political 'plum' to be handed out to some party colleague in Australia—then, of course, with every change of government the appointment of the Governor-General would be terminated and some other politician put in his place. I ask, if not honourable members, at any rate the people of Australia, to consider what will happen to the Governor-Generalship if it is to be regarded as an office, occupancy of which should fluctuate with every change of the constitution of the Commonwealth Parliament? This is degrading the Governor-Generalship by making it the direct product of the party politics of the country.

These arguments, though I still believe them to be sound, were, of course, in the then state of the House, unsuccessful. But there was an interesting sequel. The appointment being duly and formally made, I advised my party that we should treat the new Governor-General with all the respect due to his office, and that we should not allow our constitutional views to colour our relations with him.

Most of the members of my party acted upon this advice. I myself saw the Governor-General quite regularly and had many valuable talks with him. The remarkable and rather disgraceful thing was that Labour Ministers and Members treated him in a casual way, still continuing to regard him as a mere job-holder. This, I know, was properly resented by McKell, who learned to appreciate the strange paradox that he was treated with respectful friendliness only by those who had opposed his appointment. The whole experience was striking evidence of what could happen to the Governor-Generalship if this vulgar conception of its significance were allowed to prevail.

On one occasion, when Field-Marshal Montgomery was visiting Canberra as McKell's guest, a dinner was put on at Government House.

At the dining table my ears were assailed by the noise of Ministers, young and old, addressing our host as 'Bill', and treating him as if they were back in the Caucus Room. All this, as I knew, angered and disappointed McKell very much. He himself, apart from what I thought the initial error of his appointment, worked manfully to discharge his duties in an impartial way. In my opinion he succeeded. Behind his normal informality he had a great natural dignity; he understood his duties; and he performed them extremely well.

But throughout his term of office he was essentially a lonely man, since most of his contacts in life had been political and he felt that those contacts must be sharply limited in his new sphere.

I will always regard Sir William McKell as a distinguished Australian, and look back on his term of office with personal pleasure. But at the same time, I feel sure that the grossness of his treatment by those who appointed him confirms my belief that no serving Australian political leader ought ever to be appointed the Queen's representative in Australia.

In December 1952, the time had come to secure the appointment of a Governor-General in succession to McKell, who had run for more than a normal five-years' term. Being in London, I saw the Queen and discussed the matter with her. I will give a brief account of our conversations, because they will sufficiently explain my views of the constitutional practice.

When I had broached the subject, the Queen, with a twinkle in her eye, said: 'Well, Mr Prime Minister, I understand that the Constitutional Rule is that you will nominate somebody and that I have no choice in the matter.'

I smiled in my turn and said: 'Well, Ma'am, they tell me that that is the position. But as a Constitutional lawyer myself, it is not a position that I like very much. After all, the Governor-General is to be *your* representative in Australia, not mine. What I suggest we should do is this. Let us first have a talk about the kind of person we are looking for. Then, when we have agreed on that, perhaps Your Majesty might, over the next few days, think of say three people; I will do the same. And, as I am going down to Cranbourne to spend the weekend with 'Bobbety' Salisbury and as he knows everybody of consequence and has great judgement, I will, with your permission, ask him to think of three names.'

'And what will happen then?' asked the Queen.

'Then, Ma'am,' I said, with what might be described as a broad Australian grin, 'we will discuss these names. It may be that somebody I approve of would be personally unacceptable to you. It may be that somebody selected by you might, in my judgement, do badly in Australia, in which case I would be bound to tell you, and I think you would take notice of my opinion. But we will undoubtedly agree on somebody. When we have in fact done so, and the name is one completely acceptable to *both of us*, I will then nominate him and Your Majesty will be bound to accept my nomination!'

The Queen liked this very much and said that she thought it quite a charming way of resolving constitutional problems.

I went off for the weekend. I wrote down three names on a piece of paper. I got 'Bobbety' Salisbury to write down three and close them up in an envelope.

Two days later, I repaired to Buckingham Palace and saw the Queen once more. She had written down her three names. I said: 'Ma'am, my Number One name is Sir William Slim.' She said: 'So is mine.' I then opened Salisbury's envelope and said: 'He is also Number One on Salisbury's list.' 'So now, Ma'am,' I said, 'I nominate Slim and you are bound to approve!'

Armed with this singularly happy conclusion, I got the authority of the Queen to speak to Sir William Slim; drove straight down to the Map Room; got him out of a Conference, and on behalf of Her Majesty offered him the post.

It is interesting to recall what happened. I said: 'Sir, I gather that you are about to finish your term as Chief of the Imperial General Staff.' 'That is so,' he said. 'Under these circumstances, I have the authority of the Queen to ask you whether you would care to be Governor-General of Australia.' 'Are you serious?' 'Never more so. We should all be delighted.' 'Could I have a talk with my wife? Of course you have not met my wife. She is very important in this matter. For, if I accept this post, which I would like to do, you must understand that I have a considerable faculty for dropping bricks. But she has a genius for catching them before they hit the floor!'

Next day, to my pleasure and the immense satisfaction of the Australian people, he accepted.

My conclusion about these matters can be stated very briefly:

1. In the last resort, the Queen must be guided by the advice of her Prime Minister in the Commonwealth country concerned, since constitutional practice forbids a purely personal and unadvised appointment; while, if there is to be advice, it must clearly come from the Prime Minister of, for example, Australia, and *not* from the Prime Minister of the United Kingdom.

2. But this does not mean that any Prime Minister should simply force one person's appointment, without adequate discussion and without any genuine exchange of views with the Queen.

To do what had been done by two of my predecessors would be, in my opinion, rather offensive to the Crown. There must be a genuine exchange of views and a genuine consideration of the available people. After all, as I said to the Queen, the Governor-General is *her* representative not ours.

3. In considering names in his own mind, a Prime Minister should, in my opinion, consider, among other things, two factors.

Is any proposed nominee personally known to the Queen? It is very desirable that he should be since, in Australia, or wherever it may be, he will stand in the place of the Queen and carry with him as he goes around the country some derivative atmosphere of Royalty. In other words, the presence of a Governor-General should evoke some at least of the emotions which we have when we contemplate the Crown.

If the Governor-General is notoriously completely unknown to the Queen, he will have some difficulty in carrying with him the atmosphere I have described.

The other factor is this. As the Governor-General may well be called upon to deal with political crises and to deal with applications by governments for dissolutions, it is in the highest degree important that his impartiality should be undoubted. Once he is powerfully suspected of partiality, not only will his moral authority be reduced but his own loss of reputation may seriously and adversely affect the position of the Crown itself. And that position, as I have tried to show earlier, is vital to any structural conception of the British Commonwealth.

Doubtless an Australian Prime Minister could later be a Governor-General of some other Commonwealth country because, to him, their political disputes would be remote. I have no doubt that Australia produces just as high a percentage of men of distinction as any other country in the world, but to regard the Governor-Generalship as a pension or promotion for a serving local party politician seems to me to degrade the conception of the office, to destroy its significance in the public mind and to damage the Crown itself. I merely add that, in the subsequent appointments of Lord Dunrossil, Lord De L'Isle and then Lord Casey, I followed the procedure I have described, in direct personal discussion with Her Majesty.

CHAPTER ELEVEN

OUR RELATIONS WITH THE UNITED STATES OF AMERICA

(with some comments on the American system of Government)

A N IMPORTANT PORTION of my time since 1949 has been devoted to Australia's relations with the United States of America. Indeed, I like to think that they grew stronger and closer during my long term of office as Prime Minister, and that today, in spite of the great disparity between our population and physical resources, we have a warm place in many American hearts and a respected position in Washington. And this has happened while we have maintained our British inheritance and our allegiance to the throne!

I would like to look back over these developments by writing the story in two parts.

In the first, I will examine the nature and form of our association, in order to discover on what it is based. This is something which is even now not always understood either in Australia or in America. Yet it is important that it should be understood; for friendly sentiments, though they unquestionably exist and flourish, can occasionally change, sometimes for the most superficial reasons.

In my second part, I will examine some of our differences, which are in some ways quite profound. A continuing friendship between two nations depends just as much upon a common understanding of differences as it does upon a fundamental sense of unity.

1. *The nature and form of our association*

I shall begin with a little bit of history. When I made the Jefferson 'oration' at Monticello on 4 July 1963, I took the opportunity to point out that when the famous American Declaration of Independence was made and followed up by a successful War of Independence, the American colonies actually created, without knowing it at the time, two new nations. One was, of course, the United States. The other was. Australia! Up to that time the American colonies had been the recipients of convicts transported from England; many thousands of them;

though, as I have sometimes pointed out to English audiences, most of the persons convicted over the period of transportation remained in England! When the American colonies became independent, transportation naturally ended. So another destination had to be found. Thus it came about that the Southern Continent of Australia, especially made known to Great Britain by Captain Cook, received, at Botany Bay and Sydney, the first white settlers, the convicted persons and their military custodians, in the fleet commanded by Captain Phillip in 1788! From this somewhat murky origin has grown a nation of life, character and purpose. This is what I mean when I say that two nations were created by the one act.

Again, Australia, sixty-five years ago, became a Federation with a Constitution in some material ways modelled upon that of the U.S.A. We have much experience in common of the problems which are presented in adjusting the relations between a Nation and its constituent States. As a lawyer engaged in Constitutional cases in Australia, I used to read, and occasionally quote, decisions of the United States Supreme Court. I think the traffic was reciprocal; I know in particular that my late friend Mr Justice Felix Frankfurter was an avid and prompt reader of the judgements of the High Court of Australia.

And, most eloquent of all facts, American and Australian troops have fought together in two great wars, and since in Korea and Vietnam, in the common cause.

If we recall that these elements in our common history have an enormous background of inheritance of a common history before the late eighteenth century, of language and literature, of the Common Law, of the great principles enshrined in the phrase 'the Rule of Law', of popular self-government, of religious faith, and of a common passion for individual and national freedom, we will at once see that enmity between the United States and Australia would be not only unthinkable, but 'most foul, strange and unnatural'.

I have wearied the reader with this elementary recital only because I have occasionally encountered Americans of standing and repute who have made it courteously clear that they regard Australia's modern friendship and close association with the United States as representing no more than a sort of cupboard love. 'You Australians cultivate us because you want us to defend you!' I believe that this is a minority view. But I shall say something about it, because such a view not only misconceives Australian opinion, but does a disservice to the United States itself.

In the late eighteenth century, in the nineteenth century, and at the turn of the twentieth century, Britain was the greatest power in the world, partly because of her Industrial Revolution, but particularly because she had command of the Seas. Like all great powers, she inspired jealousies and occasionally hatreds.

But a great and civilized power must accept world responsibilities, must set out to discharge them, not priggishly, but with a real vision of what the world needs for the prosperity and happiness of its people. In the performance of its duties, it will need patience and tolerance. It will encounter selfish objections in various quarters. It should never seek to make excuses, but if objections arise, it must have no fear of them. A true consciousness of destiny is not to be brushed aside as 'imperialism'. For a great nation without a sense of purpose will not remain great very long. What it gives to the world will be the true measure of its greatness.

Americans should never fall into the error of thinking or speaking patronizingly of Britain and her now disappearing Empire. For, though her colonial days are almost over, and new nations, once colonies, have emerged, it remains true that the best elements and institutions in those new nations have been derived from their former masters. There is a species of immortality about good things. It is human belief in this great truth which gives us courage and persistence.

It follows that great powers should welcome small friends who think as they do, and who are warmed by the same inner fires. The relations between the United States and Australia illustrate this to perfection.

True, as I have said many times in America, Australia is a small nation, with no more than two or three times the population the American colonies had when they became a young, proud and ambitious Republic; twice the population of the time of Thomas Jefferson's Presidency. We have, roughly, the same land area. We have far more material resources than we knew of twenty years ago. Their development taxes our strength, but assures us, if peace can be preserved, of a great future, and the capacity to sustain a very large population. At our best, we still have the pioneering spirit. The early pioneers are buried in many old cemeteries; but their descendants are not degenerate. They may *look* different from their predecessors seen in old and faded photographs or engravings (though beards seem to be coming back!), but they have the spirit of discovery in new fields of enterprise.

Australians would be the last people to adopt a *set of principles* just to please the United States and secure its help. Our principles are ours. It is not to be wondered or scoffed at that we have a friendship with Americans, for we know that they have the same principles. Our unwritten alliance with the United States is therefore a spiritual one. The American nation can never be lonely or isolated, or be successfully accused of being the sole bastion of out-dated individualism and democratic freedom, so long as there are other nations which share its faith and are not afraid to say so.

Thus it is that even small friends are important for a great power. It is an *a fortiori* case when a small friend may well become a large friend as time goes on.

But there are some more formal aspects of our association.

Australia and the United States have two pacts, both, I am proud to say, negotiated and achieved during my own term of office as Australian Prime Minister. They are, in order, the ANZUS Pact, and the South East Asia Treaty, SEATO. Each represents a remarkable development in American foreign policy, probably unthinkable before the Great Wars.

The ANZUS Pact is the Security Treaty, signed at San Francisco on 1 September 1951, duly ratified, and coming into force on 29 April 1952. It was executed between Australia, New Zealand and the United States.

Nothing could better demonstrate the role which the United States has accepted since the Second World War, and its willingness to accept great responsibilities, than this brief but significant Treaty. The United States has sixteen times the population of Australia, and almost sixty times the population of New Zealand. Clearly what Australia and New Zealand could do to assist the United States would be a very small fraction of what it could do for us. But the United States still made the treaty. The Preamble sets the stage in words which I think it important to quote in full:

The Parties to this Treaty,

Reaffirming their faith in the purposes and principles of the Charter of the United Nations and their desire to live in peace with all peoples and all Governments, and desiring to strengthen the fabric of peace in the Pacific Area,

Noting that the United States already has arrangements pursuant to which its armed forces are stationed in the Philippines, and has armed forces and administrative responsibilities in the Ryukus, and upon the coming into force of the Japanese Peace Treaty may also station armed forces in and about Japan to assist in the preservation of peace and security in the Japan Area,

Recognizing that Australia and New Zealand as members of the British Commonwealth of Nations have military obligations outside as well as within the Pacific Area,

Desiring to declare publicly and formally their sense of unity, so that no potential aggressor could be under the illusion that any of them stand alone in the Pacific Area, and

Desiring further to co-ordinate their efforts for collective defence for the preservation of peace and security pending the development of a more comprehensive system of regional security in the Pacific Area,

Therefore *declare and agree* as follows:

I direct attention to two aspects of these recitals.

The first is that the United States recognized the existence of military obligations between members of the British Commonwealth of Nations. As these obligations do not arise under treaty, but rather out of the nature of the Commonwealth association, they were clearly contemplating such military obligations as, say, Australia might voluntarily assume towards Malaya (or Malaysia) out of a sense of Commonwealth duty and mutual Commonwealth interest.

Australia and New Zealand in fact, some years after the ANZUS Pact, sent forces into Malaysia to help to resist Indonesian 'confrontation'. In the case of Australia, I announced, as Prime Minister in Parliament, our commitment in these words:

For the benefit of all concerned, honourable members would not wish me to create or permit any ambiguity about Australia's position in relation to Malaysia. I therefore, after close deliberation by the Cabinet, and on its behalf, inform the House that we are resolved, and have so informed the Government of Malaysia, and the Governments of the United Kingdom and New Zealand and others concerned, that if, in the circumstances that now exist, and which may continue for a long time, there occurs, in relation to Malaysia or any of its constituent States, armed invasion or subversive activity—supported or directed or inspired

from outside Malaysia—we shall to the best of our powers and by such means
as shall be agreed upon with the Government of Malaysia, add our military
assistance to the efforts of Malaysia and the United Kingdom in the defence of
Malaysia's territorial integrity and political independence.

The activities so instituted were clearly in 'the Pacific area' referred
to in the ANZUS Pact, and were therefore technically capable of
bringing into the field of possibility the performance of the provisions
of the Pact. We knew, however, that American leaders felt that the
Malaysian matter was especially one for Commonwealth countries,
and we understood and respected that view.

The second aspect is that potential aggressors are warned that they are
to be under no illusion that any of the three parties 'stand alone' in the
Pacific area.

From the outset of American military operations against aggressors
in Vietnam I, as Prime Minister of Australia, found it impossible to
contemplate that Australia could allow the United States to 'stand
alone' in that enterprise. My successor in the Prime Ministership,
Mr Harold Holt, has the same state of mind, and has acted upon it with
great spirit, and with the clear support of the Australian electors.

Several of the principle operative articles of ANZUS deserve to be
better known.

Article I: The Parties undertake, as set forth in the Charter of the United
Nations, to settle any international disputes in which they may be involved by
peaceful means in such a manner that international peace and security and
justice are not endangered and to refrain in their international relations from
the threat or use of force in any manner inconsistent with the purposes of the
United Nations.

All three of us in varying degrees are using force in Vietnam for
purposes of defence and clearly pursuant to and consistent with
Articles 2, 51, 52 of the Charter of the United Nations.

Article II: In order more effectively to achieve the objective of this Treaty the
Parties separately and jointly by means of continuous and effective self-help and
mutual aid will maintain and develop their individual and collective capacity
to resist armed attack.

Article IV: Each Party recognizes that an armed attack in the Pacific Area on any of the Parties would be dangerous to its own peace and safety and declares that it would act to meet the common danger in accordance with its constitutional processes.

Any such armed attack and all measures taken as a result thereof shall be immediately reported to the Security Council of the United Nations. Such measures shall be terminated when the Security Council has taken the measures necessary to restore and maintain international peace and security.

I must at once say something about this Article. Some people, both in America and Australia, challenged the action of my government in putting troops into Malaysia, saying that we were trying to use the ANZUS Pact to involve the United States in Indonesian confrontation; or, in short, that we were trying to make the tail wag the dog. It was said that the Australian Government was assuming that, under the ANZUS Pact, the United States would, under particular circumstances, be *automatically* at war.

On 21 April 1964, in a major Parliamentary debate on this matter, I explained the position as I understood it. I said:

When the question arose as to whether Malaysia was to be threatened by somebody else, this was obviously and instantly a matter for discussion between the United States of America and ourselves, Great Britain, and so on. The United States of America did not ever withdraw its support for Malaysia. It has approved of Malaysia and has recognised Malaysia, and it wants Malaysia to be maintained. But I very well remember America saying to us—I took no exception to it; I thought it was pretty sensible—that when it came to the immediate defence of Malaysia this was perhaps primarily a Commonwealth responsibility, because we are all members of the Commonwealth together. I would not quarrel with that. The Government has not quarrelled with it.

I then proceeded:

When we get to the next step, which is what happens if in the course of this defence of Malaysia we face a genuine attack on the territorial integrity or political independence of Malaysia—a matter which invokes our promise—I want to remind the House and the people of the terms of the ANZUS Treaty.

I then read the relevant Articles, which I have just been putting before you, and emphasized the significance of the phrase 'in accordance with the constitutional processes'.

I knew that it was important that there should be no misunderstanding between ourselves and Washington, and I chose my language
with great care:

> Of course this should be in accordance with constitutional processes. Very
> few countries go automatically into a state of war. They all have certain pro-
> cedures to go through but, subject to constitutional processes, which can
> operate here just as much as they can anywhere else, there is a clear statement
> that the parties will act to meet the common danger in accordance with their
> constitutional processes.

I thus rejected the idea of automatic and instant hostilities, while
leaving open the broad implications of the Pact.

Article V: For the purpose of Article IV, an armed attack on any of the
Parties is deemed to include an armed attack on the metropolitan territory of
any of the Parties, or on the island territories under its jurisdiction in the Pacific
or on its armed forces, public vessels or aircraft in the Pacific.

I dealt with this provision—necessarily, since Australian forces were
under fire in Malaysia—in the statement I have already partly quoted,
in this way:

> Those words do not produce automatic hostilities, because reference is made
> to constitutional processes, but they contain in the clearest terms a high-level
> acceptance of responsibility. It is not for us to assume that any great ally of ours
> will avoid that any more than we will avoid it. It is a great mistake to talk
> dogmatically of what the United States of America will do. All I point out to
> the House is that this is the Treaty, and never has one word been said to this
> Government or any member of it by any member of the American Adminis-
> tration, from the President down, to water down or weaken the force and
> significance of that treaty. Consequently, without conducting extravagant
> ideas as to when, how and what forces will be involved—I do not profess to
> engage myself in these matters—I merely point out to the House that if we want
> to have a sensible, balanced view of the international position of this country it
> is essential that we should understand the nature, terms and significance of the
> ANZUS Treaty.

And then, having pointed out that the reference to 'island territories'
in Article V clearly covered the Australian territories of East New
Guinea and Papua—an opinion subsequently and explicitly confirmed

by the Ambassador for the United States—I went on, in words to which I invite special attention:

I am not going to have anybody in the United States of America think that we are trying to force the cards. We are not. I am not going to have anybody in the United States of America believe that we are trying in a rather cheap way to involve the United States in something. We have too much respect for the United States to resort to any such strategy. We have too much faith in its friendship for this country to feel that it is necessary to try to involve it. All I do is point out, as I am sure any member of the American Administration would, that there is a contract between Australia and America. It is a contract based on the utmost goodwill, the utmost good faith and unqualified friendship. Each of us will stand by it.

I have some reason to believe that this explanation, which was promptly reported in full to Washington, was in line with official United States opinion. I do not wish to create an impression that, in the Australian Parliament, there was complete unanimity. There seldom is. Americans know something about this themselves.

Mr Casey (now Lord Casey, and Governor-General) handled the Bill as Minister for External Affairs. He pointed out that:

'. . . the precise action to be taken by each party is not specified. There is no obligation on Australia to make any immediate formal declaration of war; the United States, for its part, could not constitutionally accept such a binding obligation. But the broad intention is that an attack on one shall be regarded as an attack on all.

Dr Evatt, the then Leader of the Opposition, said that the Bill to ratify the Treaty had the support of the Opposition. But he expressed his fears that the Peace Treaty with Japan, enabling Japan to re-arm, could worsen the defence position of Australia. He said:

The Pacific Pact will be a step in the direction that we have always favoured, but the tragedy of it is that it is linked up, because of a separate bill, with a situation that the security of the South Pacific may well be endangered by the very thing with which this agreement deals. That is the Japanese peace treaty which provides for the unlimited rearmament of Japan.

It would be idle to deny that the acceptance of a 'soft' treaty of peace

[267]

with Japan gave impetus to the negotiating of ANZUS. But, so far as Japan is concerned, subsequent history has justified the Peace Treaty. Relations between Japan and Australia, embittered by the horrible experiences of the war, have sensibly improved, as have our trade relations, to our mutual advantage. Japan has not engaged in massive rearmament. Like so many other defeated countries, she has had much more money for beating swords into plough-shares, keeping her people profitably employed, and selling her products to the world.

The South-East Asia Collective Defence Treaty (to give it its full title), compendiously referred to nowadays as SEATO, was executed on 8 September 1954—the year of the Geneva Accords—by the plenipotentiaries of Australia, France, New Zealand, Pakistan, the Philippines, Thailand, the United Kingdom and the United States. It was ratified by the Australian Parliament on 18 November 1954. It is a binding and authoritative Treaty in each of the countries concerned.

A few passages from the Preamble of the Treaty deserve to be remembered today.

Reaffirming that, in accordance with the Charter of the United Nations, they uphold the principle of equal rights and self-determination of peoples, and declaring that they will earnestly strive by every peaceful means to promote self-government and to secure the independence of all countries whose people desire it and are able to undertake its responsibilities.

Intending to declare publicly and formally their sense of unity, so that any potential agressor will appreciate that the Parties stand together in the area, and

Desiring further to co-ordinate their efforts for collective defence for the preservation of peace and security.

The Articles of the Treaty set out to apply these principles. I quote some of the more important of them.

Article II: In order more effectively to achieve the objectives of this Treaty, the Parties, separately and jointly, by means of continuous and effective self-help and mutual aid will maintain and develop their individual and collective capacity to resist armed attack and to prevent and counter subversive activities directed from without against their territorial integrity and political stability.

There should be noted, in particular, the phrase '*separately and jointly'*. Not one of us can avoid the Treaty obligations by making our performance dependent upon the action of any other Party. Properly considered, unanimity in any particular decision is legally irrelevant. The United States and Australia accept this, and are at this very time acting under it in Vietnam!

And then, the words *'to resist armed attack and to prevent and counter subversive activities directed from without against their territorial integrity and political stability'*. The events there contemplated have since occurred, as nobody can reasonably deny, in Vietnam.

It is interesting to note that the Leader of the Opposition in Canberra, whose party, the Australian Labour Party, in the election campaign of November 1966, opposed Australian military participation in South Vietnam, said in the House in 1965:

> That there has long been and still is aggression from the North and subversion inspired from the North, I do not for one moment deny.

Here was a precise acceptance of the relevance of Article II of the Treaty.

Article IV:
1. Each Party recognises that aggression by means of armed attack in the treaty area against any of the Parties or against any State or territory with the Parties by unanimous agreement may hereafter designate, would endanger its own peace and safety, and agrees that it will in that event act to meet the common danger in accordance with its constitutional processes. Measures taken under this paragraph shall be immediately reported to the Security Council of the United Nations.

(This was, of course, done.)

3. It is understood that no action on the territory of any State designated by unanimous agreement under paragraph 1 of this Article or on any territory so designated shall be taken except at the invitation or with the consent of the government concerned.

It was under Article IV that the parties, by unanimous agreement, designated South Vietnam as a 'protocol State', thus bringing it within the protection of the Treaty. When the United States went into South

Vietnam, it did so at the invitation of the government. The same procedure was followed when Australia participated.

The recital of these historic treaties does, I submit, dispose of the last shreds of the cynic's argument! For if a great power sees fit to make a pact or treaty with other powers, some of them small, it must be in the expectation that the other contracting parties will perform their obligations. It would be strange if their performance were to be accounted a selfish act, founded upon narrow self-interest, and nothing more.

To sum up, I think that there is mutual dignity and fidelity in the relations between the United States and Australia, and that those relations offer advantages to both parties; not quantitatively equal, of course, but in quality a true benefit both ways.

2. *Some of our differences*

Over the last thirty years, I have become increasingly aware of profound differences between the American system of government and our own. It is easy to say that the Australian Constitution was 'modelled' on that of the United States; that we each have a Senate and a House of Representatives; that the powers of government are divided between the centre and the States; that specific powers are given to the central (or Commonwealth) Parliament (or Congress), and the residue of power remains with the States; that in each Constitution distinction is made between the Legislature, the Executive, and the Judicature; and that the boundaries of power are policed by the Supreme Court of the U.S.A. or the High Court of Australia with complete authority. These things are all true in substance, and of course have great significance. Yet there is one great difference. It concerns the machinery of government.

Now, it has been my experience, over many years of activity and observation, that the machinery of government is not something of merely technical interest; on the contrary, it has enormous practical significance, and may well affect the course of history.

Thirty years ago, I discussed this matter with Paul Reynaud in Paris. We both agreed that the absence of a power to dissolve the *Chambre des Députés* in France was a prime cause of the notorious instability of French politics. Every few months the current government fell and, after tedious bargaining, another emerged, to give way, not long afterwards, to another.

In Australia, if I had been defeated in the House of Representatives, where governments are made or unmade, I could, under most circumstances, have sought and obtained a dissolution and a fresh popular election. The incoming government would then have a mandate and a good expectation of life. This was not the position in France, where one compromise government followed another with a highly precarious tenure, to the detriment of long-term policies and the enhancement of bureaucratic power.

For many years, nothing did more harm to France.

So we should not think of problems of government machinery as if they were of interest only to mechanicians. And the United States and Australia (or for that matter Great Britain, whose practice we have followed) will not fully understand each other unless the differences of machinery are understood. This is not an academic matter.

Inherent in the Australian Constitution, we have the system and principle of 'Responsible Government'. In practice, this means that:

The Prime Minister and other Commonwealth Ministers of State are and must be *Members of the Parliament,* elected as such by the people.

They are *accountable to Parliament;* are in fact questioned by Members at the beginning of each daily sitting; present and argue their own legislative proposals; and are subject to the votes of Parliament. *Should the Government be defeated on the floor of the House* on a major measure declared by it to be vital, or on a financial measure of substance, the Prime Minister resigns, and all Ministers with him in consequence. In some rare circumstances, another Government might be formed; in most cases there would be a dissolution and a new General Election.

This is the British practice, and ours.

The Australian 'founding fathers' were familiar with the Constitution of the United States, and were in many important ways greatly influenced by it. But, as *Sir Owen Dixon* said to the American Bar Association in 1942:

They all lived under a system of responsible government. That is to say, they knew and believed in the British system by which the Ministers are responsible to the Parliament and must go out of office whenever they lose the confidence of the legislature . . . .

They found themselves unable to accept the principle by which the executive government is made independent of the legislature. Responsible government, that is, the system by which the executive is responsible to the legislature, was therefore introduced with all its necessary consequences.

Yet the interesting fact is that the Australian Constitution contains no express reference to Responsible Government *eo nomine*. It has to be inferred. But its existence as an Australian constitutional provision has been authoritatively established by the Courts.

The principle provides a background to the Australian Constitutional provisions relating to the Executive. Thus:

61. The Executive power of the Commonwealth is vested in the Queen, and is exercisable by the Governor-General as the Queen's representative, and extends to the execution and maintenance of this Constitution, and of the laws of the Commonwealth.

64. The Governor-General may appoint officers to administer such departments of State of the Commonwealth as the Governor-General in Council may establish.

Such officers shall hold office during the pleasure of the Governor-General. They shall be members of the Federal Executive Council, and shall be the *Queen's Ministers of State* for the Commonwealth.

After the first General Elections no Minister of State shall hold office for a longer period than three months unless *he is or becomes a Senator or a Member of the House of Representatives.*

Thus, Ministers must be serving Members of Parliament, attending its sittings, participating in its debates, and voting in its divisions.

Compare this with the United States Constitutional provisions:

Article 2, Section 1
The Executive power shall be vested in a President of the United States of America.

So far, this may seem similar to our Section 61, substituting the President for the Queen. But in reality, there is a great difference. As a result of a long British constitutional development, the Queen is a 'constitutional monarch', with, for all material purposes, no direct executive authority; such authority being in substance exercised in her name by her Ministers. But the President is, of course, himself the Chief Executive in his own constitutional right.

He has, in fact, more points of resemblance to a British or an Australian Prime Minister; though his powers are much greater.

But here again there is a material difference. The American President *'shall hold his office* "during the term of four years", which now can be renewed once. He cannot be *voted out* by Congress, except by impeachment under Section 4 for convicted "treason, bribery, or other high crimes and misdemeanours" '.

In Britain and Australia, a Prime Minister has no set term; he continues in office until Parliament votes him out, or until he resigns. We have had Prime Ministers who lasted for only a matter of weeks.

Again, our Section 64 requires the Members of the Political Executive, the Ministers of State, to be in Parliament. America has attached itself deeply to the principle of the *Separation of Powers*—for example, the separation of the legislative power from the Executive, believing with *Montesquieu* that 'there can be no liberty where the legislative and executive powers are united in the same person or body of magistrates'. If I may be impertinent enough to say it, I have never thought that either *Montesquieu* or *de Tocqueville,* brilliant though they were, really understood the British political organism, which was after all itself the product of a long struggle for freedom. But it had not been fully explained in writing!

But be that as it may, American practice is firmly established, although I have observed that proposals have sometimes been made (but not advanced very far) to permit members of Congress to serve in the President's Cabinet.

There are of course advantages and disadvantages in each system.

In forming a non-Congressional Cabinet, the President has the widest possible choice. He can reach out into the high places of business and scholarship. He may even, as I have occasionally noticed with surprise, choose somebody of the opposite political party. Such a phenomenon could not occur in Australia, where Governments are party governments, and the party lines are strictly drawn.

Looking at the Congressional Division Lists, an Australian is interested to see how much 'cross-voting' there is; hardly ever a strict division on party lines. This is, I would think, inherent in the system, for the President's government will go on even though some or perhaps all of its important measures may be defeated. Departure from the party vote does not frequently happen under our system of Responsible Government, for the party of the ruling government knows that to defeat that government on a material measure would be to force its resignation, with either a consequential formation of another different government, or much more probably a dissolution and a fresh general election.

That, I believe, is the great reason why our party lines are more tightly drawn, and party discipline so active.

It is well to keep this aspect of the matter in mind when we view our respective political methods from afar. There will be fewer misunderstandings if we do.

To return to the matter of Cabinet selection, the field of choice for an Australian Prime Minister in a system of Responsible Government is restricted. His Ministers must be Members of Parliament elected as such. No others need apply, or are available for selection. Clearly this method has its disadvantages. This is particularly true in a Federation like Australia, where State feelings run high and there is almost an unwritten rule that each of the six States is entitled to at least one Minister! Under such a practice, one able man may not find a place in the Cabinet, while another, perhaps less able, goes in.

But, though our system presents the Prime Minister with a restricted and possibly distorted choice, its end results are good. I could claim without pretentiousness that leading Ministers in the Australian Government, several of whom are well known and respected in Washington, will hold their own in any political company.

In comparing the two systems, I must, as, naturally, a great believer in Responsible Government for my own country, emphasize one aspect of the matter. Every Minister in the Australian Cabinet has been through the political mill. He knows the Members. He knows their enthusiasms and their prejudices. In brief, he knows what they will take and what they will want to reject.

When I first became Prime Minister in 1939, I was only 44 years of age but I had sat in the Victorian State Parliament for six years, half of them as a Minister; and had thereafter been Attorney-General in the

Commonwealth Government for over four years. So whatever else I was, I was not a novice. From 1941 to 1949 I sat in Opposition, six years of the eight as Leader of a heavily outnumbered Opposition. This was difficult, but it was rich tactical training. By the time I came back as Prime Minister at the end of 1949, I had learned a lot more about the conducting of parliamentary business and the influencing of public opinion, and remained in office for another sixteen years. A Cabinet made up of people with experience like this, particularly experience on the floor of the House, has a pretty practical outlook on legislative programmes. Before a proposal is adopted, it is thrashed out in Cabinet. Then it goes to the Government parties (Parliamentary members), is expounded and debated. When it is produced in Parliament by the relevant Minister, the Cabinet *knows* that nine times out of ten it will go through! These remarks are on the assumption that the Government has a majority in both Houses. If, in fact, it has a hostile Senate, its programme can be frustrated.

Now, the American method is different; the proposals of the Administration are sometimes rejected, not infrequently modified, and sometimes 'suffer a sea-change, into something rich and strange'.

I am not concerned to prove that one system is better than the other. The U.S.A. has operated its system for many decades, and the results have put the whole of the free world under obligation.

But these differences of method and of machinery must be recognized and understood. For a misunderstanding among friends can be more serious than a misunderstanding between enemies.

One particular result of the American system has been the development of the Committee system. Since American 'Ministers' do not and cannot sit in Congress and therefore do not handle their own legislative proposals, the Chairman of the appropriate Committee, which argues out and ultimately drafts and produces the Bill, does what a Minister would do in my country. Yet the Committee Chairman is not a member of the Administration; he is in a very real sense independent.

But there is another aspect of the matter which is so important that a failure to understand it, internationally, has given rise to great international misapprehensions.

Under the American system, the natural ambition of one going into Congress is to become a Committee member, or even a Committee

Chairman. Except in the rarest cases, he does not reach the Cabinet by
this route.

America has developed a practice of Congressional Committees
sitting in public, sometimes with the adventitious aids (or handicaps) of
television and broadcasting. These Committees have also felt free to
call before them not only the great political Officers of State, but
Chiefs of Staff and other military gentlemen from the Pentagon. Even
before any official policy has been announced from the White House,
or the State Department, or Defence, there is thus a public debate, in
which some of the advisers of the President, or the Secretary, as the
case may be, are questioned on matters of opinion, and are required to
answer.

This, I must say, has always astonished me. I can recall John Foster
Dulles telling me of what happened after he had attended the 1954
Conference on Indo-China in Geneva. He flew back home and, *en
route,* compiled his report for the President. On arriving in the evening
at his house in Washington, he sent his report to the White House, and
then found lying on his hall table a summons to appear before the
appropriate Committee next morning. Inheritor as I am of the tradition
and practice of Responsible Government, I expressed surprise. 'Foster,'
I said, 'do you mean to say that you would be cross-examined on a
policy not yet discussed with your President?' The answer was 'Yes'.
'But,' I said, 'why don't you tell them to jump into the Potomac? They
surely would not commit you for contempt, and deprive the United
States of its Foreign Minister for weeks!' Dulles's reply was illuminating. 'I would hate to have my estimates cut about!'

This American practice of working out policy by public debate
is not, I suppose, to be criticized by an outsider bred in other methods.
But it does give rise to misunderstandings in other countries. For
example, Senator X, a member of an important Committee, offers a
pungent sentiment. This receives great publicity on the international
news services. Somebody in England says, 'You see what these Americans think'. He becomes hostile. When the official policy emerges, and
is contrary to the views of Senator X, the same somebody says, 'How
inconsistent these Americans are!' This kind of thing leads to more heat
than light!

Conversely, in Australia (or Great Britain), policies are evolved in

Cabinet, sitting without television or radio. Rumours and press speculations there may be a-plenty, but when the policy is announced by the Prime Minister or the appropriate Minister, everybody in Australia knows that that is *the policy,* and that critical or alternative individual remarks by private Members of Parliament have no official weight or authority, but must be evaluated strictly on the individual merits. But is this equally understood in the United States? Will there be a temptation to believe that the critic, Mr Y, being (as he may be) a member of some Parliamentary Committee, is speaking with official authority?

This brings me back to the Committee system, which is one of the great matters of difference between the American machinery of Government and ours.

I hope I am right in believing that the American Committee system derives from the Constitutional Separation of Powers, and affords a sort of *nexus* between Administration and Legislature.

So that the comparison I am making will be clear, I will begin by explaining the extent to which Committees are used in the Australian Parliamentary system.

We have several types of Committee:

1. The House of Representatives sits as 'a Committee of *the whole*', that is, every Member is a member of the Committee:

   (*a*) at the Committee stage of a Bill, that is, after the Second Reading has been passed and the Bill then calls for consideration clause by clause;

   (*b*) to consider any matter which may be referred to it by the House.

2. *Standing Committees of the House*
   The House Committee
   The Library Committee
   The Printing Committee
   The Privileges Committee
   The Standing Orders Committee, with corresponding *Standing Committees of the Senate.*

These Committees do not deal with any aspect of political policy.

3. *Joint Statutory Committees* (that is Joint with the Senate)
   The Broadcasting of Parliamentary Proceedings Committee
   The Public Accounts Committee
   The Public Works Committee

The second and third of these Committees conduct critical examinations, and produce material of great value to the Cabinet and to Parliament. But they do not deal with political policy in the broad.

4. *Other Joint Committees*
   The Committee on the Australian Capital Territory
   The Foreign Affairs Committee
   The Parliamentary and Government Publications Committee

Of these, the second deals broadly with matters referred to it by the Minister for External Affairs, and provides a valuable means, assisted by the Department of External Affairs, for the study of current international problems. But when I wrote this book the Opposition Party, the Australian Labour Party, had declined to be represented on the Committee, the significance of the work of which was correspondingly diminished. In the result, it does not compare with the American Foreign Relations Committee of the Senate or Foreign Affairs Committee of the House.

5. *Select Committees*
   These are appointed *ad hoc* by either House, or both Houses, and are limited by their terms of reference.

6. *Party Committees*
   In the nature of things, these have no Parliamentary authority or recognition, but exist to advise their own parties.

Clearly, these Committees have little in common with those of Congress, which have what could be properly described as organic and constitutional functions.

There is at present in the Australian Parliament a movement among some private Members to develop the Committee system somewhat on the American model. I have never favoured this. I do not think that the American Committee System could be reconciled with Responsible Government. It certainly could not, without such modifications of

Responsible Government as would completely alter its character. I will briefly indicate my principal reasons for this view:

Under the American system, legislation is in effect framed by a Committee and presented by it to Congress. Where does the 'Minister' come in, except by the process of consultation? In our system, the Minister produces the Bill and moves its first, second, and third readings. He explains it, and debates it. He speaks for the Cabinet, on whose authority the Bill has come forward. Should the Bill, under an adaptation of the American system, emerge from a Committee (of which he would not be even a member), it would be no longer his, or the Cabinet's. He would become almost a cypher. Should the Bill be rejected, it could not be counted a defeat for the Minister or the Government. There could be no question of resignation, for the authority of Minister and Government would not be at issue.

This might occasionally be an agreeable and even comfortable state of affairs, but it would not be Responsible Government.

The American system works because Americans have never adopted 'Responsible Government'; they have preserved the separate authority of the Legislature and the detachment of the Executive; and their people understand this.

The two systems are basically different.

The whole point of Responsible Government may be expressed in this way.

General Elections are contests between parties and party policies announced by the rival leaders. The party which secures a majority in the House of Representatives (or the parties, since, as in Australia, there may be two parties working in alliance) establishes a Government, the Prime Minister of which is the Party Leader who declared the policy and led the campaign. He and his Ministers are responsible for the performance of the policy. If the House refuses to vote for legislation giving effect to any vital item in that policy, the Prime Minister will resign. The Government cannot off-load its responsibility by asking Parliament to set up Committees with power to decide the extent, if any, to which the election promises are to be performed.

Suppose such committees were set up, on the American model; they would of necessity be made up of members of all parties. As Committees, they would not have made or issued any election policy and would therefore feel free to exercise their own current joint judgement in their own way. The Australian elector, accustomed to election mandates and Responsible Government, would protest bitterly if he saw Ministers (as he would express it) 'running for cover'.

The committees, if we adopted the American system, would need to be committees of private members. In any matter of any political significance, no Minister could sit on the Committee with private members, for it is of the essence of Responsible or Cabinet Government that Cabinet should speak with one voice, differences of opinion being kept private. But for this rule, governments would, with us, fall to pieces very rapidly. Stability of government and continuity of policy would alike be sacrificed. It follows that we could not accept the spectacle of a Minister offering a personal view in a substantially private members' committee and then hearing another view put forward by the Cabinet of which he was a member.

Men and women of talent go into Parliament in Australia with a proper ambition some day to be chosen as Ministers. There have been able people in our Parliament who have never become Ministers; but on the whole it is reasonable to believe that (subject to the complications which arise from six States, two Houses of Parliament, and two government parties) the best qualified tend to become Ministers. It would be indeed strange if the business of preparing and passing Parliamentary measures could be taken out of their hands by Parliamentary Committees composed of non-Ministers!

In the United States, everything is different. American men and women of talent, as I have said, go into Congress not to achieve Ministerial rank, but to become leaders or members of important Committees and so influence the currents of great national events. The cream of the membership is therefore to be found on the Committees; with us it is to be found on the Treasury (that is, Ministerial) Bench.

I have offered these observations in no critical or impertinent sense. But as I wrote at the outset, Australian-American friendship will be richer and better-informed if we understand our differences of method and so avoid misunderstandings.

CHAPTER TWELVE

THE REVIVAL OF LIBERALISM
IN AUSTRALIA

THIS CHAPTER RECOUNTS VERY BRIEFLY some of the political events which were subsequent to my election to the leadership of the Opposition in Australia at the end of 1943. It describes the creation of a new party with a modern philosophy, and its ultimate succession to power. If, in this book, I say but little about Australia's political history since 1949, it is not because that history has not been one of problems overcome and in many ways dramatic success, well worth recording, but because of two considerations. The first is that the political history of seventeen years cannot be compressed into a single essay. It will, I hope, be written and documented in broad substance and in close detail by some scholar with the full facilities of research. I cannot attempt so great a task in this book. The second consideration concerns myself. I am still so close to the political events and was so much involved in most of them that, as a still, though fadingly, controversial figure, I could be found lacking in objectivity. The pulse of party politics has not yet entirely subsided in my blood, though I am happily conscious of an increasing detachment and a more relaxed outlook.

In any case, no man is a good judge in his own cause; that is the great reason why I have no wish to write an autobiography.

But the history of a political movement is a different matter, and I think I should very briefly sketch it.

Strangely enough, as it might appear, I had never, even as a student, been attracted by State Socialism. To me, human beings were individuals, and not statistics. And I was an individual, with my own ambitions. From my earliest days until now, I have found 'Socialism' a dreary and essentially reactionary doctrine.

On 6 July 1964, I delivered the first Baillieu Lecture, founded in London in honour of that very great Australian, Lord Baillieu. I made it the occasion for an expression of my own philosophy about Socialism.

It is frequently charged against those of us who are not Socialists that we are reactionaries; that we want to turn the clock back; that we yearn for a restoration of *laissez-faire*. In the modern world, this is quite untrue. The truth is that it is the non-Socialists who have moved with the times. I can understand, as an intellectual and historical exercise, how Socialism attracted the support of radical thinkers after the industrial revolution in Great Britain, the creation of 'dark satanic mills', the horrors of child labour, when industrial power was in a limited number of hands, when the rights of employed people were either denied or imperfectly recognized, when the infant Trade Unions were too commonly regarded as subversive bodies, when social services as we now know them were almost non-existent. It is not strange that under these circumstances there grew up in many thoughtful minds the egalitarian belief that the creation of social and industrial justice demanded a high measure of uniformity, and that uniformity could be achieved only by the mastery and management of the State.

But we know, and occasionally admit, that there is no uniformity among personalities, or talents, or energy. We have learned that true rising standards of living are the product of progressive enterprise, the acceptance of risks, the encouragement of adventure, the prospect of rewards. These are all individual matters. There is no Government department which can create these things.

These, though recently expressed, were my views as far back as 1944, when I set about the revival of Liberalism in Australia. The one virtue I may claim is that I foresaw that, in the post-war years, Australia would be presented with a choice between a continuation of government control on the Socialist model and a society based upon free and encouraged private enterprise. The latter could not, if social justice was to be achieved, be an irresponsible enterprise. There was to be nothing doctrinaire about our policies. If I were to become the leader of a great non-Socialist party, I must look at everything in a practical way. My associates and I knew perfectly well that, in Australia at any rate, there have been and are certain elements which, in the very nature of our geography and history, lend themselves to government management or control. Take, for example, the railways, which are for all practical purposes, government-owned and controlled. The development of a young and sparsely populated country would clearly be assisted by the creation of means of transport. New and developmental railway lines would almost certainly begin by operating at a loss; a loss which no private entrepreneur could contemplate. And so, Governments came into the picture, footed the bill, and opened up vast tracts of productive land.

Again, we have for many years lived with government control of postal, telegraphic, and telephonic services. I know that many of these services are in private hands in America; but that has its origins in American history.

But, looking to the future in a rapidly developing country like Australia, it seemed eminently desirable to look more to the citizen and less to government. A great reliance must be made on the creative genius of the individual, assisted, and sometimes controlled by the government in the general social interest, but encouraged and rewarded. The 'profit motive', so vehemently attacked by the Socialists, must be seen as one of the most powerful factors in growth.

The United Australia Party, of which I was a private member at the time of the débâcle of the 1943 General Election, had behind it (more or less) a whole series of unrelated organizations, without cohesion or common purpose.

When we met at Parliament House after the election, the Parliamentary Party at once and unanimously pressed me to resume the leadership. I said that I would do so on two conditions. One was that our party, being the majority opposition party, should assert its right to the Leadership of the Opposition, without which I believed we could not move forward effectively. The other was that I should have *carte blanche* to take all necessary steps towards gathering up all the existing organizations into one Australia-wide organization, with a new name—the 'United Australia' name having ceased to be up-to-date or self-explanatory—and a carefully prepared platform.

Both of these conditions were agreed to, and I began six years of incessant labour in the study, in the House, and all over Australia. And the labour *was* incessant. As Leader of a depleted Opposition, I had to carry great burdens in the debating of measures introduced by the Government and in the working out of our own ideas. In the Parliamentary recesses I had to travel inter-state and address meetings, and 'keep the flag flying'. This was expensive, not only financially but in terms of nervous energy. The time was to come, under the Menzies Government, where the Leader of the Opposition became entitled to the same emoluments and privileges as a Minister. In my years, I drew a private member's salary, plus an allowance of, I think, £300 a year, and, except on rare official occasions, provided my own transport.

For about a month in each year, I accepted a few briefs, partly to keep my hand in at my own profession, and partly to replenish the domestic larder. In the result, I drew heavily upon my limited private capital.

By October 1944, I convened a meeting of the organizations at the Masonic Hall in Canberra. It interests me very much to read that one non-ranking Junior Senator in the United States has a personal staff of over sixty. As Leader of the Opposition (and a former Prime Minister) in the National Parliament of Australia, I had a staff of two. All the work which had to be done to convene this meeting was done by myself, with the aid of a devoted Secretary, Miss Eileen Lenihan. I sent out letters to all of the organizations concerned, found favourable responses, and received many valuable suggestions. I felt much encouraged. Clearly, the fields were ready for the sowing, and we could hope for a great harvest. So, with much zest, I completed my preparatory work for a meeting which just had to succeed if we were to have any political significance in the years to come. When the conference met on 13 October 1944, the 'parade state' was as follows. From *New South Wales,* there were the Democratic Party and the Liberal Democratic Party. In *Queensland,* there were the Country National Organization, the Queensland People's Party (not represented at the Conference, but coming in later), and the Queensland Women's Electoral League. From *Victoria,* there were representatives of the United Australia Organization, the Australian Women's National League, and the Young Nationalist Organization (of which I had been one of the founders fifteen years before), the Services and Citizens Party. Another body, the Middle Class Organization, was not represented, preferring to maintain a non-political character.

South Australia had a single organization, the Liberal and Country League.

West Australia had a 'Nationalist Organization'; *Tasmania* had 'Nationalist' and 'United Australia', and the Australian Women's National League.

I had with me twelve Members of the Federal Parliament. From each State there were Members of Parliament.

In short, I faced a state of affairs in which I must dedicate myself to bringing fourteen organizations into one, under one banner, and with one body of ideas.

Why had we become so fragmented? The reason is not far to seek. All of the organizations were in opposition, but no doubt for different reasons. Lacking membership of a common body, and the guidance of well-formulated common ideas, we were destined for continued defeat. The Labour Party was in a powerful position to 'divide and conquer'.

As I said at the Canberra Conference, having taken the Chair as Convenor:

The Labour Party, though its policy and administration are repugnant to us, is not something which exists under a different name and with a different set-up in each State. It is the Australian Labour Party. Its membership depends upon common considerations all over the continent. It has State Branches and local branches. It has State executives and a Federal executive. It has all over Australia a system of journals so effective that it has been my experience that the same point of view in almost the same words will be produced by a Labour supporter in Bunbury as by one in Rockhampton.

The result of this unanimity and cohesion on the organizational side has been that the disunities which exist in Labour circles are usually below the surface, are not advertised, and so have nothing like the public effect that is produced by the well-advertised minor differences of opinion that may exist in our own ranks.

When I consider the structure of the Australian Labour Party and realize that the political warfare to which we have been committed for a long time past by no choice of our own is a struggle between political armies, I am driven to wonder how we could ever imagine that a concerted force under one command and with one staff is to be defeated by divided units under separate commands, and with no general staff.

(It must be remembered that these words were spoken before the time, years later, when Labour, in opposition, became deeply divided.)

I set out to inject into the meeting a sense of significance and urgency. If we could not get together then, we might not see success for our political views for many years. There were one or two doubters, who were naturally attached to their own particular groups, but their doubts were soon swept away by the general enthusiasm.

In the upshot, we passed a resolution to say that we would proceed to form one party, to be known as the Liberal Party of Australia; and that, later in the year, we would have a Special Conference to adopt a Constitution and a Platform.

Why 'Liberal'? This will need explaining to both English and American readers.

The Liberal Party in the United Kingdom is a survival of the great party of Gladstone and Asquith which for so many generations had disputed the field with the Conservative Party. When the Labour Party became, first, a force and then a major force, the Liberal Party became a residual party, destined to be a small group at Westminster. It continues to make an intellectual appeal in University circles, for it always seems to me (and I speak with respect to its leaders) to represent a state of attractive philosophic doubt; to expound its ideas in the general, but seldom to condescend to particulars. It certainly does not constitute an alternative government.

Now, though its intellectual qualities may be high, this can produce its own defects in practical politics.

It casts itself for the role of a third party, hoping, under some circumstances of close numbers in the House of Commons between Labour and Conservative, to represent the balance of power. But, and my experience confirms this conclusion, a party which aims at power in its own right, and therefore looks for the acceptance of national responsibility, must formulate and advocate its own policies of action with both broadness and particularity. It is not hoping simply to play off one great party against another.

When, therefore, we decided to call the new and united party the Liberal Party, we were adopting no analogy to the Liberal Party in the United Kingdom. On the contrary, we were aiming at political progress and power in our own right. We took the name 'Liberal' because we were determined to be a progressive party, willing to make experiments, in no sense reactionary but believing in the individual, his rights, and his enterprise, and rejecting the Socialist panacea.

In the United States of America, the word 'liberal' is used in contradistinction to 'conservative', but it seems, in recent years, to have acquired a special connotation. When I resided in America for some months in 1966-7, I thought that it threatened to become a word which had special reference to racial relations; to 'civil rights'; to the vexed questions of 'integration' and 'segregation'.

Thanks to a wise immigration policy, we are free of this problem in Australia, and I hope that we shall never permit ourselves to acquire it.

The next matter which required emphasis at the Canberra meeting was, 'what should be the substance of a Liberal policy?'

It was quite plain that 1944 was a crucial year for Australian politics. Labour had just had a smashing victory, and the Opposition, in the country though not in the House, was dejected and divided. Labour could afford to look to the future with great Socialist hopes. For the war, under both party administrations, had caused a tremendous growth in the powers of Government, in the all-pervading habit of receiving and obeying government orders. Private enterprise had grown accustomed to its chains. Private citizens had become familiar with the manifestations of the planned state; investment control, food rationing, petrol rationing, very high rates of taxation, government organization of industry and transport.

If things were allowed to settle down into a continuance of this political pattern, Labour's future would be bright, and that of its opponents shadowy indeed.

It is a political fact, well known in all parliamentary democracies, that defeat, unless it is defeat by a very narrow margin, tends to disunite the defeated. If one defeat is followed by others, disunity becomes a certainty. In Australia, even the massive monolithic unity of the Labour Party, to which I had referred at the Canberra Conference, could not survive the successive defeats suffered by it after 1949. It suffered grave internal divisions; a large group split off from it and formed a new Democratic Labour Party. It had conflicts in its branches; open conflict about its leaders; in short, everything that a political opponent could desire.

In 1944, it was clear that my main task, as Leader of the Opposition, was to secure the organic and mental unity of fourteen fractions. This, of course, was far more than a problem of mechanics. A unity artificially attained will not last long if there is no genuine community of thought; of basic principles and applied ideas. It was therefore necessary for me, as the promoter, to prepare the foundations for a comprehensive statement of political objectives. As I said to the Canberra Conference in October 1944:

We have, partly by our own fault and partly by some extremely clever propaganda by the Labour Party, been put into the position of appearing to resist political and economic progress. In other words, on far too many questions we have found our role to be simply that of the man who says 'no'.

Once this atmosphere is created, it is quite simple for us to be branded as reactionaries, and, indeed, if we are not careful the very unsoundness of so many of Labour's political proposals may accustom us so much to the role of critic that we become unduly satisfied with our existing state of affairs.

There is no room in Australia for a party of reaction. There is no useful place for a policy of negation.

I then proceeded to set out what I believed should be our 'ultimate objectives'. It would be tedious to repeat them in detail; but in substance they amounted to a series of propositions relating to international and domestic, political and economic affairs.

Internationally, we should seek peace and security from external aggression by living 'in the closest communion with Commonwealth and other like countries'. That meant that we saw a wise foreign policy as part of our defence, though we also came out clearly for treating National defence, in the military field, as a matter of universal duty. At that time, of course, with the war going on, we were not in conflict with Labour on these points.

I therefore concentrated a good deal of attention on the domestic principles which the Australian people should be asked to adopt, so that, when peace came, Australia could move into an era in which there should be both rapid development and growth, and a high degree of financial stability; two ideals thought by many to be irreconcilable.

Now, how were we to secure development? Clearly, we were to encourage thrift and saving, investment, and reward.

The principle of such reward, sometimes sneered at as exhibiting the profit motive, is the dynamic force of social progress and is of the essence of what we call private or individual enterprise.

I will quote a few more passages from my speech on that historic occasion. I am not doing this in any spirit of vanity, or because I think that I was the sole Apostle (though I did have both the initiative and the chief responsibility). I record them because, as it happened, I wrote them in my own crabbed hand in my own office.

At the time, they were an individual effort. Later events were to show that I was by no means alone: I will come to them.

We must aim at the growing exploitation of our natural resources. *Governments do not provide enterprise; they provide controls.* No sensible person can doubt that the revival of private enterprise is essential to post-war recovery and progress. . . .

There cannot be rising living standards if all we propose to do is to redistribute what we now have. We must produce more and produce it more cheaply if we are to survive and grow.

I recognized, of course, that the State had its part to play, in major public works, in fiscal policy, in the provision of basic services, in the providing of national research and leadership. But it was not to be the Master.

In a vision of the future, therefore, I see the individual and his encouragement and recognition as the *prime motive force* for the building of a better world. Socialism means high costs, inefficiency, the constant intrusion of political considerations, the damping down of enterprise, the overlordship of routine. None of these elements can produce progress, and without progress security will turn out to be a delusion.

These views did not represent a belief that private enterprise should have an 'open go'. Not at all. My friends and I recognized the economic responsibilities of the State to assist in preventing the recurrence of large-scale unemployment by appropriate economic and monetary measures; to secure, through social legislation, a decent and reasonable measure of economic security and material well-being for all responsible citizens; and to succeed in both of these purposes by creating a state of affairs which would encourage the enterprise, resourcefulness, and efficiency of individuals and to lead to the greatest possible output of the needed goods and services.

This seems commonplace now. It expresses views which were held by many in 1944; but it needed saying in a public and comprehensive way.

That Conference was a great success; a success to which many delegates made a valuable contribution. It would be self-defeating to name most or all of them. But I shall always remember two people who typified the prevailing spirit; Mrs Couchman (later Dame Elizabeth) and W. H. (later Sir William) Anderson.

'May' Couchman (as I knew her) had a clear mind and a practical grasp of politics. She had for a long time been President of the Australian Women's National League in Victoria. It was a fine body; its members did far more electoral work than most men; it had a history and tradition, and a natural pride in its own identity. It was not easy for it to merge itself into a new nation-wide organization and become part of the Women's Section of the Liberal Party.

Yet within six months, Mrs Couchman, with the aid of loyal colleagues, had achieved it!

W. H. Anderson was, and is, a man of seemingly dry but precise mind, a patriot with a lifetime of service in war and peace. He had been sufficiently dissatisfied with the Opposition to form and lead the Services and Citizens Party, one of the fourteen 'fractions' called to Canberra.

I had discussed the problem with him in my home at Kew, in Melbourne, and was greatly stimulated by his pungent remarks. He played a great hand at Canberra, and later at Albury. With no personal ambitions for Parliamentary office, he has remained a driving force in the Liberal Party organization ever since. He was Federal President for some years. One could always get up an argument with him; but, to me, he typifies the whole spirit of the 'founding fathers' (and mothers) of the Great Australian Liberal Revival.

Well, as I have recounted, the Canberra Conference not only declared for unity, but decided on a name and on broadly-stated objectives.

It was agreed that the delegates would report back to their respective organizations and recommend that the decisions of the Conference be carried into effect. A further plenary Conference would then be held at Albury, in New South Wales, at which, it was anticipated, the new Party would be formally constituted, and a Constitution adopted.

So promptly did all the delegations act and report back that by 31 October I was able to send out from my legal Chambers in Melbourne a circular letter to each organization represented at the Canberra Conference, indicating the nature of the responses I had received.

It gives me pleasure to recall them. The President of the Liberal Democratic Party in New South Wales, E. K. White, a most resolute character; Neville Harding, Chairman of the Democratic Party of New South Wales (who became Lord Mayor of Sydney); W. H. Anderson and the General Secretary of the United Australia Organization in

Victoria, and Mrs Couchman; the Queensland, South Australian, and Tasmanian organizations, had all come enthusiastically into line.

Fortified by these events, I sat down to do a mort of work, though I was now assisted by many carefully considered suggestions and drafts, on the preparation of a Constitution and a Platform. I am grateful to recall that, with much debate and proper amendments, my efforts were in general approved.

Three matters properly engaged much attention and inspired most lively contributions.

The first was the proposal that we should have a Federal organization, meaning by that one in which State Divisions should have complete autonomy on State political matters; Federal matters being the special concern of a Federal Executive, Council, and Secretariat. This, in a country very sensitive about 'State Rights', was not easy of achievement; but it was accepted.

The second concerned the ways and means of working out policy. There should be a Policy Committee in each State, and, for the Commonwealth, a Committee partly Parliamentary and partly representing the Branches or the Divisions. We provided for these Committees. But it took a few years, and a good deal of discussion, to establish what was to me basic; that is, that the Federal platform of the Party, its broad objectives, should be moulded, with recommendations by the Committees, by the Annual Federal Council, but that the particular Election policy must be propounded by the Federal Leader in consultation with his Parliamentary colleagues. It was very important to establish this principle, since one of our great criticisms of the Labour Party was that every Labour Member of Parliament, from the leader down, was bound to accept the directions of the non-Parliamentary Federal Executive of the Labour Party; the 'thirty-six faceless men', as we were later to describe them with devastating effect.

And so, the twin ideas of Organization control of the Platform and Parliamentary Party control of Election policy within the broad principles of the Platform, were established.

The third problem concerned the ways and means of financing the new party. The old United Australia Party, except for a very nominal membership fee, had been financed by special and largely self-appointed bodies. Thus, in Sydney there was a Consultative Council made up of eminent businessmen, who 'raised the wind' and met the expenses of the State Organization, and, in my experience, did not hesitate to say what policies should be pursued. In Melbourne, there was a similar body, the 'National Union', also composed of eminent citizens, which paid the expenses of the State organization but did not, in my experience, give orders. But the position was most unsatisfactory. The Liberal Party was bound to be accused, by the Labour Party propagandists, of being the servants of 'Big Business'. It must be made evident that we were not; it must be made expressly clear that the new Party organization would raise and control its own finances. This was done.

By this time, we were about to enter 1946, a General Election Year. Our Joint Standing Committee met in Canberra in January 1946, and composed, for the first time, the 'Federal Platform of the Liberal Party of Australia'.

We stated our objectives.

In the light of subsequent developments, I should quote a few of them. We declared that we wanted to have an Australian Nation

In which an intelligent, free, and liberal Australian democracy shall be maintained by

(a) Parliament controlling the Executive and the Law controlling all;

(b) Freedom of speech, religion, and association;

(c) Freedom of citizens to choose their own way of life, subject to the rights of others;

(d) Protecting the people against exploitation;

(e) Looking primarily to the encouragement of individual initiative and enterprise as the dynamic force of re-construction and progress.

As so much was to turn upon domestic economic policy in the succeeding years, I should go on to quote a few relevant passages of the Platform. Increased production was clearly going to be needed after the austerities of war. So we used such phrases as:

Favouring the principles that wages should be the highest and conditions the best that the industry concerned can provide, and that good work is the essential condition of good pay, we shall conduct a constant educational campaign against the doctrine that the interests of employer and employee are opposed. . . .

. . . Increased, more efficient and cheaper production are the essential conditions of new and increased markets, regular employment, and rising standards of living for those engaged in industry. . . .

. . . Increasing production demands increasing markets. Increasing markets can be won if production of commodities is both good and cheap. Cheap production depends upon effort and efficiency, not upon wage-slashing. We believe that high wages and high production are natural and inevitable allies.

In that same year, the Labour Government introduced and carried a Law for the broadcasting of Parliamentary proceedings. I make some personal reference to this in a subsequent chapter. But politically, it proved to be a Government mistake. Those citizens who 'listened in'— and, except on a few extraordinary occasions, they were a small minority—were fascinated by the attack, and somewhat uninterested in the defence. So, on the air, we, the Opposition, made headway.

Numerically, we were a small Opposition, though we developed a considerable *esprit de corps*, organized our debates, and heartily enjoyed them.

The General Election of 1946 fell in September. Our organization was relatively new; there were still some teething troubles. It was not reasonable to expect to win the many seats that would be needed to put the Government out. We won a few seats, and were unlucky not to win a few more. As I wrote to Arthur Fadden shortly afterwards: 'When you consider that the task was to arrest the momentum of Labour, and then to secure some movement in the opposite direction, the result of the election is not unsatisfactory.'

I might have added, in the old French aphorism, that 'it is the first step that counts'.

But although those of us who were the toilers in the vineyard were not depressed, we had plenty of onlookers who, having contributed little or nothing to victory, at once became critical. Before long, the word went around that 'You can't win with Menzies!' It received no acceptance from my Parliamentary colleagues; but in a few newspaper circles it had powerful support.

One newspaper of large circulation published, having, I suspected, promoted it, a Public Opinion Poll which found that most people would like to replace me. This newspaper sent a reporter (a man whom I knew and liked) to get my comments. 'We have a story that at your Party meeting your leadership is coming under review and possibly challenge.'

As this story was completely false, I spoke my mind, and went so far as to say that it was quite characteristic of his employers, who were by nature destructive.

He reported this back, as I knew and intended that he should. A day or two later, I received a withering blast by letter, a letter in which I was accused of promoting my own 'supposed interests', to which I replied. It is an old controversy, and I have no desire to mention names now that I am out of the arena. But I did say two things which are worth recording for the benefit of my successors in politics, and, in particular, of my family.

My correspondent had, as I have said, made a slighting reference to my 'supposed interests'. My reply on that point was:

Why *my* supposed interests? Can you really believe that you can strike down the leader of a Party (when you do not suggest any alternative leader in the Parliamentary ranks) and do no injury to the Party? Do you really believe that I have preferred my own interests?

If the Prime Ministership is the crown of political ambition, I have worn it. After many years of thankless public work, in which my character and reputation have been assailed publicly and privately, I might with reason have returned to a profession in which, had I remained at it, I should have been relatively well-off and immune from malice and abuse. But instead of returning to a private life, I undertook the leadership of a defeated Opposition, the creation of a new Liberal Party and the formulation of a policy which has received high praise from your own newspaper. With all respect, I dispute your right to make slighting references to my 'supposed interests' under the circumstances. . . . The truth is that you have a notion that it is the privilege of the press to give criticism and the function of the politician to receive it meekly and with gratitude. When you have had to suffer one tiny fraction of the criticism and personal attack to which I have been subjected for years, you will perhaps be less ready to resent a gesture of annoyance and a little more appreciative of public service which, however human and frequently mistaken, has at any rate been honest and sustained.

Meanwhile, political history in Australia was being made. As I have tried to make clear, it was our firmly-held belief that the great issue to which Liberalism must direct itself was that of Socialism. It must be taken out of the academic realms of the debating society, and presented as a real issue of practical politics.

This would not be easy, for, as I have said, people had become accustomed to government control. But our opponents, not for the first or last time, raised the issue for us, and made it a living thing.

The incoming Chifley Government, in 1945, had decided to nationalize the Civil Air Services, which had in fact been pioneered by private enterprise with notable success. I remind my readers that the Labour scheme was, first to create a National Airlines Commission with power to conduct air services on behalf of the Government, and then, by a series of Statutory devices, give it a monopoly, thus eliminating the private services. On challenge, the High Court had found that the creation of a monopoly in inter-state air services violated Section 92 of the Australian Constitution, which guarantees the freedom of inter-state trade, commerce, and intercourse.

But the Socialist Objective, in which Chifley firmly believed, had been given a practical significance in the public mind.

By 1948, the next great example had emerged. The Government passed laws to nationalize banking, under the circumstances and with the results I have earlier described.

The issue of Socialism was no longer academic. It came alive, and the critics subsided.

The 1949 General Election in Australia needs some special mention in any book of mine. The Labour Government had, in relation to both aviation and banking, prepared the ground for the kind of political battle which my colleagues and I had sought. We decided, with the complete concurrence of the Country Party, our close and almost indistinguishable ally, to fight the battle on the obvious ground. In the Policy Speech, which I wrote after consultation with my colleagues in the Opposition Executive, I stated the case as clearly, indeed as starkly, as I could; for I knew that we were at the crossroads.

I will quote just a few paragraphs:

This is our great year of decision. Are we for the Socialist State, with its subordination of the individual to the universal officialdom of government, or are we for the ancient British faith that governments are the servants of the people? . . .

... The case against Socialism is a deadly one. It concerns the spiritual, mental, and physical future of our families. ...

... The best people in this community are not those who 'leave it to the other fellow', but those who by thrift and self-sacrifice establish homes and bring up families and add to the national pool of savings and hope some day to sit 'under their own vine and fig-tree', owing nothing to anybody. ...

And then, to go to the heart of Liberalism, I said:

... The real freedoms are to worship, to think, to speak, to choose, to be ambitious, to be independent, to be industrious, to acquire skill, to seek reward. These are the real freedoms, for these are of the essence of the nature of man.

I have never regretted or qualified these words. The electors agreed with them.

And so, in December 1949, we achieved office and responsibility. We have retained it, with popular approval, ever since. In our first years, in the early fifties, we were to find ourselves coping with very great financial instability, with waves of inflation and an unhealthy loan market. But a steadfast adherence to our beliefs carried us through troubled waters; so successfully that for many years now Australia has (in spite of the sceptics) enjoyed a period of unexampled growth with great financial stability and high credit, both domestically and internationally. 'Luck,' our opponents used to say. But I always remember the frequently forgotten words of the Book of Common Prayer—'Good luck have thou with thine honour!' A little luck is no bad thing to have; I have had some experience of its opposite; but ideas and determination are of the essence.

To such of my readers as have attended to this narrative, I would wish to add one observation. If my story seems to dwell on my own actions and words in this period of Liberal Revival, the simple reason is that, in the events that had happened, the duty and the initiative fell upon me. I had to do that duty and maintain that initiative. With great help, as I proudly acknowledge; but the task imposed burdens which were, in a real sense, mine. If, in my retirement, I permit myself to cast myself for the role of the 'founding father' of a great and enduring Australian party, I hope that this will be attributed, not to a species of vanity, but to a just pride in a result which many 'practical' people would have dismissed from their imaginations twenty-three years ago.

CHAPTER THIRTEEN

TWO AUSTRALIAN EPISODES IN THE MATTER OF PARLIAMENTARY PRIVILEGE

Two particular experiences have induced me to set down these recollections. Each concerns Parliamentary Privilege— one directly and one indirectly. As each has some historic significance, my account of them may have value for the future student. The one that concerned Parliamentary Privilege directly was the celebrated Australian case of Browne and Fitzpatrick.

I will begin the story by reciting the provisions of Section 49 of the Constitution of the Commonwealth of Australia. That Section says:

The powers, privileges, and immunities of the Senate and of the House of Representatives, and of the members and the committees of each House, shall be such as are declared by the Parliament, and until declared shall be those of the Commons House of Parliament of the United Kingdom, and of its members and committees, at the establishment of the Commonwealth.

In 1955, when this *cause célèbre* arose, the Australian Parliament had not thought it necessary to declare any special 'powers, privileges and immunities' but had been content to rest upon those already established by the House of Commons over the centuries.

The most important privilege is of course to speak freely in Parliament on behalf of the electors, without fear or favour. Such a privilege is not the personal property of an individual member. He is not selfish when he defends it. The privilege is that of the people, the electors speaking through Parliament. As I said myself in Parliament on 13 June 1955, 'It must not be forgotten that the vital conflict in the seventeenth century was between the power and privilege of the King and the power and privilege of the Parliament.'

Modern parliamentary democracy is the product of the victory of Parliament in that conflict. Can that supremacy of Parliament be sustained if a member of Parliament can be threatened by somebody outside Parliament in order to induce or compel his silence on matters which he would otherwise regard it as his duty to lay before Parliament?

This was the basic question in the case of Browne and Fitzpatrick. It arose in this way.

On 28 April 1955, a Sydney suburban newspaper the *Bankstown Observer*, which was owned by Fitzpatrick, a man generally regarded as exercising a considerable political influence in that part of Sydney, published a statement about Charles Morgan, M.P., the Labour Member for a Federal Constituency which included Bankstown. The statement was that 'some people were claiming' that Charles Morgan, a solicitor, was mixed up in 'an immigration racket' by charging alien immigrants a fee for procuring their entry into Australia. There was a great interest in immigration. After the Second World War it had been a notable feature of Australian development. The newspaper, having retailed these 'charges', added, with the usual piety of the public defamer, that it did not know whether the charges were true or false but that there should be an inquiry.

On 3 May, Morgan, with great spirit, raised the matter in Parliament and secured the passage of a resolution, that the article be referred to the Parliamentary Committee of Privileges for investigation and report.

The *Bankstown Observer*, professing to be shocked at this action, returned to the attack on 5 May. It boldly described Morgan's action (which was in fact a courageous one, for he knew that he was giving wide circulation to a libel), as 'a cowardly Canberra attack' and accused him of 'slandering people that he does not like'. The writer concluded on an heroic note: 'We will go to Canberra. *And we will take with us proof of the charges against Morgan.*' In later issues of this journal, the work of defamation was carried on.

The Committee of Privileges heard evidence from Morgan, from Raymond Edmund Fitzpatrick, the owner of the newspaper, and Frank Browne, a free-lance journalist who had written the articles. The Committee reported to the House on 8 June 1955. It found that there was a breach of privilege 'in that an attempt had been made, through the newspaper articles, to influence and intimidate' Morgan in his conduct in the House. That the charges were groundless was clearly established. *No evidence was adduced to substantiate them.*

The Committee reported Browne as saying to it 'that he did not have the proof with him', and that he did not possess the proof at the time the article was written.

Fitzpatrick was asked: 'Have you any personal evidence of any charges against Mr Morgan?' He replied: 'No.'

The Committee reported that 'the evidence showed that Mr Fitzpatrick had employed Mr Browne as author of the articles concerning the honourable Member for Reid, at the fee of £30 per week for the express purpose of attacking the honourable Member for Reid, that he had implicit trust in whatever he (Browne) wrote and that he left the writing of the articles to Mr Browne.'

The reason for this commission quickly appeared. Mr Joske, a legal member of the Committee (now Mr Justice Joske) referred to a statement by Mr Morgan in the House: 'I regard it as a brazen attempt to intimidate me in the course of my public duties on behalf of the people whom I represent', and then said to Fitzpatrick: 'What do you say about that?'

Mr Fitzpatrick: 'That was our idea in printing it.'

Mr Joske: 'To prevent him saying things in Parliament?'

Mr Fitzpatrick: 'Yes.'

Mr Joske: 'Mr Morgan then said: "No doubt it has been caused by fears about disclosures that will be made in the near future as a result of inquiries that have been set in train." What is your comment on that?'

Mr Fitzpatrick: 'That is the burning of the "Torch".'

Mr Joske: 'You agree that that is the true reason why it was published?'

Mr Fitzpatrick: 'Yes, that is so.'

(The reference to the burning of the 'Torch' was a reference to a somewhat mysterious fire which had occurred in the Bankstown district and about which great local controversy had occurred and some unpleasant suggestions, not against Morgan, had been made.)

The report having been presented, the House of Representatives on 9 June passed a resolution 'that the House agrees with the Committee in its report'. In moving this, as Prime Minister, I suggested that if the

House agreed with the report 'these two men, Fitzpatrick and Browne, should be given the benefit of what we call natural justice in these matters. Before the House proceeds to decide what penalty it will impose, it should give them, first thing tomorrow morning, an opportunity of being present at the bar of the House, and speaking to the House before the House passes sentence on them.' The motion was carried without dissent.

A resolution was then carried:

That Raymond E. Fitzpatrick and Frank C. Browne be notified that at 10 a.m. tomorrow the House will hear them at the Bar before proceeding to decide what action it will take in respect of their breaches of privilege.

On 10 June, at 10 a.m., the two men appeared separately at the Bar of the House of Representatives and were heard, Fitzpatrick briefly and apologetically, Browne at length and truculently. Browne's address was marred by one unfortunate incident. The Bar of the House had been lowered (it was literally a wooden bar) across the entrance to the Chamber, a species of wide doorway recess. I do not think any of us had seen it lowered before. Browne, leaning forward so as to be seen and heard, very naturally placed his hands on the Bar. Thereupon suddenly and loudly the Speaker, Cameron, ordered him 'to take his hands off the Bar'. This was harsh and unnecessary. (It must be confessed that Cameron did, from time to time, act like a Regimental Sergeant-Major.) It could have grievously disturbed and confused anybody less self-confident than Browne turned out to be.

He argued at length and offensively about the rights of Parliament and said vehemently that he had been denied a fair trial.

The House adjourned at about 10.20 a.m. until 11.10 a.m. I then moved two resolutions, the material portion of each of which was that the person concerned (i.e. Fitzpatrick and then Browne) should be imprisoned 'until the tenth day of September 1955, or until earlier prorogation or dissolution, unless this House shall sooner order his discharge'.

In submitting the motions, I first of all dealt with the powers of Parliament and the nature of Parliamentary Privilege. Having quoted Section 49 of the Commonwealth Constitution, I went on to refer to 'the very sound principle that, unless the Parliament itself remains an institution in which members are free to speak, it ceases to perform one of the greatest of the functions of the Parliament, which is the free expression of opinion and the free debating of ideas concerning the public good'.

As Browne and some of his outside journalistic supporters had fiercely criticized what was described as Parliament being a judge in its own cause, I then went on to make some observations which, as they secured wide acceptance in the House, I venture to reproduce.

A right to punish for contempt is not peculiar to the Parliament. The courts of law have a right to punish for contempts of court. Indeed, I remind honourable members that, in the case of a contempt of court committed in the face of the court, the judge who is at the time presiding over the proceedings deals with the matter himself, there and then, and has power instantly to commit for contempt the person guilty of it. I mention that very well-known fact merely to point out that some of the remarks about trials to which we listened this morning are entirely misconceived. In the case to which I have referred, the court is a judge, if one likes, in its own cause. Parliament, if one likes, is the judge in its own cause, because no one except the Parliament can protect the Parliament. The case with which we are now dealing is a perfect illustration of the differences that must be kept clearly in mind not only by us here in this place of privilege, but also by people outside this chamber. Criticism of the Parliament, of course, is well justified by experience and well warranted in point of right. Violent criticism and attacks, perhaps of a highly personal sort, on individual members of Parliament are not unknown. No Parliament has ever taken action to prevent those things, and I do not think any parliament will ever do so. The freedom known as the freedom of criticism is something that neither the Government nor, I suppose, any member of this House proposes to touch.

If this were merely a case of criticism, even of violent criticism, and if the matter had followed what one might call the pattern of controversial journalism, it would never have engaged the attention of the Committee of Privileges, or if it had done so, would never have been made the subject of a finding by the Committee in the terms in which a finding has been made. This happens to be a case in which the Committee has found, in substance, a conspiracy to blackmail a member of the Parliament into silence. Let us be perfectly clear about this matter. If these tactics had succeeded, and if the honourable member for Reid (Mr Morgan) had not invoked the consideration of the House on this matter but had been silenced and forced to conceal what, no doubt, would be his views, this conspiracy would have succeeded. A member of Parliament would have been silenced. Something that, perhaps, ought to have been made known and ought to have been discussed would not have been made known and would not have been discussed. Here we have something that is completely outside the realm of criticism as we understand the term. It is a conspiracy to blackmail a member into silence. If that objective can be achieved, that member's capacity to represent his electors has, to that degree, been destroyed; he has been silenced. And, then, one has only to silence enough people by those methods to reduce this Parliament to impotence. I have emphasized that matter because, in some minds, there is always a little disposition to be sceptical about the Parliament as if it were an odd place in which only odd people were to be found. I am proud to say that this institution is the representative body of the nation. It is the flower of Australian democracy, and the degree to which this House preserves the freedom of its members to speak and to think will be the measure of its service to democracy.

The debate was conducted for the most part, with one or two exceptions, on a remarkably high level, and with an absence of passion, which did great credit to members, some of whom had been violently attacked by Browne on other occasions.

Knowing that it might be thought by some that a fine would be an appropriate punishment, I referred to the history of these matters in the House of Commons, pointed out that the imposing of a fine had long since fallen into disuse, and that it could not, therefore, in 1901 when the Commonwealth Constitution began to operate, be included among the powers of the Commons House of Parliament. I concluded by saying: 'the historic remedy, adopted repeatedly over the course of history by the House of Commons, and, indeed, by one or two parliaments at least in Australia, is the remedy of committing to prison.'

Dr Evatt, then Leader of the Opposition, though he agreed that the imposition of a fine 'had long since fallen into desuetude in Great Britain' thought that the appropriate punishment would be a very substantial fine. He agreed with the report of the Committee and thought the Committee justified in saying that there had been a serious breach of the privileges of the House. But he thought imprisonment excessive and that the amount of the fines and the procedure for enforcing them should forthwith be determined by the House.

I will not elaborate the course of the debate. In the result an amendment moved by Dr Evatt to substitute a fine was defeated by 52 to 16, and my own motion was agreed to by 55 to 12. In each division it was to be noted that some members of the Labour Opposition voted with the Government and that some others rather conspicuously abstained. I mention this to show that the matter was not dealt with on orthodox Party lines.

The case created a great sensation. There were in some newspapers bitter attacks upon what Parliament had done; most of them being based upon the view that nobody should be sent to prison except under the order of one of the ordinary courts of law.

I have no doubt that this was a wrong view. It arose in reality from a confusion about the nature of the Commonwealth Constitution, a confusion which I have observed many times in the course of my own public life.

There are, in fact, three great organs of Government established by the Constitution—one, the Legislature; one, the Executive; and one, the Judicature. It is part of the very history of British constitutional development that, while the judiciary deals exclusively with litigation, the privileges of Parliament are created by and enforced by Parliament itself. It would indeed be strange if it were otherwise.

Parliament consists of people freely chosen by the electors. It is responsible to those electors and to nobody else. It should not tolerate the imposing upon it of restrictions in the performance of that duty. If it were to delegate to some judge or magistrate the determination of its privileges or the enforcement of them, conflicts could arise which could have a most damaging effect upon the whole Parliamentary institution.

It was, of course, freely said by some newspapers that the privileges and immunities of Parliament were either inconsistent with or a threat to the freedom of the press.

The reply to that was quite simple; so simple that I made it myself. The historic fact was that the modern protection of the freedom of Parliament and the even more modern freedom of the press have gone hand in hand. One cannot exist adequately without the other. Parliament makes no challenge to the rights of newspapers or citizens to criticize Members of Parliament closely or even bitterly. But just as any attempt (except under the pressures of war) to close the mouth of a newspaper would be a violation of free speech, so no reputable newspaper either demands or expects the right to threaten into silence a Member of Parliament speaking in his place in the House.

Looking back on it all, I think that what we did was right; that there was no undue haste; that the House itself maintained a high standard of responsibility; and that the punishment inflicted served as a proper warning to people that the freedom of a newspaper or writer is freedom and not licence, and that it can be lost when it is abused.

The other notable event or series of events in my political lifetime bearing upon Parliamentary Privilege has concerned the introduction of the broadcasting of Parliamentary debates at Canberra.

This experiment, which is now settled practice, began in 1946. I call it an experiment because it contained in itself certain inherent dangers of which some members were perhaps not fully aware. The chief political danger was that some members read well and sound badly. I was leader of the Opposition at the time. I thought that if sufficient people listened in to Parliamentary debates some unexpected changes might occur at the next election! Why then did the Chifley Labour Government introduce the scheme and why was it substantially supported by the Members of the Opposition?

I think that basically the principal reason was that there was widespread dissatisfaction with the way in which most Australian newspapers report Parliament. The art of reporting, in my political lifetime, has declined out of all sight. I remember saying to John Curtin once, when I was Prime Minister in 1940 and he was the Leader of the Labour Opposition, that I was disappointed that somebody who could speak as well as he could should have fallen into the habit of reading carefully prepared typed speeches to the House. Curtin had been a journalist himself and was *persona grata* with the average member of the Canberra Gallery. Most of them indeed were his political supporters. But with a wry smile he said to me, 'Well, old man, the trouble is that they don't report any longer. If you hand out the full text of your speech, it has a fair chance of getting into the newspapers; if you don't, it's just a gamble as to what you will find you said.'

This was, I fear, quite true. It was, in 1946, widely believed to be true by Members of Parliament. They believed that not only was the most serious speech quite inadequately reported but that there was a tendency in the news columns to devote undue attention to the silly little incidents which occur in Parliament and to which nobody in the House pays much attention until it turns out that they have reached the headlines next day. Members had also realized that there is a disposition nowadays, in the interests of what is called 'colour', to interlard what the speaker said with what the reporter thought and, not infrequently, to base denunciatory leading articles upon something which in fact the Member of Parliament did not say at all. I had a great deal of experience of this myself. It was, therefore, thought that the people should be given the opportunity to hear exactly what the Member of Parliament said, without suppression or alteration or comment.

On the whole I approved of the innovation, though with considerable reservation. I could see quite clearly the great advantage of being able to speak to electors direct. Broadcasting would provide a better form of reporting. It would help listeners to assess the personality and significance of the speaker as well as the accuracy of his views. It was also thought by some that the fact that many thousands of people would be listening in would tend to restrain extravagances of speech and occasional outbursts of vituperation.

On the other hand, of course, some of us realized that broadcasting, with its development of *prima donna* outlook at 'good listening-in times', would tend to destroy the intimate quality of Parliamentary debate and tend to convert it into a series of set speeches to the electors.

It is for this latter reason that Sir Winston Churchill always told me that he was against broadcasting of Parliament; and I know that he spoke for a great body of Parliamentary opinion.

After many years of experience, I have serious doubts about the value of Parliamentary broadcasting, for I don't think that it has, of itself, in the slightest degree improved the standard of Parliamentary behaviour; on the contrary, I would think that the few men who see in Parliament a glorious opportunity for unrestrained defamation of character have been encouraged by broadcasting and not restrained by it. But these reflections are not entirely relevant to the main purpose which I have in mind.

How has broadcasting of the Australian Parliament affected the broad question of Parliamentary and legal privilege?

Clearly, Parliamentary privilege is unaffected by it, since it is governed by the considerations which I have discussed in the earlier portion of this chapter. But from the beginning an interesting question arose as to the privilege to be enjoyed by the Australian Broadcasting

Commission which was to conduct the broadcasting. A Bill was introduced, the Parliamentary Proceedings Broadcasting Bill 1946; one of its provisions was that the privileges and immunities applying to debates within the Parliament should apply to the broadcasts of Parliamentary proceedings. In other words, the Broadcasting Commission was to be in the same position from the point of view of privilege as the Hansard writers and those who published Hansard as a Parliamentary Paper. That meant 'absolute' privilege. So far so good. The proposal was inherent in the very idea of broadcasting. But in my own speech, I raised a question of the broader aspects of this matter. I pointed out that the broadcast was in a sense a substitute for, or an alternative to, reporting in the press; and reminded members that newspapers did not have absolute privilege in respect of reports of Parliamentary proceedings.

The legal position was, I thought, clear enough. From the point of view of a newspaper, it is only a 'fair and accurate' report of any debate or proceedings in Parliament that has protection. If the report is not fair and accurate, because, for example, it reports a charge and suppresses the answer, then the privilege is lost. This is something frequently overlooked by Members of Parliament, some of whom rather like, particularly at election time, to publish extracts of some violent attack made by them or somebody else in the House and do so under the naïve belief that so long as they quote their own words accurately from Hansard they are safe. What they have left out of account is that their electoral document is privileged only if it is a fair and accurate report of Parliamentary Proceedings and that a partial report which gives an unfair picture of the total is not privileged.

I offered the view that if Parliamentary proceedings were to be broadcast then the whole debate must be on the air, and not small selected portions of it.

Nothing I believed, and still believe, could be more unfair than to pass out over the air an attacking speech and to find that the reply is not on the air at all. This, as it seemed to me, would give to the broadcasting authority, as the reporter for this purpose, a privilege denied to any newspaper.

What is more, the Act set up a Committee, and the time over the air is allocated between the House of Representatives and the Senate.

Thus, the House may be on the air on Tuesday, the Senate on Wednesday, and the House again on Thursday. This inevitably means that what is broadcast on Tuesday may find itself effectively answered on Wednesday without broadcast. This is not fair. I have no doubt whatever that there is much more popular interest in the debates in the House of Representatives than in the debates in the Senate. As complete fairness cannot be achieved if each House has only occasional access to the air, it seems to me that broadcasting should be confined to one house, and that the House of Representatives, which in Australia is the House which makes and unmakes governments, and has a major responsibility for public affairs, should be the selected House. The alternative would be to have two broadcasting channels, which even a long-suffering Australian public would not tolerate.

There is another defect about the broadcasting of Parliament. It is that the broadcast ceases when, at the end of the day's debates, the Minister-in-charge of the House moves 'that the House do now adjourn'. Now, very frequently in Australia a lengthy debate occurs upon this motion. Various grievances are ventilated, and sometimes a most vigorous discussion takes place. Although the Standing Orders are supposed to prevent discussion on the adjournment on matters which have been before the House that day, the rule is frequently broken. It may well be, therefore, that a Member of Parliament, speaking on the adjournment, may make a most vigorous counter to what he regards as offensive observations which were made earlier, but the defence will not be broadcast, though the original observations were.

But the whole point of my narrative is that I think that the sound rules which at Common Law and by Statute have defined the privileges of reporters and commentators have been exposed to some material and undesirable modifications by the Broadcasting of Parliament Law.

As I write, there is a good deal of reason to suppose that the day will come when there will be pressure by Members of Parliament in Australia to have Parliamentary proceedings televised. I am old-fashioned enough to believe that the great quality of Parliamentary debate must reside in its intimacy, in its parry and thrust, in the desire of the good Parliamentarian to feel the atmosphere of the House and to establish some personal influence upon it. If those considerations disappear, and we are all to look upon ourselves with simple vanity as television stars, we will find in Parliament more and more people who are not a bit concerned about their influence upon their fellow members but are concentrating upon satisfying their own particular public. One has only to look occasionally upon the popular television commentators, with all their vanities and affectations and superficialities, to realize how important it is that in the supreme forum of the nation there should be people who can match their knowledge and their wits with those of their peers, and so thrash out what we call the combined wisdom of Parliament which is, in my experience and at its best, a very remarkable wisdom indeed.

I have always maintained, and I am sure that this goes for every British Parliament, that on great occasions, when a sense of national responsibility rides high, the total judgement of Parliament exceeds the sum of the individual judgements of its members.

It is just because that corporate sense of responsibility is so vital to the functioning of Parliament that I hope that the time will not come when Parliament consists of no more than so many individuals who do not address and seek to influence their fellow members at all, but are seeking to deal with the passions of thousands, or, on a lucky day, millions of people outside.

CHAPTER FOURTEEN

TWO GREAT AMERICANS

I T IS ONE THING TO WRITE about Presidents and Prime Ministers. They are, *ex officio*, fair game. But one hesitates to write about other individuals, because to do so involves selection; and selection brings up comparison; and, to borrow the famous phrase from *Much Ado About Nothing*—'Comparisons are odorous!'

There are quite a few notable but non-Presidential Americans who have a warm place in my memory. Take, for example, my old friend Averell Harriman, who has never occupied the highest place, but whose devoted, able, and continuing services to his country and to the world are, in a real sense, unique. And take others, such as . . . but I must not go on. This short chapter is about two great Americans who were themselves close friends, and, to my lasting joy, friends of mine. I always think of them together, and would think any book of mine incomplete if I did not record some story about them as a pair of unforgettable characters. One of them is now dead; the other will give a wry smile if he reads this chapter, but will, I trust, forgive me.

I write about Felix Frankfurter and Dean Acheson, who between them (and I rarely think of them separately) have done as much for my mind and spirit as any two Americans ever did.

I first met Felix Frankfurter in May 1941 when, having attended Churchill's war cabinet for ten weeks, I was on my way home through the United States. In New York I made a speech about the significance of the war to Americans. It was no doubt a breach of official protocol; but I thought it worth doing. A day or two later, I spoke to the National Press Club in Washington and, for the first time—and perhaps for the last—was given an ovation as I described the war in the Middle East, in which Australian troops were playing a most significant part, and the behaviour of the British people under the Blitz. It was there I met Mr Justice Felix Frankfurter, of the Supreme Court of the United States, who bestowed on me his enthusiastic blessing. He was particularly delighted with one observation. I had been speaking about the financial sacrifices which were being made in the defence of freedom and which were bound to become more severe as the war went on. 'It doesn't matter if we have to scratch gravel, so long as it is our own gravel!' I recall that just before I went in, a few days later, to do my third speech, to a thousand people at the Stephens Hotel in Chicago, I received a telegram from him which included a quotation from Lincoln on 'liberty', which he thought would be appropriate in Lincoln's own State; and which I was of course delighted to use.

From 1948 on, I had occasion to pass through Washington about twice a year. On each occasion, up to the time of his death, I had the joy of dining with him and Dean Acheson at what Dean described as 'Felix's cliff-hanging dwelling' in Georgetown, the fourth diner being the Australian Ambassador, first Sir Percy Spender and then Sir Howard Beale. These were, for me, unforgettable occasions. For I was meeting and talking intimately with two of the greatest Americans of our time. I had little to give, but much to receive. They were united by a great friendship. Felix treated Dean as he would have a son whose talents had delighted him. Dean treated Felix with an affection which shone through every intellectual dispute—and there were many.

After dinner, Felix sat in a winged arm-chair, and talked. Each time he became excited, and this meant every few minutes, he would hitch his legs up under him on the chair, his eyes shining, and the words pouring out. For Felix Frankfurter had the old-fashioned characteristic of enthusiasm. When he believed, he believed intensely. He was, of course, as the greatest of his legal contemporaries in the United States, in England, and in Australia (where I think particularly of the unsurpassed Owen Dixon) agreed, a magnificent lawyer, who added to a faculty of analysis, which is not so rare among good lawyers, the rare faculties of synthesis and judgement.

Dean Acheson, with (as I hope he will allow me to say) a somewhat Mephistophelian appearance, was the perfect foil. For, though he has deep convictions and a rare capacity and courage to speak his own mind, he would occasionally produce a sceptical and almost cynical observation of some astringency, which gave piquancy to the dialogue and served, at the end, to enlarge the boundaries of my own understanding.

The gentleman in the Bible who 'sat at the feet of Gamaliel the prophet' was not as well-off as I was. For I sat at the feet of two prophets.

In the summer 1966 number of the *Virginia Quarterly Review*, Dean Acheson wrote:

One is certain to be excluded from the sainted company of idealists. For the first rule of controversy is to steal the dictionary and appropriate the best words. And too many forget that an idealist can be good, bad, or indifferent, depending on his ideas.

This remark is pure Acheson; there were and are no cloudy patches in his mind.

I remember that, at the time when Senator McCarthy was conducting his evil campaign of intimidation and suspicion against Acheson, who was in every way, morally, intellectually, and in true patriotism, infinitely McCarthy's superior, I found myself, in Canberra, having a long and fascinating talk with Madariaga, the great Spanish thinker and writer. I proudly mentioned Dean Acheson, and asked Madariaga whether he had met him. He said, 'No. But I have carefully followed his words and his actions, just as I have studied the words and actions of his predecessors at the State Department in this century. And in my opinion he takes his place as the greatest of them all.'

Next day, I wrote to Felix and reported this, so that he might give some comfort to Dean. I did not write direct to Dean, but Felix, as I learned, conveyed the story to him. Even the bravest of men needs an occasional word of comfort and approval.

I thought this period in Dean Acheson's public career quite shocking. It was redeemed to some extent in my eyes by the magnificent mutual loyalty between him and President Truman.

Both Frankfurter and Acheson were much too individual and forthright to escape violent criticism.

When Felix went to the Supreme Court, he went there as the result of a political decision; as indeed all judges do in all democratic countries. But in the United States the Supreme Court (if I may say so with bated breath) is more influenced by political considerations than is, for example, the High Court of Australia. I think I have detected two reasons for this.

The first is that in the United States the 'Bill of Rights' Amendments to the Constitution, themselves possessing binding constitutional authority and therefore incapable of amendment by a Congressional Statute, contain a series of express guarantees of individual rights and freedoms which have no place in the Australian Constitution, which is written, or in the British Constitution which, as we know, does not exist. When litigation comes before the U.S. Supreme Court on such matters as 'freedom of speech, or of the press', or 'the right of the people peaceably to assemble', or the provision that 'no person shall be deprived of life, liberty, or property, without due process of law', there is obviously more scope for subjective tests, and the political philosophy of the judge comes into play. On the contrary, the High Court of Australia, dealing primarily, in the constitutional field, with problems of the demarcation of Commonwealth and State powers, tends to be more objective and technical.

The second reason for the introduction of politics into U.S. Supreme Court constitutional decisions, and therefore the marked tendency to make party political appointments, is that there is, as I have observed it, a disposition in America to resent the invalidation of some popular measure by the Supreme Court. This is somewhat surprising to the Australian observer, who is disposed to think that the power of the High Court to declare a Commonwealth law invalid is a good guarantee of the endurance of the Federal system; who likes to believe that only the best lawyers, *as lawyers,* find their way to the highest court; and who wants them to make their decisions as such.

The appointment of Felix Frankfurter to the Supreme Court of the United States was no doubt not uninfluenced by his political beliefs. But if anybody ever thought that Felix would be the talented exponent of a political point of view, and nothing more, he was doomed to disappointment. For the time was to come when Frankfurter came to be regarded as a Conservative! The law has its own disciplines. No lawyer so scholarly and devoted as Frankfurter will distort what he believes to be the legal position to serve some political end fashioned by others or by himself.

Until Frankfurter's physical vigour began to diminish, he lived in a tall, narrow house in Georgetown, the historic area of Washington. His charming wife was semi-invalid, and a mechanical stairway had been fitted in. She did not attend our dinner parties, where our physical needs were attended to by a genial and dusky woman, Matilda.

[312]

But the time came, after his first severe illness, when Felix should be relieved of the strain of stairs. Dean Acheson, the 'cold', the 'unapproachable', the 'almost inhuman', took the matter in hand. The next time my wife and I called on Felix, he was in a splendid apartment on the ground floor of a block in a near area. It was characteristic of Dean Acheson (and he will not thank me for mentioning it) that he should have attended to this problem himself, with all the warmth and enthusiasm of a practically filial affection.

I have sometimes wondered how it came about that Felix, once thought to be a radical and 'new dealer', ended his judicial career under the dreadful charge of being a Conservative. To me, as a distant observer of the Supreme Court of the United States, the answer seems clear. Frankfurter did not change, the Court did. For Frankfurter was above all a lawyer, and brought to the task of interpreting the American Constitution a set of deeply held principles; legal, not political, principles. He approached the problems of interpretation more as an Australian High Court Justice would, with a stock of legal concepts which would never permit any constitutional case to be decided by the exercise of a purely personal discretion.

Jean Monnet, the French economist, in a volume published by Reynal and Co. in 1964, entitled *Felix Frankfurter: A Tribute,* and edited by Professor Wallace Mendelson, said this about Felix. It strongly supports what I have just said:

When he retired from the Supreme Court, many of those who paid tributes to him claimed that over the years he had changed from a liberal into a traditionalist. This was not so. It is the times that have changed, not he. Throughout the years that I have known him, his fundamental beliefs have remained firm.

His conception of the role of the Justice is deceptively simple, but it is very profound. He has always believed that the duty of a judge in a democratic society is to interpret the law without partiality or prejudice, because the law is the expression of the people's will. Whatever his own feelings, they must not deter him; nor must the pressure of political expediency stand in the way of justice and democracy. Only thus, through the supremacy of laws and institutions, can civilized society be built, developed, and freedom preserved.

In recent years some of the Supreme Court Justices of the United States have increasingly handed down opinions which seem to me to reflect, in some measure, the individual Justice's own political and sociological ideas.

For all I know, this—which comes with something of a shock to a traditional Australian lawyer—may be inevitable in dealing with a constitution which is so rich in general phrases about human freedom that the conflict between giving them their full literal meaning and giving them some more restricted meaning, which will enable the ordered business of society to go on, becomes one which cannot readily be resolved by the usual rules of statutory interpretation.

I will take one example only, which will, I think, explain to non-American readers the significance of what I have written earlier in this sketch. The First Amendment provides that 'Congress shall make no law . . . abridging the freedom of speech, or of the press. . . .'

Taken literally, here could be a guarantee of the right to speak treason and to print without censorship in time of war. But the words have never been taken *au pied de la lettre*. How far the exceptions may extend is inevitably, as the decisions run, a subjective rather than an objective problem. Yet there have been decisions excepting some cases of sedition and subversion and even obscenity from the rolling words of the declaration.

I think that as the Court ventured further into sociological considerations, Felix tended to move apart, to dissent or to modify.

Certainly, he had the clear intellectual integrity of the best type of judicial lawyer. He had no love of labels. He had no instinct to 'line-up' with 'liberals' or 'conservatives' as if his vote on the Bench would be determined by some immutable law of political predestination.

Nobody could sit down as frequently as I was lucky enough to do with Frankfurter and Acheson without realizing that he was in the presence of two men of indomitable activity of mind; two duellists each doubly armed with the sword of the mind and the sword of the spirit. They left no room for woolly notions or the vagaries of unfettered discretion. They jointly served one master; the law; though Dean had also served a not always grateful country on the battlefield of politics.

The whole point I want to make about Felix Frankfurter is that his heart was in the law and that is why I believe that just as no American student can understand the early history of his country without becoming familiar with the great name and work of Chief Justice John Marshall, so will he fail in his understanding if he fails, in this century, to become familiar with the name and work of Mr Justice Felix Frankfurter.

CHAPTER FIFTEEN

A LAWYER LOOKS BACK

W HEN I WAS ABOUT TEN OR ELEVEN YEARS OLD, a phrenologist visited my birthplace, Jeparit, a township in the north-west of Victoria, and, for a modest fee 'read my head'! He said I would be a barrister and public speaker. I knew what a public speaker was, for my father was, in a sense, the local politician and a speaker of renown. But what was a barrister? I went home and was told. From that day on, my course was charted and my mind clear, provided that I could win enough free passages, that is, scholarships and exhibitions, to bring me to port.

And so, in due course, I became a barrister. It was my good fortune to 'read' in the Chambers of Mr Owen Dixon, then the leading junior at the Victorian Bar, and later Justice and Chief Justice of the High Court of Australia.

When, years afterwards, I called on him to tell him that I was about to stand for Parliament, he delivered a quick judgement. 'Well, Menzies, it is probably easy to convert a good lawyer into a good politician; but re-conversion is impossible!'

Well, why did I, in the face of such a discouraging opinion from the greatest lawyer in Australia, one of the very greatest men in my life, make this move? It could not be for what are called economic reasons, for I had attained both rank and practice at the Bar, and Australian politics are comparatively poorly rewarded.

It is probably true that most people, seeing a tolerably successful lawyer go into politics, think that he is gladly escaping from a dry and tedious occupation into one which offers light and colour and movement. My own experience was quite opposite.

The practice of the law in court was and remains my first love. A large practice at the Bar means much concentrated and hard work. For some years before I took silk at the age of thirty-four, and for some years thereafter, my weekly hours of work would average not less than eighty. Either in court or in his Chambers, the advocate must never lose his concentration upon the job in hand.

Can it be, then, that politics is attractive because it offers opportunities for idleness? My answer to this is that the task of a political leader, indeed of anybody with real political responsibilities, is immeasurably more difficult and wearing than that of the greatest advocate at the Bar. This statement is so contrary to popular legend that I will set down my reasons for it.

First, the advocate prepares his case interrupted only by his clerk, whom he can order out, and not by constituents, whom he must invite in. He may, in short, concentrate at will.

Second, he knows that in the presentation of the case, the examining and cross-examining of witnesses, the argument of questions of law, he will be his own master, exercising his own judgement, accepting his own responsibility, and not be the perhaps unwilling servant of the judgement of others.

Third, he knows that he will be presenting his case to one judge, or a few, or a handful of people in a jury box, instead of to thousands or millions of people most of whom he will never see. The seen and 'felt' audience of the advocate is a much easier one to judge and influence than the unseen constituency of the politician.

Fourth, he stands before a judge or judges trained in objective analysis and judgement, and can therefore concentrate upon the legal and applied merits of his case. Even when there is also a jury, the influence of the judge will not be insignificant, though it is to be confessed that in criminal cases an advocate is permitted and sometimes expected to advance arguments of such maudlin sentimentality that no politician would readily use them for fear of losing his more intelligent supporters.

Fifth, when he completes a case, it is over. 'Tomorrow is another day.' The next case is just about to begin. 'Thank you, Mr X.' 'Very sorry, Mr Y.' But for a political leader, no case is ever finished. Post-mortems, recriminations, controversy about whether he was right or wrong, will in some matters pursue him to the grave and beyond it. The truth is that when a man enlists himself in the army of politics and achieves high rank in it, he ceases to be his own master; 'there's no discharge in the war'. Even if and when he retires, he will not be outside the firing range of his critics.

But there are, of course, great compensations in politics, as I have tried to show elsewhere, and a great challenge; for I shall always believe that of all civil vocations that of politics is the greatest and most responsible.

No doubt I would have found it difficult to escape politics indefinitely. My father and two uncles, and my wife's father, had all sat in Parliament, State or Federal. At my paternal home, political discussion was in the air. Yet for years after I began practice, I thought about politics very little.

And then, I was assailed by two thoughts which it is difficult to record without the appearance of affectation.

One was that, as I looked around my leading contemporaries and saw some of them so exclusively devoted to law books that they read nothing else, such industrious apprentices of the law that no other civilizing influence had any place in their lives, I began to fear that if my mind grew more technically acute it would cut a more and more narrow groove; make me a more skilled practitioner, but detach me from a broad and humane life. This, I know, sounds affected and pompous; but it is true. I admired men of versatile talents; and felt an impulse to imitate them.

My second reason was that I owed a great deal to my country, which had, by its educational policies, done a great deal for me. I would, I thought, put in a tour of public duty in Parliament; six or seven years would, I considered, be enough, and if I went into the State Parliament I could still largely maintain my practice, and hope, some day, to reach the Bench.

There were, as you see, limits to my virtue. But alas for human expectations—I went into the Victorian Parliament, soon proved to be a thoroughly controversial creature, went to Canberra, retired after over thirty-seven years in Parliament, eighteen of them as Prime Minister; and had not opened my mouth in Court for very many years.

Politics proved to be my greatest duty. But the law remained my first love.

What I have set down will perhaps explain why it is that, after so many rewarding years in Parliament and in high office, my memory turns to those years when I knew the joys of forensic advocacy, the fine *petillant* flavour of cross-examination, the thrust and counter-thrust of argument, the quirks and quiddities of individual judges and opponents, the rich occasions for humour, the whole arresting pattern of oratory and rhodomontade, reason and sentiment, subtlety and the claymore, truth and falsehood under the microscope, the fierce but bloodless battles between 'learned friends'.

I suppose that, after years of intense experience, I am a fairly well-furnished repository of first-hand legal anecdotes. I cannot fit them into this volume. But I warn my legal readers that with the slightest encouragement I will some day commit them to printer's ink. Meanwhile, I resist the temptation.

But no general volume even of some of my memoirs would be complete, or even representative, if I failed to make a bow to what I have described as my 'first love', in whose happy service I recently interrupted my retirement to become, for some months, a 'Visiting Scholar' in the Law Faculty of the University of Virginia, preparing and delivering, and since publishing, a series of lectures on Australian Constitutional developments.

I will therefore, primarily in a non-anecdotal way, set down some concentrated views, based on my own experience on three aspects of court work in Australia.

First, I will make some respectful comments on the High Court of Australia. I will then go downstairs in the judicial building, and offer a few iconoclastic remarks on the Jury System. To conclude, I will yield to the temptation, to which all senior lawyers are subject, to give some unasked advice to young advocates.

1. *The High Court of Australia*

At the founding of the Australian Federation, attention was properly given to the creation of a Judicature. Clearly, if there was to be a division of powers between the new National Parliament and the Parliaments of the States—the pre-existing self-governing colonies—there must be an umpire to interpret and enforce the rules. So, quite clearly, there must be a superior court which could, in a proper case, declare valid or invalid a law passed by a Federal or State Parliament, or an executive act purporting to be done under the authority of that law.

Section 71 of the new Australian Constitution provided that 'the judicial power' of the Commonwealth should be vested in a Federal

Supreme Court to be called the High Court of Australia. The new court was not, however, to be confined to Constitutional cases. It was given an extensive original and appellate jurisdiction; so that every branch of the law, criminal and civil, common law and equity, would fall within its scope.

I mention this fact because there are still people who appear to think that the High Court deals with constitutional cases and nothing else. This error explains, I think, why so many, realizing that constitutional law is a unique mixture of history, statutory interpretation, and some political philosophy, have thought that the political views of prospective High Court judges should be canvassed before their appointment. The Australian Labour Party has made little secret of its belief in this doctrine. The fallacy is that the great bulk of the work before the High Court is not constitutional, attracts no headlines, and calls for the very highest kind of general legal learning and equipment.

The creation of the new High Court having been attended to, and its jurisdiction defined, it became necessary to set down the rules which were to relate to the carrying of appeals to the Judicial Committee of the Privy Council, the highest court of appeal in the then British Empire. There had been spectacular arguments both in Australia and London before a compromise provision ultimately took shape as Section 74 of the Constitution, as follows:

74. No appeal shall be permitted to the Queen in Council from a decision of the High Court upon any question, howsoever arising, as to the limits inter se of the Constitutional powers of the Commonwealth and those of any State or States, or as to the limits inter se of the Constitutional powers of any two or more States, unless the High Court shall certify that the question is one which ought to be determined by Her Majesty in Council.

The High Court may so certify if satisfied that for any special reason the certificate should be granted, and thereupon an appeal shall lie to Her Majesty in Council on the question without further leave.

Except as provided in this section, this Constitution shall not impair any right which the Queen may be pleased to exercise by virtue of Her Royal prerogative to grant special leave of appeal from the High Court to Her Majesty in Council. The Parliament may make laws limiting the matters in which such leave may be asked, but proposed laws containing any such limitation shall be reserved by the Governor-General for Her Majesty's pleasure.

By subsequent provisions in the *Judiciary Act,* the new Parliament took steps to see that, in substance, cases in a State Court which involved the interpretation of the Commonwealth Constitution or the limits *inter se* of the powers of any two or more governments, should be dealt with in the High Court, so that such constitutional cases should not be taken from a State Supreme Court direct to the Privy Council! I am not writing a legal treatise and will not attempt to explain the technical problems which emerged. It is sufficient for my purpose to say that for many years constitutional and other cases have been dealt with, in Australia, by the High Court; that the Privy Council has freely exercised its power to grant special leave to appeal against High Court decisions in such cases; but that in constitutional cases found to be *'inter se'* cases, only one certificate has been granted by the High Court, and that nearly fifty-five years ago!

It is just on forty years since I first found myself appearing as Counsel before the High Court. For many years I was in that jurisdiction a great deal. The Court is only sixty-five years old. I did not ever appear before Chief Justice Griffith and Mr Justice O'Connor, of the first High Court. But I have appeared a great deal before most of the other judges in the Court's history, and think that I know something of their character and talents.

In addition, in my political capacity, first as Attorney-General and later as Prime Minister, I was largely responsible for the appointment of eight of the judges.

For the sake of good order, I will arrange my ideas around two central questions:

(a) Has the High Court turned out to be of a quality adequate for the performance of its very great judicial responsibilities?

(b) If it has, should the Privy Council appeal be abolished or modified by the Commonwealth Parliament under the concluding provision of Section 74?

As to the first question, my answer is unhesitatingly YES. To support this answer, I will offer some views, not, I hope impertinent, about High Court judges as I have seen and heard and known them.

The first High Court, Chief Justice Griffith, Mr Justice Barton, and Mr Justice O'Connor, was made up of men who were among the 'founding fathers' of the Constitution. They had played a great part, not only in the drafting of the Constitution but in the long controversies which were involved in getting self-governing colonies to accept a federal system and the paramountcy of Commonwealth legislation on matters assigned to the new Commonwealth Parliament. The task had not been easy, for it had not been assisted by the existence of imminent external threats or, as in the case of the United States, by the prior happening of a revolution against overseas control.

Under these circumstances, it is not surprising that the first Court was strongly disposed to protect 'State rights' by giving a somewhat restricted interpretation of Commonwealth powers.

Barton was still a judge when I first appeared at the High Court bar. He had been the greatest popular champion of Federation. He had been, after some amazing moves on behalf of others, Australia's first Prime Minister. He had a fine brow and a lambent eye, a great natural dignity, an admirable capacity for good living, a not extensive technical learning in the law, but a sound legal approach, a human but scholarly mind. I have heard him rebuke an over-aggressive counsel with quiet and courteous devastation. As he had much the same cast of mind on constitutional interpretation as Griffith, he not infrequently confined his decision to two words—'I concur'. This gave him a reputation for indolence, though in later years it might have given him a reputation for good sense, and might have saved some of the confusion which arises when judges who agree in the result are driven by their individual *daemon* to an over-elaboration of their reasons for agreement. Personally, I had a quite unexpected reason for being grateful to him. When Griffith died, Adrian Knox, K.C., of the Sydney Bar was appointed Chief Justice. The Melbourne Bar gave him a dinner. As the most recently called barrister present, I was Mr Junior. At Melbourne, Mr Junior, by tradition, proposes the health of the distinguished guest. H. E. Starke, later Mr Justice, was not, and never was, a silk. But he had a commanding practice in the courts of appeal, was a prominent man at the dinner, had given me a quick scrutiny, and thought little of me.

So the toast was not proposed by me, but by the Chairman, Sir

Edward Mitchell, K.C., who was long both in figure and in words, and had never become acquainted with the joyous art of the after-dinner speech. So Starke had second thoughts, scribbled on his place-card, and sent it round to me. It was quite curt—'Menzies, propose Barton's health!' Within two minutes I was doing so, probably the better for having had no warning. I remember quoting Swinburne's verse to Walter Savage Landor:

> I came as one whose thoughts half linger,
> Half run before;
> The youngest to the oldest singer
> That England bore.

The speech had a *succès fou*; made me known to the judges; and restored me, permanently, I believe, to Starke's good graces; though I should add, in justice to that great lawyer, that he practised in its fullness the maxim 'Whom the Lord loveth, he chasteneth'.

In more recent times, two very important things have happened in the High Court.

The first, which I have discussed in another book* is that the historical preconceptions of the earliest Justices have disappeared with them. Much broader principles of interpreting the Constitution have been adopted, but at the same time they have been principles of law, not of politics. For myself, I have found immense pleasure, as a quondam constitutional lawyer myself, in seeing how the High Court, particularly under Chief Justices Latham and Dixon, has recognized that 'federalism is legalism'; that the High Court is a court of law and not one of sociological opinion; and that legal concepts must control the interpretation of powers; with a broad and sensible recognition of the basic fact that the Constitution was not born dead, but is a living instrument for the regulating of the affairs of new generations of men in new circumstances not reasonably to have been foreseen by the 'founding fathers'. In brief, the legal principles will continue to be applied, but will be brought to bear on evolving and changing circumstances.

* *Central Power in the Australian Commonwealth* (Cassell, and University of Virginia Press).

I have no doubt, and most lawyers would I think agree, that the High Court of Australia is, and has been for a long time, composed of a body of judicial lawyers which has no superior in the English-speaking world.

The second question which I have set myself concerns the appeal to the Judicial Committee of the Privy Council, sitting in London.

I have cited the language of Section 74. For fifty years, the practice of the High Court has been to refuse to grant a certificate to permit an appeal to the Privy Council on questions as to the limits *inter se* of the powers of Commonwealth and State, or State and State. But there has been, especially in recent years, some professional opinion that the whole system of appeals to the Privy Council needs review. Why should not the High Court be the final arbiter?

I have some views on this matter, and will set them down as concisely as possible.

I can see no reason why the Privy Council should have power to entertain an appeal from *any* decision of the High Court on the interpretation of the Australian Constitution, whether it involves the demarcation of powers *inter se* or not, unless the High Court itself grants leave. The distinction between questions of power which arise between Commonwealth and State, or State and State, and any other question of Constitutional interpretation, is now quite artificial. It derives from the fears of the federating Australian colonies, which had to be overcome by such compromises as we see in Section 74. Clearly, if the High Court can (without appeal, save by its own choice) competently deal with one type of constitutional problem, it can deal with all.

In all other respects, I would preserve the power of the Privy Council to grant leave; in matters of common law and equity, and all matters (excluding constitutional questions) in which the decision is on a point of general interest and application in what we call the 'Common Law' countries, which include not only Australia and New Zealand and the United States but also a considerable number of Commonwealth countries.

In these fields of law, broad uniformity of decision has positive value, to students, practitioners, and courts alike. A sort of central clearing-house is of advantage. If it disappeared, by the complete abolition of the Judicial Committee appeal, separate lines of decision would soon begin to emerge. Each country would in time develop its own body of principles, and could afford to ignore development elsewhere. Standard text-books, those invaluable adjuncts to practice which are now used in many countries, would be replaced by purely local productions. 'Why not?' you may ask. 'Let's be patriotic and have pride in ourselves!'

This is an engaging sentiment. But before we are carried away by it, we should remember that such great elements as the Common Law, though they began in the vicinity of Westminster Hall, are part of a common inheritance which has much to do (as I think) with true civilization. To break this inheritance into fragments may please the immediate beneficiaries, but, before long, the estate will have gone.

In my own closing period of office, an arrangement was made which may well improve the present position. All Australian High Court judges are now appointed Privy Councillors. They are, in consequence, eligible to sit on the Judicial Committee. Over the past two years, two of them have done so and taken an active and valuable part in the proceedings and decisions. I would like to see a High Court judge go to London once a year under this arrangement.

2. Some frank words about juries

The jury has been exuberantly described as 'the palladium of English liberty'. To challenge its virtue is still to provoke hostility. Yet my own experience has persuaded me that this venerable institution needs critical examination.

The jury in criminal cases has, I believe, much to commend it. No doubt under the impact of persuasive emotion, or that evasion of moral responsibility which is endemic in human nature, or simple prejudice against policemen, it acquits quite a few guilty persons. Far better that this should be so than that innocent men should be convicted. So regarded, the criminal jury is an historic device for tempering the natural severities of the criminal code. Its function is not so much to do justice, as to avoid injustice.

I could perhaps enliven this sapient conclusion by recalling that the best criminal judges have always perceived this; that prosecutors too eager for a conviction have found themselves rebuked from the

Bench; that, on the other hand, over-acting 'prosecuting judges' have frequently, to their surprise, procured an acquittal; and that the English law has, wherever not constrained by statute, always insisted that guilt has to be proved, not innocence established.

One of the great criminal judges of the Supreme Court of Victoria in my early days was the late Sir Joseph Hood. He had a face like an eagle, a mind like a razor, and could deal severely with a convicted person. But, in the course of the trial, he was at all times tender of the rights of the accused.

Thus, one day, he presided at the trial of a man who was being defended (if that is the right word) by a young barrister who was making his first appearance before a jury, and had brought, for good measure, his mother and his father, his sister and his fiancée, to witness his new-found skill. The Crown case was weak, and was, oddly and fortunately, not made stronger by cross-examination. When it ended, Hood promptly asked the prosecuting counsel whether he thought the case one on which a jury could properly be asked to convict. The prosecutor replied that he had no strong views. The judge was about to direct an acquittal when the young defending counsel arose. He was not very coherent, but from his frequent glances at his family circle, Hood could see that the last thing he wanted was to be deprived of his first chance to address a jury. So, leaning foward, Hood said, in a gruff but human voice, 'Yes, I understand. I have been young myself. I will allow you to address.' Up rose the wig and gown, with the young man enclosed. The throat was cleared. And then Hood leaned further forward, tapped on the edge of the bench, and said clearly to his associate—'Robinson, as a matter of precaution, discharge the prisoner first!'

So much for juries in criminal cases. On balance, I would keep them.

But for juries in civil cases I have a very different verdict. It is my considered opinion that in most cases they are an instrument of injustice. Be it remembered that in civil cases between individuals or corporations, the kind of case litigated before a jury is just the same kind of case as is frequently litigated before a judge. The jury is to find the facts, by processes with which it is not familiar and which require an objectivity of mind not commonly found, but it is to find those facts under judicial direction as to the law, of which the jury is presumed to know nothing (and of which the judge is presumed to know all). Under these circumstances, why put six or twelve citizens into a jury box to do with uncertainty and difficulty what a judge has been trained to do for many years? Take an action of libel in which publication and reference to the plaintiff are admitted, but justification is pleaded. The questions for decision are whether the words complained of are capable of a defamatory meaning (which is a pure question of law for the presiding judge), whether they are in fact defamatory (which is a question for the jury, but which any judge could decide in half the time), and whether they are true in substance and in fact. On this last issue a judge is familiar with the rules of proof. He knows that the defendant must establish truth, and that if he fails, on reasonable balance, to do so, the plea must fail. But what happens with a jury? It goes into the box with a stock of varying experience and of accumulated prejudice. The plaintiff is a well-known politician. He has made friends, but has inevitably acquired enemies. In these days when we are taught daily to regard political champions as all good or as all bad, it will require a singular effort on the part of a juryman to find in favour of the 'all-bad' plaintiff. Of course it can be done, and no doubt is done on occasions, but it is more likely to be done by a judge trained in objective judgement than by an untrained citizen unwillingly temporarily snatched away from his normal and highly subjective life.

In short, those who defend the use of juries in civil cases must be prepared to assert that 'men of the world' can, in the light of nature, decide judicially questions of fact more sensibly than trained men. Is it really believed that judges live in an ivory tower and know nothing of what goes on in the ordinary human mind? The truth is that a barrister with years of experience and considerable skill gets to know far more of human psychology and human behaviour than most men. He really gets to know a great deal about truth and falsehood, and what makes people 'tick'. He is not easily deceived by plausible stories. And above all, he is trained to distinguish between the relevant and the irrelevant.

I can illustrate my point by an actual case in which I once appeared in Bendigo, in Victoria.

The action was one in which I appeared for the defendant, who owned and conducted a cool-store. The plaintiff had put into the store a large quantity of eggs which were to be kept at an indicated temperature. When the eggs were re-delivered, many of them were bad. So far, the facts were not in dispute. The real issue was whether the eggs were bad on delivery to the store, or whether the temperature control had been inaccurate, so that the eggs had gone bad in store.

The determining question was therefore one of fact, and many witnesses, technical and otherwise, were called and cross-examined. Opposing counsel and I addressed the local jury at length, with great subtlety and persuasiveness. The judge summed up. During my own address, I observed a certain appearance of impatience, not to say hostility, on the faces of the jury. I was therefore not optimistic. When the jury retired, my opponent and I went to the robing room. We had scarcely removed our wigs when a messenger came hastily in and said that the jury had agreed. We returned to court. The foreman said that the jury found for the defendant. Judgement was then entered our way, with costs.

We changed, and went across the way (it was late afternoon) to the Shamrock Hotel. My instructing solicitor, very prominent in Bendigo, hastily excused himself to have a word, in the street, with a member of the jury whom he knew, and from whom he hoped to obtain some gratifying account of the impact made by my powerful and convincing presentation of the case. He returned, convulsed with mirth. 'Menzies,' he said, 'it will be good for your soul if I tell you the truth. At the very beginning of the case the foreman told his colleagues that the only difficulty in the way of the defendant was that his barrister was an incompetent fool. "Look," he said, "years ago I left a saddle and harness at a local livery stable, which was shortly afterwards burned down. I consulted a lawyer. He asked me whether I had any written evidence of the deposit. When I said that I had not, he advised me not to proceed. Now, there is nothing in writing here, yet this fool Menzies has failed to take the point!" '

Fortified by this legal opinion, the jury, in a case in which no question had ever arisen as to the terms of the contract or the fact of the deposit, had regarded all the evidence and the argument as tedious and irrelevant!

One must not, of course, generalize from a single instance. But it is, I think, permissible to think that civil juries do not commonly direct themselves strictly to the objective issue. Two particular types of case recall themselves to my mind.

One is the action in which an insurance company is the presumed defendant. The modern statutory fashion is to provide for the compulsory taking out by motorists of 'third party' insurance. As such insurance is compulsory, and as in Australia very many persons are owners and drivers of motor vehicles an action for damages arising from collision is almost a commonplace. The jury knows full well that some insurance company will pay. And insurance companies are fair game. Thus it has come about that the passenger in the car, frequently a relative or sometimes a prospective one, sues the driver, in the most friendly way, for damages for negligent driving leading to personal injury! The nominal defendant is genial and frank, and the plaintiff wins. The insurer pays!

Another type of case, of a sort in which I found myself appearing many times for the defendant, is that in which a medical man is sued for damages for negligent treatment. The plaintiff has suffered a compound fracture of the arm, and the injury has resulted in a permanent distortion. All the most competent technical evidence will not easily defeat the argument that 'you can't tell me that there has not been carelessness somewhere!' It is, indeed, one of the oddities of human nature that, while we go off to a doctor when we are injured or ill, with supreme, if somewhat nervous, confidence in his mysterious skill, we tend, if he is sued for alleged negligence, to regard him not just as a man doing his best, sometimes against odds, but as one who guarantees success! I well remember a case in which a tall Irish Australian lawyer, opening his case to the jury, was heard to say—'Look at the plaintiff, gentlemen. Before this wicked treatment, she was a foine buxom lass, curved in all the proper places. And today, look at her! All straight up and down like you or me!' The jury awarded damages so generously that they exceeded the claim, so that the summons had to be amended.

I would not wish to be thought to decry sentiment, which in a real sense makes the world go round. But sentiment must be distinguished from sentimentality. In the great and civilized process of administering justice according to law, sentimentality can be as powerful an enemy of justice as lying or fraud.

There is another aspect of the civil jury system, in Australia at any rate, which should be noted. When the jury has made its findings and has given its verdict either general or particular, rights of appeal are extremely restricted. In effect, apart from alleged misdirection on the law, what the jury says on the facts is virtually sacrosanct. Was there *some* evidence on which reasonable men *could* have found for A.B. or found the libel true?

A judge's findings of fact, though made, as I believe, by a tribunal much more likely to be impartial and skilled to detect truth and falsehood, are much more open to scrutiny in a Court of Appeal. This is for two reasons.

One is that a judge, trying issues of fact alone, will as a rule state his reasons for accepting A or rejecting B. If the Court of Appeal finds these reasons unsatisfactory, the conclusions of fact are easily rejected. It is true that Courts of Appeal do tend to modify their own impressions of the evidence in 'the court below' by reference to the sensible principle that the demeanour of a witness cannot (until T.V. comes to court) be transcribed, and that the trial judge's views on individual credibility of witnesses ought not lightly to be rejected. Apart from this, appeals on the facts not infrequently succeed. It is little wonder that it used to be common advice to newly appointed magistrates to 'make up your mind clearly, but resolutely refuse to state your reasons'.

This naturally reminds me of the late Sir John Madden, Chief Justice of Victoria for many years. As students we gazed at him with awe. A handsome appearance, a white moustache, a rich and rolling voice, an actor's enjoyment in a fine rhetorical phrase, an air of supreme confidence had made him a renowned judge. It was said of him that his law was shaky; and that may be conceded. But for picturesqueness and impressiveness he provides a cheerful memory for my generation, now that dullness and correctness have come to be thought by many observers to be cardinal judicial virtues.

It was said of the young Shakespeare that he was once apprenticed to a butcher, and that when he slaughtered a calf he did it 'with an high pompe'. Well, in Victoria, the process known as an Order to Review exists, by which a Supreme Court Judge can be asked to review a decision of magistrates. Where the latter had lapsed into the giving of reasons, some slaughter would occur in the Supreme Court. When Madden was the judge, all slaughter was done 'with an high pompe'.

Witness the delightful case of HARVEY *v*. OTTOWAY.

It is reported in the 1915 volume of the Victorian Law Reports. The magistrates of Preston, a suburb of Melbourne, heard a case in which a husband was sued for the price of household necessaries ordered by his wife, who was living with him. In the circumstances established, it was clear that the husband was liable. The case was flatly covered by the decision of the House of Lords itself in PAQUIN *v*. BEAUCLERK in 1906. But the magistrates refused to listen to authorities, saying, tersely but imprudently, 'Those are no good to two old married men!' So judgement went for the defendant, and the case went, on Order to Review, before Madden. How he enjoyed it, and the ornate character of his verbal architecture, both appear in the concluding passage of his reasons.

In this case the justices would not hear the law expounded, because they claimed that the experience of two old married men was a better guide in these matters than the law presented to them. But one must always remember that in judicial proceedings magistrates have undertaken to administer justice according to law, and they, and indeed every one of us, would do well to listen to the House of Lords—a tribunal not only composed of the greatest lawyers but also the most authoritative, for they speak last. And if it be said that the magistrates here acted on an inspiration springing from the antiquity of their domestic relations, they ought still to remember that the Judges of the House of Lords, in addition to being great lawyers, are probably no less old and no less married than themselves, and that acting on the inspiration in question is certain to lead to confusion and appeals and costs in the administration of justice.

3. *Some advice to young advocates*

'They' tell me (I hope wrongly) that the standard of advocacy is declining and that the great art of cross-examination is falling into decay. 'They' tell me that the chief reasons are that counsel are too busy, that the courts are pressed for time because the lists are so heavy, and that in consequence the accent is on 'getting on with the job'.

If 'they' are right, then it is time somebody explained what good advocacy is. For good advocacy saves time, helps judges, and forwards the paramount cause of justice as nothing else can.

I will treat the business of advocacy as including everything from the drawing of the 'pleadings' to the final exhortations in court.

In most States of Australia the Judicature Act applies. Common Law and Equity are administered by the same judges. Pleadings, those written statements of claim and defence which are exchanged before hearing, and are designed to identify the true issues to be decided, became less technical. An error in a form of action became, if I may use so villainous a phrase, less fatal. Judges exercised powers of amendment more freely, even during the actual hearing.

I think it is clear (or at least it was in my time) that, in consequence, pleadings are now drawn more carelessly; amendments are quite frequent; delays are increased and the cost of litigation increased. More than this, looseness of pleading leads to confusion at the hearing, the introduction of much matter subsequently found to be irrelevant, and added burdens for the judge who has to seek for a few needles in a fairly large haystack. If a meticulous consideration of the case by counsel had been engaged in before he drew his pleading, no doubt from the point of view of a busy junior some hours would have been 'lost' but, from the point of view of his client and of the Court, many more hours would have been saved. At the very beginning, therefore, good advocacy saves time.

When the pleadings have been closed, junior counsel will frequently be asked to advise on evidence; that is, to advise the solicitor as to the nature of the evidence which will be relevant to the issues, the burden of proof, and the witnesses whose evidence will be required. He can do this with greater certainty and economy if the pleadings are in good shape.

In Victoria, interrogatories are commonly administered by the parties before trial. These are written questions which the other party must answer on oath. Clearly, if admissions are to be obtained which will obviate the calling of some witnesses at the actual hearing, the drawing of interrogatories must be done with great care and precision, so that, to take an instance, an unfavourable or unexpected answer to the first interrogatory will not render the subsequent interrogations futile. In my own time as a junior, we did not suffer the disadvantages of having stenographers to whom to dictate. We drafted our interrogatories laboriously in long-hand on blue draft

paper, and sent them out to the solicitor. We concentrated our in-
quisitiveness into eight or ten questions, and we not infrequently
got useful answers to them. But modernity prevailed. Chambers
became studded with stenographers. Learned junior counsel, unable to
dictate to judges, restored the balance by dictating to young women.
And, as dictating lends itself to wordiness, the number of interrogatories grew, and their effectiveness declined.

There is, however, yet another stage of advocacy of which the
newspaper readers know nothing, but of which a really competent
advocate should know a great deal. In Victoria, a conference is commonly arranged by the solicitor between counsel and the witnesses for
his side. I know that many people, bemused by reading picturesque
fiction, think that such conferences are held so that counsel may
instruct witnesses as to what they are to say in the witness-box; in
short, so that some carefully considered perjury can be arranged. This
kind of thing, I believe, very seldom occurs. On the contrary, I fear
that too many of such conferences are mere formalities. My own
practice was, in conference, to cross-examine my own witnesses; first,
so that they might not be taken at a sudden disadvantage in the witness-
box, where most of them would otherwise face cross-examination for
the first time, and second, so that, if the evidence proved quite unlikely
to be accepted, some settlement could be sought.

On one occasion this practice of mine had somewhat remarkable
results. It was a County Court action for the rectification of a written
contract. I was for the nominal defendant, the real defendant being his
wife, a thin-lipped and determined character who had the effective
voice in the transaction. As sometimes happens, the conference
occurred at the last moment, first thing on the morning of the day on
which the case was listed for hearing before a celebrated County Court
Judge, who was something of a comedian. In conference, I cross-
examined the lady, and soon involved her in a most obvious lie.
Before long, I disclosed her in another. She glared at me angrily—
'Are you on my side?' I assured her that, with some regret, I was; that
if time permitted I would return my brief so that she could have the
services of somebody more to her taste; that as the case would be on
within the hour I could not decently do this; that I would do my duty
by her, but hoped that the judge would do likewise. On this unhappy

note we repaired to the court, and presented ourselves before the judge, whose countenance resembled the harvest moon, and whose sentimentality, as we were to learn, was in full command of him. In due course, I called my lady, to whom the judge, for some reason, took an immediate fancy. She was cross-examined by my opponent, and out came the lies. Plaintiff's counsel then said, 'So, Mrs X, you would not mind telling lies to help your husband?' At once she said, 'No, I would do it!' The judge's face registered horror. Looking reproachfully at the witness, he said, 'Look, Mrs X, I had formed a very good opinion of you! Surely you don't mean that last answer!' Like a flash, she realized that the judge would be putty in her hands. Raising her eyes somewhat piously towards heaven (a ray of sunlight was coming through a high window), she said, 'Your Honour, if I thought that by telling a lie I could help my husband into the Kingdom of Heaven, I would gladly tell that lie!' Such are the vagaries of mankind, and even of judges, that, to my complete bewilderment, the judge sighed his relief, and gave judgement for the defendant.

This is a somewhat scandalous story. Whether it contains a moral or not, I do not know. Perhaps it was one of those cases in which, in spite of my earlier criticisms, a jury would have done better!

And now I come to the conduct of a case in Court. Here we come to the supreme test of advocacy.

First, a good advocate must be a good judge. This may seem paradoxical, and I will therefore explain it. There can be nothing more irritating to a judge than to have before him an advocate who cannot distinguish good argument from bad, who argues everything, who recognizes and concedes no weakness in his case, who goes on and on and finally leaves the court with a confused mess of ideas and arguments from which the judge must endeavour to extract some relevance and some help. There are some such advocates. Either they have not adequately mastered their case and isolated the points upon which judgement will turn; or they are afraid to exercise their own judgement by discarding bad arguments; or they weakly believe that the quantity of their words will, in the ears of their client, make up for the paucity of their quality.

What a judge, say, in a Court of Appeal, needs is counsel who will, after outlining the facts and the nature of the decision in the court below, say, 'The decision in this case will clearly depend upon the view taken about points A and B. I have one difficulty, a decision given in the Chancery Division which is against my argument. I propose to meet that difficulty by showing that that decision either ought not to be followed or ought to be distinguished on the facts. I will not waste the court's time on other matters, unless I am requested to do so. On the contrary, I will go to the point on which, as I see it, I must either succeed or fail!'

That sort of thing is good advocacy, because it depends upon enough ability to select the real point, and enough courage to abide by the selection.

I could illustrate the point about facing up to the weaknesses by an experience which I once had before the late Sir William Irvine when he was Chief Justice of Victoria. Irvine had been Premier of Victoria and later Attorney-General of Australia. His long sojourn in politics had detached him a little from the law, but had enriched his knowledge of men. He was not infrequently overruled, on appeal, on questions of law. But he was, in my opinion, a first-class trial judge, dignified, upright, cold in manner (they called him 'Iceberg' Irvine in politics!) but perceptive, and devoted to justice. It was always a great pleasure to appear before him.

I was for the plaintiff in an action of fraudulent misrepresentation. There was, I thought, no doubt that the defendants had engaged in some hard lying, and that the plaintiff was blazingly indignant about it. In the result, under cross-examination by my learned opponent, the plaintiff told a few pretty obvious lies on his own account. When we got to the final address, I had a problem to face. If I endeavoured to explain away my client's 'errors', I would tend to make them important matters in issue, and the whole case might turn upon them. I therefore (it being clearly one of my better days) adopted the quite unusual course of saying, at the very outset, 'Your Honour, in this case my client has, in the course of his evidence, told several lies which would, if you looked no further, justify you in rejecting his evidence and giving judgement for the defendants. But I invite you to look more closely, and try to find out *why* he told lies to support a good case. What I put to you is that you have seen and heard the defendants under cross-examination. You must have formed a low opinion of them. They clearly set out to defraud the plaintiff. The plaintiff, knowing this, and being himself under close cross-examination, gave way to resentment, felt that the world was against him, and did some counter-lying. This was foolish, unnecessary, and deplorable. But the essential fact is that my client did his lying in the witness-box. The defendants did theirs long ago, when they were fraudulently inducing him to make the contract!'

The judge agreed, and we had our judgment. The moral for the young advocate is clear. Never dodge a weakness in your case. Meet it. It may turn out to be a source of strength.

Second a good advocate at *nisi prius* should seek and obtain a real proficiency in cross-examination, which is a great art, not to be mastered by inadvertence. When I first went to the Victorian Bar, forty years ago, the best cross-examiner was a dark complexioned, dashing, sporting man, who still had a good pair of hands with a witness, and could cajole, entrap, or threaten with considerable flexibility. A few years later, he seemed to me to have deteriorated, and to have become one of those swashbuckling cross-examiners who get headlines rather than success. I spoke to Owen Dixon, who was still at the Bar, and who was, nearly enough, this man's contemporary. 'Ah,' said Dixon with that nervous laugh which many of us know so well, 'he was even better before you knew him. But his trouble is that he has been listening to the applause of junior clerks!' There is a moral in that story. Let the young advocate be his own best judge. He will know in his heart whether his cross-examination succeeded, because he must know better than anybody else what he was after; what points he wanted to fix; what difficulties for the *next* witness he wanted to create. So, you see, the good cross-examiner must be a better judge than the common law clerk sitting opposite at the Bar table. But perhaps you may say—Why have cross-examination at all? Isn't it just an excuse for bullying and brow-beating? Isn't it designed to make an honest witness look and sound like a liar? Isn't it unfair?

These are good questions, and they deserve an answer. You would perhaps not put them so vehemently if you had sat in court and actually listened to a good cross-examination. You are probably going on either the somewhat unorthodox court proceedings of most of the detective-story writers, or the newspaper reports of cases. The latter are fractional, concentrated for sensation, and for the most part written by reporters unaware of the true nature of the procedures of the law.

But I will answer the questions. Why have cross-examination? Because without it, evidence is almost worthless. It was cynically observed that 'truth will out, even in an affidavit'. But any experienced lawyer could relate how, under cross-examination, the dogmatic statements in the affidavit have been whittled away, and an entirely different set of facts has emerged. I will go so far as to say that, if cross-examination were abolished, much false evidence would be accepted and much injustice would be done. Bad cross-examiners may, and do, resort to insult and bullying; and a good judge will restrain them. But the good cross-examiner does things in a different way.

What do I mean by a 'good' cross-examiner? This question deserves an analytical answer, particularly for the guidance of those apprentices to the art who, by the reading of lives of the great advocates, have been beguiled into thinking that the brilliant and daring and crucial question put by an F. E. Smith or a Norman Birkett comes by intuition from the soil of genius.

To show what I mean by a good cross-examiner, let me begin by describing a bad one; bad, though by no means uncommon. He is counsel for the defendant in a civil action, with witnesses. He comes into court and hears the evidence of the plaintiff. He has not, in his study or in his chambers, worked out what it is that he should endeavour to elicit from the plaintiff which will help the defendant's case. He has not cleared his own mind to the point where he knows that he must establish A, B and C, and whether he will succeed or not will to an extent depend upon the kind of witness the plaintiff turns out to be.

So, in the event, he sits in court during the plaintiff's evidence-in-chief, writing busily—as if he were the Court reporter—without looking much at the witness, without studying his personality.

When plaintiff's counsel sits down, he gets to his feet, has nothing but his scribbled notes to go upon, and, not infrequently, takes the witness right through his evidence again, garnishing his alleged cross-examination with such fatuities as 'Do you know you are on oath?' 'Do you swear to that?' In the result the plaintiff's evidence acquires emphasis by repetition, and the defendant's case is well on the road to ruin. But the cross-examination has taken a long time, and the 'junior clerks' are delighted.

The good cross-examiner for the defendant will have prepared his own mind, and will have endeavoured to get inside the mind of his opponent. During the plaintiff's evidence-in-chief, he will no doubt make a few notes as reminders of vital points. But for the most part he will study the plaintiff. If he seems aggressive and self-confident, he is much less likely to be dislodged by a frontal attack than by an almost timid and gentle cross-examination which will encourage him in boldness, will develop his self-confidence into arrogance, and may so induce him into extravagances of evidence which will prove his undoing. If, on the other hand, he is a timid witness, he will produce the ultimate truth under courteous persuasion much more probably than under a bullying approach which will secure him the sympathy of both judge and jury. It was my experience that pedantic witnesses were frequently confounded by their own pedantry; that theoretical witnesses could be cut down to size by a cheerful invitation to examine some practical instance; that emotional witnesses would, under proper treatment, exhibit their emotions and prejudices to the point of bias.

In short, it is better for the cross-examiner to study his witness, after studying his brief, than to act as an unobservant but meticulous recording clerk.

'Ah,' you may say, 'this is merely a system of sophisticated trickery. What chance does an honest man have in the witness-box?'

Well, in my experience honest witnesses are not defeated. The truth has a faculty for emerging in both word and demeanour. Judges are not such fools as to reject a man's evidence simply because he has become involved in some verbal inconsistency. But the plausibly false and the cunning can be brought most properly to defeat only by a good cross-examiner. In my time, I can recall a few liars 'getting away with it'. But I cannot recall a truly honest witness being refused credibility.

The importance of careful preparation by the cross-examiner before the hearing begins can be illustrated by the cross-examination technique which I will call 'closing the gaps in the fence'. The cross-examiner has among his papers a letter or other document signed by the witness and relating to the matter in issue. The reasonable implication from the document is one inconsistent with what the witness has sworn to in his evidence-in-chief. But there may, of course, be other explanations of an inconvenient but not fatal kind. A bad cross-examiner will at once produce the document and confront the witness with it. Thereupon the witness will proffer one of the non-fatal explanations, and a great deal of the effect of the document is destroyed. The good cross-examiner will start, not with the document, but with the explanations. He will ask the witness whether he ever intended or contemplated such and such—not fatal, but inconvenient. The witness says 'No'. One gateway of escape is closed. And so the cross-examiner goes on, eliminating one non-fatal explanation after another, closing one gateway after another. And finally, when there can be no explanation save the damaging one, he produces the document, gets the witness to verify its signature and authenticity, and mildly asks him to 'explain what it meant'. The witness finds that he has already denied on oath all the non-fatal explanations, that the gates are shut, and that there is no escape.

There is one other thing about cross-examination which leaps to my mind out of the past.

In my early days at the Bar, there was a leading Silk who had a notable jury practice. He was a well set-up, impressive man, with a good voice and a most composed manner. He had a little trick of playing with a length of white tape while he was speaking. When he was cross-examining he conveyed, by sheer manner, the idea that he had a great deal up his sleeve. For the first half hour of a cross-examination, he was one of the most masterly I ever heard. But he did not know when to stop. Having shaken and discredited the witness, he would keep going. He would, in fact, keep going so long that by the end, a couple of hours later, the witness would have recovered his ground, would have won sympathy, and would, in effect, have emphasized his original evidence-in-chief.

Cross-examination must be considered and cautious. Recklessness can destroy the cross-examiner's own case. A cross-examiner, like a public speaker, must know when and how to stop.

Fairly early in my own practice, at a time when I was getting a great deal of work in the civil courts, a well-known solicitor named N. H. Sonenberg, who did a lot of criminal court work himself, came to see me. He had never briefed me, for I was not in his jurisdiction. But I knew him. He was a short, whimsical man of great humour and character, completely trusted by the courts, and properly so. To my surprise, he offered me a brief, as junior to the late 'X', for the defence of one of the accused in the famous conspiracy prosecution in what was known as the BADAK tin-mining scandal. I was honest enough to say that he could find juniors much more competent in criminal matters than I was. His reply was characteristic. 'That's all right, son. I've watched you in court, and I think you know when to stop. "X" does a lot of work for me, and he's good with a jury. But there are some complications in this case, and Mr Justice Cussen is presiding. I don't want you to utter a single word, son. But whenever "X" is up, and you think that he ought to sit down, you pull him by the gown, and make him stop! For that, son, I will gladly pay the proper junior fee!' I took the brief. The case lasted twenty-eight days. I did a lot of work on the case outside court, but my curial activities were purely muscular. The accused were acquitted. 'Sonny' was delighted, and I bought a new carpet for the dining-room!

CRICKET—A DIVERSION

(not compulsory reading in the United States)

SHAKESPEARE'S FALSTAFF and I have two elements in common; one, over-weight (to which I now plead guilty), the second, the famous passage in *Henry V*, Act II, Scene iii, in which his death is described so graphically; though I am not yet come to that pass.

A'parted even just between twelve and one, even at the turning o' the tide: for after I saw him fumble with the sheets and play with flowers and smile upon his fingers' ends, I knew there was but one way; for his nose was as sharp as a pen, and a'babbled of green fields.

I will not enter the lists with those Shakespearian scholars who find this passage corrupt; like most unscholarly people, I prefer its errors if it suits my purpose.

For here sit I, thinking about past events and people, fumbling with sheets of paper, a sharp pen (or more accurately pencil) in hand, and about to babble of the green fields of the great game of cricket.

Cricket is a game well understood and frequently well enjoyed by hundreds of thousands of players in a dozen countries, and well understood and sometimes enjoyed by hundreds of writers, to whose numbers I am now a recruit.

Unfortunately, cricket is, save in Philadelphia and a few other civilized places in the United States, not a widely known game in that great country. The late Aubrey Smith, a noted actor and cricketer, gave it some currency in Hollywood, where its essential romanticism had some appeal. But, on the whole, its failure to achieve major status in America is one of those things that have operated to limit that full mutual understanding between the United States and the other English-speaking countries which is so vital in this difficult and dangerous world.

In my time, I must have written a dozen or more 'forewords' for books by celebrated cricketers. I was even honoured by being asked by the famous Wisden to write a piece for its Centenary Year number in 1963.

I am not an expert cricketer. As I said, with, I hope, engaging frankness, in a foreword to Keith Miller and R. S. Whitington's *Bumper* (Latimer House, 1953):

> As a cricket executant, I fell and fall below all standards of decency. The feet, the eyes, the hands, the head, are all no doubt excellent of their kind, but they lack harmony. Yet here is one of the fascinating mysteries of life; so many of my betters have made their centuries and passed on to golf or dog-racing as if cricket had never been. It is occasionally left to people like me to carry with them through life a love and growing understanding of the great game—a feeling in the heart and mind and the eye which neither time nor chance can utterly destroy.

In spite of this serious lack of qualification, the love of cricket has been one of the great loves of my life; and no book of my memoirs would be either complete or credible without some reference to it. Not a whole book (as yet) but at least a chapter.

For cricket has stored my memory with unforgettable images of play and players. It may be of comfort to the philosophic mind to read on the old sundial '*Horas non numero nisi serenas*'. But after all, a sundial is a static thing which is uncommunicative when the sun is not shining. It is one of the glories of cricket that, when one looks back at it, one remembers the hours, not as something static but as something alive, and vivid, and full of action.

Further, I enjoy the company of cricketers; they are, in Dr Johnson's famous word (though cricket meant nothing to him), the most 'clubbable' of people, full of anecdote and, almost always, of genial goodwill. Without exception, they have always been pleasant to me, admitting me to the dressing-room and the brotherhood, and symbolically promoting me to their own ranks; they have no snobbery.

What is more, I know most of the cricket writers, some of whom are highly literate and literary people, and I read and keep their books, scores and scores of them.

Yet I repeat my confession that I am no expert, except in the sense that I flatter myself that I know a good cricketer when I see one, and find it difficult to forget the great incidents of play.

My American friends cannot understand my strange passion for cricket. 'How slow it is,' they say. 'A game goes on for days, frequently without a final decision. How futile, and how boring!'

I understand this. For in the world of sport, Americans are hustlers. Results count, and results must be got quickly. Take two of their most popular games, American football and basketball, to both of which I was introduced in Virginia last year.

With an interval at half-time, there is an hour's play. In football, there is a minimum of kicking and a maximum of throwing and grappling. The players wear a sort of protective armour around their heads and shoulders and legs; they need it, for there is much assault and battery of a legalized kind; each player will spend a high percentage of his time as one of a piled up heap of players on the ground. Should he become weary of well-doing, the coach takes him off, replaces him, and may later return him at will. But to me the striking feature was that each side has two complete teams, one 'offensive' and one 'defensive', plus, of course, a number of 'spare parts'. When the state of the game seems to require it, the 'defensive' team runs off, and the 'offensive' team runs on, or *vice versa*.

If cricket in England or Australia could command the financial resources of football in America, the adoption of this principle could have fascinating results. Each side could pick two elevens; one consisting of batsmen only, and the other of ten bowlers and a wicket-keeper!

In basketball, a remarkably fast game, the incessant demand for victory puts a premium on players of inordinate tallness. I saw young men of six feet ten inches as a commonplace; one little fellow of six feet and thirteen stone evoked my sympathy; he looked like a dwarf. One would almost think that players are specially bred for this game. Speed, reach, height are of the essence. Even the onlooker has no time or desire for reflection.

Cricket is entirely different. Except for those playing it, it seems to be a slow and leisurely game. The onlooker has plenty of time for reflection. He can watch the artistry of a batsman without interruption. He is concerned to know what the bowler is doing in pace or spin or turn. He can get an exquisite pleasure from the speed and accuracy and beauty of movement of a great fieldsman. Between the overs (I dislike neighbours who want to talk during an over) he can comment on the present and draw parallels with the past, to his heart's content.

Cricket, in short, is illustrative of the character of player and

[343]

onlooker alike. It evokes a quiet humour, and expresses both patience and endurance.

Because a player is on view for a relatively long time he becomes a known personality. If he is in the deep field, he exchanges a little badinage with the nearest spectators. And in Australia, if they report that X is 'a good bloke', the word goes round. If he is a batsman, his popular reputation will depend much more on how he makes his runs than on how many runs he makes. He does not need to be even popular, so long as he is 'a character'. For, as every experienced politician knows, it is better to be vigorously hated than to be tepidly admired. For example, I cannot recall any deep public affection for that great Australian all-rounder and captain, Warwick Armstrong; but he was such a 'character' that when he retired from cricket he left a gap like a volcanic crater.

If the cricketer is a bowler, his chances of inspiring hatred or affection are approximately equal. I will illustrate by taking two extremes. I have seen many great fast bowlers, some of them, like Gregory, MacDonald and Lindwall, Australians; but the greatest fast bowler I ever saw was Harold Larwood, who bowled Australia out in the 'bodyline' series of 1932-3. But, under the somewhat extreme and humourless leadership of Douglas Jardine, he carried out his orders with such devastating speed and accuracy that he quickly became 'Public Enemy No. 1'. Yet, underneath all the passion and furore, Australians took time off from cursing him, to admire him. I know, for I was one of them.

My second extreme is Arthur Mailey, Armstrong's great 'googly' bowler. What a man! He didn't need to be one of the great slow bowlers of cricket history; his talents were manifold—a superbly comic cartoonist, a whimsical writer, a witty conversationalist, a warm friend. Somebody once wrote that his Australian successor, 'Clarrie' Grimmett, the tiny embodiment of accuracy, bowled 'like a miser', while Mailey bowled 'like a millionaire'. These similes are just. That is why, to me, Arthur Mailey was one of the great 'characters' of cricket, a gentle but destructive humorist who could never (I think) have been produced by any other game. I will illustrate this by two first-hand personal observations.

The first concerns the great Master of batsmanship, J. B. Hobbs, playing in a Test Match at Melbourne. When play ended for the day,

Hobbs was—as usual—not out, with a century under his belt. Would he ever go out? The next morning, Mailey opened the bowling from the Southern end. Those were the good old days when the Melbourne Cricket Ground had not been converted into a football stadium. At the Southern end, there were elm trees whose leaves, above the sightscreen, twinkled in the sunny breeze. So Mailey, with a bland smile, walked back to his mark, tossing the ball from one hand to the other; turned, ambled in, and sent up a full toss so high that the sightscreen knew it no more. Hobbs bowed respectfully as the ball went overhead. The ball dropped suddenly and steeply, and the bails came off!

My second memory is of a match many years later, when a Test Trial was played at Sydney as a somewhat belated benefit to the veteran Mailey and that great batsman of older years, 'Johnny' Taylor. Neither had played for many years. On the Saturday, with forty thousand spectators, Ian Johnson, who captained one of the teams, and who was one of the great gentlemen of the game, had an inspiration. After the luncheon adjournment, he brought both teams out on to the ground, and invited Mailey and Taylor, both dressed in their ordinary civilian clothes, to come out to the middle. Both teams lined up at the pitch, and applauded. Ian Johnson then handed the bat to Johnny, and tossed the ball to Arthur. Arthur stood at the stumps, waved both teams back to the boundary, walked back, ambled up with the same old action, and clean bowled Taylor. It was a sensational moment, and we all roared our approval. Five minutes later, Mailey arrived in the New South Wales Cricket Association reserve, stood at the end of the row in which I was seated, and said to me, 'You remember that day at Melbourne when I took four wickets for 364 runs! I now realize the mistake I made. I should have bowled with my coat on!'

It is an amusing fashion among cricket writers, in the off-season, to select 'All-time World XI's', or to name as the 'greatest ever' some batsman, or bowler, or wicketkeeper. I confess that such exercises leave me cold.

Failing any other objective test, the selection has recourse to the averages. Even my friend, E. W. Swanton, in *The Cricketer* of October 1966, while he concedes that 'career records must be treated with reserve, since there is so much in the way of opposition strengths and

[345]

other factors that they do not disclose', goes on to say that 'they are a prime source of evidence'.

Averages cannot, of course, be overlooked. Brilliant failures cannot be carried indefinitely. And matches are, after all, to be won. And I can claim no authority, for nobody has less. Yet, as I look back over my life, so frequently lit up as it has been by the highlights of cricket, I know that to me the 'greatest' bowler will prove to be that one who achieved his success against the most powerful batsmen (I can still see Maurice Tate bowling to Ponsford and Woodfull!) while the 'greatest' batsman is the one who handled the best bowling under a variety of conditions with success.

If, as in the case of the incomparable Bradman, both averages and success against great bowlers concur, the question falls. (I could write a great deal about Bradman, the master batsman, the superb captain, the very able man of many talents; but I refrain, for I want 'mere mortals' to have a chance. Not that Victor Trumper was in this category, as will appear.) But, though I saw Victor Trumper but once, when I was a boy, I subsequently learned from older and experienced friends of competent judgement enough to realize that the prosaic fact that his career Test average against England was, on wickets good, bad, and indifferent (by modern standards), the modest figure of thirty-odd, he really 'bestrode the narrow world like a Colossus', and left an imperishable memory behind him.

But, as I have made clear, I am not writing this chapter as an expert, but as an onlooker. For me 'Beauty is in the eye of the beholder'. I have been actively and laboriously engaged in many notable matters, some of which are recorded in this book. But when it comes to cricket, I am that harmless, necessary thing, a born spectator. It follows that I will not profess to offer impertinent judgements as to who were the 'best', or the 'greatest'.

For to me, let me confess it with apologies to my American friends, cricket has been and is a great entertainment. This needs explanation, and perhaps apology. It was once said of the English that 'they take their pleasures sadly'. Well, to the player out in the middle, there may be something dour about a great match. But to me, there is joy in the eye, and in the mind, and in the heart.

It follows that in this brief chapter of reminiscences of cricket as an entertainment, many will be remembered, but few chosen. I will therefore defy chronology and abjure authority, and write something of some of the 'characters' who have entertained me, making my humble apologies to those equally interesting 'characters' whom the demands of space require me to omit.

There have been, I will be told, greater fast bowlers than 'Freddie' Trueman, of Yorkshire and England. Indeed, I can remember some of them; 'Ted' MacDonald, whose run up to the wicket was like the bobbling of silk over a spool; Jack Gregory, whose final kangaroo leap was enough to strike terror into the stoutest English heart; Harold Larwood, whose somewhat ascetic appearance was matched with a degree of accuracy and control which I have never seen equalled, (he was the only fast bowler extant who could have carried out Douglas Jardine's orders); and Ray Lindwall, every yard of whose run mattered since he developed speed as he went.

But, of all these, my 'character' is Freddie Trueman, with his curving run, his lank dark locks, his facial ferocity. He must have been a hard man for a captain to control, but he always fascinated me. He will, I hope, allow me to refer to three events.

On the Saturday night of a Test Match at Adelaide, the Australian Board of Cricket Control gave a dinner at the lovely Adelaide Cricket Ground. I was invited on the usual terms; I was to sing for my supper. The weather was hot; Trueman had been bowling from the Lake Torrens end. As he beat his way back to his mark, his head could be seen wagging and his lips moving, perhaps profanely. The genial 'barrackers' of Adelaide—the 'City of Churches'—raucously inquired whether he could 'do with a pint'. His lips moved more eloquently. At the dinner, I hypocritically came to his rescue:

You know, gentlemen, many people may have thought that on his way back into the wind Freddie was using bad language. This idea did him a grave injustice! He was, in fact, reciting Greek iambics!

Great laughter. But for the next few weeks Freddie's stock question was—'What did that old b—— mean about Greek iambics? And what the hell are they, anyhow?' But all I know is that he became my friend.

[347]

The second event was at my match at Canberra, Prime Minister's XI *v.* M.C.C., a match which I had first established against the West Indies in 1951, and which has become, I think I may claim, a happy feature of each visiting tour. It was my practice, at the end of this one-day 'festival' match, to give a dinner to both teams, a dinner of much hilarity and some superb, if incredible, post-prandial oratory. On this occasion, the Duke of Norfolk was present as M.C.C. Manager, and sat on my right. Ted Dexter, as Captain, was on my left. For the first time in the history of these games, a player's birthday coincided with the date of the match. The player was 'Freddie'.

I had a splendid pewter pot suitably inscribed and, at a suitable time during the dinner, called Freddie up to the top table, said a few words, and presented him with this trophy, on which my signature was duly engraved. Freddie was much affected by this, made a very brief but pleasant acknowledgement, and retreated to his place, muttering quite audibly, 'First time a b—— Prime Minister ever did this to a b—— professional cricketer. It's b—— wonderful.' He was in reality quite moved. But Norfolk, who is the master of the 'dead-pan' face, turned to me and said: 'That was very generous of you, Menzies, but I would like you to know that you have undone the hard disciplinary work of six weeks!' Well, perhaps!

My third anecdote about Freddie concerns the Test Match at Headingley in July 1964. I had dined with the Australian team at their hotel. On arriving at the ground the next morning, I went round to see the M.C.C. team, most of whom I had got to know in Australia. When I had gone round them, and had settled into a talk with Ted Dexter about politics (of all things!), I said, 'Where is Freddie?' A noise behind me identified him, so I turned around. Freddie was just getting into his cricket clothes. I noticed that he had had a haircut; not a close one, of course, but the marks of the scissors were plain. So, in a heavy-footed way, I said: 'Fred, you are a traitor to your country!' He bristled up at once. 'What do you mean?' 'Fred,' I said, 'the answer is simple. You have had your hair cut. And you must know what happened to Samson when Delilah cut his hair off!' A broad grin swept across Freddie's face. 'Ah,' he said, with a gleam in the eye, 'I could have done with a piece of that Delilah myself!'

Another great 'character' in my gallery of memories is 'Sam'

Loxton, of Victoria and Australia, now a Member of the Victorian Parliament. 'Sam' is a powerful athlete with, on suitable occasions, a countenance of unexampled fierceness, a heart of gold, and a rare taste for the humour of situations.

I was at Headingley in 1948 when he and Neil Harvey, that quiet artist, were playing their first Test Match against England. In that match Neil got a lovely century. 'Sam' was in great form, and hit the ball all over the ground. When he was ninety-three he swung wildly at one delivery, and was clean-bowled. Knowing how bitterly disappointed he must be, I repaired to the Australian dressing-room. Sam had just emerged from the shower, and greeted me.

'Sam,' I said, 'if ever I see you try to hit a *seven* before the ball is half-way down the pitch, I will run out and attack you!'

A diabolical grin accompanied his rejoinder. 'Well, you see, Boss, the skipper's instructions were to have a go' (the skipper was Don Bradman) 'and that's just what I did. It's all in the game. After all, Boss' (with a broader grin), 'you've probably made some bloody big errors in your own time yourself!'

It has been very rarely that a player, batting in his first Anglo-Australian Test Match, has made a century. Most men who had got so near to that honour and then failed would have been the dejected victims of self-pity. But not 'Sam' Loxton. That is why he is in my collection of 'characters'.

Later in that season, I was able to tell him of a delicious conversation at Lord's. It occurred as Sam went out from the Member's Pavilion to bat. I was sitting between two fairly venerable peers. They were both, as I knew, Bank Directors. 'Sam' was a bank clerk in an Anglo-Australian bank in Australia.

A. 'Who is this fella?'
B. 'Our colleague, Loxton, my dear boy.'
A. 'What do you mean, "colleague"?'
B. 'A banker, my dear boy, and in my bank!'
A. 'Oh, splendid! An attractive fella.
Good luck to you, Sa!'

And that reminds me. When I get to thinking about cricketers, one thing inevitably leads to another, and not necessarily in chronological order.

In 1938, I had the great good fortune to be in the delightful company of 'Plum' Warner, as a guest of Lord Belper, then the President of Notts, at the Trent Bridge Test Match. And so I saw the great 'Tiger' O'Reilly toiling in vain on the deadest of dead wickets whilst those then youthful masters, Hutton and Compton, made a packet of runs. When England finally declared, with something over six hundred runs on the board, a leg-weary and mentally exhausted O'Reilly came off, only to be greeted by me in a most offensive way—this is a method which the Tiger perfectly understands and practises:

'I always thought you were a spin bowler. How is it that you didn't turn the ball at all?'

O'Reilly: 'D'you know what that wicket is like? You dig a deep trench 22 yards long. You put in a layer of "manure"; you add a layer of soil; you then put down a series of feather mattresses; and you then top it up with more soil; water it and roll it, and then say to us bowlers, "Come on!" '

(He was one of the greatest Australian bowlers; a picturesque talker, and a great 'character'.)

Australia went into bat, at odds. The pitch had, under the flailing of bat and ball, broken up a little. Puffs of dust began to signal each stroke. A couple of wickets fell. Then McCabe moved into the attack, and played the greatest innings I have ever seen. As usual, he was not overawed by the occasion; he was there to get the runs, and he got them—232 in 240 minutes! A film of that innings would have afforded a complete course of instruction in the art of batting. If Farnes, who was an accomplished fast bowler, kept the ball up, McCabe drove it along the ground or in the air to unguarded spaces, with deadly ferocity. If he dropped the ball shorter, the rearing delivery found the ropes at fine leg or late through the slips. If he compromised on length, he was pulled or square driven. It was fantastic, and unforgettable. It is credibly reported that Don Bradman called on his players to watch, saying 'You will never see an innings like this again.' I always thought that McCabe's secret was that he loved batting, and was not obsessed by 'averages'. He was a supreme artist, and practised art for its own sake.

I saw one day of the next Test Match, at Lord's. When McCabe went in, he took 'block' at the Nursery end, facing the pavilion, where no sightscreen was allowed to obstruct the spectator's view. The pitch was (and I dare say still is) canted—higher on the 'Father Time' side, so that even a straight ball from the pavilion end would move to the batsman's leg side. Down came a fast delivery, swinging across. McCabe's feet moved a few inches, his wrists turned, and the ball was cracked into the Tavern for six. There was some feeling near me that this was an irreverent action, especially at Lord's. But that was McCabe!

William Maldon Woodfull, Captain of Australia and famous partner of 'Bill' Ponsford in many notable opening partnerships for Victoria and Australia, had the shortest back-lift to be seen before 'Slasher' Mackay. He became known as the 'unbowlable'. His demeanour was modest, but his character was so clear that it was understood by every onlooker. He embodied the spirit of cricket at its best, and was a great leader by example rather than by precept. I will never forget that, just before he was selected to go to England for the first time, the selectors, for some reason best known to themselves, had chosen the bulk of the team before Victoria played New South Wales at Sydney. I was there. For the remaining batting vacancy the choice was (believe it or not) between Woodfull and that great artist, Alan Kippax. Woodfull made a defensive century, to which Kippax's retort was a brilliant double century. In Victoria's second innings, Woodfull made another century, so aggressive in its quality, that he was chosen. They both should have been in the team; but that is (or was) the way of the world.

Woodfull, of course, figured in the great 'body-line' explosion of 1932-3. Woodfull was Captain of Australia. Douglas Jardine, whom I later got to know very well and to like very much, captained England. There had to be some way to defeat the Bradmans and the Ponsfords, and Jardine set about discovering it with almost military method and ruthlessness. The answer was the fast attack, with a fiercely rising ball, on or outside the leg-stump, with a tightly packed leg field. The batsman would be desperately concerned to protect his head and body, and false strokes would be almost a certainty.

Jardine had his instrument to hand. Larwood was a magnificent fast bowler, with a superb control of length, rise and direction. Australia

12*

had nobody to compare with him, and therefore could not retaliate. Now, McCabe had shown in Sydney that 'body-line' could be hit to leg with a vengeance; but for that kind of buccaneering business there has been, in my time, only one McCabe.

Up came the Adelaide Test Match. When Jardine marched on to the ground, wearing his inevitable Harlequin Cap, he was roundly hooted. This was an astonishingly bad piece of misbehaviour for Adelaide, which admits to being the most respectable city in Australia. But Jardine had, in the homely phrase, 'bought it'. In every step, in every gesture, in every tilt of the head, on every cricket ground, he showed his contempt for the crowd. He was a cricketing Coriolanus.

I shall never forget the incident which provoked the ultimate crisis, for I saw it all. Up to that time, I confess, I had been on Jardine's side. Why should the fast-rising ball, outside the leg-stump, be any less legitimate than the fast-rising ball outside the off-stump? True, most of the strokes of fine art are on the off; but Jardine had come out to win, not to contribute to art. Something had to be done to counter the all-powerful Bradman.

But what happened? Larwood opened the bowling from the Torrens end, and had early success outside the off-stump. But the in-domitable Woodfull was still there, partnered by Victor Richardson. Woodfull moved across rather awkwardly to get over a rising ball on the off, the last ball of the over, was struck over the heart, and fell to the ground. There never was anything bogus about Woodfull; the onlookers knew that he was hurt. Jardine, fielding at point, tactlessly complimented Larwood. 'Gubby' Allen, who was to bowl the next over, ran off the ground for a glass of water. After a minute or two, Woodfull stood up, but was obviously shaken. Then followed one of the most agreeable exhibitions of the true spirit of cricket which I have ever seen. Gubby bowled a series of almost long-hops, and Victor Richardson played them defensively straight back along the pitch!

Then it was once more Larwood's turn, to Woodfull. An orthodox off-field fell into place, Jardine at point. Suddenly Jardine signalled to Larwood, and swung the field to the body-line setting. It was almost as if he had said—'This man is a bit groggy; let's dispose of him!' A roar of rage went up from forty thousand spectators. If it had been Sydney or Melbourne, I believe, and said so at the time to 'Plum' Warner, who was next to me in the Committee Box, the crowd would have invaded the ground, and the Test Match might have ended in tumult and disorder.

What happened thereafter is a part of cricket history; angry cables were exchanged; there was much bad feeling; all pleasure went out of the series. Jardine's action was a blunder of the first magnitude. He had in effect announced that 'body-line' was designed as a physical attack; no more and no less. Many years afterwards, he conceded to me that he would like those five minutes over again!

Victor Richardson, of South Australia, was one of those rare athletes who captained his State in both cricket and football, who played cricket for Australia and captained Australia in South Africa! He was a courageous batsman, as the records will attest. But it is as a fieldsman that he lives in my gallery of immortals. Like all very great players of ball-games, he had an eye like a hawk. As a captain, he liked nothing better than to place himself at 'silly mid-off' five or six yards away from the bat. I think that I can confidently say that, in that impossible position, he was never known to miss a catch. I don't say 'drop'; I say 'miss'; for he collected all catches, possible and impossible alike.

In his last year for Australia against England in Australia, some 'expert' commentator in the Melbourne press said that it was 'time for Richardson to go', since, obviously his eye-sight was not as good as it used to be. At the cricket dinner at the Melbourne Cricket Ground on the Saturday of the Test Match (in 1932-3) I was, as usual, put up to speak. To the astonishment of most of those present, I referred to this press attack, and said that, most reluctantly, I had to agree with it. 'After all,' I said, 'we who have been watching Vic at silly mid-off have not failed to notice that he stands six feet nearer to the bat than he did once. True, he never misses; but clearly his eye-sight is not what it used to be!' Loud cheers from the players; a baleful glare in the eye of the journalist!

Lindsay Hassett was one of the great batsmen of cricket history. To see him play a scoreless and defensive over against Alec Bedser at his top was a memorable experience for any onlooker who had enough wit to know that 'slogging' is not all. But it was even better to see this short, nimble man, reduce the great 'Tiger' O'Reilly to impotence by driving him through the covers and past mid-off time after time. Which recollection reminds me that, some years after they had both retired from first-class cricket, I saw them, during a Test Match at Melbourne, having a friendly drink in the Committee Rooms of the Melbourne Cricket Club. I approached them with all the brutal confidence of a Prime Minister with a majority, and gave tongue. 'I'm just remembering, Lindsay, the day I saw you hit "Tiger" for a century on the Sydney ground.' (Now, don't forget that O'Reilly was the greatest Australian bowler of his time!) 'Oh,' said Lindsay, his face as immovable as that of a dead cod-fish, 'to which of the three occasions are you referring?'

I knew that they were famous antagonists and therefore, in the world of cricket, close friends. I remembered, but refrained from saying so, for even I have had my good moments, that it was a received legend that, on the occasion which I had witnessed, the Tiger, who hated all batsmen on principle, having been roughly treated by Lindsay, walked back past him and said, with all the clarity of a schoolteacher (for that is what he was), 'You little b—— it's not even that you're good looking!'

I remember, many years ago, reading a whimsical description by Neville Cardus (now, happily, Sir Neville), the undisputed Dean of the faculty of cricket writers, of 'Johnny' Briggs. But I still believe that Lindsay Hassett was the greatest wit in the cricket world.

So you will readily see why he has a double claim upon my affectionate memory.

Then there is that rich character 'Ernie' McCormick, the Australian fast bowler. For a fast bowler, he had, and has, a genial philosophy and a pretty wit. In the opening match against Worcester in 1938, McCormick was no-balled nineteen times in three overs for dragging over.

When the players came off at the luncheon adjournment, the sensation hunters clustered around, hoping for some pithy remarks about the standard of umpiring. They came to the wrong shop for those goods. 'Oh,' said Ernie with a spacious grin, 'it's all very understandable. You see, I come from a country where the States cover enormous areas of land. Here it is different—a great number of small counties. That was where I, as a new-comer, got into trouble. I could never make up my mind *in which county* I was bowling!'

Or again, take the cricketing Indian Prince, the Nawab of Pataudi, who made a century in his first Test Match against Australia. He was fielding in the deep at Melbourne, and receiving good-natured banter from the nearest onlookers. Suddenly a raucous voice rang out from some ill-mannered and beer-laden lout—'Hey, Gandhi, where's your goat?'

Pataudi turned quietly, gazed speculatively around, and said, 'Ah! there you are. Could somebody lend me a piece of string?' Laughter won the day.

It was on the same tour that Pataudi was warned that 'Eddie' Gilbert, an aboriginal fast bowler who played for Queensland, and whose action was suspect, would possibly 'knock him out' in Brisbane. Pataudi's reply was superb. 'Not at all,' he said, 'when Eddie sees me standing at the wicket, he will say "No, I cannot kill a brother!" and will bowl slow.'

One of the regrettable modern developments in big cricket is that there is too much talk outside the playing arena. For this, the sporting press must accept the major responsibility.

A captain who won't talk to the press is branded as unco-operative, and a 'bad ambassador'. So nowadays he talks; not just at official functions, which is inevitable, but before and after the day's play. He is expected to give his opinion on the appropriate tactics and on his opponents both jointly and severally. He will become an author either in right of his own talent or (very commonly) by trafficking with a 'ghost' who is determined to be neither dull nor prosaic. The teams' dressing-rooms are compassed about by a great cloud of witnesses, many of whom have only the remotest interest in the game or the play. The result of all this is to represent cricket as a sort of warfare inspiring bitter enmities, warfare in which the national honour seems to be at stake; victory creditable, and defeat disgraceful.

What nonsense this all is; and how unjust to the greatest of all games, in which the best players, as I have known hundreds of them, are distinguished by character and geniality; warm and sometimes whimsical personalities. It is this fact which has served to make cricket so wonderful an entertainment, so great a source of happy memories for people like me.

When I was a boy, the only way in which a cricket match could be reported was by the printed word in the newspapers. And it wasn't a bad way either; the reporter stuck to the facts, and did not try to write a gossip column!

Then came broadcasting, which worked like a charm when the matches were within broadcasting range, but encountered great problems before the days of short-wave transmission. A Test Match was being played in England. A broadcasting station in Australia undertook to describe it. How? A series of cables was arranged, converted into a sort of direct description at the Australian end. These 'fake' broadcasts were the funniest things in cricket history. Former players were engaged as commentators. Over by over we heard a description, interspersed with a click of bat on ball, arranged in the studio. Then, when twenty runs had been laboriously accounted for, in the better part of an hour, the studio voice would say, 'We have just had a flash score from Leeds; Australia is "no wicket for sixty"!'

After that, it was odd to be taken back forty runs, and pretend not to know what was to come!

Some of the old cricketers found it difficult. The broadcasts on the 'commercial' stations were of course sponsored by advertisers.

At suitable intervals, a laboriously impromptu remark would be made—'I say, Jack, have an XY cigarette!' But, as I was listening in, Jack, forgetting his cue, replied—'No thanks, old man; I can't stand them. They give me a sore throat!' So Jack's career ended.

Things are different now, with short-wave and non-stop talk. Some of the broadcasters are very good, though there are some who reduce me to an irritated despair by concealing the score under a cloud of eloquence about irrelevant matters such as the habits of seagulls, the density of the air-traffic overhead, or the antics of the inevitable small dog!

In my County Court days, I had been appearing a good deal before an elderly judge who was not a great lawyer but who had for a brief period been a better than average cricketer. He was somewhat pernickety and abhorred slang expressions, but he was always approachable through his three special hobbies; roses, poultry and cricket. I suppose that purists will say that no advocate should play upon the weaknesses or foibles of a judge. My reply is that any advocate who does not study and know his judge or judges is going to lose many cases, most needlessly.

Anyhow, my story is this. I was for the defendant in a civil action which arose out of events in the neighbourhood of Ballarat, the famous old gold-mining city. My client, as I discovered after a conference with him and his solicitor, was a very decent and honest, but dull, man, quite incapable of stating the facts in any consecutive fashion. Right through the first day of the hearing, the plaintiff and his witnesses were heard. I cross-examined with no particular success. Yet I had a feeling that my bucolic client was right, if he could only be coherent, and register himself with the judge. The plaintiff's case closed just on the adjournment. The judge looked at me, kindly enough (he approved of me because he thought I spoke good English!) and said: 'Mr Menzies, I think I should tell you that I find the plaintiff's case and witnesses most impressive.' With my usual air of confidence, I replied: 'I would ask Your Honour to suspend judgment until you have heard my client, who will, I am sure, impress you very much!'

After the adjournment, I led the solicitor and client (we had no other witness) down to my chambers. All efforts to extract coherence from the client failed. I then produced my cards.

M. 'Mr X, have you ever grown roses?'

X. 'I think my wife has some in the garden.'

M. 'But can you distinguish a La Belle France from a Frau Carl Drushki?'

X. 'Not a hope!'

M. 'Do you keep fowls?'

X. 'The wife has a few.'

M. 'Can you distinguish between a White Leghorn and an Orpington?'

X. 'Not for the life of me!'

M. 'Have you ever played cricket?'

X. 'Ah! Now you're talking. I played for Ballarat and District against Ivo Bligh's Eleven!'

M. 'Good. Conference ended!'

The next morning I opened my case and called the defendant. He was quite dreadful as a witness. At one stage it became necessary to ask him about a date. Before he could reply I said, in the most helpful manner: 'Take your time, witness. I know that dates are not always easy to remember. Now, if I were to ask you about the date when you played cricket for Ballarat and District against Ivo Bligh's Eleven, that would be much easier!'

The judge, beaming with excitement and delight, switched round in his chair and said, 'Is that so? Tell me about the match. Were you batsman or a bowler?' And at once they were into it. For half an hour we had cricket reminiscences galore. By the time my client, completely relaxed, had returned to and concluded his evidence, the judge turned to the plaintiff's astonished counsel and said: 'Of course, Mr Y., you may cross-examine if you like. You have a perfect right to do so. But I think I should tell you that in all my years on the bench I have never been more favourably impressed by any witness.'

It is hardly necessary to add that the defendant won and, I think, rightly, on the merits. But it was cricket that did it!

While I am in this mood, I crave leave to record another reminiscence of cricket and the law.

A case had occurred, well over thirty years ago, in the local court at Mildura, the famous irrigation settlement in the far north-west of Victoria, on the River Murray. The Mildura solicitor concerned on the losing side, an old friend of mine, wanted to obtain, in the Supreme Court, an Order Nisi to review the decision. But he overlooked the time factor—the Order had to be applied for within thirty days—and filed his papers and briefed me almost at the last moment. Alas! It was Christmas time, and the Supreme Court was not sitting! But there was a Test Match on at the Melbourne Cricket Ground, and Mr Justice Cussen was the President of the Club.

I hared off to the ground; it was my only hope. The judge was in the Committee Box. I found my way in, waited until the end of the over, and then caught the eye of the judge. Happily he was a patient and generous man. I told him the circumstances. He at once caught on. 'I quite see the position. Have I your assurance that the necessary papers are filed?' I assured him that they were. 'Very well,' he said, 'I think the rule is that if you formally apply within the time, and the papers are in order, I can note the fact that you have applied, and adjourn the actual argument to a future date!' I vigorously agreed. He noted the application, turned to the field, and said with a smile: 'That was a fine bit of bowling wasn't it?'

I could not set down any cricket memoirs without some affectionate references to two of the great men of Lord's, Sir Pelham (Plum) Warner, and Harry Altham. Both were off the playing list when I first met them. Each had become a cricket administrator and a cricket historian; Plum with a clear and vivid memory of events in which he had played a part, Altham with rare literary charm and the graces of classical scholarship. Each has now departed to the Elysian fields.

Over the years, I got to know 'Plum' very well, and learned without difficulty to love him. He was, in Chaucer's famous phrase, a 'verray parfit gentil knight'. Cricket was his life. He had been a great batsman and a celebrated Captain of England. But he detested rude controversy, was sensitive on all points of honour, and spoke well of all men, provided they were lovers of what he used to call 'cricket, the beautiful game with the beautiful name'.

He knew how cricket was going, all round the world. One year I took to London with me my great friend and colleague, Athol Townley, now, to my enduring sorrow, dead and gone. Athol had played for my Prime Minister's XI against the West Indies at Canberra, and had hit a couple of towering 'sixers'. I had 'Plum' and a few others to dinner at the Savoy. When Athol walked in and I mentioned his name, 'Plum' at once came forward with outstretched hand— 'Ha! Sixer Townley!'

For many years, I have had the respectable habit of putting on a dinner party in London for my cricketing friends. I always treated 'Plum' as the special guest of honour, and seated him on my right. I then placed 'Gubby' Allen directly opposite, and had disposed on the table between them a variety of small movable articles like salt-cellars and pepper pots. These tactical dispositions made the party a guaranteed success. All I had to do was to toss in the apple of discord about fast bowling, or the new l.b.w. rule, and the contest was on. For you must know that, though 'Plum' was gentle, he was pertinacious in his views, while my friend 'Gubby' Allen thrives on controversy, and never has to be talked into offering an opinion.

What a gallery of memories I have of these dinners, with great and good companions like 'Freddy' Brown, Ian Peebles, 'Jim' Swanton, Harry Altham, Rait Kerr and Ronnie Aird, *et hoc genus omne*, and once Lord Birkett, the greatest after-dinner speaker I ever heard.

I rather think that I made a poor start with 'Plum' at Lord's thirty years ago. He had taken me out to see the famous ground. The leather-jackets(?) had been in; the grass was rough, patchy, and worn. I offered the brash view that football should be played on the ground during the winter. Cutting up the ground, I suggested, would let the air in and improve the health of the grass. I delicately mentioned that the Melbourne ground, which sometimes looked like a mudheap after the Football Grand Final, was promptly harrowed, top-dressed, and so attended to that six weeks later cricket was in full swing. 'Plum' was shocked at this blasphemy. His good opinion of me was restored only when, some years later, in the course of a speech, I referred to Lord's as the 'Cathedral of Cricket'.

Indeed, I must tell of my last talk with 'Plum' at the home of his son, John, a close friend of mine, who will, I know, not object to my narrative. The old man was sick, and frail. In fact, I was never to see him again. But John suggested I should come to see him.

'Plum' was seated in an armchair. He gazed vaguely at me; clearly he did not recognize me. But he knew that I was somewhere in his failing memory, and that he must have talked cricket with me. Suddenly he said, loud and clear, 'Who was that splendid statesman from the colonies who described Lord's as the Cathedral of Cricket?'

John promptly identified me, the shadows cleared away, and we launched into cricket talk, which, peace to old Sam Johnson, is just about the best talk in the world.

MEMORANDUM SENT TO COLONEL NASSER
ON 7 SEPTEMBER 1956

Our discussions have been conducted in an atmosphere of courteous frankness and responsibility. But they have, in our opinion, disclosed deep differences of approach and principle which it seems clear that no repetition of debate can affect. In these circumstances, we consider that it would now be helpful that my committee should now set down, in summary and objective form, the underlying purposes of the 18-power proposals and the nature of the reasons underlying them. This seems desirable because, as our talks have been conducted in private without records and with great informality, neither you nor we would desire that there should be in future any misunderstanding on the part of our principals or of yourself as to what we were proposing to your government.

We were authorised to present those proposals on behalf of the following nations represented at the London Conference as follows (I put them into alphabetical order):

Australia Denmark, Ethiopia, France, the Federal Republic of Germany, Iran, Italy, Japan, the Netherlands, New Zealand, Norway, Pakistan, Portugal, Spain, Sweden, Turkey, the United Kingdom and the United States of America. (Spain at the London conference made a reservation which has been conveyed to you.)

From the outset, you will have observed that the 18 nations have not attempted to arrive at any joint opinion as to the validity or otherwise of Egypt's nationalisation decree. The London conference felt that to have a debate on this point would be fruitless, since the conference possessed no authority to make any judicial determination. It was therefore considered much more practical to work out constructive proposals which assumed that the act of nationalisation had occurred and that the problem of payment of compensation to the Suez Canal

[361]

Company would be properly dealt with, with provision for arbitration in the event of difference, and that what was needed was the establishment of principles and methods for the future. These should be such as would both in law and in fact, ensure that the Suez Canal would continue to be an international waterway operated free of politics or national discrimination, and with a financial structure so secure, and an international confidence so high, that an expanding and improving future for the Canal could be guaranteed.

The proposals evolved in this atmosphere have been placed before you and have been much debated between us. We have, as you know, gone beyond the mere presentation of the proposals and have sought to apply and establish what we believe to be the large questions of principle involved.

It would be tedious and unnecessary in this document to recapitulate all the discussions that have occurred on all the points of interpretation that have arisen. The simple truth is that we quite early realized on both sides of the table that there were certain central matters without agreement upon which subsidiary matters could not usefully be determined.

The two crucial proposals emerging from London are:

1. that the operation of the Canal should be insulated from the influence of the politics of any nation;
2. that, to enable this to be done, there should be established under an international convention to which Egypt would be a party, a body charged with the operation, maintenance, and development of the Canal.

Such a body, we propose, should be constituted of people from various countries, including Egypt. The members would not be subject to political direction, and should be given in covenant, with the free consent of Egypt, wide powers of management and finance so that it could inspire confidence and deal with the future financial requirements of the Canal, and ensure a non-discriminatory and non-political management of Canal traffic. The proposed body would naturally have due regard for the laws and institutions of Egypt.

You have with complete frankness made it clear to us that the existence of such a body operating the Suez Canal would, in the view of Egypt, be a derogation from Egyptian sovereignty; that it would in substance represent a reversal of the policy announced by you on 26th July.

We cannot agree with this view. Nowhere in our proposals is there any denial of Egypt's territorial sovereignty. On the contrary, the London proposals expressly recognized these rights in paragraph two of the Resolution. The whole essence of what we have put forward is, to use a homely illustration, that Egypt's position as the landlord of the Canal being completely accepted, she should proceed by international agreement to install a tenant so constituted that the future of the Canal would be satisfactory both to its owners and to those many nations who use it. We believe, as we have pointed out, that it cannot seriously be maintained that when a landlord grants a lease of premises, that lease derogates from his ownership. The fact is that the lease is an expression of, and conditional upon, his ownership. On this analogy our proposals would mean that the tenant of the Canal would pay to Egypt a substantial rental which must unquestionably grow as the traffic through the Canal increases, and that in the meantime, the tenant would, in exercise of its managerial and financial powers, be constantly improving the value of Egypt's asset. Indeed, as the 'tenant' in this analogy would be a body which includes Egypt, herself, the position of Egypt would be even stronger.

In Paragraph 3A of our proposals, there is a reference to 'institutional arrangements'. As we felt that this phrase might be regarded as admitting of a variety of applications, we undertook the task of illustrating what it meant. We pointed out that what we were saying was merely illustrative and was not designed to narrow the broad significance of the proposals themselves. But, as we have said, one form of 'institutional arrangement' which comes readily to mind is to be seen by reference to the case of the International Bank for Reconstruction and Development. That Bank was created by agreement among a considerable number of nations. It was not incorporated under the law of any one country. It owes its existence to the agreement of many countries. Its powers are defined by an international document. Without being in the technical sense incorporated under some pre-existing law it has, in fact, by its articles wide powers of borrowing and lending, and banking generally. The International Bank succeeds in its purpose, not only because it has extensive powers, but also because in its capital structure and growth it has enjoyed the unquestioned confidence of a great variety of member nations. Its existence has not, so far as we know, been regarded as derogating from the sovereignty of any nation, even though it enjoys a wide immunity from national laws.

We have become conscious of your firmly held view that there is no occasion for a canal authority possessing an international character, because of Your Excellency's belief that Egypt is herself capable of conducting and ensuring the future of the Canal, and has never challenged the 1888 Convention or its declarations about the freedom of the Canal.

To answer this point, we found it necessary to put before you quite frankly and objectively, certain considerations which, from the point of view of the 18 nations we represent, nations who among them represent over 90 per cent. of the traffic passing through the Canal, are of vital significance. The traffic through the Canal has almost reached what might be described as saturation point. Even to maintain it in its present shape, requires the constant services of a highly skilled, ex-perienced, and specialised engineering and transportation staff. This staff has been built up over a long period of years. There has been an increasing intake of Egyptian personnel, but the great majority of the key employees are still nationals of other countries. From the point of view of Egypt herself it is desirable that there should be a continuity of skilled operation. Such continuity, in our judgment, cannot be assured unless there is complete mutual confidence among those actually operating the Canal, the Government of Egypt, and the users of the Canal.

But the matter does not end there. It is clear that as a result of increased traffic Egypt can enjoy very substantial and increasing benefits from the Canal if the Canal can retain the confidence of its principal users. The number of tankers passing through the Canal could double or treble in a few years if such confidence exists. To deal with such traffic, expansion of the Canal will be necessary. Whether expansion consists of widening, deepening, constructing by-passes or even duplicating the Canal, the capital costs will be substantial. If these costs are to be met over a period of time from Canal revenues without serious current reductions in Egypt's income from the Canal or without the imposition of burdensome increases of dues, they must be derived from funds accruing from an increase in traffic—an increase which would come only if the users would maintain confidence in the Canal, and it must be remembered that increased dues would impose grievous burdens upon those many millions of people in the world who, in the long run, pay the costs and charges incurred by the cargoes they ultimately buy or sell. If expansion would not be necessary, it would be because the users' confidence would be lacking and many of them would have found ways to avoid remaining dependent on the Canal. The benefit, therefore, which Egypt might have gained would be materially lessened.

We have, therefore, in the interest of Egypt and the users, urged that the structure of the body actually conducting the Canal operations should be such as to inspire world-wide confidence and bring about a capacity to raise the necessary capital sums because of a prevailing feeling of security on the part of those who may be asked to provide them.

In short, what we have proposed is that, Egypt's sovereignty being fully recognised, the actual operation, maintenance and expansion of the Canal should be reposed in a body (established under international convention), which would include people from various nations, including of course Egypt, with extensive financial powers and responsibilities. As we believe that an international waterway like the Suez Canal should not become an instrument of the political policy of any nation or nations, we proposed that the members of this body should not be the mere delegates of any nation or be under any obligation to observe political instructions. On the contrary, we proposed that the parties to the convention should select them with regard to their personal qualities of ability, integrity and experience. It is true in a sense, that our proposed convention would be an arrangement made between governments, and that original appointments to the proposed authority would be made by governments. But we firmly believe that, with goodwill and good faith, persons so appointed could serve in a non-political manner in this case as readily, for instance, as do the judges of the permanent International Court of Justice.

As we have throughout emphasised, it is essential that if it is to be a truly international waterway as envisaged by the 1888 Convention, there should be no politics in the Suez Canal, whether those of Egypt or of any other nation.

Your Excellency has told us with clarity and frankness that you do not believe that the Canal could be excluded from the politics of Egypt, since it is part of Egyptian territory and assets. To this we have pointed out that, if the Canal is to remain fully available for any of Egypt's political purposes, subject only to the 1888 Convention, then the many nations using the Canal will have to realise that their pattern of overseas trade will be at any time subject to the decision of Egypt alone. We are, of course, conscious of your own view that these considerations are adequately met by the guarantee of freedom under the 1888 Convention. But if that Convention is to contain the only limitation, it seems clear to us, as we have pointed out, that there could be for political purposes, many discriminations in traffic and marshalling control which did not fall foul of the Convention; that, Canal dues being within Egypt's sole control, differences of opinion as to their level will almost inevitably be fixed by reference to Egyptian budgetary needs with the strong possibility that they would be raised to the maximum that the traffic could bear; and that future development of the Canal might well be controlled by local budget considerations; a danger which independent finance by a special international body would entirely avert.

We have stated and restated, that the setting up of such a body as we have proposed, would create such a feeling of assurance in the minds of all user nations, that the necessary financial provision could be secured, the burden of such matters being no longer the sole responsibility of Egypt herself. We have further emphasized that, under our proposals, there would no longer be private shareholders or dividends. The one nation which would obtain an assured annual net revenue from the Canal would be Egypt.

Your Excellency has repeatedly and vigorously explained to us that the setting up of a Suez Canal body of the kind envisaged in our proposals would, to the eyes of Egypt, represent either foreign domination or seizure. We have pointed out that the truth is that no arrangement for the tenancy of the Canal can be either domination or seizure if it is freely agreed to by Egypt. And it is, as you know, that willing and free agreement which all of our negotiations have been designed to secure.

It remains only to emphasise two other large matters which arose in the course of our proposals.

The first was our proposal that the new body, having been constructed by international convention, should be brought into relationship with the United Nations. This was done in the case of the International Bank by an agreement with the United Nations which had the effect of making the bank a 'closed agency' under the charter but which, of course, did not affect the freedom of the Bank in the conduct of its business. Association between our proposed body and the United Nations in a similar fashion could, we believe, give great satisfaction all around the world and, if adopted, would considerably strengthen international confidence and security.

We also proposed an arbitral commission to settle disputes. There might be disputes as to the equitable return which Egypt should have from the Canal. There might, in the course of the years, be other disputes involving one or more of the constituent nations. Any such matters, if they could not be resolved by agreement, could be arbitrated upon by an independent commission enjoying international confidence. Our proposal did not mean that such an arbitral commission would be the authority to deal with the normal problems which arise in the course of management, such as claims which might arise in relation to the employment of people or contracts with subsidiary contractors. To the extent to which contracts might be entered into in respect of such normal matters they would be contracts made for the most part in Egypt and we did not contemplate that in respect of such matters the normal jurisdiction of the Egyptian courts should be excluded. It would be only in any dispute of a genuine international character that the jurisdiction of the arbitral commission would be invoked.

At the London conference it was agreed by all the nations represented that any arrangement entered into must be completely fair to Egypt and must pay scrupulous regard to Egypt's territorial sovereignty. Our whole presentation of the matter to Your Excellency has been made in that spirit and with that desire. It is for this reason that we have

[367]

repeatedly pointed out that while representing nations who are users of the Canal, we are deeply and urgently concerned in obtaining the highest possible measure of confidence and an effective and practical guaranteed freedom and future for the Canal. There are in our proposals marked advantages for Egypt which we have discussed at length but which we now summarise as follows:

(A) Egypt's ownership of the Canal being recognised it is to her great advantage to have the Canal maintained and improved and made more profitable as the years go on.

(B) The future financial burden involved in such maintenance and improvement would be carried and handled by the new body and therefore Egypt would in fact be relieved of them.

(C) Egypt alone would draw profit from the Canal.

(D) A just and fair method of compensating the shareholders of the Suez Canal Company would have been agreed upon.

(E) The dangerous tension now existing internationally would be relaxed on terms satisfactory to the user nations and entirely consistent with Egypt's proper dignity, independence and ownership and thus a real contribution would be made to the peaceful settlement of international problems.

It is the understanding of the committee that you have taken the position that you are unable to accept the basic proposals put before you. I would be grateful if Your Excellency would inform the committee whether or not its understanding is correct supplementing your statement with such views as you may care to express. If, unfortunately, the understanding of the committee is correct the task entrusted to the committee by the 18 powers of presenting and explaining these proposals and ascertaining the attitude of the Egyptian Government with respect to them would have been carried out. In such an event, there would appear to be no alternative other than for the committee to request Your Excellency to receive it at your early convenience so that it may be prepared, after a final conversation with you, to take its leave.

LETTER OF 9 SEPTEMBER 1956 FROM PRESIDENT NASSER TO THE CHAIRMAN OF THE FIVE-NATIONS COMMITTEE

Your Excellency,

I have received your letter of September 7, 1956, relating to the meetings held between us and the committee headed by you and representing 18 of the Governments which participated in the London Conference on the Suez Canal. Your committee will recall that during those meetings, I took up various basic points and commented upon them. You have referred to the 18 countries as representing over 90% of the users of the Canal. Beside this being distinctly a statistical exaggeration, our understanding of the 'users of the Canal' includes those countries which, even though they have no ships passing through the Canal, use the Canal for the passage of the bulk of their foreign trade. An illustration of this would be such countries as Australia, Thailand, Indonesia, India, Pakistan, Iran, Iraq, Saudi Arabia, Ethiopia and the Sudan. Furthermore, the principle of sovereignty, the right of ownership and the dignity of nations are all deeply involved in this problem. At least in appearance, the starting point of the present crisis was July 26, 1956 when, in the exercise of one of its prerogatives, the Government of Egypt nationalized the Company which bore the name of 'The Universal Maritime Company of the Suez Canal'.

That the Government of Egypt was fully entitled to nationalize that Egyptian company cannot be seriously contested. In nationalizing that company the Government of Egypt stated unequivocally that it considers itself bound by the 1888 Convention guaranteeing the freedom of passage through the Suez Canal and its readiness to give full and equitable compensation to the shareholders. Furthermore, on August 12 the Government of Egypt announced its willingness to sponsor with the other Governments, signatories to the Constantinople Convention of 1888, a conference to which would be invited the other Governments whose ships pass through the Suez Canal for the purpose of reviewing the Constantinople Convention and considering the concluding of an agreement between all these Governments reaffirming and guaranteeing the freedom of passage through the Suez Canal. Parallel to this nowhere and no date could be found where or when the

Government of Egypt violated any of its international obligations concerning the Suez Canal. At the same time, for nearly fifty days, and in spite of the difficulties created by France and the United Kingdom and by segments of the former Suez Canal Company, the traffic through the Canal has been going with regularity and efficiency. The crisis and the so-called 'grave situation' are, therefore, artificially created by the above mentioned quarters as witness among other things

(a) statements containing threat of force;
(b) mobilization and movements of troops by France and the United Kingdom;
(c) inciting employees and pilots working in the Suez Canal to abruptly abandon their work by France and the United Kingdom and some officials of the former Suez Canal Company; and
(d) hostile economic measures taken against Egypt.

With all this going on we have been repeatedly made to listen to references to a 'peaceful solution' and to 'free negotiations' in order to achieve such a solution. Need one emphasize the contradiction between the palpitating reality and professed aim? If there is anything which flagrantly violated and disdained the letter and spirit of the Charter of the United Nations it is such acts of attempted intimidation, economic pressure and incitement of sabotage. In distinct contrast to this the Government of Egypt has announced its full readiness to negotiate a peaceful solution in conformity with the purposes and principles of the Charter of the United Nations. This remains to be the policy and the intent of the Egyptian Government. We have studied most carefully all those proposals submitted in and outside the London Conference with regard to this problem including the proposals of the 18 countries which the Committee represents. We find ourselves in agreement with the 18 countries when they state that the solution must

(a) respect the sovereign right of Egypt;
(b) safeguard the freedom of passage through the Suez Canal in accordance with the Suez Canal Convention of October 29, 1888;

(c) respect Egypt's right of ownership;
(d) ensure the efficient and dependable operation, maintenance and development of the Canal.

When however, we come to consider the ways and means proposed by the committee to attack these objectives we find that they are self-defeating and that they lead to opposite results from those aimed at. The 'definite system' as proposed by the committee would, in fact, mean 'taking over the operation of the Canal' as circulated by the sponsoring Government immediately before the conference among the Governments invited and in substance maintained throughout, in spite of the variance of expression. The system proposed is bound to be considered and treated by the people of Egypt as the hostile infringing upon their rights and their sovereignty all of which precludes real cooperation. It can, moreover, be asked whether it was the Suez Canal Company which guaranteed the freedom of passage through the Canal? Was it not indeed the Government of Egypt who safeguarded, and still safeguards, that freedom of passage? Would this freedom be, or could its actual practice be, safeguarded by the proposed Suez Canal Board? Is it not to be expected that this board be not a source of comfort and help, but a source of misunderstanding and trouble? In all this we keep constantly in our mind the vital importance of genuine international cooperation as distinct from domination of any country, be it single domination as the one which Egypt just got rid of, or collective domination, as would inevitably be considered the system proposed by the committee. Any attempt to impose such a system would indeed be the signal for incalculable strife and would plunge the Suez Canal into the turmoil of politics, instead of as the committee professed to want, insulating it from politics. Whatever the system of operation of the Canal is going to be, it will depend on the close, full and willing cooperation of the people of Egypt, among whom and through whose country the Canal runs. It is obvious that such indispensable cooperation cannot be had if the people will consider the operating body as hostile and as against their sovereignty, their rights and their dignity. Strangely enough, those who pose as protagonists of 'insulating' the Suez Canal from politics have been the authors of many acts which diametrically contradict this announced purpose.

What is the 'internationalization' of the Suez Canal, the convening of the London Conference on the Suez Canal within the most part tactically selected invitees, the delegating of the Five Member Committee, the threats, the deployment of armed forces and the economic measures—what are all these, if not politics? You have mentioned that the delegates of any nation represented in the proposed Suez Canal Board should not be under any obligation to observe political instructions. They will, nevertheless, be nationals of their respective countries and subjects of their respective Governments and it will be extremely unlikely that they will be immune from the influence of such relationships. The similes you have put forth of the International Bank and the International Court of Justice do not, in our opinion, either hold or convince. We believe that the real insulation of the Canal from politics would best be guaranteed by a solemn and internationally binding commitment in the form of a reaffirmation or a renewal of the 1888 Convention either of which, as we have already declared, is acceptable to us. It has been alleged that the Government of Egypt aims at discriminating against one of the countries you represent, namely the United Kingdom, and that the Government of Egypt has among its objectives the disruption of British economy and the interruption of the line of trade and supply of the United Kingdom through the Suez Canal. It is clear beyond cavil that nothing could be farther from the truth and no one could validly point out one single reason why, and for what useful purpose, the Government of Egypt should entertain such policy. International confidence was mentioned by you. I have in this connexion called your attention to the fact that confidence is a two way proposition and that, while the confidence of other nations is important, that of the Egyptian people is at least of equal importance in this respect, and it cannot be had if the Egyptian people are, as a result of certain acts and policies, imperilled to doubt and lose faith in the existence of international justice and the rule of law in international relations. If the real objective is to secure the freedom of passage through the Suez Canal the answer is there, namely that passage through the Canal has always been and continues to be free. The only danger to this freedom of passage stems from the threats, the re-deployment of armed forces, the incitation of employees and workers to sabotage the operation of the Canal and the economic measures against Egypt. If, on the other hand as it seems, the objective is to amputate and to sever from the very body of Egypt one of its main points, if the aim is to deprive Egypt from an integral part of its territory, we should be told of it. It should be abundantly clear by now that Egypt by the very nature of things is vitally interested in the maintenance of peace and security, not only around the Suez Canal but also throughout the area in which it exists and all over the world. It should be equally clear that, if only by sheer self interest, Egypt is devoted to the freedom of passage through the Canal and is equally devoted to the concept of an efficient enlightened and progressive operation of the Canal without any discrimination or any exploitation whatsoever. I wish to refer in this last connexion to my having mentioned to the committee that the Government of Egypt is ready to enter into a binding arrangement concerning the establishment of just and equitable tolls and charges. As for the future development of the Suez Canal to which you referred, I wish to reiterate that the Government of Egypt is determined to do everything possible in this respect, that it has already announced its intention to carry out the development programme which was planned by the former Canal Company and other programmes of much wider scope and longer range. It is our announced policy that the Suez Canal authority is an independent authority with an independent budget empowered with all the necessary powers without being limited by Government rules and systems. We have also announced our intention to earmark an adequate percentage of the revenues of the Canal to its future development and to deviate none of the revenues needed for such development to other channels. Both for the development and for the operation of the Canal, the Government of Egypt does, and will always be ready to, benefit by the knowledge and experience of highly qualified experts from all over the world. The crux of the present situation is, in our opinion, that the proposed system, in itself and, in what has accompanied it, and what it involves, aims at securing for a group of the users of the Canal control of it by their taking over its operation. The paper which was circulated among the countries invited to the London Conference shortly before it was convened and which seems to be until now a guide as to the still maintained objectives of the sponsoring countries reads: Proposal for the establishment of an International Authority for the Suez Canal.

France, the United Kingdom and the United States are in agreement that at the conference a resolution shall be tabled for setting up an International Authority for the Suez Canal on the following lines.

1. The purposes and functions of this International Authority would be

    (i)   to take over the operation of the Canal;

    (ii)   to ensure its efficient functioning as a free, open and secure international waterway in accordance with the principles of the Suez Canal Convention of 1888;

    (iii) to arrange for the payment of fair compensation to the Suez Canal Company;

    (iv) to ensure to Egypt an equitable return which will take into account all legitimate Egyptian rights and interests. Failing agreement with the company or with Egypt on either of the last two points, the matter would be referred to an Arbitral Commission of 3 members to be appointed by the International Court of Justice.

2. The constituent organs of the International Authority would be

    (i)   a Council of Administration, the members of which would be nominated by the Powers chiefly interested in navigation and sea-born trade through the Canal;

    (ii)   the necessary technical, working and administrative organs.

3. The Powers of the International Authority would, in particular, include

    (i)   the carrying out of all necessary works;

    (ii)   the determination of the tolls, dues and other charges on a just and equitable basis;

    (iii) all questions of finance;

    (iv) general powers of administration and control.

We are convinced that any unbiased study of this circular would leave the reader with but one conviction, namely, that the purpose is to take the Suez Canal out of the hands of Egypt and put it into some other hands. It is difficult to imagine anything more provocative to the people of Egypt than this. An act of such a nature is both self-defeating and of a nature to generate friction, misunderstanding and continuous strife. It would be, in other words not the end, but the beginning of trouble. I would like, on the other hand, to reaffirm that the policy of my Government remains to be:

(a) —the freedom of passage through the Suez Canal and its secure use without discrimination;

(b) —the development of the Suez Canal to meet the future requirements of navigation;

(c) —the establishment of just and equitable tolls and charges; and

(d) —technical efficiency of the Suez Canal.

We trust that the Suez Canal will thus be insulated from politics and will, instead of being a source of conflict, become again a link of cooperation and of mutual benefit and better understanding between the nations of the earth. Furthermore, we are confident that, by carrying out this policy, and extending its good will in every direction, Egypt will best be able to contribute to the welfare and happiness of the world as well as to its own happiness and welfare.

INDEX

INDEX
Richardson, Victor, 352, 353
Ritchie, General, 86
Rodwell, Sir Cecil, 217
Rommel, General, 34
Roosevelt, F. D., 35, 90, 132–7, 138
Rootes, Sir William (later Lord), 72–73

Sabry, Wing-Commander Aly, 162
Salisbury, 3rd Marquess of, 3
Salisbury, 5th Marquess of, 30, 45, 83, 256
Sampson, John (grandfather), 6–7
Sampson, John (uncle), 10
Sampson, Kate (mother), 6–8, 12
Sampson, Sydney (uncle), 6, 10, 109
'Scrap iron' flotilla, 17, 112
Scullin, J. H., 109, 116, 117–21, 122, 123, 251, 252
SEATO, 60, 147, 228, 262, 268–70
Sellers, Lord Justice, 85–6
Sharpeville shootings, 192, 200
Shedden, F. G. (later Sir Frederick), 20, 24, 30
Simon Commission, 106
Simon, Sir John (later Lord), 89, 97, 151
Simpson, Mrs Wallis (later Duchess of Windsor), 242–4
Singapore, 17, 20, 30, 31, 60, 134
Sirry Pasha, 23–4
Slim, Field-Marshal Sir William (later Lord), 86, 256–7
Smith, Aubrey, 341
Smith, F. E. (Earl of Birkenhead), 337
Smith, Ian, 218, 221, 223, 226
Smuts, J. C., 29, 92, 188
Soames, Christopher, 83
Soames, Mary, 68, 81, 82
Sonenberg, N. H., 339–40
South Africa, 16, 187, 189, 191–215, 246
South-West Africa, 197, 201
Southern Rhodesia. See Rhodesia

Spence, W. G., 6
Spender, Sir Percy, 310
Spooner, E. S., 49
Starke, H. E. (later Mr Justice), 322–3
Stonehaven, Lord, 251
Storey, John (later Sir John), 20
Street, Geoffrey, 18
Stuart, H.M.A.S., 24
Suez Canal: nationalization of, and the proposals of the London Conference, 149–51, 153–5; the legal position, 151–3; the Suez Committee established, 155–9; personnel of the Committee, 158–61; the Menzies Mission, 161–71; the Anglo-French expedition and U.N. intervention, 172–85; exchange of letters with Nasser, 361–75
Suez Canal Convention (1888), 151
Suez Canal Users' Association, 175
Sukarno, President, 232
'Sunshine' harvester, 6
Supreme Court (U.S.A.), 136
Swanton, E. W., 345, 360
Swinton, Philip, 104
Sydney, 260
Sydney, H.M.A.S., 17
Sydney Morning Herald, 19
Sydney Worker, 6

Tanganyika, 205
Tate, Maurice, 346
Taylor, 'Johnny', 345
Tenby, Lord (Gwilym Lloyd George), 75
Thailand, 31, 52, 268
Thant, U, 145
Theodore, E. G., 120, 122
Thomas, J. H., 39, 329–40
Thomas, Sir Shenton, 21
Tobruk, 17, 27, 29, 127
Tocqueville, Alexis de, 273
Townley, Athol, 359

[383]